Christianity and Monasticism
in Wadi al-Natrun

Essays from the 2002 International Symposium
of the Saint Mark Foundation and the Saint
Shenouda the Archimandrite Coptic Society

Edited by
Maged S.A. Mikhail
and Mark Moussa

A Saint Mark Foundation Book
The American University in Cairo Press
Cairo • New York

Christianity and Monasticism
in Wadi al-Natrun

Dedicated to the memory of
Bishop Samuel of Shibin al-Qanatar

Copyright © 2009 by
The American University in Cairo Press
113 Sharia Kasr el Aini, Cairo, Egypt
420 Fifth Avenue, New York, NY 10018
www.aucpress.com

The chapters in the History section were first published in *Coptica* volume 2, 2003.
The chapters in the Art and Architecture section were first published in *Coptica* volume 3, 2004.

Dar el Kutub No. 16941/08
ISBN 978 977 416 260 2

Dar el Kutub Cataloging-in-Publication Data

Mikhail, Maged S.A.
        Christianity and Monasticism in Wadi al-Natrun / edited by Maged S.A. Mikhail and
    Mark Moussa.—Cairo: The American University in Cairo Press, 2009
                p.   cm.
        ISBN 977 416 260 9
        1. Monasteries, coptic— Wadi al-Natrun   I. Mikhail, Maged S.A. (ed.)
        II. Moussa, Mark (jt. ed.)
        255

1 2 3 4 5 6 7 8   14 13 12 11 10 09

Printed in Egypt

Contents

Foreword   vii
Fawzy Estafanous

Introduction   viii
Hany N. Takla

History
The Importance of Wadi al-Natrun for Coptology   1
Martin Krause

The Multiethnic Character of the Wadi al-Natrun   12
Karl-Heinz Brune

Wādī al-Naṭrūn and the History of the Patriarchs of Alexandria   24
Johannes den Heijer

Wadi al-Natrun and Coptic Literature   43
S.G. Richter

Wadi Natrun in Geologic History   63
Rushdi Said

Figures in the Carpet: Macarius the Great, Isaiah of Scetis,
Daniel of Scetis, and Monastic Spirituality in the
Wadi al-Natrun (Scetis) from the Fourth to the Sixth Century   69
Tim Vivian

Consecration of the Myron at Saint Macarius Monastery
(MS 106 Lit.)   106
Youhanna Nessim Youssef

Liturgy at Wadi al-Natrun   122
Ugo Zanetti

Art and Architecture

Scetis at the Red Sea: Depictions of Monastic Genealogy
in the Monastery of St. Antony   143
Elizabeth S. Bolman

On the Architecture at Wādī al-Naṭrūn   159
Peter Grossmann

The Ornamental Repertoire in the Wall-paintings of
Wadi al-Natrun: Remarks on a Methodical Approach   185
Suzana Hodak

Art in the Wadi al-Natrun: An Assessment of the Earliest
Wallpaintings in the Church of Abu Makar, Dayr Abu Makar   211
Lucy-Anne Hunt

A Play of Light and Shadow: The Stuccoes of Dayr
al-Suryan and their Historical Context   246
Mat Immerzeel

Results of the Recent Restoration Campaigns (1995–2000)
at Dayr al-Suryan   272
Ewa Parandowska

Indigo and Madder, Finger Prints and Brush Strokes:
Notes on Six Byzantine Great Deesis Icons of Wadi
al-Natrun Monasteries and their Egyptian Origin   283
Zuzana Skalova

History Through Inscriptions: Coptic Epigraphy
in the Wadi al-Natrun   329
Jacques van der Vliet

Foreword

This third volume of *Christianity and Monasticism in Egypt* contains the proceedings of one of the symposia organized by the St. Mark Foundation for Coptic History Studies and the St. Shenouda the Archimandrite Coptic Society. But this volume is of special importance, for Wadi al-Natrun boasts some of the oldest monastic settlements in the world, which developed into the most significant monastic center in Egypt. Many ascetics, whose spiritual truths have been kept alive in the "Sayings of the Fathers," lived here in the fourth and fifth centuries and provided us with significant material for understanding the cultural and social milieus of the ascetic life. Their wisdom influenced monastic life in both the east and the west. European, Syrian, Ethiopian, and Armenian monks joined the monasteries of Wadi al-Natrun, endowing the place with a multi-ethnic character, and these monasteries have always provided the Coptic Church with the greater number of its patriarchs and bishops. The spiritual and artistic heritage of this unique Coptic site is beyond estimation.

In addition to the acknowledgments expressed by Hany Takla on page x, I would like to thank all the scholars who came from all over the world to Wadi al-Natrun and enriched this volume with their contributions. Heartfelt thanks are also due to the supporters of the symposium, especially to Sherif Doss and Shahira Loza. And my thanks go to Fahim Wassef and Neven Ramzy for their help in organizing the symposium.

Fawzy Estafanous
President, The Saint Mark Foundation for Coptic History Studies

Introduction

Hany N. Takla

In August 1999, at the conclusion of the first day of the second St. Shenouda Conference of Coptic Studies at UCLA, Dr. Gawdat Gabra made a strange yet intriguing proposal in his communication to the conference attendees. In it he proposed the rekindling of the scholarly interest in the Wadi al-Natrun monastic site after decades of relative neglect since the monumental study of Hugh Evelyn-White. This bold proposal included, in detail, the convening of an international symposium on the subject to be held on the site in early 2002. This visionary idea quickly found favor with Dr. Fawzy Estafanous, founder of the St. Mark Foundation. Later that evening at a reception hosted at the local Coptic Church, he quickly set up a steering committee to coordinate such effort. Beside Dr. Gabra, the committee included Dr. Bastiaan Van Elderen of Michigan, Rev. Dr. Tim Vivian of California, and myself as representative of St. Shenouda the Archimandrite Coptic Society. Shortly after that, Dr. Estafanous and Dr. Van Elderen presented the idea to H.H. Pope Shenouda III during his visit to Ohio later that year. The Pope, who had spent his monastic days in Wadi al-Natrun, welcomed the idea. Then the difficult work began. After numerous organizational meetings, including a very significant one held during the Seventh Coptic Congress at Leiden in 2000, and hundreds of laboring hours by Dr. Gabra and the team assembled by the St. Mark Foundation in Egypt, the dream became a reality.

In early February 2002, scholars and members of both organizing entities came to Egypt from as near as Lebanon and as far as Australia. They were joined by many prominent Copts from among the clergy as well as the laity. Together they converged on the revered site of Wadi al-Natrun, the subject of this momentous gathering. The exclusivity of the attendees, the serenity of the papal residence where we stayed, and the scholarly level of the presentations and ensuing discussions made this symposium a resounding success. The field trips that were scheduled during that period significantly enhanced the attendees' appreciation for the value of the site as a testimony to both early and contemporary monasticism in Egypt, the birthplace of Christian monasticism.

This volume contains sixteen of the twenty-three papers presented at the symposium, divided into two sections, "History" and "Art and Architecture." Opening the History section, Martin Krause, the father of modern-day Coptology, deals with the role that monasticism and Wadi al-Natrun have played in Coptology. Karl-Heinz Brune then explores in particular the inhabitants of this place, who came from several ethnic groups other than native Egyptians or Copts. Johannes den Heijer deals with the mention of the area in *The History of the Patriarchs of Alexandria*, also recounting interesting historical events that were witnessed there by the authors of this important historical work. Siegfried G. Richter surveys the literary works found in the ancient libraries of Wadi al-Natrun, as well as the scholarly works and studies being done on them. Rushdi Said looks at the geological environment of the area that made it possible to establish and sustain such a vibrant community in that part of the Western Desert of Egypt. Tim Vivian examines the role that Macarius the Great, Isaiah of Scetis, and Daniel of Scetis played in laying the foundation of this great center of monastic life, as observed in their writings. Youhanna Nessim Youssef explores some aspects of the sacred service of preparing the Holy Chrism Oil, as performed in the Monastery of St. Macarius in the Middle Ages; this study is based on his work on a unique manuscript, housed in the Patriarchal Library in Cairo. And Ugo Zanetti surveys the types of liturgical services that have been found in the area and their eventual influence on the liturgical tradition of the Coptic Church, as observed in the contents of the Library of the Monastery of St. Macarius.

The second group of eight papers deals with the art, architecture, and inscriptions of Wadi al-Natrun. In the first of these, Elizabeth Bolman draws attention to the influence of Wadi al-Natrun and its monks as found in the recently restored icons of the Monastery of St. Antony at the Red Sea. Peter Grossmann then gives an overall survey of the architectural features found in the excavations of the monastic settlements in the region, including the recent excavations at the Monastery of St. John the Little. Suzana Hodak introduces her systematic work in the cataloging of the motifs and ornaments found in the wall paintings of the region. Lucy-Anne Hunt provides a general introduction to her work on the art in the Church of St. Macarius. Mat Immerzeel discusses the impressive stuccoes found in Dayr al-Suryan, tracing the origin of such decorative motifs to Syria. Eva Parandowska explains the work that was done in uncovering, cleaning, and restoring the iconographic programs in the ancient Church of the Virgin at Dayr al-Suryan: the earliest layer of wall paintings is dated to around the time of the Arab invasion of Egypt in the seventh century, later ones as late as the thirteenth century; the eighteenth-century layer was primarily added to cover the wall paintings. Zuzana Skalova examines in detail some of the Byzantine icons found in Wadi al-Natrun, arguing for their Egyptian origin. And finally, Jacques van der Vliet investigates the multilingual inscriptions found in the region: his remarks show how these inscriptions can be used to uncover the history of monasticism in Wadi al-Natrun.

The organizers especially thank H.H. Pope Shenouda III for the role he played in the success of this historic meeting. In addition to welcoming and accommodating the participants and attendees in his serene residence, he dedicated time to attend and participate in many of the symposium's sessions. The organizers would also like to recognize the selfless efforts of Dr. Hoda Garas, which contributed to the success of the symposium, and the tremendous efforts of the editors of this volume, Maged S.A. Mikhail and Mark S. Moussa. Thanks are due too to the publishers of *Coptica* for granting permission to republish these papers here. Special thanks are also due to Dr. Gawdat Gabra for proposing and negotiating the publication of this volume as part of the series of symposium proceedings on Christianity and Monasticism in Egypt, organized primarily by the St. Mark Foundation. Finally they express their thanks to the staff of the American University in Cairo Press for their tireless work in producing this volume.

The Importance of Wadi al-Natrun
for Coptology

Martin Krause

First of all, I must say some words about the history of Coptological studies[1] and the definition of Coptology.[2] I start in the 19th century, when the first professorship for Coptic language and literature was appointed at a German university. For the beginning of Coptological studies I point to my article "Coptological Studies" in the *Coptic Encyclopedia*.

It was Wilhelm von Humboldt, who advised Friedrich Wilhelm IVth, King of Prussia, to establish in 1845 a professorship for Coptic language and literature at the newly founded university of Berlin and to nominate Moritz Gotthilf Schwartze[3] as a candidate. Coptology thus became an independent scientific discipline at a German university, limited to Coptic language and literature, the areas in which Schwartze had worked. Schwartze died only three years after the establishment of Coptology in Berlin. Colleagues in related disciplines published manuscripts he had left after his death.

In Berlin, Coptology was replaced by Egyptology, also a newly founded discipline. K.R. Lepsius was the first representative. And the professors of Egyptology at Berlin University since A. Erman included the Coptic language in their teaching program while at other German universities the teaching program of Egyptology no longer includes Coptic language. The field of Egyptological research is now so extensive that in many universities Egyptology is divided into at least two fields, into philology and archaeology. Even the philologist normally does not care for the Coptic language. In his opinion it should be a language of the discipline of Christian oriental languages (Oriens christianus)[4] beside Syriac, Christian Arabic, Nubian, Ethiopic, Armenian and Georgian. This discipline we find now in

---

[1] M. Krause, "Coptological Studies," *CoptEncyc* 2: 613-16.
[2] M. Krause, "Coptology," *CoptEncyc* 2: 616-18.
[3] M. Krause, "Schwartze, Moritz Gotthilf," *CoptEncyc* 7: 2107.
[4] M. Krause, "Oriens Christianus," *CoptEncyc* 6: 1845.

Germany only in four universities: in Bonn, Munich, Tübingen and Halle. The University of Tübingen has already decided, that for financial reasons, the present holder of this professorship might not have a successor when he will retire.

According to a definition of Coptology in 1960,[5] the Coptic language belongs to Egyptology, and Coptic literature to Church history and to New Testament studies. This definition does not care for Coptic culture at all.

About 120 years after the death of Schwartze in Berlin another German institution, Münster university, decided to give Coptology a home beside Egyptology: My professorship was called: "Egyptology, especially Coptology,"[6] and since my retirement in 1995 it is now called "Coptology." I felt the definition of Coptology as only "Coptic language and literature" is too narrow. So my definition of Coptology is:[7]

> Coptology is a scientific discipline in Oriental studies that investigates the language and culture of Egypt and Nubia in the widest sense: literature, religion, history, archaeology, and art. Its range extends from late antiquity to the Middle Ages, or even down to the present. It touches on and intersects with a number of neighboring disciplines.

The greater part of its vocabulary connects it with Egyptology, with which it is still reckoned in many countries, because Coptic is the last branch of the Egyptian language; about four-fifths of Coptic words derive from Egyptian, as their etymologies show.[8] The reproduction of the vowels in Coptic is important to the Egyptologist for the reconstruction of the vowels that were not written in Egyptian, and for the investigation of verbal accent, syllable structure, and metrics in Egyptian.

In terms of content, continuity can be observed between the ancient Egyptian and the Christian period in the survival of ancient

---

[5] Prof. Dr. A. Falkenstein, *Denkschrift zur Lage der Orientalistik. Im Auftrage der Deutschen Forschungsgemeinschaft in Zusammenarbeit mit zahlreichen Fachvertretern* (Wiesbaden, 1960), 5.

[6] Ägyptologie mit besonderer Berücksichtigung der Koptologie.

[7] See note 2.

[8] J. Cerny, *Coptic Etymological Dictionary* (Cambridge, 1976); and W. Vycichl, *Dictionnaire Étymologique de la langue copte* (Leuven 1983).

Egyptian elements (concepts, ideas, and usages), particularly in religion, literature, and art, but also in Coptic medicine.

Coptology is linked with classical philology by the stock of Greek and Latin loanwords in the Coptic Language; the Greek, accounting for about 20 percent, far surpass the Latin. Their examination has begun, the discipline will experience a new florescence when all the loanwords have been collected.

In addition, there are texts preserved in Coptic that were originally composed in Greek, but whose Greek version either has not survived or exists only in fragments or in a Latin translation. Here Gnostic and Hermetic writings from the Nag Hammadi discovery should especially be mentioned.

In association with Byzantine studies, Coptology investigates the Byzantine period in Egypt. Work on the examination of Coptic codicology and paleography connects Coptology with papyrology. In addition to a few scrolls, early Coptic codices in particular have been preserved; they are roughly contemporary with the Greek. While Greek paleography has been well investigated, the Coptic has not advanced beyond preliminary work. Only with the appearance of colophons[9] do we find ourselves on firm ground. Collaboration with Greek papyrologists is necessary because Greek and Coptic documents often belong to the same archives.[10]

The Coptic nonliterary texts are important sources for the history and the cultural and economic developments of late antiquity. Especially from the sixth century on, they take their place alongside the Greek sources, later replace them, and are then the only sources.

The same holds good for epigraphy:[11] gravestones, inscriptions on buildings, and graffiti are couched in Coptic as well as Greek. In the forms used, we can often demonstrate the translation of Greek models. While Greek inscriptions in Egypt become fewer after the sixth century, in Nubia they alternated with Coptic for another five hundred years.

In association with the history of religions, Coptology examines the Gnostic,[12] Hermetic, and Manichaean texts, which often are

---

[9] M. Krause, "Colophon," *CoptEncyc* 2: 577-78.
[10] M. Krause, "Archives," *CoptEncyc* 1: 226-28.
[11] M. Krause, "Inscriptions," *CoptEncyc* 4: 1290-99.
[12] St. Emmel, "Nag Hammadi Library," *CoptEncyc* 6: 1771-73.

preserved only in Coptic translation and have been lost in their original language. Coptic magical texts and spells also belong here.[13]

Describing the content of Coptological studies does not mean that each Coptologist is a master in all fields of Coptology, but he should try to be so. In German universities, Coptology belongs to the faculty of humanities, and the student has to study three disciplines, one main and two subsidiaries. One of them can be in another faculty, for instance theology. Thus, he is free to decide whether he wants to concentrate on Egypt, studying two other disciplines in addition to Coptology, namely Egyptology and Arabic Studies. Or he may choose to study theology and another discipline intersecting Coptology to broaden his knowledge.

The work of the Coptologist intersects with various theological disciplines (Old and New Testament, church history and history of dogma, confessional lore, and liturgics). Here reference should be made above all to the work on editions of the Coptic Old and New Testaments; to work in textual criticism, and to the editing of apocryphal and pseudepigraphical writings of both Testaments.[14]

In church history,[15] the origins of Christianity in Egypt, its history beyond the split from the imperial church[16] after the Council of Chalcedon,[17] and the theological disputes that were dealt with at the early Christian councils are all the objects of Coptological research. A special investigative task force is at work on monasticism[18] in Egypt and the hagiography of Coptic Christianity.[19] The investigation of local Egyptian church history is still in its beginnings.

The confessional historian, in association with the Coptologist, examines the history of the Coptic church and its dogmas after its separation from the imperial church.[20]

We thus come to the period that extends from the Arab conquest of Egypt down to the present.[21] Here there are connections with

---

[13] W. Vycichl, "Magic," *CoptEncyc* 5: 1499-1509.

[14] T. Orlandi, "Literature, Coptic," *CoptEncyc* 5: 1450-60.

[15] J. den Heijer, "History of the Patriarchs of Alexandria," *CoptEncyc* 4: 1238-42.

[16] D.W. Winkler, *Koptische Kirche und Reichskirche. Altes Schisma und neuer Dialog* (Innsbruck-Wien, 1997).

[17] W.H.C. Frend, "Chalcedon, Council of," *CoptEncyc* 2: 512-5.

[18] A. Guillaumont, "Monasticism, Egyptian," *CoptEncyc* 5: 1661-6.

[19] T. Orlandi, "Haiographic, Coptic," *CoptEncyc* 4: 1191-7.

[20] A. Gerhards and H. Brakmann, eds., *Die koptische Kirche. Einführung in das ägyptische Christentum* (Stuttgart-Berlin-Köln 1994).

Arabic studies and with the study of Islam. The Coptic language gradually lost its significance as a colloquial and literary language and was replaced, except as the language of the church, by Arabic. The Copts translated their literary works into Arabic, and prepared Coptic-Arabic word lists, the *scalae*,[22] and grammatical summaries, in order to preserve the knowledge of their language. Part of the Coptic literature is preserved only in Arabic translation. The Coptic language had previously influenced Egyptian Arabic in its phonology, and Coptic words had been accepted into Arabic as loanwords.[23] The relations between Copts and Moslems are also a subject for research in both disciplines.[24]

Along with classical, early Christian, and Byzantine archaeologists, those concerned with provincial archaeology, and historians of architecture, Coptologists are concerned with the study of Coptic art, iconography, and architecture.[25] Here, on the one hand, they have established the survival of Egyptian building tradition in Coptic architecture, for instance at the White Monastery in Sohag, which Shenute had built at the beginning of the fifth century in the style of an Egyptian temple. Pictorial themes from late antiquity appear, above all on Coptic textiles.[26]

Coptology is linked with Nubiology, a discipline only a few decades old, in the investigation of Nubia in the Christian period,[27] which spans a period more than a thousand years. The Christian epoch in Nubia came to an end only in the sixteenth century. Like the Ethiopian church,[28] the Nubian was dependent on the patriarch of the Coptic church. The excavations carried out in Nubia before the building of the High Dam at Aswan have brought to light abundant source material (written and archaeological), which also sheds new light on the relations between the Coptic and Nubian churches.

Research into the relation between the Coptic church and the Ethiopian church links Coptology with Ethiopic studies. The

---

[21] P. M. Fraser, "Arab Conquest of Egypt," *CoptEncyc* 1: 183-9.

[22] W. Vycichl, *CoptEncyc* 8: 204-7.

[23] Emile Maher Ishaq, "Egyptian Arabic Vocabulary; Coptic Influence on," *CoptEncyc* 8: 112-8.

[24] C.F. Petry, "Copts in late Medieval Egypt," *CoptEncyc* 2: 618-35.

[25] P. Grossmann, *Christliche Architektur in Ägypten* (Leiden, 2002).

[26] P. du Bourguet, "Textiles, Coptic," *CoptEncyc* 7: 2210-30.

[27] See the articles of W.Y. Adams in *CoptEncyc* 6: 1800-20.

[28] Mirrit Boutros Ghali, "Ethiopian Church Autocephaly," *CoptEncyc* 3: 980-4 and the articles *CoptEncyc* 3: 984-4, 1056.

Ethiopian patriarch was an Egyptian Copt until Emperor Haile
Selassie broke with this ancient tradition. Coptic literature was
translated from Arabic into Ethiopic.

The field of Coptology also intersects with the study of the
Christian East (Oriens christianus),[29] which is concerned with
languages, and literature of the Eastern Christian churches, including
the Coptic.

We may link the investigation of the Coptic language with
linguistics, which is still in its infancy, since it is only in recent years
that linguists, following Hans Jakob Polotsky,[30] have concerned
themselves with this task.

Coptology is connected with the history of law through
investigation of Coptic law[31] of the Coptic documents. So far only
some of the sources, Coptic nonliterary papyri and ostraca, have been
published. The older publications need to be replaced by new ones,
since they no longer correspond to the requirements of modern text
editions.

The investigation of Coptic medical texts links Coptology with
the history of medicine.[32] Although ancient Egyptian medicine was
treated in nine volumes by Hermann Grapow and his collaborators,
many texts in the Greek and Coptic languages still await treatment.

As you may have seen Coptology is not a small, but a very large
discipline and needs many scholars for research. Although the
number of scholars interested in the fields of Coptology has increased
since the founding of the International Association for Coptic
Studies[33] in Cairo 1976—also the number of participants in the
international congresses[34] increased considerably—but there are no
new positions for Coptology at universities or institutes of research.
We remind ourselves of Jesus' saying in Matthew 9:38 or Luke 10:2,
that the harvest is plentiful, but that the workmen are few. Therefore
we are very glad that the American University in Cairo plans a
professorship for Coptology, but at the same time we are sorry, that

---

[29] See note 4.
[30] H.J. Polotsky, *Grundlagen des koptischen Satzbaus* (Decatur, Georgia 1987
u.1990); A. Shisha-Halevy, *Coptic Grammatical Categories: Structural Studies in the
Syntax of Shenutian Sahidic* (Rome, 1986).
[31] L.S.B. MacCoull, "Law, Coptic," *CoptEncyc* 5: 1428-32.
[32] K.S. Kolta, "Medicine, Coptic," *CoptEncyc* 5: 1578-82.
[33] M.B. Ghali, "International Association for Coptic Studies," *CoptEncyc* 4: 1299.
[34] M. Krause, "International Congresses of Coptic Studies," *CoptEncyc* 4: 1300-1.

we lost a position for Coptic architecture and archeology in the German Institute of Archaeology in Cairo after the retirement of our college Peter Grossmann.[35]

In any case, Coptology needs the help of scholars of disciplines neighboring Coptology which I named. So we are very glad to welcome here scholars of the faculties of theology and humanities, who work with us, helping us in our research of the Wadi al-Natrun, as well as colleagues from disciplines neighboring Coptology. As they have already collaborated with us in 1980 and 1991 as editors—I name only our colleague Khalil Samir—helping us to complete the *Coptic Encyclopedia*.[36]

This symposium corresponds to the Kellia symposium at Geneva in 1984[37] and to the congresses of Nubian Studies 1969.[38] It was there that scientists of Coptology and related disciplines, such as archeology, excavators, historians of art, and restorers of paintings working in Kellia or in Nubia met and reported about the results of their excavation and restoration work and discussed problems with colleagues.

This time Wadi al-Natrun[39] is not only the subject of this symposium, but also the place where we meet to report and discuss thanks to His Holiness Pope Shenouda III and the organizing committee. This is only the beginning of new period of research of one of the most important centers of Coptology.

The Wadi al Natrun enriches nearly all fields of Coptology and it also covers a very long period from the 4th century of the Christian era up to the present day and—I am sure—also for the coming centuries. The excavation of lauras are going on and also new wall paintings are uncovered. They must be preserved, studied, and also published.

The geology of Wadi al-Natrun will be described by Professor Rouchdi Said. The old period of research of the Wadi al-Natrun ends with the publication of the results of the so called "Egyptian

---

[35] M. Krause and S. Schaten, ΘΕΜΕΛΙΑ. *Spätantike und koptologische Studien Peter Grossmann zum 65. Geburtstag* (Wiesbaden, 1998), 9 f.

[36] A.S. Atiya (Editor in Chief), *The Coptic Encyclopedia*, 8 vols., (New York, 1991).

[37] Ph. Bridel, ed., *Le site monastique copte des Kellia: Sources historiques et explorations archéologiques. Actes du Colloque de Genève 13 au 15 aout 1984* (Genève, 1986).

[38] E. Dinkler, ed., *Kunst und Geschichte Nubiens in christlicher Zeit. Ergebnisse und Probleme auf Grund der jüngsten Ausgrabungen* (Recklinghausen, 1970).

[39] A. Cody, "Scetis," *CoptEncyc* 7: 2102-6.

expedition of the Metropolitan Museum of Art," published in three
volumes "The Monasteries of the Wadi 'n Natrun" in 1926, 1932, and
1933. The publication was prepared by Hugh G. Evelyn-White and
after Evelyn-White's death in the summer of 1924 published by
Walter Hauser. Between 1909 and 1921 members of the Museum of
New York had photographed and described the architecture and
archaeology of the three monasteries of Wadi al-Natrun in volume 3,
published 1933. "The history of the Monasteries of Nitria and of
Scetis" was published in 1932 in volume 2.

Here, in the Wadi al-Natrun, in Kellia, and Nitria are centers of
hermits since the beginning of the fourth century. The life of
Macarius and of other hermits is described in the *Apophthegmata
patrum*. Also the *Lausiac History* of Palladius and John Cassian's
Institutes and *Conferences* show how the monks of Scetis lived in the
late fourth and early fifth centuries, and how their settlements were
organized. These reports were done by Christians, who came to Wadi
al-Natrun and to other places in Egypt in order to study the famous
monasticism of Egypt and to practice it here, and persisting in it after
their return in their countries. The history of monasticism at Wadi al-
Natrun will be sketched by Reverend Dr. Tim Vivian, and the paper
of Dr. Brune "The Multi-Ethnic Character of Wadi al-Natrun" will
show that people from many countries came to become monks in
Wadi al-Natrun. His Holiness Pope Shenouda III has already
informed us about the "Current Monasticism in Wadi al-Natrun."

Already in 1926 Evelyn-White published the first volume "New
Coptic Texts from the Monastery of Saint Macarius with an
Appendix on a Copto-Arabic Ms. by G.P.G. Sobhy." Evelyn-White
also included in his publication leaves and fragments, "once
belonging to the same manuscripts, which were recovered by Tattam
in 1839 and Tischendorf in 1844."[40]

Evelyn-White's publication is the standard publication of the
Wadi al-Natrun for Coptic studies up till now. But the research did
not stop. Evelyn-White had asked Marcos Simaika to include the
Arabic manuscripts in the "Catalogue of the Coptic and Arabic
Manuscripts in the Coptic Museum, the Patriarchate, the Principal

---

[40] H.G. Evelyn-White, *The Monasteries of the Wadi 'n Natrun: Part I. New Coptic
Texts from the Monastery of Saint Macarius edited with an introduction on the library
at the monastery of Saint Macarius with an appendix on a Copto-Arabic Ms by G.P.G.
Sobhy* (New York, 1926), VII.

Churches of Cairo and Alexandria and the Monasteries of Egypt," which was completed in March 1929 and published in 1939 and 1942.[41]

In 1986 our colleague Ugo Zanetti published "Les manuscrits de Dair Abu Maqar. Inventaire." Kent Brown of Brigham Young University has microfilmed the Arabic manuscripts. So the project of the Christian Arabic manuscripts is progressing.

In 1975, Oswald Hugh Ewart KHS-Burmester published a catalogue of Coptic and Copto-Arabic manuscripts of the library of the Abba Pshoi monastery.[42] His work was continued by Lothar Störk, who, after Burmester's death in 1977, corrected and published Burmester's notes of a catalogue of Coptic manuscripts from Dair Anba Maqar in 1995,[43] and in 1996 he published a booklet of "Addenda and corrigenda" to Burmesters catalogue.[44] During his first travel to Egypt (1853/4), Heinrich K. Brugsch saw Coptic manuscripts in the Syrian monastery of the Wadi al-Natrun. In 1870 he bought Coptic manuscripts in the monastery of Apa Pshoi, which are in the library of Göttingen university.[45] The manuscripts of these catalogues must be studied and published in the future. They once belonged to the libraries of the monasteries of the Wadi al-Natrun.

Since the middle ages, European travelers had come to Egypt and visited also the monasteries of Wadi al-Natrun and brought back to Europe books from these libraries in Coptic and Arabic, which were deposed in various European libraries. I name only the Vatican library[46] and the libraries of the universities of Cambridge[47] and of

---

[41] M. Simaika Pasha, *Catalogue of the Coptic and Arabic Manuscripts in the Coptic Museum, the Patriarchate, the Principal Churches of Cairo and Alexandria and the Monasteries of Egypt*. Vol. I (Cairo, 1939), XIX.

[42] *Koptische Handschriften 1: Die Handschriftenfragmente der Staats- und Universitätsbibliothek Hamburg Teil 1 beschrieben von O.H.E. Khs-Burmester* (Wiesbaden, 1975).

[43] *Koptische Handschriften 2: Die Handschriften der Staats- und Universitätsbibliothek Hamburg. Teil 2: Die Handschriften aus Dair anba Maqar* beschrieben von L. Störk unter Verwendung der Aufzeichnungen von O.H.E. KHS-Burmester, (Stuttgart, 1995).

[44] L. Störk, *Koptische Handschriften 3. Die Handschriften der Staats- und Universitätsbibliothek Hamburg: Teil 3: Addenda und Corrigenda zu Teil 1*, (Stuttgart, 1996).

[45] H. Brugsch, *Wanderung nach den Natronklöstern in Ägypten* (Berlin, 1855), 47 f. and L. Störk, *Koptische Handschriften 4. Die Handschriften der Staatsbibliothek zu Berlin. Teil 1: Liturgische Handschriften* (Stuttgart 2002), 21 ff.

[46] A. Hebbelynck and A. Lantschoot, *Codices coptici Vaticana, Barberiniani, Borgiani, Rossiani, Bibliotheca Vaticana*, tom. I, 1937; tom. II, 1947.

Leipzig.[48] Here, the manuscripts were studied and sometimes published and roused also the interest in the Christians living in Egypt and the Coptic church and Egyptian monasticism. Moritz Gotthilf Schwartze,[49] who in 1845 was appointed Professor of Coptology in Berlin, had copied and studied Coptic manuscripts in various European libraries and planned an edition of the Bohairic New Testament, of which only the four gospels appeared in his lifetime. We can conclude: while Egyptian monastic libraries lost manuscripts these manuscripts aroused the interest in Coptology, Coptic monasticism and the Coptic Church.

Siegfried Richter's paper will show "Wadi al-Natrun and Coptic Literature." Dr. Johannes Den Heijer's lecture, "Wadi al-Natrun and the History of Patriarchs," will show what we can learn from these reports.

The importance of the Greek, Coptic, and Syriac inscriptions for the history of Wadi al-Natrun we can see from the paper of Dr. Jacques van der Vliet.

From further new excavations of ruins in the neighborhood of the four still existing monasteries we expect more archaeological evidence of their dwellings. Many of them were destroyed by invasions of barbarians from the Libyan desert in the years 407, 434, 444, and at the end of the sixth century. The paper of Dr. Peter Grossmann about the architecture at Wadi al-Natrun will show what we know about the early and later periods of archaeology and architecture of Wadi al-Natrun.

The discovery and the excavations of the monastic settlements of the nearby Kellia and the publications of our French, Swiss and Egyptian colleges have shown the transition from eremetism-(one father-eremit living with a younger pupil-eremit) to monasticism (eremits or monks living together in one building with more rooms) in archaeology. Validating what we knew from the literary sources.

As many eremits or monks were killed by invaders during the already quoted barbarian invasions, walls were built to protect the lives of the monks, and also towers inside the monasteries. Open to

---

[47] M.R. James, *Supplement to the catalogue of manuscripts in the library of Gonville and Gaius College* (Cambridge, 1914).

[48] J. Leipoldt, "Verzeichnis der koptischen Handschriften der Universitäts-bibliothek zu Leipzig," in C. Vollers, *Katalog der Handschriften der Universitätsbibliothek zu Leipzig*, vol. 2, (Leipzig, 1906), 383-427.

[49] See note 3.

question is the proposal of our college Georges Descoeudres from Switzerland that the towers in monastic buildings of Kellia could also have served as cells for monks.

When the Coptic church agreed to include the publication of the wall paintings of the Wadi al-Natrun into the French corpus "la peinture murale chez les coptes" and permitted restorers to start their work, a series of unexpected and beautiful new wall paintings were discovered. The late Paul van Moorsel[50] and his pupils, Dr. Karel Innemée and Dr. Matt Immerzeel, our Dutch colleges, who continue the work will show us a part of these wall paintings in their lectures "New discoveries of Wall Paintings at Dayr al-Surian" and "Stucco Work at Dayr al-Syrian." Dr. Ewa Parandowska will inform us about the "Results of the last Restoration Campaign."

Professor Lucy-Ann Hunt will lecture about the "Art at Wadi al-Natrun," and Suzana Hodak about "The ornamental Repertoire in the Art of Wadi al- Natrun."

With Professor Murad Kamil, I visited the monasteries in 1959 for the first time, and the last time with my students in 1988. So I saw the big progress of development of monasticism and the monasteries within 30 years and I was informed that it is progressing.

During the symposium we will also have the chance to see in 2002 all the enlarged monasteries, the new excavations and uncovered wall paintings and have the chance to take part in the Coptic liturgy by His Grace Bishop Youanes and later we will listen to the paper of father Ugo Zanetti about the liturgy of the Coptic church and the preparation, and the consecration of the holy chrism at Wadi al-Natrun by Dr. Youhanna Nessim Youssef.

All lectures are part of Coptological studies and show the importance of Wadi al-Natrun for the many fields of Coptology from the beginning of monasticism in the fourth century to the present time and—with God's help—the coming centuries.

---

[50] P. van Moorsel, *Called to Egypt. Collected Studies on Painting in Christian Egypt* (Leiden, 2000).

The Multiethnic Character of the Wadi al-Natrun

Karl-Heinz Brune

The history of the Wadi al-Natrun can be traced back to earlier pharaonic times when the trade route from Buhaira and Farāfrah Oases passed through the valley on the way to the Nile delta.[1] The oldest Egyptian term for the region, *sh.t-p.t* (Lake of Heaven) occurs in the Pyramid Texts (approx. 2360– 2160 B.C.).[2] A description of the Wadi al-Natrun is found in "the Eloquent Peasant," a literary work dating to the Middle Kingdom (approx. 1940 – 1760 B.C.).[3] The story is set in a somewhat earlier epoch, towards the end of the third millennium B.C. during the reign of King Nebkaure (Dyn. IX/X). The peasant of the title comes from the "Field of Salt," i.e. the Wadi al-Natrun, and he is on his way to sell the products of the valley in Hierakleopolis Magna (= Ahnas).[4] His wares also included merchandise from Farāfrah Oasis (called Cattle Country in the text).[5] Thanks to this tale, we know that the Wadi al-Natrun was not only an agricultural center but a transshipment point for products from oases in the Libyan Desert as early as the Middle Kingdom. Archaeological finds dating to the reign of Amenemhet I (first ruler of Dyn. XII, approx. 1920 B.C.)[6] and from Dyn. XVII (approx. 1625 – 1540 B.C.)[7] show that the Wadi al-Natrun was a site of military and religious activities as well.

---

[1] O.F.A. Meinardus, *Monks and Monasteries of the Egyptian Deserts* (Cairo 1961), 117; O.F.A. Meinardus, *Christian Egypt: Ancient and Modern* (Cairo 1965), 146.

[2] A. Fakhry, "Wadi-El-Natrun," *Annales du Service des Antiquités de l'Égypt* 40 (1940), 837-853.

[3] Publications of this text include, e.g., A. Erman, *Die Literatur der Ägypter* (Leipzig 1923), 157-176; M. Lichtheim, *Ancient Egyptian Literature Vol. I: The Old and Middle Kingdom* (Berkeley-Los Angeles-London 1973), 169-184; R.B. Parkinson, *The Tale of Sinuhe and other Ancient Egyptian Poems, 1940-1640 BC*, (Oxford 1997), 44-88.

[4] Herakleopolis Magna was a town in the 20th nome of Upper Egypt and the capital of Egypt in the 9th and 10th Dynasty.

[5] Erman 1923 [note 3], 158 f. Lichtheim 1973 [note 3], 170, 182; Parkinson 1997 [note 3], 58.

[6] Fakhry 1940 [note 2], 845-847; A. Fakhry, A., *Bahria Oasis*, Vol. I (Cairo 1942); A. Fakhry, *Siwa Oasis* (Cairo 1944), 12, 24.

[7] Fakhry 1940 [note 2], 845-847; Fakhry 1944 [note 6] 12, 24.

Many centuries later, the geographer Strabo referred to the Wadi al-Natrun in the following passage:

Above Momemphis are two nitre-beds which contain large quantities of nitre and the Nitriote Nome. Here Sarapis is held in honour and they are the only people in Aegypt who sacrifice a sheep.[8]

The old Coptic names are ϣⲓⲏⲧ and ϣⲓⲉϩⲏⲧ while Σκῆτις was the Greek designation for the Wadi al-Natrun. Beginning in the 7th century, another Coptic name became popular: ⲡⲧⲱⲟⲩ ⲙ̄ⲡⲓϩⲟⲥⲉⲙ (= the Mountain of Natron).[9] This designation is also rendered in Arabic (*Djebel al-Natrun*) in the Synaxarion under the 24th of Pachons.[10] Additional names used in the Synaxarion in particular are Desert of Shīhāt and Desert of Asqit.[11] In the Middle Ages, the term Wadi Habib was also well known for the region. El-Maqrizi, who lived in the 15th century, was the first to employ Wadi al-Natrun, the name current nowadays.[12]

The Multiethnic Character in Early Monastic Times

The multiethnic character of the Wadi al-Natrun is reflected in the names of two monasteries which are still active today: Dayr as-Surian, the Syrian Monastery, and Dayr al-Baramus, the Monastery of the Romans. But if Coptic tradition be credited, the earliest evidence for multiethnicity goes back to the time following shortly on the birth of Christ when the Holy Family sojourned in Egypt. In the Synaxarion under the 24th of Pachons, mentioned above, we read: "They crossed the river to the west bank and then saw from afar the Gabal 'n-Natrun. The Blessed Virgin Mary blessed it, knowing the effect of angelic Services that would be rendered there."[13] According

---

[8] Strabo, *Geography* XVII, 1, 23; He had accompanied Aelius Gallus, Prefect of Egypt, on a tour of the country in 25-24 B.C.
[9] Fakhry 1940 [note 2], 843 f.
[10] *Le Synaxaire Arabe Jacobite, Patrolologia orientalis* Vol. XVI, 24 de Bachons, 409.
[11] E.g. 2nd and 13th of Bābah, 26th of Ṭūbah, 27th of Baramhāt, 7th and 8th of Bashans, 19th of Ba'ūnah, 8th of Abīb. Another designation is Mizān el-Qolub, see F. Wüstenfeld, (Ed.), *Macrizi's Geschichte der Copten*, (Göttingen 1845; repr. Hildesheim-New York 1979), 109; Fakhry 1940 [note 2], 843.
[12] Wüstenfeld 1979 [note 11], 109.
[13] English translation after Meinardus 1961 [note 1], 118.

to this tradition then, it was Christ's mother Mary, a "foreigner," who played the decisive role in the first significant "event" of the Christian era associated with the Wadi al-Natrun.

Remaining in Coptic tradition and in the Synaxarion, we find a series of episodes in which other foreigners figure in the Scetis, including, for example, the visit of Severus, Patriarch of Antioch, to the desert of Shihat,[14] and the raid conducted by a horde of Berbers during the visit of an emissary from Emperor Theodosius. There was Saint Anastasia from Constantinople who hid for 28 years in the desert Shihat near the cell of Amba Daniel to escape the unwelcome attentions of Emperor Justinian.[15] We even learn that the actual founder of the Scetis Apa Makarius was called a truthful Israelite by Saint Antonius.[16] But in this last case, the reference is not to his nationality, since Makarius was an Egyptian, but rather to his piety, since Israelite pilgrims were well known to be emphatically more devout than Egyptian pilgrims.

Even if the historicity of some information from the Synaxarion is doubtful, nevertheless these examples show that contacts between the monks of the Scetis and foreigners occurred regularly from the beginning, and, furthermore, that the population of the valley included foreigners.

We tread on historically somewhat more solid ground when we turn our attention to the *Apophthegmata patrum*. This source confirms the impression gained from the Synaxarion. Numerous episodes document the presence of strangers from almost the entire Mediterranean world and eastwards as far as Persia. There is, for example, the episode concerning Basileios the Great, who is reported to have chosen a servant from among the monks.[17] Basileios, brother of Gregor of Nyssa, became archbishop of Caesarea and metropolitan of Cappadocia, in 370. Another episode mentions a man who arrived from abroad to visit Apa Poimen.[18]

Several foreigners became desert fathers and led a monk's life, either permanently or intermittently. An example is the learned

---

[14] Synaxarium, 2nd of Bābah.

[15] Synaxarium, 26th of Ṭūbah; 8th of Bashans.

[16] Synaxarium, 27th of Baramhāt.

[17] J.B. Cotelier, "Apophthegmata Patrum," in J.P. Migne (ed.), *Patrologia, series graeca* (PG), LXV, 137-138.

[18] PG, LXV, 321-324.

Arsenios (354-445),[19] tutor of Arcadius and Honorius, the sons of Emperor Theodosius. (Arsenios, who came from a Roman senatorial family, lived in the Scetis between 395 and 410.) Others include: Gregorius of Nazianz (330-390),[20] a friend of Gregory of Nyssa and of Basileios; Apa Gelasios from Palestine;[21] Epiphanios,[22] later bishop of Salamis, on Cyprus; Apa Zenon from Syria;[23] Apa Johannes, the Persian;[24] and Apa Cassian from Scythia (*360)[25] who spent much time in the Scetis on his second trip to Egypt. The final quarter of the 4th century, the classical period of Egyptian monasticism, witnessed a veritable tourist boom in the Egyptian desert which seems to have held a special attraction for foreign visitors.[26]

Ethnic problems in the Scetis

The nationality or ethnic origin of the desert fathers is only rarely mentioned in the *Apophthegmata patrum*. Generally speaking, the information we possess is derived from other sources, which might be interpreted to suggest that these factors played absolutely no role in the monastic community. But the case of the Apa named Moses shows that this surmise is questionable. The *Apophthegmata* contain no fewer than 38 episodes in which Moses features,[27] making him one of the most important protagonists in the collection. It is unnecessary to review the details of his biography, since Gawdat Gabra has thoroughly dealt with this material.[28] In the present context, it is important to note that Moses was an Ethiopian, i.e. a black man, a fact confirmed by several other sources.[29] In general

---

[19] PG, LXV, 87-108.
[20] PG, LXV, 87-108.
[21] PG, LXV, 145-154.
[22] PG, LXV, 161-168.
[23] PG, LXV, 175-180.
[24] PG, LXV, 235-239.
[25] PG, LXV, 243-246.
[26] E.R. Hardy, *Christian Egypt: Church and People* (New York 1952), 87.
[27] PG, LXV, 105 f., 179 f., 271 f., 281-290, 361 f., 371 f.; H. Rosweyde, "Apophthegmata Patrum," in J.P. Migne, *Patrologia, series latina* (PL), LXXIII, 867, 937, 957, 1027, 1034, 1049, 1053, 1058 f.; App., PL LXXIV, 383, 387, 389, 394.
[28] G. Gabra, "Bemerkungen zu Moses dem Schwarzen," in *Spätantike und koptologische Studien, Peter Grossmann zum 65. Geburtstag*, Sprachen und Kulturen des christlichen Orients Vol 3, (Wiesbaden 1998), 117-126.
[29] The most important are: E. Amélineau, "Histoire des Monastères de la Basse-Égypt," *Annales Musée Guimet* XXV (Paris 1894), 262; M. Chaine, "Le Manuscrit de

Moses is treated with the utmost reverence. Above all, his piety and
his affinity to asceticism are praised in superlatives. But two episodes
of the *Apophthegmata patrum*[30] show that because Moses was a black
man, his relationship to the other desert-fathers was not entirely easy.
The episodes in question are:

> (1) Another time there was a meeting in the Scetis, and the others
> wanted to test him and treated him like a cipher, saying: "Why
> does this Ethiopian come into our midst?" He listened silently.
> After the end of the meeting, they said to him. "Abba, did you
> not become upset there?" He answered: "Yes, I was upset but I
> didn't know what to say."

> (2) They told about the Abba Moses: When he became a cleric,
> they put the shoulder-cloth on him. The archbishop spoke to him:
> "Look, you have become quite white, Abba Moses!" The Abba
> answered him: "Yes, on the outside, Papa – but what of the
> inside!?" Then the archbishop wanted now to test him and said to
> the clerics: "When the Abba Moses enters the sanctuary, order
> him out and follow him so that you can hear what he says." The
> monks now entered, and they heaped reproaches upon him and
> chased him out with the words: "Away, out you Ethiopian!"
> Going out, he said to himself: "It serves me right, me with my
> ash-colored face, a nigger! After all, I am not a human being,
> why do I go among humans?!"

The situation is unambiguous. The Scetis was hardly an
unproblematic melting pot of different races. The decisive point is not
that Moses was tempted by his brothers - this also happened to other

---

la Version Copte en Dialecte Sahidique des "Apophthegmata Patrum," *Bibliothèque
d'Études Coptes* VI (Cairo 1960), 45 f.; G. Zoega, *Catalogus codicum copticorum
manuscriptorum qui in Museo Borgiane Velitris adservantur* (Rome 1810), 318 f.;
Palladius, "Historia Lausiaca," PG XXXIV, 991-1278, 1063-1070 (New ed. C. Butler,
The Lausiac History of Palladius (Cambridge 1898; Reprint, Hildesheim 1967), Vol. I
u. II. II, 58-62; E.A.W. Budge, *The Paradise of the Holy Fathers* (London 1907;
reprint, Seattle 1984), Vol. I u. II. I, 215 ff., 228, 267; II, 7, 8, 9, 12 f., 16, 50, 83, 102
f., 112, 122 f., 143 f., 165, 180, 203, 284 f., 289 f., 317, 325; Synaxarium, 24th of
Ba'ūnah; E.A.W. Budge, *The Book of the Saints of the Ethiopian Church* (Cambridge
1928; Reprint, Hildesheim – New York 1976), 1030-1032; B. Pirone, *Vita di Mosè
l'Etiope* = SOCC XXIV, 1991; Wüstenfeld 1845 [note 11], 111 f. Further sources in
Gabra 1998 [note 28].
[30] PG LXV, 283 f.; PL LXXIII, 959 f.

monks, for it was a common practice employed to demonstrate the humility and sanctity of an abba. At issue was rather Moses's skin color as a source of humiliation. The astonishing thing is not Moses's acceptance of racist humiliation, but rather that he heaps more humiliation upon himself, thereby increasing his humility and holiness in the eyes of the others. As a black, and thus a priori inferior, Moses had to suffer a greater humiliation than all the other fathers in order to be finally accepted by them as an equal. (Subsequently, he even became one of the most popular martyrs of the Coptic church). This tendency, which is clearly perceptible in the early documents, became less and less pronounced over the following centuries. Ultimately, in the Synaxarion, the two episodes have become harmlessly conflated, abrogating their ethnic overtones.[31]

The examination of only two Coptic religious-historical sources, namely the *Apophthegmata patrum* and the Synaxarion, shows that since the first monastic settlement in the Wadi al-Natrun, not only were international relationships cultivated, but that foreigners comprised a significant part of the population. However, these relationships, as in the case of Moses, cannot have always been free of problems.

The Foundation of the al-Baramus Monastery

I have already mentioned that the al-Baramus Monastery is the Monastery of the Romans. Etymologically, "Baramus" derives from the Coptic ⲡⲁ-ⲣⲱⲙⲉⲟⲥ "belonging to the Romans." What does the name signify? In order to answer this question, we must again turn to legend. The Romans to which the name of the monastery refers are two ahistorical sons of the emperor Valentian I (d. 379),[32] Maximus and Domitius, who are still revered today as saints in the Coptic church.[33] According to tradition, they arrived in the Wadi al-Natrun after a long pilgrimage through Asia Minor and Palestine. In the Scetis, Makarius ordained them to the priesthood. When they died, a church was built for them and, at the instigation of Makarius, its name was made to refer to them (Monastery of the Romans).[34] But

---

[31] 24th of Ba'ūnah.

[32] Amélineau 1894 [note 29], 262-315.

[33] Amélineau 1894 [note 29], 262-315.

[34] Amélineau 1894 [note 28], 311. The origins and development of the legends are not very clear. More on this there is a confusion with Arcadius and Honorius, the sons

the label "Romans" does not designate Maximus and Domitius "citizens" of Rome.

Their purported father Valentian was born in what is nowadays Croatia. Legend calls him an emperor from Greece, which, historically speaking, is not quite correct, since Valentian, shortly after his assumption of power in 364, turned over the administration of the eastern part of the empire to his brother Valens. Valentian spent most of his reign in the German town of Trier, and it was from Trier that he organized the struggle against the Alemannians who were rebellious at the time. Accordingly, his sons of legend, Maximus and Domitius, like his historical son Gratianus, should have been born in Trier. Thus, in contemporary terms, they would be Germans who, as Roman princes, engendered by a Croatian, became Egyptian monks. In other words, legend concerning the foundation of al-Baramus, the first monastery in the Wadi al-Natrun, also reflects the multiethnic character of the valley.

Early Historical Developments in the Wadi al-Natrun

Following on the foundation of more monasteries in the Scetis,[35] their history was intimately affected by the influence of foreigners. For example, foreign contacts which involved the Scetis as a whole were the repeated devastations at the hands of Berber tribesmen - thrice in the first half of the 5th century alone.[36] Further destruction occurred at the end of the 6th century and in 817. These disasters were also, of course, a kind of contact with foreign peoples. The chronological distribution of these raids shows that relative peace prevailed in the Scetis from the mid-5th century until the end of the 6th.

The Wadi al-Natrun was not spared theological conflicts. I mention here only confrontations with the followers of Origen at the end of the 4th century and the split of Egyptian Christians into anti- and pro-Chalcedonian factions after the Council of Chalcedon. The

---

of Theodosius mentioned immediately above. For subject, see H.G. Evelyn-White, *The Monasteries of the Wādi 'n Natrūn*, Vol. II (New York 1932; Reprint 1973), 98-104; Meinardus 1961 [note 1], 125 f.

[35] By the end of the 4th century there were four monastic settlements, which all became monasteries. Besides the Al-Baramus-Monastery, these were Dayr Anbā Maqār, Dayr Anbā Bishoi and the monastery of St. John the Short; *The Coptic Encyclopaedia* [*CoptEncyc*], (New York – Toronto – Oxford – Singapore – Sydney 1991), VII, 2103.

[36] 407, 434, 444 A.C.

monks of the Scetis sided with the anti-Chalcedonians and they profited from it, being rewarded by Emperor Zenon, an Isaurien, with foundations and donations[37] after he gave up his pro-Chalcedonian policy in 482. This type of foreign aid for the development of the Scetis secured the monks' prosperity for several decades. There was no renewal of religious/political tensions until the first half of the 6th century when the leaders of competing factions were two non-Egyptians: Severus of Antioch, who was born in southeastern Turkey at Pisidia, and Julian of Halicarnassus. Their theological dispute took place not far from the Scetis, in Alexandria, to which city Emperor Justinian had banished them both.[38] Scholars have assumed that Severus's adherents established four monasteries in the Scetis in the course of these confrontations, as counterparts to the four extant monasteries, three of which are known to have been dedicated to the Virgin Mother of God.[39] This probably occurred after 535, the year in which the anti-Chalcedonian church of Egypt split into a Severian (or Theodosian) faction, led by Patriarch Theodosius, and the Julianists (or Gaianits), led by the anti-Patriarch Gaianus. Of the four monasteries established in this connection, only one survived. If it was the monastery now known as Dayr as-Surian, which continues to exist down to the present, it is remarkable that a community of foreign monks could endure during the intervening centuries. Theological conflicts dragged on for decades, with the Gaianic movement ceasing only after the fourth destruction of the Scetis, at the end of the 6th century, although some individual Gaianites would hold out until the beginning of the 8th century.[40]

The next significant contact with foreigners affected the entire Wadi al-Natrun: the Arab conquest of Egypt, 640/641. At first, relations between the monks and the conquerors were not difficult. It was only at the beginning of the 8th century that the first conflicts occurred. The problems which arose were not the immediate result of, but they were indirectly related to ethnic and/or religious differences, since it was a matter of the taxes levied against non-Muslims. But despite reprisals and a decline in the number of monks,[41] the Scetis

---

[37] *CoptEncyc*, Vol. VII, 2104.
[38] *Lexikon für Theologie und Kirche* (LThK) (Freiburg 1986), Vol. I, 702 f. Vol. V, 1198; *Lexikon der antiken christlichen Literatur* (LACL) (Freiburg² 1999), 362, 555 f.
[39] *CoptEncyc*, Vol. VII, 2104.
[40] *CoptEncyc*, Vol. VII, 2104.
[41] *CoptEncyc*, Vol. VII, 2104.

remained the most important refuge and bulwark against the increasing expansion of Islam during these times, as evidenced by the many patriarch-bishops who were appointed from among the local communities. The situation led to another wave of internationalization within Egyptian monasticism. Many strangers came into the Wadi al-Natrun, not for the sake of monastic ideals but to use the Scetis as a springboard for a career in the church.[42]

The desert fathers' next contact with uninvited guests occurred in the first half of the 9th century when marauding gangs of Arabs invaded the Scetis. These waves of destruction, the fifth and sixth in the series, contributed to a persistent precarious condition of the monasteries with long-range consequences for monastic life. The way the monks had traditionally built their settlements was abandoned after their experience with predatory hordes. Now they surrounded the nuclei of their monasteries with walls to provide better protection from marauders than afforded by the fortified towers they had previously relied upon. And they began to give up living in individual, scattered cells in favor of life inside walled enclosures. In the final analysis, the movement away from the anchoritic towards a cenobitical way of life[43] in the Scetis was not only motivated by religious change but prompted by the pressure of external forces on the anchorites as well. Reinforced by reprisals directed against non-Muslims, the survival of monasticism became possible only within a protected community.

Various Religious Communities in the Scetis

The new, cenobitic form of monastic life fostered the establishment of other religious communities in the Scetis. Dayr as-Surian, the name still current today for one of these communities, shows that it was originally a colony of Syrian monks. Scholars followed Evelyn-White in dating the origin of the monastery to the beginning of the 8th century,[44] down until the discovery of new Syrian texts on older layers of paintings in 1995/96.[45] The early history of the Syrian

---

[42] So reported by Dionysius von Tellmahrē, Patriarch of Antiochia, who visited the Scetis around 830 (*CoptEncyc*, Vol. VII, 2104).

[43] *CoptEncyc*, Vol. VII, 2104.

[44] Evelyn-White 1932 [note 34], 318.

[45] K.D. Jenner and L. van Rompay, "New Syriac Texts on the Walls of the al-ʿAdra' Church of Dayr al-Suryān," in K. Innemée, P. Grossmann, K.D. Jenner, and L. van Rompay, "New Discoveries in the al-ʿAdra' Church of Dayr as-Suryān in the Wādī al-

colony in the Wadi al-Natrun can now be reconstructed using this and all other available textual sources. By 816 several Takritic[46] monks had arrived in the Wadi al-Natrun[47] to effect monastic reform and to engage in building projects. In particular, they intended to create a home for Syrian monks in Egypt, a plan supported by the Coptic Church. The newly established monastery was neither a private Takritic foundation nor an official "dependence" of the Syrian Orthodox Church, but rather erected within the organization of the Coptic Church. In view of the doctrinal agreement between both religious communities at the time, this did not present a problem.[48]

In addition to the Syrians, Ethiopians and a community of Armenian monks were also present in the Scetis during the medieval period. There are many manuscripts, especially in the Syrian language, but little is known of these communities, apart from their existence, which nevertheless adds to our knowledge about the enduring multiethnic character of the Wadi al-Natrun.

From the Middle Ages to Modern Times

Periods of relative peace were punctuated intermittently by instances of persecution and destruction, initially at the hands of nomadic Arabs. Beginning in the 14th century the greatest threat to monastic life in the Scetis was not posed by incursions of foreigners but by the "Black Death" which decimated the communities.[49] As a consequence of these years of tribulation, the Wadi al-Natrun became secluded from the outside world. Significant encounters with strangers to the desert began to occur again in the 17th century when the first European travelers came to Egypt. The descriptions these

---

Natrūn," *Mitteilungen zur Christlichen Archäologie* 4 (1998), 96-103, 96; K. Innemee and L. van Rompay, "La présence des Syriens dans le Wadi al-Natrun (Égypte). À propos des découvertes récentes de peintures et de textes muraux dans l'Église de la Vierge du Couvent de Syriens," *Parole de l'Orient* 23 (1998), 167-202, 186.

[46] Takrit was a city in Iraq with a sizable Syrian-Orthodox community. "We do not know why they left their hometown in Iraq or whether the (later) Monastery of the Syrians was their first destination in Egypt" in L. van Rompay and A.B. Schmidt, "Takritans in the Egyptian Desert: The Monastery of the Syrians in the ninth Century," *Journal of the Canadian Society for Syriac Studies* 1 (2001), 41-60, 42.

[47] K. Innemée and L. van Rompay, 1998 [note 45], 182.

[48] L. van Rompay and A.B. Schmidt, 2001 [note 46], 52. See also K. Innemée, L. van Rompay, E. Sobczynski, "Deir al-Surian (Egypt): Its Wall-paintings, Wall-texts, and Manuscripts," at <http://syrcom.cua.edu/Hugoye/ Vol2No2/index.html>.

[49] Meinardus 1961 [note 1], 135 f.

early "tourists" left of their visits are important sources for the history of the monasteries in the Wadi al-Natrun, but the travelers themselves made no lasting impression on monastic life.[50] By contrast, the activities of the next major wave of foreigners, which began in the 19th century,[51] significantly affected the settlements, for these visitors were primarily after manuscripts. Most of the Coptic manuscripts now dispersed in museums throughout Europe and North America were acquired during this period, sometimes not entirely by legal means. Such disagreeable experiences naturally led the monks to exercise reserve towards strangers and to suspect their curiosity and craving for knowledge about the monastic way of life. But western interest in Egypt steadily increased, and in 1880, the first guide with advice for tourists visiting the monasteries of the Wadi al-Natrun appeared. There we read, for example, about Dayr al-Baramus:

> A ride of two hours from Der es Syrian brings us to Deyr
> Baramus, a large convent, for which an antiquity of 1600 years is
> claimed. It boasts of four churches and one monk (in 1874) who
> was an Abyssinian.[52]

At the end of the 19th century the number of monks in the valley grew again, paralleled by an increase in internationalization of the communities as is shown, for example, by the fact that a Syrian monk became hegoumenos of the Dayr al-Baramus monastery in 1897.[53] And in 1920, when Evelyn-White visited the Wadi al-Natrun, seven Abyssinian monks lived there.[54] I think it can be said that there was an uninterrupted connection to the Ethiopian church since the time of Moses the Black, a connection which was very important for the Christianization of Ethiopia.

In spite of the many visitors who came to the Scetis throughout its monastic history, the religious communities there enjoyed the relative isolation that the desert provided until 1936 when the desert highway linking Cairo and Alexandria was completed. While the road

---

[50] Meinardus 1961 [note 1], 136-140.
[51] Meinardus 1961 [note 1], 140-150.
[52] Quoted after Meinardus 1961 [note 1], 142.
[53] Meinardus 1961 [note 1], 145.
[54] Meinardus 1961 [note 1], 153-154.

undermined the cherished isolation of the monks,[55] it also improved the accessibility of the monasteries to the Coptic population of Egypt, especially those Copts living in Alexandria and Cairo. (Nowadays the Monastery of St. Bishoi is the ecumenical center of the Coptic Church). Furthermore, the opening facilitated international contacts and thus fostered the Wadi al-Natrun's multiethnic character which had been a fundamental component of life in the valley since earliest times, a phenomenon that continues down into present.

---

[55] Meinardus 1961 [note 1], 122.

Wādī al-Naṭrūn
and the
History of the Patriarchs of Alexandria

Johannes den Heijer

1. Introduction

For a paper about the importance of the monasteries of the Wādī al-Naṭrūn as illustrated in the famous *History of the Patriarchs of Alexandria*, there cannot be a more appropriate introduction than a quotation from its editorial preface written in the year 1088 A.D. by the compiler of this work, Mawhūb Ibn Manṣūr Ibn Mufarrij of Alexandria:[1]

Mawhūb Ibn Manṣūr Ibn Mufarrij, the Alexandrian, the deacon, said: "Since those who have gone before (us) from among the righteous predecessors have written the biographies of the Church and arranged them, and explained the affairs of the patriarchs of the city of Alexandria, and what befell them, and what God – praised be He! – manifested at their hands in the way

---

[1] I am grateful to Dr. Mark Swanson for his corrections and his manifold suggestions to improve this text. All quotations from the *History of the Patriarchs* in this paper are given according to the translation by O.H.E. KHS-Burmester c.s., with some adaptations, mainly based on the older, unpublished manuscript Coptic Orthodox Patriarchate Hist. 12, which contains the third volume of the primitive redaction of the text. See J. den Heijer, "L'*Histoire des Patriarches d'Alexandrie*, recension primitive et Vulgate," *Bulletin de la Société d'Archéologie Copte* 27 (1985), 1-29; idem, *Mawhūb Ibn Manṣūr Ibn Mufarriğ (XIe siècle) et la rédaction du texte arabe de l'*Histoire des Patriarches d'Alexandrie (= *Corpus Scriptorum Christianorum Orientalium*, vol. 513, Subsidia, tomus 81 (Lovanii 1989), 14-80. In the present study, the Cairo manuscript in question will be referred to as Ms. C. The edition and translation of the relevant parts of the better-known but secondary "Vulgate" version appears in *History of the Patriarchs of the Egyptian Church, known as the History of the Holy Church, by* Sawīrus Ibn al-Muḳaffa', bishop of al-Ashmūnīn, Vol. II Part II and Part III, [edited,] translated and annotated by A.S. Atiya, Y. 'Abd al-Masīḥ & O.H.E. KHS-Burmester (*Publications de la Société d'Archéologie Copte*. Textes et Documents (Le Caire 1948-1959). The titles of the two relevant parts of this edition will be abbreviated here as *HPC* II ii and *HPC* II iii, respectively.

of miracles, and (how) He fortified them with patience and zeal and power of faith to guide their flocks and to lead them to the Orthodox Faith and to teach them the Evangelic commandments, as the Lord – Whose name be magnified ! – ordered them ; I, the sinner, the wretched (one), yearned to collect their biographies and to write them down so that this might be of profit to me and to him who shall read them after me. Then I asked help of God – may His remembrance be exalted! – and I journeyed to the monastery of Saint Macarius (*al-qiddīs* Abū Maqār) in the holy Wādī Habīb. I found the deacon Abū Ḥabīb Mīkhā'īl Ibn Badīr al-Damanhūrī, and the saintly and pure father, Anbā Cyril (Kirullus) was there, and with him three bishops, namely, Anbā Ghubriyāl, bishop of al-Buḥayra, and Anbā Awrahām, bishop of Dibqū', and Anbā Khā'īl, bishop of Nawasā, who was from Būra. This was in Baramhāt of the year eight hundred and four of the Martyrs, which corresponds to the year four hundred and seventy-six of the tax (calendar) which is the (month of) Muḥarram of the year four hundred and eighty of the lunar (calendar) which is the tenth year of his patriarchate. In the aforesaid desert (there were) at that time about seven hundred monks of whom (there were) in the monastery of Saint Macarius (*al-qiddīs* Abū Maqār) four hundred, in the monastery of Anba John (John the Little = Abū Yuḥannis) one hundred and sixty-five, in the monastery of John Kamā (John the Black = Abū Kamā) twenty-five and this is Yūḥannā, in the monastery of Anbā Bishoi (Abū Bishāyh) forty, in the monastery of the Syrians (as-Suryān) sixty, in the monastery of the Romans (*Nīrūmā'ūs*) twenty, and in the Cave of Abba Moses (*maghārat* Abū Mūsā) and his church two monks – a Syrian and a Copt – besides the saintly anchorites whom we did not see and did not get to know. (...)"[2]

Mawhūb goes on to mention the Fatimid caliph of his time, the *imām* al-Mustanṣir Billāh, and the all-powerful vizier Badr al-Jamālī, known as the Amīr al-Juyūsh (Commander of the Armies), to whom he refers by using one of his honorific titles, Sayf al-Islām. Subsequently, Mawhūb returns to discussing his project of collecting the source material—mainly Coptic source material, as we can infer

---

[2] Ms. C 1r5-2r3 / *HPC* II ii 159.9-160.7 transl. 241-242.

from other editorial and scribal notes—for what was to become the
History of the Patriarchs of Alexandria, in Arabic.[3] He mentions the
monasteries where he found specific materials, including the
monasteries of the Mistress at Nahyā and of the Martyr Theodore at
al-Manhā, which are, of course, located outside the Wādī al-Naṭrūn.
But the last Coptic source text that he was able to retrieve and use in
his Arabic work was found in the monastery of Saint Macarius itself.
This is the original series of biographies of the patriarchs Khā'īl, the
56th since Saint Mark the Evangelist, to Shenoute (Shanūda), the 65th,
written by Anbā Mīkhā'īl, bishop of Tinnīs, whom we shall mention
again later:

> And we found in the monastery of Saint Macarius (Dayr Abū
> Maqār) the biographies of ten patriarchs from Khael (Khā'īl), the
> fifty-sixth, to Shenoute (Sānūtiyūs), the sixty-fifth, which Anba
> Michael (Mīkhā'īl) bishop of Tinnis, wrote, and they are in the
> handwriting of Luqūṭ, the monk, his son.[4]

Mawhūb Ibn Manṣūr's preface eloquently illustrates how intimately
the Wādī al-Naṭrūn – or Wādī Habīb, as it was usually called in the
mediaeval period – is linked to the Coptic historiographical tradition.
For it was in the monastery of Saint Macarius, in this area, that
Mawhūb, the leading notable (*protos*) of the Alexandrian community
in his times, initiated his project of compiling his Arabic text, which
would later be continued by subsequent generations up to the 20th
century, and which would also be quoted or expanded in other
important Arabic texts by Coptic authors.[5] Moreover, the presence of
the patriarch, Cyril II, and several bishops as well as another

---

[3] On these Coptic sources, see den Heijer, *Mawhūb Ibn Manṣūr Ibn Mufarriǧ* (see
above, note 1), 2-10.

[4] Ms. C 2v10-14 / *HPC* II ii 161.2-4 transl. 244.

[5] See J. den Heijer, "The influence of the «History of the Patriarchs of Alexandria»
on the «History of the Churches and Monasteries of Egypt» by Abū al-Makārim (and
Abū Ṣāliḥ?)", in Samir Khalil Samir, S.J., ed., *Actes du 4ᵉ congrès international
d'études arabes chrétiennes*. Cambridge, septembre 1992 = *Parole de l'Orient* 19
(1994), 415-439; idem, "Coptic Historiography in the Fāṭimid, Ayyūbid and Early
Mamlūk Periods," D. Thomas, ed., *Second Woodbrooke-Mingana Symposium on Arab
Christianity and Islam, 19-22 September 1994: "Coptic Arabic Christianity before the
Ottomans: Text and Context*," Leiden etc. 1996 = *Medieval Encounters: Jewish,
Christian and Muslim Culture in Confluence and Dialogue* 2 (1996), 67-98.

prominent layman, Abū Ḥabī Mīkhā'īl Ibn Badīr al-Damanhūrī, suggests that Mawhūb's project was an official mission of the Church, approved and encouraged by a committee of great stature, and prompted by the need to collect, to preserve, and to transmit the historical heritage of the Coptic community in a coherent and continuous Arabic text, at a time when the original Coptic sources were no longer generally understood.[6]

The general purpose of this paper is to shed some light on the monasteries and monks of the Wādī al-Naṭrūn as they are mentioned and described in the *History of the Patriarchs of Alexandria*. Now if we look at the work as a whole, we indeed find abundant material on this area and its monasteries. We read about many patriarchs who previously had been monks in one of the Wādī's monasteries, or of patriarchs who were consecrated there; but there is also plenty of interesting information about the monasteries that does not concern the patriarchs themselves. If we realize, however, that the Arabic text of the *History of the Patriarchs* as we know it today extends from the first to the 20th century A.D., and we combine this with our awareness of the prominent position that the monasteries of the Wādī al-Naṭrūn have always occupied in the life of the Coptic Church, we will readily understand that the text contains so many data on the Wādī al-Naṭrūn throughout the ages that, even if we limited our account to those episodes that directly concern the patriarchs, we would still have to review so many cases that the resulting account would inevitably be utterly superficial. Hence, it is more useful, within this very large theme, to concentrate on one particular period. The period chosen here is that of the Fatimids (969-1171 A.D.), which is generally considered one of the periods in which the Coptic community flourished. It was a time when many Copts held high positions in the administration and when the Coptic proportion of the Egyptian population was still very considerable.[7] It was also a time when a fascinating process of arabization was in full swing, in which the

---

[6] See J. den Heijer, "History of the Patriarchs of Alexandria," in A.S. Atiya, ed., *Coptic Encyclopedia* (New York 1991), 4: 1238-1242 and "Mawhūb Ibn Manṣūr Ibn Mufarrij al-Iskandarānī (c. 1025-1100)," *Coptic Encyclopedia* 5: 1573-1574 [hereafter *CoptEncyc*].

[7] Samir Khalil Samir, "The Role of Christians in the Fāṭimid Government Services of Egypt to the Reign of al-Ḥāfiẓ," in D. Thomas, ed., *Second Woodbrooke-Mingana Symposium* (see note 5), 177-192.

tasks of collecting, translating, editing and transmitting earlier (Coptic) texts were undertaken vigorously, with an aim to help the Coptic community adapt to a changing social and cultural environment, while conserving its religious and cultural identity.[8]

Within the Fatimid era, the most suitable period for our investigation consists of the patriarchates of Christodoulos, the 66th patriarch, and his successor, Cyril (Kirullus) II, the 67th. In the first place, Mawhūb Ibn Manṣūr's own contribution to the *History of the Patriarchs*, i.e. the part that he himself compiled in Arabic,[9] consists precisely of their two biographies, which cover a time span stretching from 1046 to 1092 A.D. In the second place, these two patriarchs were themselves important exponents of the ongoing process of community and identity building. Both issued new sets of canons for the Church, and the canons of Christodoulos are actually considered to be the first systematical codification of Coptic religious law since the Arab conquest of Egypt in the seventh century.[10]

Accordingly, what follows here is a number of remarks on the patriarchs Christodoulos and Cyril II, and on what their biographer, Mawhūb, has to say about them and about the monks and the monasteries of the Wādī al-Naṭrūn in their days.

2. Patriarchs and Wādī al-Naṭrūn in the Fatimid Period
(Particularly in the second half of the eleventh century)

2.1 *The Patriarchate of Christodoulos*

2.1.1 *Election and consecration*

In the opening paragraphs of the *Vita* (*Sīra*) of Anbā Christodoulos, Mawhūb tells us how a new candidate had to be found following the death of Anba Shenoute II (in 1046 A.D.). It was, as Mawhūb has it, the turn of the Alexandrians, their priests and their notables (*ahl al-Iskandariyya wa l-kahana wa l-arākhina*), to identify and nominate a new patriarch. This was actually the beginning of a custom that would remain in use for quite some time: the inhabitants of the two

---

[8] Cf. S. Rubenson, "Translating the Tradition: Some Remarks on the Arabization of the Patristic Heritage in Egypt," in D. Thomas, ed., *Second Woodbrooke-Mingana Symposium* (see note 5), 16-27, particularly p. 6-8.

[9] Den Heijer, *Mawhūb Ibn Manṣūr Ibn Mufarriǧ* (see above, note 1), 153.

[10] Cf. O.F.A. Meinardus, *Two Thousand Years of Coptic Christianity* (Cairo 1999), 45-52, part. p. 50.

main cities of Egypt, Cairo (Miṣr) and Alexandria, would take turns in playing the leading role in appointing a patriarch.[11]

As Mawhūb tells the story, a council is formed, which eventually settles on electing Christodoulos, a monk of the monastery of Dayr Baramūs, who had, however, left his monastery to live in solitude as a hermit at Nastarawa, on the Mediterranean shore. In order to go and fetch him from his hermitage, the Alexandrians dispatch ten notables (*muqaddamūn*), as well as a prefect (*'āmil*), and the priest Sīmūn, of the church of Saint Mark - who, incidentally, later was to become bishop of Tinnīs. When they approach him with their request, Christodoulos refuses, as was customary, but his godfather, one of the Alexandrian notables named Abū Zikrī Ibn Marqūra, convinces him to accept. The Alexandrians clothe him with the patriarchal dress and take him to Alexandria, where he is consecrated in the month of Kiyahk 763 AM (Nov.-Dec. 1046 A.D.).[12] Subsequently - and this is important for the present investigation - the new patriarch journeys to the Wādī al-Naṭrūn, where, according to Mawhūb, he is consecrated again, in the monastery of Saint Macarius.[13] After this confirmation of his consecration he travels to Cairo to be consecrated another time, an event that is reported in quite an interesting account, which, however, does not concern us here.[14]

2.1.2 *Christodoulos' patriarchate and the "Great Crisis" of 1066-73*

Anbā Christodoulos has become famous for his Canons, mentioned earlier, but this is not the occasion to dwell upon this important

---

[11] H.G. Evelyn White, *The Monasteries of the Wādi 'n Natrūn*, vol. II (New York 1932), 351; O.F.A. Meinardus, *Christian Egypt Faith and Life* (Cairo 1970), 95-96, 98-105.

[12] Ms. C 4r-4v / *HPC* II iii 1645-10; transl. 246-247; Ms. C 5r-5v / *HPC* II iii 16420-1658; transl. 248.

[13] Ms. C 5v / *HPC* II iii 165.9-10; transl. 248.

[14] This contemporary description of more than one consecration confronts the modern historian with a difficult problem. On the one hand, the *CoptEncyc* refers to Christodoulos' repeated consecration in Cairo as "according to established tradition," see S.Y. Labib, "Christodoulos," *CoptEncyc* 2: 544-547, part. p. 545. On the other hand, during the symposium at the Wādī al-Naṭrūn, it was His Holiness Pope Shenouda III himself who declared that this account of a second and a third consecration must be based on a misunderstanding by Mawhūb, since according to Coptic Canon Law the consecration of a patriarch or a bishop can only take place once. See also the report by H.N. Takla in the *St. Shenouda Newsletter*, 8 (N.S. 5), No. 3 (April, 2002), 2-11, particularly p. 3-4.

contribution to the history of the Coptic Church. A more sobering aspect of his patriarchate is that it was marked by great difficulties, which to a high degree were related to the general social, political and economic climate during the first part of the caliphate of al-Mustanṣir Billāh.

In many passages of his biography of Christodoulos, Mawhūb stresses this patriarch's financial difficulties. Without complaining, Christodoulos undertook to pay the Coptic community of Alexandria 350 dinars a year for the construction (or restoration) of their churches and for the production of the Eucharist.[15] For this he had to find sources of revenue, since he definitely did not have a "working capital" at the time of his appointment. Although he had previously been a hermit, obviously living in absolute poverty, at the time of his election the Alexandrians apparently found it necessary to assess his belongings. They thereby established that he only owned two dirhams and three quarters of a dirham.[16]

In order to face his financial challenges, Christodoulos was strongly tempted to resort to simony, as several of his predecessors had been forced to do under equally harsh circumstances. In an attempt to avoid this, he introduced a new arrangement according to which newly consecrated bishops were expected to cede 50 % of the income of their dioceses to the Cell (qallāya) of Saint Mark, i.e., to the Patriarchate.[17]

More significantly, much of Christodoulos' patriarchate was affected dramatically by the "Great Crisis" of 1066-1073, a period of instability, pestilence and starvation that was to be remembered by Egyptian historians for centuries. The term "Great Crisis" (al-shidda al-'uẓmā) was still used by al-Maqrīzī some 300 years later. During this crisis, marauding army regiments violently fought each other, wrought havoc and attacked the civilian population, particularly in the Delta. The central Fatimid government was too weak to secure the roads and the land, so that trade and agriculture came to standstill. On top of all this, in some of these seven years, the Nile did not rise sufficiently to irrigate the land. The army regiments in question were ethnically defined: there were the African slaves ('abīd), the Turks and the Lawāta Berbers. The latter group of tribesman made a

---

[15] Ms. C 23v16-24r4 / HPC II iii 181.1-3; transl. 275.
[16] Ms. C 5v4-7 / HPC II iii 165.6-8; transl. 248.
[17] Ms. C 19r16-19v12 / HPC II iii 177.3-12; transl. 268-269.

coalition with the Turkish general Nāṣir ad-Dawla Ibn Ḥamdān and actively tried to put an end to the Ismaili Fatimid dynasty, in order to restore the rule of Sunnite Islam in Egypt. Although their terror clearly affected the population of the Delta at large,[18] Mawhūb understandably pays particular attention to the sufferings they inflicted on the Christian population. He writes that they attacked and plundered the monasteries; those of the Wādī al-Naṭrūn were not spared. They also took the patriarch Christodoulos himself as a hostage, tortured him, and only released him against a considerable ransom.[19] Exhausted and impoverished by his tribulations, Christodoulos tried to obtain financial aid from the king of Nubia.[20]

Furthermore, the rebel leader, Nāṣir ad-Dawla ibn Ḥamdān, had actually developed plans to get rid of Christodoulos and to appoint his own counter-patriarch, a monk called Abū Yaʿqūb. Perhaps— although this is by no means certain—this monk is identical to the Abū Yaʿqūb who is mentioned in Mawhūb's biography as *qummuṣ* at the Dayr Baramūs, who had become a monk late in life, and who as a layman had been quite well off.[21]

2.1.3 *Christodoulos and the Monks of Wādī al-Naṭrūn*

One episode in Anbā Christodoulos' biography is interesting in that it illustrates the actual functioning of a monastic library. For some time, the monks of Saint Macarius had maintained the habit of keeping the Holy Eucharist after the mass. In the presence of several bishop and one prominent layman from Cairo (the *wakīl* Baqīra), the patriarch solemnly forbids this habit. When the monks react furiously and oppose his ruling, he has a manuscript taken out of the library (*khizānat al-kutub*), which contains a homily (*mīmar*) supporting his opinion. He charges his secretary, the well-known bishop Anbā

---

[18] As-Sayyid ʿAbd al-ʿAzīz Sālim, *Tārīkh al-Iskandariyya wa-ḥaḍāratuhā fī l-ʿaṣr al-islāmī* (al-Iskandariyya 1972), 187-188.

[19] J. den Heijer, "Considérations sur les communautés chrétiennes en Égypte fatimide: l'État et l'Église sous le vizirat de Badr al-Jamālī (1074-1094)," in M. Barrucand, ed., *L'Égypte Fatimide, son art et son histoire. Actes du colloque organisé à Paris les 28, 29 et 30 mai 1998* (Paris 1999), 569-578, part. p. 571.

[20] Ms. C 28r6-9 / *HPC* II iii 184.18-19; transl. 281.

[21] Ms. C 31v11-13 / *HPC* II iii 188.1-2; transl. 286.

Mīkhā'īl of Tinnīs, to read this homily aloud before the monks. With this action, he puts an end to the anomalous practice.[22]

2.1.4 Death

A final indication of the importance of the Wādī al-Naṭrūn for Anbā Christodoulos, and indeed, for many other Coptic patriarchs, is that when he died, on 14 Kiyahk 794 AM (=10 December 1077), he was initially buried in the al-Muʿallaqa church in Old Cairo, but later his remains were transferred to the monastery of Saint Macarius.[23]

2.2 Patriarchate of Cyril II

2.2.1 Election and consecration

After Christodoulos's death, it was the turn of the notables and priests of Cairo (Miṣr) to elect a new patriarch. We must point out, however, that things were arranged somewhat differently than thirty years earlier, for in this case the Cairenes were joined in the election process by the monks of Saint Macarius. This monastery plays a central role in the procedure. A council is installed, which consists of a number of bishops (twelve are mentioned by name), some priests, including several from Alexandria, and a group of laymen from Miṣr. This council spends no less than two months at Saint Macarius, trying in vain to find a suitable candidate.

Some of the bishops, together with the monk Sharūt, archdeacon at the monastery, go to the neighboring monastery of John Kama (Abū Kamā) to try to convince the famous monk Bessus (Bisūs) to accept the patriarchate. Later on in this paper we will hear more about this monk, who was known for his many miracles. He objects so vehemently that all those present understand that his protest is not just meant to observe tradition. He also makes it perfectly clear that they should not approach another well-known holy man, Maqāra al-Amnūt, the doorkeeper, either. The real successor, he says, is to be found in the skéné (iskinā) of Saint Macarius.

At this point of his narrative, our author, Mawhūb, reveals something to his readers that the bishops at that moment do not yet know: the late patriarch Christodoulos had announced to a priest

---

[22] Ms. C 14v2-15r7 / HPC II iii 172.19-173.9; transl. 261-262.
[23] Ms. C 54r11-54v12 / HPC II iii 207.6-11; transl. 320-321. Quoted by White, *Monasteries*, II: 351.

called Rajā' that his successor would be a monk called Jirja, a thresher (*jarrān*) from a village called Iflāqa in the district of al-Buḥayra. This flashback by Mawhūb is interrupted by a later scribe's interpolation, which confirms that Christodoulos himself had secretly identified the next patriarch.

Turning back to the events, Mawhūb relates how the bishops who had stayed behind at Saint Macarius lost all hope of finding a suitable candidate when they learned what had happened at the monastery of John Kamā. But then Jirja appears, who turns out to be a monk of the very monastery of Saint Macarius, in accordance with what the monk Bisūs had exclaimed earlier but which the members of the council had failed to understand. Incidentally, in another passage Jirja's link with the monastery is underlined by Mawhūb's remark that he was an able priest, because he had served at the *skéné* (*iskinā*) of Saint Macarius.[24]

When Jirja enters, the council recognizes the new patriarch in him, or as Mawhūb puts it:

When they saw him, God, Whose Name (is) exalted, put it into the hearts of all of them to agree on appointing him. All of them arose, (and they went) to him, and they took him by force, and they clothed him with the robe (*thawb*), and they named him Cyril, while he wept and said: "I am the son of a second (wife). I am not fit for this state," but they did not relinquish him.[25]

In this account by Mawhūb, the monastery of Saint Macarius is much more closely connected to the election of the new patriarch than in Christodoulos' case. For even though the passage just quoted does not explicitly refer to a consecration rite, but only to clothing the monk with the robe and renaming him Cyril, it is quite clear from the conclusion of the biography that Mawhūb is actually talking here about the ritual of laying on of hands, because in that conclusion he refers to the ritual in question in the following words:

(…) from the time of the laying on of hands upon him in the Monastery of Saint Macarius (…)[26]

---

[24] Ms. C 60v15-16 / *HPC* II iii 213.13; transl. 333.
[25] Ms. C 54v6-56r11 / *HPC* II iii 207.13-209.12; transl. 321-325.
[26] Ms. C 82r6 / *HPC* II iii 232.4-5; transl. 369. /// (H/V z 22/01/2002).

In the context, it is obvious that this ceremony, whatever its ritual
status may have been, is considered the real beginning of his
patriarchate. From the monastery, the bishops and priests take their
new patriarch to Alexandria, where he is consecrated on 22 Baramhāt
794 A.M. (=18 March 1078 A.D.).[27] Subsequently, he is taken to
Cairo, where he is received ceremonially, first by the caliph al-
Mustanṣir and his family—which is significant, because subjects
were rarely admitted to the court of the Fatimid caliphs,[28] who
claimed descent from the Prophet Mohammed—and then by the
vizier Badr al-Jamālī. Only after these occasions he is consecrated, as
Mawhūb has it, in the churches of Cairo: first in the al-Muʿallaqa
church at Qaṣr ash-Shamʿ (Old Cairo), and a few days later in the
church of Ḥārat al-Rūm in Cairo proper.[29]

2.2.2 Cyril and the vizier Badr al-Jamālī

The relations with the new all-powerful ruler are a central issue in
Anbā Cyril's patriarchate, as described by Mawhūb, his biographer.
These relations are also what contrast his patriarchate to that of his
predecessor. Whereas Christodoulos had suffered greatly from the
political chaos of the "Great Crisis," and initially had not enjoyed
very cordial contacts with Badr al-Jamālī (although he later did gain
his confidence), Cyril generally was on good terms with the military
dictator, even though the latter went quite far in applying his
centralist policies of law and order to all national institutions,
including the Coptic Church.

It is certain that Cyril regularly resided in the Wādī al-Naṭrūn, as
we may infer from Mawhūb's words:

The ceremony of laying on of hands (waḍʿ al-yad) upon the Patriarch also appears
with a biblical reference in Ms. C 29v13 / HPC II iii 186.4-7; transl. 283.

[27] Ms. C 56r11-14 / HPC II iii 209.12-13; transl. 325.

[28] H. Halm, "Die Zeremonien der Salbung des Nilometers und der Kanalöffnung in
fatimidischer Zeit," in U. Vermeulen & D. De Smet, eds., Egypt and Syria in the
Fatimid, Ayyubid and Mamluk Eras. Proceedings of the 1st, 2nd and 3rd International
Colloquium organized at the Katholieke Universiteit Leuven in May 1992, 1993 and
1994. Orientalia Lovaniensa Analecta 73 (Leuven 1995), 111-124, part. p. 111.

[29] For a description of this reception by the caliph and the vizier in Den Heijer,
"Communautés chrétiennes" (see above, note 19), 572-573. For the historical problem
of these accounts of multiple consecrations, see above, note 14.

The father, the patriarch, Anbā Kīrullus, had delayed to enter the desert of Abū Maqār this year (...).[30]

It would seem, then, that the patriarch would at least aspire to spend a fixed period of every year in the monastery, but his ability to do so on a regular basis was seriously hampered by the vizier Badr al-Jamālī's ambition to keep control of all Egyptian institutions firmly in his own hands. As Mawhūb states explicitly, the patriarch was forced to take up residence in Cairo, in the church of the Archangel Michael on the Island of Miṣr, because the Amīr al-Juyūsh (i.e., Badr al-Jamālī) insisted on his presence nearby at all times, particularly because of the relations of the Fatimid State with the Nubian and Ethiopian kingdoms, in which the Coptic Church was involved in a rather intricate manner. Unfortunately, this fascinating issue cannot be discussed here further.[31]

Although earlier patriarchs had occasionally resided in the Cairo area, and also in several places in the Delta, in retrospect, this order by the Fatimid vizier and military ruler marks the definitive relocation of the Patriarchate of Alexandria to the Egyptian capital. This is where the patriarchs kept their official residence for the remaining part of the Fatimid period, as well as throughout the Ayyubid, Mamluk, and Ottoman periods and until the present day. Moreover, since the 15th century, even the installation ceremony for the new patriarch is performed in Cairo, rather than in Alexandria.[32]

---

[30] Ms. C 79r15-16 / *HPC* II iii 229.13-14; transl. 365.

[31] For a brief discussion of this transfer, see Den Heijer, "Communautés chrétiennes," 573-574, and more extensively: idem, "Le patriarcat copte d'Alexandrie à l'époque fatimide," in C. Décobert, ed., *Alexandrie Médiévale 2.* Études alexandrines 8 (Le Caire 2002), 83-97, part. 84-87. For the patriarch's role with regard to Fatimid-Ethiopian relations, see E. van Donzel, "Badr al-Jamālī, the Copts in Egypt and the Muslims in Ethiopia," in I.R. Netton, ed., *Studies in Honour of Clifford Edmund Bosworth,* Vol. I, (Leiden/Boston/Köln 2000), 297-309; and M. Brett, "Al-Karāza al-Marqusiya. The Coptic Church in the Fatimid Period," paper read at the Eighth Colloquium on the History of Egypt and Syria in the Fatimid, Ayyubid and Mamluk periods, Leuven, May, 1999 (acts forthcoming), particularly section VIII (with much gratitude to Prof. Brett for making his unpublished paper available to the author).

[32] See M. Martin, "Alexandrie chrétienne à la fin du XIIe siècle d'après Abū l-Makārim," in C. Décobert et J.-Y. Empereur, eds., *Alexandrie médiévale* I. Études alexandrines 3 (Le Caire 1998), 45-49, here p. 46. According to Martin, all patriarchs were consecrated in Alexandria until John I, who was consecrated in Cairo in 1427. See also Den Heijer, "Le patriarcat copte d'Alexandrie," 87.

On the other hand, what has remained constant is that the monasteries of the Wādī al-Naṭrūn continued to function as a secondary residence, to which the patriarchs would retreat whenever they could.[33]

There are numerous other interesting aspects of Badr al-Jamālī's attitude towards the Coptic Church, an attitude which was both benign and rigid, and at any rate deeply affected its internal affairs. These relations, as interesting as they are,[34] cannot be studied here, because most of them do not directly concern the Wādī al-Naṭrūn. But it should be clear that, generally speaking, they very much marked the patriarchate of Cyril II.

2.2.3 Financial administration

As soon as Badr al-Jamālī had restored order and security in Egypt, the general situation of the Church improved significantly, particularly with regard to material matters. Nevertheless, Patriarch Cyril II maintained Christodoulos' financial arrangements, which stipulated that 50% of the episcopal revenues should be ceded to the Cell (qallāya) of Saint Mark. Again, this measure was expressed in such a way as to avoid accusations of the forbidden practice of simony. There is a new element in Cyril's financial policy, however, which seems to be connected to his special devotion to the Wādī al-Naṭrūn:

> He did not accept simony at all. He abolished it altogether, and he made an agreement with everyone whom he consecrated that half of what he should receive from the see should be for the bishop and half for the Cell of my lord Mark the Evangelist, according to the ancient rule. He dedicated what he was wont to receive from certain sees to the Monastery of the Saint Abū Maqār, and they were: Damīra, Abū Ṣīr, Banā, and Damanhūr, and al-Ihnāsiyya. He wrote documents for this, and he laid down conditions in them to confirm it, and he delivered them to the monks, the stewards, of the aforesaid monastery.[35]

---

[33] See R.-G. Coquin, "Patriarchal Residences," CoptEncyc 6: 1912-1913.
[34] See Den Heijer, "Communautés chrétiennes."
[35] Ms. C 59v12-60r3 / HPC II iii 212.13-18; transl. 330-331.

2.2.4 Death, burial, succession

Cyril II, Patriarch of Alexandria, went to his rest on 12 Ba'ūna 808 A.M. (=6 June, 1092), after a patriarchate of fourteen years and three-and-a-half months. He was buried initially in the aforementioned church of Michael the Archangel at al-Mukhtāra, where he had resided, but, just as in the case of the Patriarch Christodoulos, his bodily remains were later relocated to the monastery of Saint Macarius.[36]

3.　Other Data on the Monasteries

Mawhūb's biographies of the patriarchs Christodoulos and Cyril II also contain many data on the monasteries of the Wādī al-Naṭrūn that do not concern the patriarchs themselves. In the introduction, we have already seen Mawhūb's account of the numbers of monks who resided in the respective monasteries.[37] In a number of cases, the monasteries, or the desert of Wādī Habīb, are mentioned without further detail. Other passages, however, contain interesting information on individual monasteries, on some of the monks who resided in them and on some of the people who visited them in the period under consideration here.

3.1 Saint Bishoi

The monastery of Anbā Bishoi (Dayr Abū Bishūyh / Dayr Abū Bishāy) is only mentioned as the monastery from which hailed a monk called Sanhūt, who was to become bishop of Cairo (Miṣr) in 804 A.M. (=1088 A.D.) . According to Mawhūb, Sanhūt was consecrated on the 12th of Bāba, at the church of the Archangel Michael, at al-Mukhtāra on the Island of Miṣr, and a week later at the church of Saint Sergius (Abū Sargah).[38]

3.2 Dayr al-Suryān

In the two *Vitae* of patriarchs studied here, the only passage mentioning the "Monastery of the Syrians," Dayr al-Suryān, is

---

[36] Ms. C 81v15-82r10 / *HPC* II iii 232.1-7; transl. 368-369. Quoted by White, *Monasteries*, II, 351.

[37] See above, section 1 (introduction).

[38] Ms. C 68v13-69r14 / *HPC* II iii 220.7-16; transl. 346-347. This is one more instance of the problem of multiple consecrations. See above, note 14.

Mawhūb's preface mentioned above, where he mentions the numbers of monks living in the respective monasteries. The compiler fails to inform us about the ethnic background of these monks, but it is now known that for a good part of its history, this monastery has had a mixed population. Recently much attention has been paid to the coexistence of Coptic and Syrian monks not only there, but also in other monasteries in Egypt.[39]

3.3 *Saint John the Little*

Another candidate for the See of Cairo, who did not obtain the majority of votes in the election, was a monk called Bimīn, archdeacon at the monastery of John the Little (Dayr Abū Yuḥannis).[40] The previous bishop of Cairo, Anbā Yaʿqūb (1064 to 1088 A.D.), had also been a monk at this monastery.[41]

3.4 *Saint Macarius*

We have seen in the introduction how important the monastery of Saint Macarius, consistently referred to as Dayr Abū Maqār, was for the collection of the sources for the *History of the Patriarchs*.[42] In the light of the preceding remarks on the "Monastery of the Syrians," it is appropriate to point out that Syrian monks also lived in the monastery of Saint Macarius in Mawhūb's days.[43]

---

[39] In this symposium, the contributions by Lucas Van Rompay and Karl-Heinz Brune have dealt with this phenomenon. See also K.C. Innemée, P. Grossmann, K.D. Jenner and L. Van Rompay, "New Discoveries in the Al-ʿAdhra' Church of Dayr as-Suryān in the Wādī al-Naṭrūn," *Mitteilungen zur christlichen Archäologie* 4 (1998), 79-103; K.C. Innemée and L. Van Rompay, "La Présence des Syriens dans le Wadi al-Natrun (Égypte), à propos des découvertes récentes de peintures et de textes muraux dans l'Église de la Vierge du Couvent des Syriens," *Parole de l'Orient* 23 (1998), 167-202; K.C. Innemée, L. Van Rompay and E. Sobczynski, "Deir al-Surian (Egypt): Its Wall-paintings, Wall-texts, and Manuscripts," *Hugoye: Journal of Syriac Studies* 2, 2 (1999); K.C. Innemée and L. Van Rompay, "Deir al-Surian (Egypt): New Discoveries of January 2000," *Hugoye: Journal of Syriac Studies* 3,2 (2000); L. Van Rompay and A.B. Schmidt, "Takritans in the Egyptian Desert: The Monastery of the Syrians in the Ninth Century," *Journal of the Canadian Society for Syriac Studies* 1 (2001), 41-60; J. den Heijer, "Relations between Copts and Syrians in the light of recent discoveries at Dayr as-Suryān," in J. van der Vliet, ed., *Acts of the Seventh International Congress of Coptic Studies,* Leiden 27 August – 2 September, 2000 (forthcoming).
[40] Ms. C 68v13-69r5 / *HPC* II iii 220.7-10; transl. 346.
[41] Ms. C 68r8-13 / *HPC* II iii 220.4-7; transl. 346.
[42] See above, section 1 (introduction).
[43] Ms. C 62v14-15 / *HPC* II iii 197.14; transl.302.

One individual monk of Saint Macarius appears several times in Mawhūb's narrative. This is Maqāra, the doorkeeper (*amnūt*), who had gone into hiding in order to avoid being sought for the patriarchate after Christodoulos had died.[44] Our author, Mawhūb, was personally acquainted with this monk. Once, when he found himself in great difficulty,[45] he was helped by Maqāra, as well as by the monk Bisūs.[46]

3.5 *Baramūs*

We have seen earlier that the patriarch Christodoulos had been a monk at Dayr Baramūs, and that perhaps the monk Abū Ya'qūb, *qummus* at the same monastery, was involved in a plot to become patriarch instead of him.

Otherwise, it should be noticed that in the primitive recension of the *History of the Patriarchs* the name of the monastery is written in Arabic as دير نيروماوس, which reflects Coptic ⲑⲣⲁⲟⲩⲏ ⲛ̄ⲛⲓⲣⲱⲙⲉⲟⲥ "Cell of the Romans," whereas the later, better-known Vulgate version has changed this into the more common دير برموس, which goes back to Coptic ⲡⲁⲣⲱⲙⲉⲟⲥ, "The Roman" / "That of the Romans."[47] Later, of course, the Coptic ⲡⲁ- was no longer recognized in the Arabic *ba-*, so that the Arabic article was added to what had become a single word, yielding Dayr al-Baramūs (دير البرموس).

One last detail is that the fingers of Saint Severus of Antioch were kept among the relics of this monastery.[48]

3.6 *Saint John Kamā (the Black): the Monk Bessus*

Most of Mawhūb's passages on the monastery of Saint John Kamā (Dayr Abū Kamā) concern its most famous monk at the time, the saintly Bessus (Bisūs). No fewer than ten of his miracles are

---

[44] Ms. C 34r14-16 / *HPC* II iii 190.5-6; transl. 290; Ms. C 42v5-6 / *HPC* II iii 197.8; transl. 302; Ms. C 55r14-15 / *HPC* II iii 208.9; transl. 322.
[45] Ms. C 34r12-14 / *HPC* II iii 190.4-5; transl. 290.
[46] Ms. C 35r4-7 / *HPC* II iii 190.18-20; transl. 291.
[47] White, *Monasteries*, II, 98.
[48] Ms. C 76v10-11 / *HPC* II iii 227.3; transl. 359.

described at considerable length in Mawhūb's text, mostly in a special section of his *Vita* of Christodoulos, but also scattered elsewhere in the two patriarchal biographies. As we have seen earlier, his fame made him a sought-after candidate for the patriarchate, but he categorically refused to accept this honor.

Several of Mawhūb's miracle accounts are of considerable historical interest in that they reflect the monks' social relations with laymen, and more particularly with the notables (*arākhina*) of Cairo and Alexandria. One of these accounts stands out because of its lively description of these relations. The story in question is an autobiographical note, in which Mawhūb tells us about a trip to the Wādī al-Naṭrūn which he made with a group of twelve Alexandrian notables in the winter of 778 A.M. (1062 A.D.).

The company first visited Dayr al-Baramūs, where they obtained the blessing of the *qummuṣ* Abū Yaʿqūb, who was mentioned earlier in this study. From there, they went to the monastery of Saint John the Black (Dayr Abū Kamā), where the monk Bisūs gave them a warm welcome. The next morning, however, he informs them that there is also a group of notables from Cairo about to visit the monasteries during the Feast of the Epiphany. He implores the Alexandrians not to make him encounter these Cairenes. He actually goes as far as warning them that, if they do not make sure that the Cairenes are kept at a distance, he will withdraw to the caves of Moses the Black (*maghārāt* Abū Mūsā).

The next morning, the twelve Alexandrians go to the monastery of Saint Macarius, where they indeed meet with a large group of notables from Cairo, among them the sheikh Abū al-Badr Ibn Mīnā al-Zarāwī, who had been scribe (*kātib*) to several emirs including the later anti-Fatimid rebel leader, Nāṣir al-Dawla Ibn Ḥamdān, and who was later to be assassinated by a band of marauding Lawāta Berbers. In this account, Abū al-Badr urgently asks Mawhūb himself—who evidently is the most prominent Alexandrian in the company—to arrange for him to meet the monk Bisūs: he desires to confess his sins to him, and to present to him his nephew (*ibn ʿamm*), the sheikh Thiqat al-Thiqāt Abū al-Ṭayyib Ibn Bishōyh Ibn Yūḥannis, who had earlier taken a vow that in some way involved a sum of 500 dinars. Our author makes his way to the monastery of Saint John the Black, to explain the matter to the monk. The latter finally says he will agree to meet the sheikh Abū al-Badr at the monastery of Saint Macarius.

Mawhūb spends the night at Saint John the Little (Dayr Abū Yuḥannis), where the sheikh Abū al-Ṭayyib sleeps as well. The next morning, back at Saint John Kamā's, he learns that the monk Bisūs has been seen there, striking the semantron (*nāqūs*) at midnight to summon the monks to the Psalmody. Our author says he inferred from this that the monk had cancelled his plan to go to the monastery of Saint Macarius, because it is too far away from Saint John Kamā.

Mawhūb decides to check the matter with the monk Bisūs himself. This part of the story is better given in quotation:

Then I went in unto him smiling, and he (Bisūs) knew that I had suspected that he had not gone to the Monastery of Saint Macarius. When I had greeted him and had received his blessing, he said to me: 'I went and I met the man'. Then I asked him: 'When didst thou reach him, and (at what time didst thou) return?', since it is not possible for anyone to go to the Monastery of Saint Macarius and to return in a night. He said to me: 'Thou hast no need (to know) this. I went unto him, as it was agreed with thee'. I said to him: 'What are his characteristics?' He said: 'He is a short fat man with dark blue eyes, and I found with him thy brother, Abū al-'Alā' Fahd, and Dimyān thy kinsman with dark blue eyes also, and I conversed with him in Coptic.' When he had said this to me, I immediately went forth at sunrise, and I mounted my beast and I hastened on my journey, and I reached the Monastery of Saint Macarius at the fourth hour of the day, since it was in the month of Ṭūba. Then I went in with the sheikh Abū al-Ṭayyib, mentioned before, to the presence of the shaikh Abū al-Badr mentioned before, and he said to me: 'Did ye not have news of us from the saintly Bisūs, for he came to us?' I said to him: 'What time did he come?' He said: 'He came to us at darkness.' I said to him: 'It was the time at which he went forth from the Monastery of Abū Kamā, and I separated from him there, and he went on to thee.' He and all those who were present marveled.

The narrative goes on, telling us that at midnight the Cairene notables had actually locked the monk up in a storeroom (*khizāna*) to prevent him from returning to his monastery, Saint John Kamā. But in the morning, they no longer found him in the storeroom. Mawhūb then tells them that midnight, the time at which he was locked up in

Saint Macarius, was exactly the time when he struck the semantron at Dayr Abū Kamā.[49]

4. Conclusion

By way of conclusion, it is to be borne in mind, in the first place, that Mawhūb's two biographies of patriarchs are very much written from an urban perspective: as an eminent Alexandrian layman, our author also spent quite some time in Cairo, and many of the eyewitness reports in his text are situated in either of the two cities. For events that took place elsewhere, in the Delta or Upper Egypt, Mawhūb usually relied on informants. The great exception, as we have seen, is the Wādī al-Naṭrūn. From at least two of the episodes presented above, it should be clear that Mawhūb was very much at home in several of its monasteries. We are probably entitled to regard the monasteries in his times as spiritual centers where monks retreated from the world to devote themselves to worship, but also as places where the same monks were in contact with believers—especially with the most prominent among them—from the main urban centers.

The parallel with the present day is striking; even though a millennium ago the means of communication and transport were not like those of today. To be sure, the monks living the Wādī al-Naṭrūn in those days were definitely more withdrawn from lay society than are today's monks, since it was not as easy to travel to and between the monasteries as it is today. It would be an historical error, however, to believe that their reclusion was total. The examples cited above have adequately shown that the Coptic monasteries of the Wādī al-Naṭrūn, already in the eleventh century, provided a dynamic link between the patriarchs, bishops, priests, monks and laymen from Cairo, Alexandria and other cities. In many ways, these monasteries already were the throbbing heart of Egyptian Christianity that they are today.

---

[49] This whole episode: Ms. C 31v5-34r2 / *HPC* II iii 187.21-189.22; transl. 286-289.

Wadi al-Natrun and Coptic Literature

S.G. Richter*

In the first part of this report I give a brief overview of Coptic literature and the current status of research in this field of study. I will point out that the connection between literature and monasticism goes back to the very beginning of the Coptic period. Against this background, it is possible to understand the importance of the monasteries of the Wadi al-Natrun for Coptic literature. Naturally, the history of the libraries and the dispersal of the manuscripts into the whole world and the problem of the reconstruction of volumes has to be considered too. Of course, it will not be possible to deal with all aspects of literature in the Wadi al-Natrun in this article. It is not my intention to draw up a list of all available information and data concerning the libraries of the Wadi al-Natrun, but rather to give an overview of its history and importance. Therefore, I will try to provide a summary of interesting points and give examples for the several problems that Coptology is dealing with.

Some Remarks on Coptic Literature

A first question arises: What is Coptic literature? Texts written in the Coptic language are often translations, especially texts that come from the beginning of the history of Coptic literature. In some cases it cannot be answered without doubt, whether some fourth- (or third-) century texts are translations or not. But in principle, we have to keep in mind that not only original works but also translations are an expression of literary effort and skill, a view which was emphasized by S. Morenz.[1]

On the basis of such theoretical considerations about literature, but also for practical reasons, each text which is written in the Coptic

---

* I am grateful to Prof. S. Emmel for reading and commenting critically on a draft of this article and for revising my English style.

[1] S. Morenz, "Zum Problem einer koptischen Literaturgeschichte," in P. Nagel (ed.), *Probleme der koptischen Literatur.* Wissenschaftliche Beiträge der Martin-Luther-Universität Halle-Wittenberg 1968/1 [K 2] (Halle 1968), pp. 11–16.

language is to be counted as belonging to Coptic literature taken in its entirety. This is a point of view which one finds also in more recent articles about Coptic literature, such as those written by Tito Orlandi.[2]

Nevertheless, the first certain testimony of Coptic original literature is to be found in the monastic rules and the letters written by Pachomius.[3] The significant influence of the Rule of Pachomius on the later rules of the Occident is well known. It was already at this point in the beginning of cenobitism that the connection between monasticism and literature arose, a connection which has continued in all cultures up to the present day. Until the transition from Late Antiquity to the Middle Ages, the Christian mission depended partly on the growth of monasteries. These monasteries were important not only in religious affairs, but also for the spread of crafts and literature, that is to say for the teaching of reading and writing, the copying and collecting of books, the illumination of manuscripts and also the writing of books.

The earliest traces of this tradition, namely the connection between monasticism and books, can be found in the Pachomian rules. Nobody should leave a book open when he goes to an assembly or to a meal. In addition, the books should regularly be counted by the second, who is also charged with taking care of them.[4] In the following decades and centuries, libraries belonged to the basic equipment of monasteries. For this reason, it is no real surprise that all the monasteries of the Wadi al-Natrun had libraries.

Dealing with the roots of Coptic literature, two names have to be mentioned, who may have been writing even earlier than Pachomius. First of all Antonius, who was called "father of all monks." Several years ago, S. Rubenson proposed the thesis that Antonius (the letters bearing his name and handed down in several languages are well known) might have been the first Coptic author. Currently it is not

---

[2] T. Orlandi, "Literature, Coptic," *CoptEncyc* 5, pp. 1450–1460; T. Orlandi, "Koptische Literatur," in M. Krause (ed.), *Ägypten in spätantik-christlicher Zeit. Einführung in die koptische Kultur.* Sprachen und Kulturen des christlichen Orients 4 (Wiesbaden 1998), pp. 117–147, with references to other articles.

[3] L.-T. Lefort, *Œuvres de S. Pachôme et de ses disciples.* CSCO 159, Scriptores coptici 23; CSCO 160, Scriptores coptici 24 (Louvain 1956); H. Quecke, *Die Briefe Pachoms. Griechischer Text der Handschrift W. 145 der Chester Beatty Library eingeleitet und herausgegeben. Anhang: Die koptischen Fragmente und Zitate der Pachombriefe.* Textus patristici et liturgici 11 (Regensburg 1975).

[4] H. Bacht, *Das Vermächtnis des Ursprungs. Studien zum frühen Mönchtum, vol. 2. Pachomius – Der Mann und sein Werk* (Würzburg 1983), p. 106 (rules no. 100, 101).

possible to verify this thesis, a fact which A. Khosroyev has shown in an essay on this subject. The arguments, both pros and cons, are not strong enough to enable us to reach a clear resolution.[5]

Furthermore, Epiphanius of Salamis mentioned a certain Hierakas of Leontopolis, who lived in the last third of the third century and the first half of the fourth century. He is supposed to have composed books, commentaries, writings, and religious psalms, in Greek as well as in Coptic. However, none of his works have been transmitted, although some modern scholars have attempted to attach Hierakas's name to certain writings, but without any certainty.[6]

Apart from the early Coptic authors whom I have just mentioned, there exist a few references indicating that biblical texts were translated into Coptic—translations of a high quality—beginning perhaps already in the beginning of the third century, but certainly at least since the fourth century. The fact that biblical translations form the initial stages of the development of a literary language is common for other cultures, too. One needs only to think of the beginnings of German literature in the early Middle Ages, where among the earliest testimonies a Gospel harmony can be found, as well as magical spells. In Egypt, we find the well-known magical texts in the so-called Old Coptic language attested since the first century.[7]

In the time span of the third to the fourth centuries, a wide range of Gnostic and Manichaean literature, as well as apocryphal gospels and other religious texts were translated from Greek into Coptic—for example, apocryphal writings like the Acts of Paul and the Epistula Apostolorum, but also homilies of the early Patristic Fathers, or Acts of Martyr.

During the fifth century—apart from the translations of many important authors of the Christian neighborhood—the term Coptic literature is closely connected with Shenoute, the abbot of the so-called White Monastery near Sohag in Upper Egypt. He left behind the largest corpus of writings that originates from a native Coptic

---

[5] S. Rubenson, *The Letters of St. Antony: Monasticism and the Making of a Saint*. Studies in Antiquity and Christianity (Minneapolis 1995) earlier publication, Lund 1990; A. Khosroyev, *Die Bibliothek von Nag Hammadi. Einige Probleme des Christentums in Ägypten während der ersten Jahrhunderte*. Arbeiten zum spätantiken und koptischen Ägypten 7 (Altenberge 1995).

[6] A. Guillaumont, "Hieracas of Leontopolis," *CoptEncyc* 4, pp. 1228–1229.

[7] H. Satzinger, "Old Coptic," *CoptEncyc* 8, pp. 169–175; J. Quaegebeur, "Pre-Old Coptic," *CoptEncyc* 8, pp. 190–191.

author that we know of. His writings were found in the White Monastery but have now been scattered over many of the main libraries in Europe and North America, a fate similar to that which befell the libraries of the Wadi al-Natrun, as we shall see. Shenoute's writings can be divided into "canones" and "logoi." He wrote homilies, treatises, catecheses, letters, and so on.[8]

Especially in the sixth century, among creations which provide information about Church history or legendary stories about the lives of important persons, hagiographic stories about famous monks were written. The next two centuries are called the period of cycles, when a number of ambitious, multi-volume hagiographic epics were composed or compiled, but this fruitful period was followed by a period of decline after the Arab Conquest. These different steps in the history and development of Coptic literature have been described and put into a system in a series of articles written by Tito Orlandi.[9]

Just as the first original works in the Coptic language point to monasticism, so does the last. In the eighth century, Arabic became the language of the secular administration in Egypt.[10] Although in the next centuries many literary works were created, transmitted, or revised and reworked in Coptic, such as the cycles pertaining to certain saints, or certain groups of homilies, nevertheless the Arabic language spread gradually throughout the entire land. As a consequence, bilingual manuscripts came into being. The last literary work in Coptic is the "Triadon," written in the fourteenth century by an unknown Coptic monk in Upper Egypt. It is a poem, of a type which in German is called a "Lehrgedicht," with the function of reawakening the love for the Coptic language and the virtues of the monks.[11] But from this time on, there were only a few people who were able to speak or write Coptic, which came to be transmitted

---

[8] See S. Emmel, "Editing Shenute: Problems and Prospects," in S. Emmel, M. Krause, S.G. Richter, S. Schaten (eds.), *Ägypten und Nubien in spätantiker und christlicher Zeit. Akten des 6. Internationalen Koptologenkongresses Münster, 20.–26. Juli 1996, vol. 2: Schrifttum, Sprache und Gedankenwelt.* SKCO 6.2 (Wiesbaden 1999), pp. 109–113; S. Emmel, *Shenoute's Literary Corpus* (Ph.D. diss., Yale University, New Haven, 1993).

[9] See note 2.

[10] For this development, see E.M. Ishaq, "Coptic Language, Spoken," *CoptEncyc* 2, pp. 604–607; B. Verbeeck, "Greek Language," *CoptEncyc* 4, pp. 1165–1170.

[11] P. Nagel, *Das Triadon. Ein sahidisches Lehrgedicht des 14. Jahrhunderts.* Martin-Luther-Universität Halle-Wittenberg. Wissenschaftliche Beiträge 1983/23 [K 7] (Halle [Saale] 1983).

finally only as one of the liturgical languages of the religious services among the Copts.

In this short overview I have had to leave many details aside, but I want to refer here to the works of Martin Krause in addition to the several articles of Tito Orlandi already mentioned.[12] Since there are a lot of gaps in the material that needs to be studied, such attempts as have been made to order the sources inevitably display a lot of question marks and must be revised and updated from time to time. It is important to heed the remark of Orlandi that it is not possible to understand Coptic literature without reviewing and analyzing texts in Greek, Arabic, and other languages of the Christian Orient. The same holds true for the creation of texts, given that translating and handing on—sometimes with a great deal of alteration—was done within the framework of a network that existed among the different Christian cultures of the eastern Mediterranean world. The intersecting influences and combinations within this network were manifold.

The last stage in the history of Coptic literature, for which the libraries of the Wadi al-Natrun are an important source, came to be an important witness not only for works of the Middle Ages but also for the earlier centuries. Since we have only a few very early manuscripts which might be dated to the fourth century, such as the Nag Hammadi Codices, the Bodmer papyri, or the Manichaean codices of Medinet Madi, much of our modern knowledge about the history of Coptic literature is based on manuscripts from the ninth century and later, which are often copies, revisions, or summaries of older works. In many cases, the works of earlier Coptic literature were transmitted finally only for liturgical purposes and so were put into such codices.

But precisely because of these circumstances the libraries and manuscripts of the monasteries of the Wadi al-Natrun are important for Coptic literature not only for the later stages of its history, but also for previous stages which were thus preserved and protected.

Fate of the Libraries and Manuscripts of Wadi al-Natrun

The fate of the manuscripts of the Wadi al-Natrun has similarities to the famous collection of manuscripts from the White Monastery: the libraries were dismembered and scattered over several collections of

---

[12] See note 2, and M. Krause, "Koptische Literatur," *Lexikon für Ägyptologie* 3, pp. 694–728.

museums in Egypt, Europe and North America. In most cases, the codices were dispersed and carried out of Egypt by several travelers and scholars. Therefore, the first problems in working with these texts are codicological and paleographical, where solutions contribute to identifying the leaves and fragments that were originally parts of a single manuscript.

The libraries of the monasteries were devastated by attacks of barbarians in the fifth century (three times), as well as in the sixth century and finally also in the ninth century. As a result, the oldest preserved manuscripts date from the ninth and tenth centuries. In the ninth century, several patriarchs of Alexandria undertook to restore the monasteries and their libraries.[13]

Generally it is assumed that in the founding phase in the fourth and fifth centuries, no general library existed, but rather the monks themselves owned books. The initial impulse for assembling a general library might have been the need for a collection of books for liturgical use, like lectionaries, homilies, and the Holy Bible.[14] Testimonies like the 39th festal letter for Easter, circulated by Athanasius in the year 367, in which the patriarch wrote against the use or even reading of heretical and apocryphal scriptures, demonstrate that such books were in fact collected and read at the time, very likely in monasteries as well as elsewhere.[15]

The exact composition of the early libraries is not known. It is only possible to draw conclusions in an indirect way. R.-G. Coquin, for example, published an ostracon with a list of books belonging to the library of a certain monastery of Apa Elias. With the exception of a medical tractate, the list contains only orthodox religious books—there are no profane, heretical, or schismatic works mentioned.[16]

The reconstruction of the libraries in the 9th century was undertaken in a time of transition. At that time, the prevailing dialect

---

[13] For the history, see H.G. Evelyn-White, *The Monasteries of the Wâdi 'n Natrûn*, part 2: *The History of the Monasteries of Nitria and of Scetis* (New York 1932, reprint 1973).

[14] H.G. Evelyn-White, *The Monasteries of the Wâdi 'n Natrûn*, part 1: *New Coptic Texts from the Monastery of Saint Macarius* (New York 1926, reprint 1973), pp. xxi–xlviii.

[15] L.-T. Lefort, *S. Athanase. Lettres festales et pastorales en copte.* CSCO 150, 151; scriptores coptici 19, 20 (Louvain 1955); E. Lucchesi, "Un nouveau complément aux *Lettres festales* d'Athanase," *AB* 119 (2001) 255–260.

[16] R.-G. Coquin, "Le catalogue de la bibliothèque du couvent de Saint Élie 'du Roucher' (ostracon IFAO 13315)," BIFAO 75 (1975) 207–239; see now also *KSB* I 12.

was Bohairic, and of Greek texts only very few were still in use. Since Arabic had acceded to the position of dominant language, the production of bilingual, Copto-Arabic manuscripts had already started. One of the most famous manuscripts from the Wadi al-Natrun libraries is—without doubt—a manuscript of the Psalms known as the Barberini Psalter, which is written in Coptic, Armenian, Ethiopic, Arabic and Syriac. The book can be dated to the 13th or 14th century but was bound anew in the year 1625. The volume was owned by the Monastery of St. Macarius and bought there in 1635 by exchange for various assorted objects. The fate of the book sounds a little bit like an adventure story. In the year 1635, it was sent to the French bibliophile Nicolas-Claude Fabri de Peiresc. The volume was transported across the Mediterranean in a vessel, which had the misfortune to be attacked and captured by pirates. After a much longer journey than had been foreseen, the Psalter came into the possession of the Grand Master of the Knights of Saint John on the island of Malta. In the end the Psalter was presented to Cardinal Barberini and finally found its way to the Vatican library.[17] The book just mentioned is not the only polyglot manuscript from the Wadi al-Natrun. Evelyn-White wrote about four more fragments, for example half of a leaf bearing a part of the Gospel of Luke written in five parallel columns in Ethiopic, Syriac, Coptic, Karshuni, and Armenian.[18] Such sources impressively demonstrate the active connections that existed among the Oriental Churches at the time.

The libraries functioned not only as archives or centers of production for liturgical manuscripts. The Wadi al-Natrun with its libraries was possibly a principal source of material for the Arabic History of Patriarchs, mentioned in this way by Sawirus ibn al-Muqaffa.[19] In the 14th century the monasteries went through a period of severe crisis. Nevertheless, throughout the following centuries many manuscripts of high quality were preserved and stored in the various monastery libraries.

---

[17] Evelyn-White, *The Monasteries,* part 1 (see note 14), pp. xxxvii–xxxviii; A. Hebbelynck and A. van Lantschoot, *Bibliothecae Apostolicae Vaticanae Codices Manu Scripti Recensiti: Codices Coptici Vaticani, Barberiniani, Borgiani, Rossiani,* vol. 2.1: *Codices Barberiniani Orientales 2 et 17; Borgiani Coptici 1–108* (Vatican City 1947), pp. 1 ff.

[18] Evelyn-White, *The Monasteries,* part 1 (see note 14), p. 272.

[19] A.S. Atiya, "Sāwīrus ibn al-Muqaffa'," *CoptEncyc* 7, p. 2100.

In the 15th century, the Flemish knight Joos van Ghistele made a pilgrimage trip and told about his visit to the Monastery of St. Macarius.[20] For the period immediately thereafter, there exists little information about the Wadi al-Natrun, but beginning early in the 17th century increasing numbers of European travellers visited the monasteries there, were fascinated by the abundance of books they saw, and were responsible for carrying fragments or whole volumes away and depositing them into various libraries in Europe. The various reports of these travelers were collected by H.G. Evelyn-White and others, most recently L. Störk.[21] Only a few of them will be mentioned here.

In the 17th century, Cassien de Nantes reported that he saw three of the four libraries in the monasteries of the Wadi al-Natrun. The Frenchmen Jacques de Thou and Nicolas-Claude Fabri de Peiresc tried to acquire manuscripts with the help of diplomats or merchants. When it became known that manuscripts might be bought and sold in Cairo, a regular antiquities trade developed at an early period.[22] In the year 1712 the French Jesuit Claude Sicard visited the monasteries for his first time and wrote a short description of the four libraries. Three years later he returned with Giuseppe Simone Assemani, who worked for the libraries of the Vatican in Rome. Assemani acquired a large assortment of splendid parchment manuscripts and brought them to Rome.[23]

---

[20] Joos van Ghistele, *Voyage en Égypte, 1482–1483.* Collection des voyageurs occidentaux en Égypte 16 (Cairo 1976), pp. [132]–[135].

[21] Evelyn-White, *The Monasteries,* part 1 (see note 14), pp. xxxvi–xlii; Evelyn-White, *The Monasteries,* part 2 (see note 13), pp. 439–458; L. Störk, *Koptische Handschriften 2. Die Handschriften der Staats- und Universitätsbibliothek Hamburg,* Teil 2: *Die Handschriften aus Dair Anbâ Maqâr.* Verzeichnis der orientalischen Handschriften in Deutschland 21.2 (Stuttgart 1995), pp. 45–98. In his most recent publication (*Koptische Handschriften 4. Die Handschriften der Staatsbibliothek zu Berlin,* Teil 1: *Liturgische Handschriften 1* (Stuttgart 2002), he reported about the origin of certain manuscripts in Berlin, some of which come from the Wadi al-Natrun (pp. 21–23). See also the wealth of informations in O.V. Volkoff, *À la recherche de manuscrits en Égypte.* Recherches d'archéologie, de philologie et d'histoire 30 (Cairo 1970).

[22] See Störk, *Koptische Handschriften 2* (see note 21), pp. 63–64.

[23] A. Hebbelynck and A. van Lantschoot, *Bibliothecae Apostolicae Vaticanae Codices Manu Scripti Recensiti: Codices Coptici Vaticani, Barberiniani, Borgiani, Rossiani,* vol. 1: *Codices Coptici Vaticani* (Vatican City 1937), from Assemani: nos. 1, 5, 18, 19, 35, 55, 57–69; cf. Evelyn-White, *The Monasteries,* part 1 (see note 14), p. xxxix; Störk, *Koptische Handschriften 2* (see note 21), pp. 71–72.

In this century the number of monks diminished. In 1799, General Andréossy, who was a member of the Napoleonic mission, reported that only 59 monks inhabited the monasteries. Andréossy mentioned old books, and he took some of them away with him. The dismembering of the libraries went on. Manuscripts were taken to Turin by the antiquities dealer Drovetti and the scholar Peyron, further manuscripts were brought away by Robert Curzon and, in the year 1839, by Henry Tattam.[24] In the year 1843 Sir Gardner Wilkinson saw many manuscripts in the Wadi al-Natrun and reported on bound books in good condition, as well as innumerable leaves of paper and fragments which covered the whole ground level of the keep of the Monastery of St. Macarius. Constantin von Tischendorf, the famous biblical scholar of the University of Leipzig, visited the monasteries 1844 and reported that there were many remains of books to be seen. He brought away parchment and paper manuscripts which today are preserved in Leipzig and in Cambridge.[25] In the same century, the Egyptologist H. Brugsch bought manuscripts at the Monastery of Bishoi, now stored in Göttingen.[26] Among the visitors who passed through the Wadi al-Natrun still later, many took several manuscripts away with them and brought them to the various European collections, some of these collections being less well-known than the others. In such a manner, for example, leaves of a liturgical codex were acquired by C.M. Kaufmann at the Monastery

---

[24] Most of the manuscripts from Tattam's collection eventually became the property of the John Rylands Library; see W.E. Crum, *Catalogue of the Coptic Manuscripts in the Collection of the John Rylands Library* (Manchester and London 1909), p. vii; S. Emmel, "The Coptic Manuscript Collection of Alexander Lindsay, 25th Earl of Crawford," in S. Giversen, M. Krause, and P. Nagel (eds.), *Coptology, Past, Present, and Future: Studies in Honour of Rodolphe Kasser*. OLA 61 (Louvain 1994), pp. 317–325. Concerning Curzon's fragments from the Wadi al-Natrun in the British Museum (now in the British Library), see: W.E. Crum, *Catalogue of Coptic Manuscripts in the British Museum* (London 1905), pp. xii, xiii, xvii –xviii; B. Layton, *Catalogue of Coptic Literary Manuscripts in the British Library Acquired Since the Year 1906* (London 1987), pp. xliv–xlix etc.; S. Emmel, "Robert Curzon's Acquisition of White Monastery Manuscripts," in M. Rassart-Debergh and J. Ries (eds.), *Actes du IVᵉ congrés copte, Louvain-la-Neuve, 5–10 septembre 1988*, vol. 2: *De la linguistique au gnosticisme*. PIOL 41 (Louvain-la-Neuve 1992), pp. 224–231.

[25] Störk, *Koptische Handschriften 2* (see note 21), pp. 73 ff.

[26] P. de Lagarde, "Die koptischen Handschriften der Goettinger Bibliothek", in P. de Lagarde, *Orientalia*, part 1, (Göttingen 1879). Originally published in Abhandlungen der königlichen Gesellschaft der Wissenschaften zu Göttingen 24.1 (repr. ed. Osnabrück 1973), pp. 3–62.

of Baramus and are now exhibited in a collection in Valkenburg in
the Netherlands.[27]

Also scholars like Steindorff, Gayet, and Strzygowski visited the
Wadi al-Natrun and reported on the libraries. In 1912, when Johann
Georg, Duke of Saxony, made an expedition to the monasteries, of
course he reported a lot of entertaining episodes. At St.
Macarius, for example, he drank the best coffee of the whole Orient—and at the
end, the library with a quantity of illuminated manuscripts was shown
to him.[28]

A milestone in the history of research history on the Wadi al-
Natrun were the investigations in the years 1909–1910, 1910–1911
and 1920–1921 by the Metropolitan Museum of Art in New York. It
served as the basis for the publication of H.G. Evelyn-White, who
went to the Wadi al-Natrun three times and studied the monasteries in
great detail. He was allowed to investigate a room in the keep of the
Monastery of St. Macarius, reachable only through a trap-door, in
which many volumes, leaves of paper, and fragments were stored. He
was permitted to transfer this mass of manuscript remains to the
Coptic Museum in Cairo and also to publish them.[29]

This brief narration of the history of the libraries and their
dispersal leads straight on to the main problems in this area with
which Coptology has to deal.

Work in Progress: Cataloguing of Manuscripts

In recent years it has been a main task to catalogue and to edit the
texts in the different collections or to microfilm the manuscripts in
Egypt.[30] It is always an important step to group the manuscripts and

---

[27] P.G.J. Post, *De collectie C.M. Kaufmann van de Katakomben-Stichting
Valkenburg* (Valkenburg 1988), p. 17.

[28] Johann Georg Herzog zu Sachsen, *Streifzüge durch die Kirchen und Klöster
Ägyptens* (Leipzig, and Berlin 1914), pp. 39–41.

[29] See the description of the "oubliette," where the manuscripts were found, by
Störk, *Koptische Handschriften 2* (see note 21), pp. 75 ff.

[30] S. Kent Brown, "Microfilming Coptic records in Egypt: Report of a Research
Development Trip," in *Acts of the Second International Congress of Coptic Studies,
Roma 22–26 September 1980*, edited by T. Orlandi and F. Wisse (Rome 1985), pp. 27–
29; S.K. Brown, "A Communiqué: Microfilming the Manuscripts of the Coptic
Orthodox Church in Egypt," in *Coptic Studies: Acts of the Third International
Congress of Coptic Studies, Warsaw, 20–25 August, 1984*, edited by W. Godlewski
(Warsaw 1990), pp. 71–73; S. Kent Brown, "Preservation on Microfilm of Coptic and
Arabic Manuscripts for Posterity—a Serious Challenge," *Newsletter of the American
Research Center in Egypt* 153 (Spring 1991), pp. 7–11.

to put the scattered fragments together. In this way, with codicological and paleographical research it is possible to reconstruct the original codices. On this basis, the texts gain new value for further questions, like historical developments or liturgical practice. But in some cases, not even the first step, the cataloguing, not to mention codicological investigations and publications with photographs or microfilm, is done. It is not possible in this article to give a complete list of all known and (let alone unknown) objects that have been distributed from the Wadi al-Natrun to the collections of the world. Therefore, it is my task only to offer an introduction to some of the most recent publications to show not only the problems and new results of research today, but also the importance of future studies. And by the way, a look at the recent publications allows one to get an impression of the contents of the manuscripts as well.

Significant progress has been made, for example, by the publication of the manuscript collection in Hamburg, which contains manuscripts from the Monastery of St. Macarius and the Monastery of St. Bishoi. The publication started with a first catalogue prepared by O.H.E. Burmester in the year 1975. It contained leaves from manuscripts written in Bohairic and originating from the Monastery of Bishoi.[31] The objects were found in a kind of stone container in the second floor of the keep. The system of the catalogue orders the leaves according to different genres: biblical texts, lectionaries, euchologia (missale), horologia (breviarium), pontificale, rituale, psalmodia and scalae (grammars and vocabularies). This systematic arrangement was taken over in two following catalogues published by L. Störk in the years 1995 and 1996.[32] One need only look at these catalogues to see that the majority of texts from the Wadi al-Natrun is connected with liturgical use.

The second catalogue (Störk's first, from 1995) is based on notices made by Burmester and contains 334 manuscripts or fragments from the Monastery of St. Macarius. The group of hymnological texts is the largest one. Störk listed over 130 objects,

---

[31] O.H.E. Burmester, *Koptische Handschriften 1. Die Handschriften-fragmente der Staats- und Universitätsbibliothek Hamburg,* Teil 1, Verzeichnis der orientalischen Handschriften in Deutschland 21.1 (Wiesbaden 1975).

[32] Störk, *Koptische Handschriften 2* (see note 21); L. Störk, *Koptische Handschriften 3. Die Handschriften der Staats- und Universitätsbibliothek Hamburg,* Teil 3: *Addenda und Corrigenda zu Teil 1.* Verzeichnis der orientalischen Handschriften in Deutschland 21.3 (Stuttgart 1996).

for example: psalmodia, the Difnar, Difnar-typikon, Pascha-turuhat, hermeniai, hermeniai to the Theotokia, *hus* (a Coptic word for "song"), psali and doxologies. This shows the important role of songs and poems within the Coptic Church, sung among the Old Testament psalms. Again and again, copies of texts have been discovered which offers new branches in text critical investigations. Alongside the application of the traditional psalms of the Old Testament, a multitude of new songs were created for the liturgy as well. Manuscripts with such texts are preserved from the 10th century onwards. They show a lot of stylistic features that are characteristic for poetry, like figures of parallelism in the structure of the stanzas, or a kind of metric system based on a certain number of accentuated syllables in each verse. These elements of style, as well as the existence of acrostic hymns, prove that these songs were composed in the Coptic language.[33]

Editing Liturgical Books: The Difnar

As an example of such liturgical books of the Coptic Church bearing such pieces of poetry, the Difnar ("antiphonarium") can be mentioned here. It contains hymnic texts for each day of the year in which personalities like saints and martyrs, but bishops as well, were honored. Often biographical details are mentioned, so that the songs offer information for hagiographical questions, too. The Difnar serves as a kind of memorial book and bearer of information, preserving the tradition and ideals of the community. The book can be arranged in a historical series of liturgical texts. Comparative investigations enable us to place the book in a chronological sequence of different traditions.

Already the first scientific publication of the Difnar, by De Lacy O'Leary in 1926, included for the first four months 39 fragments—all of them originating from the Wadi al-Natrun—, which were made available to him by Evelyn-White. Also manuscript no. 435 from the John Rylands Library in Manchester was used, which had been bought in Egypt by Tattam, so that it could originate possibly from the Wadi al-Natrun too. The second part of the publication of the Difnar, in 1928, was based on a manuscript of the 18th century. A

---

[33] See H. Junker, *Koptische Poesie des 10. Jahrhunderts* (Berlin 1908–1911; repr. Hildesheim and New York 1977).

codex from the Borgia collection, no. 59 in the Vatican, which originates likewise from the libraries of the Wadi al- Natrun.[34]

In the course of research, the Difnar was first regarded as a translation of an Arabic version into Coptic or as a revision of the Synaxar compiled with a liturgical and hymnodical interest in view. But more recent preliminary investigations made by Gawdat Gabra have shown that the oldest parts of the Difnar must be older than the Synaxar itself. Therefore, the value of this source is much greater for hagiography and liturgy than was believed at the beginning of research into this Coptic liturgical work. The oldest parts reach back into the 10th century, although an exact clarification about the creation of the oldest parts still remains to be discovered. But it is known that the antiphonary of the Pierpont Morgan Library (M 757), dated 893, precedes the text of the later Difnar.[35]

The oldest manuscript of the Difnar presently known originates from the 14th century; it was found in the Monastery of St. Antony and is not yet published. Another fragment, originating from the Monastery of St. Macarius, was found in the collection of Hamburg. Seventeen leaves from what were originally two volumes, each consisting of approximately 160 leaves, written in Coptic with bilingual titles, have been published by Störk under the number 165. Störk dates the fragment likewise to the 13th or 14th century, so that there is now some known parallel material for a publication of the Difnar in the Monastery of St. Antony.[36]

Reuniting Manuscript Fragments

Establishing catalogues with thorough and exact descriptions of the manuscripts makes it possible again and again to reunite leaves or even fragments of leaves scattered across different collections.

In such a manner, L. Störk was able to prove that his fragment Hymnologie no. 32, in the collection of Hamburg, belongs to two leaves which had already been published by De Lacy O'Leary. The pieces bear orders for a common church service which was celebrated by the monks of the monasteries of St. Macarius and of John

---

[34] De Lacy O'Leary, *The Difnar (Antiphonarium) of the Coptic Church,* 3 vols. (London 1926–1930).

[35] Gawdat Gabra, "Untersuchungen zum Difnar der koptischen Kirche. II. Zur Kompilation," *BSAC* 37 (1998) pp. 49–68, especially pp. 62–64.

[36] Störk, *Koptische Handschriften 2* (see note 21), pp. 335–340.

Kolobos. After combining the pieces, it is obvious that the monks of the Monastery of St. Macarius went to the neighboring monastery for the feast of John Kolobos. The fragments are from a typikon which gives the titles of the hymns from the Difnar and the psalms of David which had to be sung on the occasion of the feast.[37]

But also, in other respects, the texts of the Wadi al-Natrun have led to new results and contribute textual material to various research projects. A constant prime example is the work of textual criticism concerning the Old and New Testaments. Since there exists no complete critical publication of the Old Testament in the Coptic language, one has to work with the diverse collections of textual witnesses, a very difficult procedure which is made easier by the contributions of Vaschalde, Till, and Nagel.[38] At this point, a project initiated by K. Schüssler can be mentioned. Up to now 141 witnesses have been collected in a system of descriptions, tables, and indices, with the existence of published editions being indicated by means of a bibliography. In principle, the work is the initial stage of a "Biblia Coptica Patristica" which the author wants to publish in the future.[39] Such works which collect manuscripts in a systematic arrangement enable scholars to reunite parts of one and the same book which was dismembered long ago and then scattered piece by piece among various libraries and museums. In what follows, I want to report on the general progress that has been made in this important field of Coptology, and to illustrate it with some examples from recent years. Work in this field concerns Coptic literature as a whole and so is not restricted to literature of the Wadi al-Natrun.

A first example for a new reuniting of manuscript fragments can be best described step by step. In the year 1996, Schüssler published the second fascicle in his project mentioned above. In this publication, manuscript "sa 32" was described as a Psalms codex with 16 leaves that are stored in Paris, Rome and Vienna. The codex is supposed to have consisted originally of 120 leaves. Proposals for

---

[37] L. Störk, "Eine gemeinsame Festfeier zweier Klöster," *Enchoria* 22 (1995) 151–157.

[38] See the most recent report about progress in this field, by P. Nagel, "Die Arbeit an den koptischen Bibeltexten 1992–1996," in *ICCoptSS 6 (Münster 1996)* (see note 8), pp. 38–48.

[39] K. Schüssler, *Biblica Coptica. Die koptischen Bibeltexte,* vol. 1: *Das sahidische Alte und Neue Testament. Lieferung 1–4: sa 1–120* (Wiesbaden 1995–2000); vol. 3: *Das sahidische Alte und Neue Testament. Vollständiges Verzeichnis mit Standorten,* Lieferung 1: sa 500–520 (Wiesbaden 2001).

dating have reached from the 7th to the 10th centuries. With the help
of intensive paleographical investigation, Schüssler was able to add
further leaves, e.g. the manuscript Oriental 8808 of the British
Library with 44 leaves, and he wrote of this result in the addenda et
corrigenda of his fascicle 4, published in 2000. Looking at the British
Library catalogue of Layton, we can read under number 13, which is
Oriental 8808, that this manuscript was found by Curzon in the
library of the Syrian Monastery and that it was obtained by him from
the monks, which in this case seems to be a correct information.[40] The
reuniting of these leaves, dispersed across four collections, is one of
the most recent positive results in this work.

L. Störk recorded similar progress in the third volume of the
catalogue of the State and University Library in Hamburg, in which
additions and corrections to Burmester's catalogue of manuscripts
and fragments from the Monastery of Bishoi are published. He was
able to reunite fragments within the collection itself and to show that
some manuscripts are to be dated as far back as the 12th and 13th
centuries. This result puts in question the old thesis of Evelyn-White
that white termites destroyed the library around about 1330.[41]

Another example not only gives an impression of the wide range
of problems that scholars have to deal with, but it also functions as
testimony for the continuity of progress in this field of scholarship.
Under number 2 (Or. 8810 ff. 1–6) in his catalogue of manuscripts in
the British Library, published in 1987, B. Layton described six leaves
of a codex bearing Exodus 16:6–19:11. In the description of the
history of the manuscript it is told that it was bought by Robert
Curzon from monks of the Syrian Monastery in the year 1838. The
text was first edited by Erman in the year 1880, on the basis of M.G.
Schwartze's copy of Tattam's transcription, which is now to be found
in the John Rylands Library in Manchester.[42] Layton noted

---

[40] Emmel, "Robert Curzon's Acquisition of White Monastery Manuscripts" (see
note 24) p. 225.
[41] Störk, Koptische Handschriften 3 (see note 31).
[42] Layton, Catalogue of Coptic Literary Manuscripts in the British Library (see note
24), pp. 6–7. ("Paris 129¹24–37" in his list of "related fragments" being apparently an
error for "Paris 129¹24–39"); Emmel, "Robert Curzon's Acquisition of White
Monastery Manuscripts" (see note 24), p. 230, but see also Emmel's addendum in "The
Coptic Manuscript Collection of Alexander Lindsay" (see note 24), pp. 323–324, A.
Erman, "Bruchstücke der oberaegyptischen Uebersetzung des alten Testamentes,"
Nachrichten von der Königl. Gesellschaft der Wissenschaften und der G.A. Universität
zu Göttingen (Jahrgang 1880), no. 12, pp. 401–440, edition on pp. 407–414.

connections with fragments in other collections, such that it would be possible to add 16 leaves from Paris (BN, Copte 129[1] ff. 24–39), 1 leaf from Naples (manuscript no. 4 in the catalogue of the Borgia collection by G. Zoega published in 1810), and—with a question mark—a leaf in Leiden ("Ins 1") with Deut 17:5–14. Some years before this catalogue was published, P. Nagel had proposed not only the association of the Exodus fragment of the British Library with the fragments listed later by Layton, but mentioned also another Deuteronomy leaf in the Bibliotheque Nationale in Paris (Copte 130[5] f. 137).[43] Further codicological and paleographical study of the handwriting and the book illumination showed that neither the Deuteronomy fragment of Leiden nor the Paris fragment BN 130/5 could belong to the Exodus fragment of London. Therefore, Nagel concluded in 1987 that it is possible to reconstruct a pergament codex (of Exodus) with 23 surviving leaves consisting of the fragments of the British Library, the Bibliothèque Nationale Copte 129/1 ff. 24–39, and the object of the Borgia collection.[44] In this particular case, it is possible to illustrate another problem in dealing with the manuscripts which were brought to various museums by travelers. Curzon wrote that the leaves now in the British Library came from the Wadi al-Natrun, but the leaves in the Borgia collection belonged originally to the White Monastery of Shenoute in Upper Egypt. The problem is obvious: one single codex is reconstructed but the information about the provenance is not compatible. In order to solve this problem, Stephen Emmel showed in a critical analysis concerning the travels of Robert Curzon that also the fragments now in the British Library must have come originally from Sohag and not from the Wadi al-Natrun.[45] The result of all this work was summarized by Schüssler in 1995. The parchment leaves now dispersed across three European collections (London, Paris, Rome), belong to an Exodus-codex with the new label "sa 8."[46]

More examples for reunited fragments can be found in studies dealing with the libraries as a whole.

---

[43] P. Nagel, "Studien zur Textüberlieferung des sahidischen Alten Testamentes," *ZÄS* 110 (1983) pp. 60–61.

[44] P. Nagel, "Textumfang und Textabfolge der sahidischen Version des Buches *Exodus*," in *P.O. Scholz, R. Stempel, Nubia et Oriens Christianus. Festschrift für C.D.G. Müller zum 60. Geburtstag.* Bibliotheca Nubica 1 (Köln 1988), pp. 187–189.

[45] St. Emmel, "Robert Curzon's" (see note 40), p. 231.

[46] K. Schüssler, *Biblica Coptica 1* (see note 39).

Attempts to Reconstruct the Libraries

Evelyn-White who made a detailed study of the Coptic texts from the Monastery of St. Macarius in volume 1 of his major work on the Wadi al-Natrun, wrote also about the other libraries, especially with an excursus concerning the one of the Syrian Monastery.[47] In 1981 S. Kent Brown published a list of the number and genre of manuscripts stored in the monasteries of the Wadi al-Natrun. In all he counted 2,036 known manuscripts in the archives.[48]

In an article titled "Reconstructing a Dismembered Coptic Library," S. Emmel undertook to illuminate the history of the manuscripts of the Monastery of St. Bishoi,—that is, the circumstances under which they came to be dispersed into a number of different collections.[49] He gave an account of the visitors to the Monastery of Bishoi and published a list of the Coptic (or Copto-Arabic) manuscripts which can be traced back to that monastery's library. In his list one can find many cases, in which leaves, stored in several countries, are belonging originally to one codex. Fragments of a lectionary for example, no. 26 in his list (p. 153), are now archived in Hamburg, London, Vienna and Oxford.

In a forthcoming review of the third volume of the Hamburg catalogue by Störk, Emmel gives an update showing the changes that need to be made to his list as a result of the progress that Störk was able to make in reuniting related fragments within the collection in Hamburg.[50]

In Emmel's first article about the library of Bishoi, he reported also on manuscripts which are known from older reports but are now lost. In the collection of the Bible scholar William Hatch, for example, who visited the Wadi al-Natrun in 1923, there were three leaves of a manuscript in Bohairic containing parts of the apocryphal

---

[47] Evelyn-White, *The Monasteries,* part 1 (see note 14), pp. 270–274, part 2 (see note 13), pp. 439–458.

[48] S. Kent Brown, "Microfilming," *Bulletin d'arabe chrétien* 5 (1981) 79–81.

[49] S. Emmel, "Reconstructing a Dismembered Coptic Library," in J.E. Goehring et al. (eds.), *Gnosticism and the Early Christian World: In Honor of James M. Robinson.* Forum Fascicles 2 (Sonoma 1990), pp. 145–161 (with bibliography on pp. 162–184 passim).

[50] S. Emmel, review of Störk, *Koptische Handschriften* 3 (see note 32), to be published in *Acta Orientalia (Sweden).* I am grateful to S. Emmel for giving me a printout of this article prior to publication.

Acts of the Apostles. In this case it is not known where the fragments are now—the worst possible case for scientific research.[51]

The Libraries—Treasuries of Different Text Genres

However, these lost leaves bring us to the last part of this overview, which deals with some aspects of special genres of texts, namely the literary importance of texts which belong to the corpus of apocryphal literature, and which are in a way typical for Egyptian Christianity.

Apart from the multitude of texts which were used for liturgical purposes, some seem to have been used for a kind of personal delight and inner edification. For all the great quantity of religious texts that were found in the libraries, secular and profane literature is almost entirely absent. The only exceptions are Coptic-Arabic word lists, which came into existence in the times when the Coptic language was in retreat from being used by the public at large.[52] Such works are philological works and were found at other places, too.

At this point I should add some remarks about the value of Arabic texts for Coptic literature. Apart from the importance of bilingual manuscripts, of which many can be found, for example, in the inventory of the current holdings of the library of the Monastery of Macarius that was prepared by U. Zanetti,[53] manuscripts written only in Arabic can be a source for older Coptic literature if the Arabic texts are Arabic versions of older Coptic texts. The different aspects of the translations from Coptic into Arabic were summed up recently by J. den Heijer in his general lecture at the Sixth International Congress of Coptic Studies in Münster.[54] In some cases, lost works of Coptic literature have survived in translations into the Arabic language. Gawdat Gabra has offered one example for the monasteries of the Wadi al-Natrun. In the Syrian Monastery, an Arabic manuscript is archived which is dated from the year 1314 and deals

---

[51] Emmel, "Reconstructing" (see note 49), pp. 150 and 160; but see also Emmel, "Recent Progress in Coptic Codicology and Paleography (1988–1992)," in *ICCoptS 5 (Washington 1992)*, vol. 1, pp. 33–49, at p. 43 n. 8, where he points that "Hatch did in fact publish his apocryphal Acts fragment" (in the Festschrift Crum), so that at least the text is known, even though the leaves themselves have disappeared.

[52] Evelyn-White, *The Monasteries*, part 1 (see note 14), p. 222.

[53] U. Zanetti, *Les manuscrits de Dair Abū Maqār. Inventaire* (CdO 11), Geneva 1986.

[54] J. den Heijer, "Recent Developments in Coptic-Arabic Studies (1992–1996)," in *ICCoptS 6 (Münster 1996)* (see note 8), pp. 49–64.

with the life of Moses the Black. Since parts of the Sahidic version of the Apophthegmata Patrum were translated word for word into Arabic, it seems likely that the surviving text goes back to an older Coptic Life of Moses the Black.[55]

It was already mentioned that the works of famous leaders of Christianity had an important place in the translation projects from Greek into Coptic. As an example for translations of such Greek Patristic Fathers, we find that in the libraries of the Vatican there are 38 excerpts from homilies of St. John Chrysostom.[56] Also numerous Acts of Martyrs were found in the libraries.[57] It would need a separate paper to give an overview or to deal with the contents of this genre, which is also a witness for the enjoyment for narratives among the monks. Apart from the stories of famous personalities of Egyptian Christianity, apocryphal histories narrating the adventures of the heroes of the Bible were also very popular. In the first of Evelyn-White's three volumes, we find, besides an apocryphal fragment on Adam and Eve, parts of the apocryphal Acts of certain Apostles, a small fragment of an apocryphal apocalypse of John, and texts about the life and death of the virgin Mary.[58]

Normally composed in the Greek language and then translated and altered, the wonders and miracles surrounding the apostles were found pleasurable by the believer. Evelyn-White published altogether 39 leaves with apocryphal Acts of the Apostles (to which W.H.P. Hatch later added three more, as mentioned above). These leaves contain parts of the Acts of John, his journeys and his death, homilies and the Martyrdom of Philipp, the Preaching of Saint Bartholomew, the Martyrdom of Saint Matthias, of Saint Mark, and of Saint Luke. These texts are Bohairic variations of older ones. The Acts of John, for example, were composed originally in the 2nd or 3rd century. The oldest indirect witnesses date from the 3rd to the 4th centuries. These apocryphal Acts were translated into many languages and were continually read by ordinary believers through the centuries. The version of the Monastery of St. Macarius demonstrates that such

---

[55] G. Gabra, "Dair Anba Musa al-Aswad. Das originale Baramus-Kloster im Wadi al-Natrun," *BSAC* 36 (1997) 71–74.

[56] Hebbelynck and Van Lantschoot, *Codices Coptici Vaticani* (see note 23) no. 57.

[57] See for instance Evelyn-White, *The Monasteries,* part 1 (see note 14), pp. 75–119.

[58] Evelyn-White, *The Monasteries.* part 1 (see note 14), pp. 3–6, 27–50, 51, 51–54.

apocryphal texts were transmitted and read in Egypt's monasteries until the 12th and 13th centuries.[59]

I hope to have shown that the old manuscripts of the Wadi al-Natrun, which transmit a history of nearly 1,000 years, hand over to us the responsibility for large parts of the heritage of Coptic literature. The surviving remnants of these venerable monastic libraries are now spread over several collections which are far away from Egypt, but nevertheless the heart of the libraries, which are slowly being reconstructed through the efforts of many scholars, continues to beat in the Wadi al-Natrun.

---

[59] The manuscript dates possibly as far back as in the 13th century (Evelyn-White, *The Monasteries.* part 1 [see note 14], 26 n. 1.

Wadi Natrun in Geologic History

Rushdi Said

Wadi Natrun is one of the many sites in the Egyptian desert, which were settled by the wandering ascetic forefathers who sought retirement in the solitude of that desert. There are literally hundreds of these sites that are distributed all over the desert. Most of these sites had a small source of water. Their abundance and wide distribution is related to an early spell of wetness that characterized the climate of Egypt for several millennia prior to the onset of the present-day dry conditions at ca. 2400 BC. That spell of wetness raised the water table and produced gushing springs in many parts of the desert. Unlike Wadi Naturn, the majority of the sites were located at some distance from the beaten paths and trading routes of the desert and did not support a large number of monks. Examples of these sites can be found in the Fayum, Farafra and the Siwa areas in the Western Desert and in the two Galala Plateaus in the Eastern Desert. The two Galalas had a large number of small and widely spread sources of water that supported a large number of solitary monks who built their cells (*gallayas*) around them. These were so numerous that the plateaus were named the northern and southern Gallayat plateaus. It was only in the 1920's that their name was changed to Galala. Most of these sites are now abandoned as their water sources ran dry. The only two extant sites of these plateaus are the large and well-known monasteries of St. Paul and St. Anthony that are hidden in the rocks of the southern mountain.

Wadi Natrun stands out among all other locations because of its ample and seemingly renewable source of water and because of its proximity to the seats of the Coptic patriarchate and the centers of learning. It is a unique place in being so near and yet so deep in the desert. The wadi is an elongate depression that runs in a northwest-southeast direction along the western edge of the Nile delta. Like all other depressions of the Western Desert part of it lies below sea level. This part extends for about 33.6 km in length and has an area of close to 240 km². The lowest part of the depression lies along its eastern rim and is occupied by a string of lakes the water surface of which is about 23 m below sea level. The lakes' waters are rich in salts; a thick bed of these salts is deposited at their bottom and also as incrustations on the ground adjacent to many of the lakes. The bed is made up of a lower layer of sodium sulfate, a thicker middle layer of sodium carbonate and an upper layer of sodium chloride. Of these, sodium carbonate or Natron was the most precious and sought after material. It was sorted out and extensively used from the most ancient of times. In ancient Egypt natron was used in purification ceremonies, especially as a mouthwash, in the manufacture of glass and glaze (possibly the green frits used as pigments) and in the bleaching of linen. It was also used extensively in mummification. Natron continued to be used throughout history until the 1970's when it was replaced by the purer and chemically produced carbonate that was made by the electrolysis of sodium chloride and the chemical reaction of the resultant sodium hydroxide and calcium carbonate (lime). This put an end to the industry of Natron collection and trade that had played an important role throughout the history of Egypt.

The geological history of Wadi Natrun is written in its rocks. It can be read by examining these rocks, putting them in chronological order and attempting to decipher the environment in which they were formed. The evolution of the present-day wadi Natrun seems to be closely knit to the drainage systems that developed over the elevated land of Egypt which had emerged as a result of the retreat of the seas that covered it until the end of the Eocene epoch (i.e. 38 million years ago). The older system of drainage lasted for about 24 million years and spanned the time of the Oligocene and Early Miocene epochs. During this long time the system underwent great changes especially toward the end of the Oligocene epoch when Egypt witnessed a period of great earthquakes and volcanic activity that dramatically changed its landscape. It raised the Red Sea mountains, led to the birth of the Red Sea and the rise of the southern part of the modern delta of the River Nile to form the South Delta Block high, along whose western edge Wadi Natrun lies (figure 1). Volcanic material in the form of basalt sheets was extruded during this period covering large parts of northern Egypt including the Wadi Natrun area. Sheets of basalt covered the South Delta Block and have been encountered in all the wells that were drilled in that block, including that which was drilled in Wadi Natrun.

Little is known about the earlier part of this old drainage system that preceded the extrusion of the basalt, but the latter part, which lasted for about 10 million years, is better known. It was dominated by a drainage system whose rivers flowed in the great Moghra Bay that skirted the fringes of the South Delta Block and occupied most of the northern Western Desert (figure 1). The bay was shallow. It received the flow of the rivers and was the receptacle of their sediments. Standing at the eastern edge of the bay the Wadi Natrun area was inundated frequently by the waters of the bay. It received a mixed range of sediments from pure fluvial (river) to mixed fluvio-marine. These sediments cover today a large part of the surface area of Wadi Natrun and the adjacent Wadi el-Faregh. They have a thickness of close to 300m as shown in the Wadi Natrun well that was drilled in the early 1960's after the search for oil. The rivers that fed the Moghra bay have long disappeared and their courses can no longer be traced or seen. They seem to have been numerous, shallow, meandering and frequently shifting their courses. We know of their existence from the sediments that they left behind. These sediments were mostly coarse-grained sands and gravels with frequent intercalations of fine-grained clays. There is good indication that the climate in Egypt at that time was extremely wet supporting a rich fauna and a thick vegetation. The stems of some of the large trees that lived at that time were preserved in the fluvial sediments of this age. In some areas in Wadi el-Faregh many of these stems cluster together forming fields that have been dubbed "petrified forests."

During the succeeding seven million years of middle Miocene time (14-7 million years ago) the climate became arid and warm. The rivers ran dry and the Moghra bay became part of the advancing sea that covered the northern part of Egypt as well as the newly formed Red Sea depression. Wadi Natrun, as well as the entire South Delta Block, stood high above the waters of that sea forming an island that stood between the deep sea that covered the North Delta Embayment and the shallow arm that covered the area to the south along the Cairo-Suez road.

The onset of the late Miocene time at about 7 million years ago saw the withdrawal of that sea and the beginning of the dramatic event that led to the total disappearance of the entire Mediterranean Sea. This disappearance happened as a result of the closure of the Gibraltar strait, the only connection of the sea to the world oceanic system. The closure converted the sea into a closed lake that shrank gradually as it lost its water by evaporation until it finally desiccated exposing the sea bed as a pan of salt. The event lasted for about two million years during which time the present-day channel of the River

Nile was excavated. The river deepened its channel in response to the lowering level of the desiccating Mediterranean forming a canyon that was probably just as awe inspiring as the present-day Grand Canyon of Colorado. This period was a time of erosion in Egypt. It saw the dissection of the South Delta Block and the lowering and excavation of the Wadi Natrun depression.

Five million years ago the Gibraltar Strait opened up to the world oceanic system and the Mediterranean Sea started to fill again. The rising waters of the sea transgressed the excavated valley of the early Nile forming a marine gulf that extended up to the latitude of Aswan. The Gulf also covered the South Delta Block and the Wadi Natrun area where it left behind a bed of marine limestone that can still be seen today covering the floor of Wadi Natrun.

The marine gulf that was converted into an estuary with the advent, some three million years ago, of a river that occupied the excavated channel of the Nile. This ancestral river (the Paleonile) lasted for about one million years. It drew its waters from the land of Egypt which saw a change of its climate and the onset of a period of extensive rains. Wadi Natrun depression lay at the western fringes of the estuary receiving deposits which seem to have filled and leveled it. These sediments were eroded away during the succeeding arid phase that ushered the Pleistocene epoch; the last remains of which are preserved in the Gar el-Muluk hill, a knoll in the middle of the Natrun depression. The hill carries a unique collection of vertebrate fauna that must have lived in that mixed environment. The fauna included several fish, crocodilian, turtle, hippopotamus, rodent and mammalian remains. With the erosion of these sediments Wadi Natrun assumed its present shape. Wind seems to have been the dominant factor that eroded these sediments. The first million years that ushered the Pleistocene epoch were extremely arid with stormy wind seasons. In one of the wet spells of this early Pleistocene, gravels of a short-lived river passed by Wadi Natrun. These gravels can be seen in the western slopes of the wadi.

The wadi remained since then and throughout the one million year of the middle and late Pleistocene epoch outside the valley of the Nile although the delta of one of the predecessors of the modern Nile (the Prenile) extended westward to its fringes. The last million years show great fluctuations of the climate. The wadi became the receptacle of dunes during the arid episodes and the site of larger lakes during the wet episodes.

This survey of the geological history of Wadi Natrun shows that the wadi lies at the confluence of two great groundwater reservoirs: the older Moghra reservoir of non-renewable fossil water and the more recent present-day Nile reservoir of renewable source of water. All indications suggest that the latter reservoir is the main source of the water of the wadi. Prior to the building of the Aswan High Dam and the tapping of the Nile floods there was an increase in the water supply entering the wadi with the incoming of the flood, which began at Cairo about the end of June and generally reached its maximum in September. This seasonal fluctuation of the water supply of the wadi affected the level and number of the string of lakes that fringe its eastern side. Their level became high during the flood season and their number increased when the supply became exceptionally high and spilled over other depressions. It is essential that the agricultural expansion in the wadi be balanced with the amount of the incoming flow.

The following is a table of the major events that led to the evolution of the present-day Wadi Natrun. The table is better read from bottom to top so that the reader may follow the events in their sequential order. The years marked are in the millions.

TABLE I

Year
Present

1 --
  Arid episode – excavation of Wadi Natrun depression
2 --
  Paleonile reaching Wadi Natrun
3 --
  Mediterranean Sea filling, invading the Nile channel
  and forming a gulf extending to Wadi Natrun
4 --
  Mediterranean Sea desiccated – excavation of the canyon
  like Eonile
7 --
  Climate becoming dry – advance of the Sea over the land of
  Egypt – South Delta Block remain uncovered forming an island
14 --
  Climate becoming wet – drainage system flowing into the
  Moghra Bay depositing sheets of sands and gravels forming
  the Moghra groundwater reservoir
24 --
  Period of earth movements and vulcanicity, South Delta Block
  elevated, basalt sheets extruded covering large tracts

  Climate wet – drainage system of shallow rivers developing
  depositing beds of sands and gravels
38 --
  Start of retreat of the sea from the land of Egypt

References
James, G.T. & B.H. Slaughter. "A primitive new Middle Pliocene Murid
  from Wadi Natrun, Egypt." *Annals Geological Survey Egypt* 4 (1974),
  319-332.
Said, Rushdi. *The Geology of Egypt.* Balkema, Rotterdam & New York,
  1990.

Figures in the Carpet:
Macarius the Great, Isaiah of Scetis, Daniel of Scetis, and Monastic Spirituality in the Wadi al-Natrun (Scetis) From the Fourth to the Sixth Century

Tim Vivian[*]

Not many years ago I read a very good scholarly book on Palestinian monasticism in Late Antiquity. In my review of that book I observed, however, that one could finish the volume and have no idea why those Palestinian Christians had become monks: Why had they chosen the monastic life? One can sometimes set down a book or leave an academic conference with the empty feeling that scholars often talk all around the subject of monasticism without really addressing the central issue: Why are monks monks? What are they doing in their monasteries? More particularly for our purposes at this symposium: Why were the early monastic fathers and mothers out in this desert?[1] What were they doing here? I respectfully suggest that if we do not at least address these questions at this symposium, then we are wasting our time here. Because these questions lead to two others: (1) Why are monks here now? and (2) Why are *we* here at this symposium?[2]

---

[*] I wish to thank Augustine Casiday and William Harmless, S.J. for their comments.

[1] I include "mothers" because tradition speaks of at least two female monastics at Scetis disguised as men, monastic "transvestites": Saint Apollonaria Syncletica, who reportedly lived in Scetis in the 4th-5th c. [see H.G. Evelyn White, ed. Walter Hauser, *The Monasteries of the Wādi 'N Natrūn*, vol. 2, *The History of the Monasteries of Nitria and of Scetis* (New York: Metropolitan Museum of Art, 1932; repr. Arno Press, 1973), 117-18], and Anastasia, the subject of a story in the dossier of material connected with Abba Daniel of Scetis (see below, Part III).

[2] I acknowledge the "gap of incomprehension" that Columba Stewart and others have emphasized between the early monastics and ourselves; Stewart, who once desired to close that gap, now says that he needs "to step back and keep the gap open." See Columba Stewart, "'We'? Reflections on Affinity and Dissonance in Reading Early Monastic Literature," *Spiritus* 1.1 (Spring 2001): 93-102. By contrast, Graham Gould, *The Desert Fathers on Monastic Community* (Oxford: Clarendon, 1993), 186, with whom I concur, acknowledges that "there is much which is alien in their teaching," but goes on to confirm that "the Desert Fathers have proved their capacity to speak clearly even sixteen centuries after the hey-day of their communities." Alan Jones has

I do not propose in this paper to answer these latter questions, at least directly, but I do intend to address the ones I raised earlier. Monks have been here in the Wadi al-Natrun for almost 1700 years. Why? Why did the early monks come to live in the forbidding desert? I was originally going to speak here today about the history of monasticism in Scetis but the more I thought about it the more I realized that history, at least monastic history, has embedded within it the concomitant question about spirituality that I posed above. I hope to answer this question, or make an effort at answering it, by looking at the spirituality of early monasticism in the Wadi al-Natrun.[3] Such an effort will, I hope, offer a history of a different sort, a history of the heart, mind, and spirit in one particular place and at one particular time. Such a history, I firmly believe, has relevance for own places and time.[4]

A paper of this length can only be suggestive, not exhaustive. In my home study, where I spend a good deal of time thinking and writing about early Christian monasticism, I have a beautiful handwoven carpet of burnished reds and oranges, made here in Egypt. That carpet has many smaller figures in it, united around a large central figure; all the figures work together to make a coherent and cohesive pattern. In my reveries I like to think of that carpet as representing the mothers and fathers of early Egyptian monasticism gathered around their Lord and Savior, listening attentively to the Word in the desert. From those ammas and abbas I will focus on three representatives of early desert monasticism in Scetis from the fourth through the sixth century, one from each century: Macarius the Great (4th c.), Isaiah of Scetis (5th c.), and Daniel of Scetis (6th c.). My hope is that by the end of the paper these three figures will have given

---

commented that Dante's *Divine Comedy* is both accessible and inaccessible; so too are the desert fathers and mothers.

[3] As Mark Sheridan has commented, "The Spiritual and Intellectual World of Early Egyptian Monasticism," *Coptica* 1 (2002): 50, "the cultivation of the interior life was effectively at the heart of" early Egyptian monasticism. His essay surveys in particular Antony, Paul of Tamma, and Pachomius.

[4] By "spirituality" I will follow Kenneth J. Collins and adopt first a broad definition, "the importance of surpassing oneself into a wider circle of meaning with its resultant enlightenment or greater knowledge of God," then add with him the specifically Christian "revelation of God manifested in *Jesus Christ* through the Holy Spirit." See Collins, ed., *Exploring Christian Spirituality: An Ecumenical Reader* (Grand Rapids, MI: Baker Books, 2000), 14 and 13. On 14, Collins notes that spirituality transcends "egocentric commitments" and leads to "sociocentric ones as well," that is, to community, which is vital to early Christian monasticism.

us a clearer picture of the intricate and beautiful carpet of early monasticism and will help us better understand why the early monks were out here and what they were hoping to accomplish.

I. SAINT MACARIUS THE GREAT (300-390)[5]
Feast Day: 27 Barmahat (5 April)

Macarius the Great, also called Macarius of Egypt to distinguish him from Macarius of Alexandria, came to Scetis (the Wadi al-Natrun) about 330 A.D., settling first, perhaps, near the present-day monastery of Deir al-Baramus to our north, and later moving near the site of the present-day monastery that bears his name: Deir Anba Maqar, the Monastery of Saint Macarius.[6] Before he came to Scetis, Macarius, like Antony the Great, was probably an *apotaktikos* or village ascetic.[7] Then, also like Antony, he withdrew (*anachôrein*) to the desert and thus became an anchorite (*anachôritês*). Soon, however, Macarius, like Antony, like Amoun in Nitria at the same time, began to attract disciples who formed a community around him. Such a community was semi-anchoritic; that is, unlike the cenobitic monks in Pachomius' *koinonia* in Upper Egypt, the monks of Scetis, Nitria, and Kellia lived alone during the week or in small groups where an abba or spiritual father directed one or more younger monks.[8] On Saturdays and Sundays all the monks would come

---

[5] On the ancient works by and about Macarius discussed below (the Coptic *Sayings*, the *Virtues of Saint Macarius*, and the *Life of Macarius of Scetis*) with introductions and translations, see Tim Vivian, *Saint Macarius the Spiritbearer: Coptic Texts Relating to Saint Macarius the Great* (Crestwood, NY: St. Vladimir's Seminary Press, 2004).

[6] Evelyn White, *Monasteries of the Wâdi 'N Natrûn*, vol. 2: 98-103; The *Life of Macarius of Scetis* 21. For a general presentation, still see Derwas Chitty, *The Desert a City* (Crestwood, NY: St. Vladimir's, 1966).

[7] For the *apotaktikoi*, see James E. Goehring, *Ascetics, Society, and the Desert: Studies in Early Egyptian Monasticism* (Studies in Antiquity and Christianity; Harrisburg, PA: Trinity, 1999), 20-25, 53-72; *Life of Macarius of Scetis* 13, in Vivian, *Saint Macarius the Spiritbearer* (n. 5 above).

[8] For a good general overview of anchoritic and semi-anchoritic monasticism, see Lucien Regnault, *La vie quotidienne des pères du désert en Égypte au IVe siècle* (Paris: Hachette, 1990), trans. Étienne Poirier, Jr., *The Day-to-Day Life of the Desert Fathers in Fourth-Century Egypt* (Petersham, MA: St. Bede's Publications, 1999).

together for worship (*synaxis*), the Eucharist, and a common meal (*agapê*).[9]

The early monastic endeavor, then, was both individual and communal; in the felicitous phrasing that French allows, the desert fathers and mothers practiced "la vie solitaire et la vie solidaire" (solitary and communal life).[10] Central to their spirituality is this symbiosis and this tension. Historians have suggested a number of reasons for the sudden rise of monasticism in Egypt, among them withdrawal (*anachôrêsis*) from oppressive taxation and disaffection from an increasingly worldly Church. But historians rarely talk about the desire to live a holy life (*eusebeia*); holiness, unlike high taxes and grasping prelates, cannot be readily quantified.[11] The *Life of Macarius of Scetis*, by contrast, written sometime before the 10th century, saw Macarius as following in the "godly footsteps" of the apostles as he "looked forward to the imperishable hope that the Savior taught us through his holy teachings in the Gospels."[12] In allegiance to the Gospel visitations to Zecheriah (Lk 1:8-20) and Mary (Lk 1:26-55), the author of the *Life of Macarius* has "Abraham, the father of Isaac who begot Jacob," declare to Macarius' father:

> Leave this land, for God has so decided it . . . . "I will not forsake you," says the Lord, "but I will bless you," he said [Dt 31:6, Josh 1:5; Gen 17:16, 20], for I too left my country of Haran and I dwelt in the land of Canaan, as the Lord told me: "And I will give you a son," said the Lord, "from this wife whom you now have, and his name will endure for generations with the children that he will beget spiritually to serve me in the place that I will show him" [Gen 17:15-19, 18:9-15].

---

[9] On the weekend synaxery and agape, see Regnault, *La vie quotidienne*, 177-88, and Cecil Donahue, "The ΑΓΑΠΗ of the Hermits of Scetis," *Studia Monastica* 1 (1959): 97-114. On instruction, see the Coptic "Life of Evagrius" 17 in Vivian, *Four Desert Fathers: Pambo, Evagrius, Macarius of Egypt, and Macarius of Alexandria* (Crestwood, NY: St. Vladimir's, 1994). For the tension between solitude and community, see Gould, 142-50.

[10] Antoine Guillaumont, "Histoire des moines aux Kellia," *Orientalia Lovaniensia Periodica* 8 (1977): 187-203, at 194.

[11] Douglas Burton-Christie, *The Word in the Desert: Scripture and the Quest for Holiness in Early Christian Monasticism* (New York & Oxford: Oxford UP, 1993), as the subtitle of his book suggests, has understood the importance of holiness in early monasticism.

[12] *Life of Macarius of Scetis* 1 (Proemium).

According to the *Life of Macarius of Scetis*, Macarius, like Abraham, will beget a new people. Abraham begot according to the flesh; Macarius, however, will beget spiritually.[13] Others, both ancient and modern, have expressed in other ways what the author of the *Life* saw biblically and typologically. In the *Life of Antony*, Athanasius enthuses that Antony and his followers were making the desert a city and a modern scholar has similarly observed that the early monks "were intent upon creating a new society."[14] As Stelios Ramfos has observed,

The anchorite is not offended primarily by the world; he is offended by futility. He needs to be part of a society which is more sensitive and more real and lives by unadulterated truths different from those of the market-place, so that instead of persisting in what is transient he decides to seek the *eschaton*, the ultimately real.[15]

The writer of the *Life of Macarius of Scetis*, whatever his merits (or demerits) as an historian, long ago understood the spirituality of Macarius' desert endeavor and particularly emphasizes the creation and sustenance of community. Any treatment of early monasticism should begin with a discussion of this early monastic spirituality of community.[16]

If community is central to monastic spirituality, then the abba, a holy person like Macarius, Antony, Amoun, and many others, is the still point of that center, the anchor, the nexus, the begetter of

---

[13] In the *Life of Macarius of Scetis* 8, an angel declares to Macarius: "Thus says God: 'This land I will give to you. You shall dwell in it and blossom and your fruits shall increase and your seed shall multiply [Gen 12:7] and you shall bear multitudes of spiritual children and rulers who will suckle at your breasts.'"

[14] *Life of Antony* 14.7; Philip Rousseau, "The Desert Fathers, Antony and Pachomius," in Cheslyn Jones, et al., eds., *The Study of Spirituality* (London: SPCK, 1992), 119-30, at 120.

[15] Stelios Ramfos, *Like a Pelican in the Wilderness: Reflections on the Sayings of the Desert Fathers*, trans. and abridged by Norman Russell (Brookline, MA: Holy Cross Orthodox Press, 2000), 11. As Ramfos adds, 21, "The morality of the desert fathers is nourished not by a set of rules about relationships with material things, but by a radical demand for inward change and purification concerning relationships with persons."

[16] Graham Gould, *The Desert Fathers on Monastic Community*, has understood this particularly well.

spiritual children.[17] The abba, of course, is inspired and guided by God. Although the *Apophthegmata*, or *Sayings* of the desert fathers and mothers, does not emphasize this, it is a given of its spirituality;[18] the *Life of Macarius of Scetis* represents and personifies God's guidance with a cherub that directs Macarius and keeps him focused.[19] The story of Maximus and Domitius, though much of it is legendary,[20] accurately illustrates both how a community could grow around a holy person and shows the relationship that developed between abba and disciple. As Macarius explains,

> When I was sitting in my dwelling in Scetis, two young men, foreigners and strangers, came to see me . . . and said, "Where is Abba Macarius' cell?" I said to them, "What do you want with him?" They said to me, "When we heard about his works and about Scetis, we came to see him." I said to them, "I am he." They begged my pardon and said, "We want to live here."[21]

Macarius thinks the two are too soft to last in the desert so he orders them to hew a cell for themselves from the rock of an abandoned quarry. This they willingly do, illustrating Macarius' authority and their humility and obedience, all important components of monastic spirituality. The two "patiently did everything" Macarius had ordered, but when they did not come to see the old man for three years he mused to himself, "What is their way of life? They haven't come to see me about their thoughts. Those who live far away come to see me but these two do not come, nor have they gone to anyone else, only to church, and only to receive the Eucharist, keeping silent all the while." The sharing of thoughts, *logismoi*, with an elder and his giving of spiritual counsel was extremely important in early

---

[17] On spiritual fatherhood, see especially Gabriel Bunge, *Geistliche Vaterschaft: Christliche Gnosis bei Evagrios Pontikos* (Regensburg: Friedrich Pustet, 1988).

[18] See Gould, 38-41. Gould points out, 11, how apposite the *Apophthegmata* are for the study of the history and spirituality of Scetis. See Burton-Christie.

[19] *Life of Macarius of Scetis* 15, 27.

[20] For a discussion, see Evelyn White, 98-104; for the text, see the *Coptic Life of Maximus and Domitius*, ed. Emile Amélineau, *Histoire des moines de la Basse-Égypte*. Annales de Musée Guimet 25 (Paris, 1894), 262ff.

[21] The Coptic *Sayings of Saint Macarius of Egypt* 8 (= Greek *Alphabetical Apophthegmata* 33), trans. Tim Vivian, "The Coptic Sayings of Saint Macarius of Egypt," *Cistercian Studies Quarterly* 35.4 (2000): 499-523, at 507-9. Reprinted in Vivian, *Saint Macarius the Spiritbearer*.

monasticism and was a vital part of monastic formation and discernment.[22] So Macarius goes to see the two young monks, learns of their holy way of life, and thus the elder is himself edified (a common theme in early monastic texts).

As the story of Maximus and Domitius shows, one of the chief characteristics of early monastic literature is "a far-reaching interest in the pattern of personal relationships within the monastic community."[23] Although the Greek and Coptic *Apophthegmata* concerning Macarius have only five or six abba-disciple sayings (out of 41 and 34 sayings respectively), where a monk explicitly asks Macarius for counsel, the *Virtues of Saint Macarius*, probably a fifth- to eighth-century compilation, has many more.[24] Both the *Apophthegmata* and the *Virtues*, however, have many more sayings— the majority in fact—where Macarius is teaching or giving advice; these presuppose monks or disciples who are listening and who must have often asked a question. It is clear from these three sources that Macarius' chief role was that of spiritual counsellor; if we utilize the epithet that the *Virtues* gives to Macarius, "Spiritbearer," then Macarius bore and passed on the Holy Spirit when he taught his charges about the spiritual life.[25]

As Graham Gould has wisely observed, the abba-disciple relationship was "not a matter of practical convenience but a divinely guaranteed means by which a monk grows, by obedience and trust in

---

[22] In the *Apophthegmata*, Abba Paphnutius reports that he went to see elders twice a month, walking some 12 miles (*Alphabetical Apophthegmata* Paphnutius 3; PG 65:380), and Abba John the Little used to sit in front of the church on weekends so that monks might approach him about their thoughts (*Alphabetical Apophthegmata* John Kolobos 8; PG 65:205). See also Tim Vivian, "Words to Live By: 'A Conversation that the Elders Had with One Another Concerning Thoughts (ΠΕΡΙ ΛΟΓΙΣΜΩΝ),'" *St. Vladimir's Theological Quarterly* 39:2 (1995), repr. in Vivian, *Words to Live By: Journeys in Ancient and Modern Monasticism* (Kalamazoo: Cistercian, forthcoming); and Columba Stewart, "Radical Honesty about the Self: the Practice of the Desert Fathers," *Sobornost* 12 (1990): 25-39. Failure to seek counsel could lead to presumptuous self-importance and ruin; see *Lausiac History* 27.2.

[23] Gould, 17, who is speaking of the *Apophthegmata*.

[24] On the dating of the *Virtues*, see Vivian, *Saint Macarius the Spiritbearer*, Introduction. About 32 out of 83 sayings in the *Virtues* involve a disciple asking Macarius for counsel.

[25] "Spiritbearer" was also applied to Saints Antony and Pachomius; see *Alphabetical Apophthegmata* Antony 30 and François Halkin, ed., *Sancti Pachomii vitae Graecae*. Subsidia Hagiographica 19 (Bruxelles, Société des Bollandistes, 1932), 153.19.

what his abba tells him to do, in his acceptability to God."[26] The first requirement (virtue) asked of the disciple was renunciation of one's own will and obedience to an abba, who represents God.[27] Perhaps the most striking example in the Macarian corpus occurs when Macarius tells a young monk to go to the cemetery and abuse, then praise, the dead, who, of course, care nothing about either praise or abuse. When the disciple returns the second time, Macarius teaches him:

> You saw how you abused them and they did not say anything to you and how you praised them and they said nothing in reply; it's the same with you: if you wish to be saved, go, be dead, take no account of people's scorn or their compliments, like the dead themselves, and you can be saved.[28]

As Macarius' final words suggest, the young monk's question/petition to the old man was "My father, tell me a word how I may be saved." Macarius' answer—and the expected change in outlook or behavior that that answer expects—shows that the abba-disciple relationship was not only formational and transformational, it was also systolically and diastolically soteriological. Just as the young man in the Gospels asks Jesus what he must do to have eternal life (Mt 19:16), over and over in the *Apophthegmata* disciples sincerely ask their spiritual fathers how they can be saved.[29] As a letter writer in Late Antique Egypt famously wrote to the holy man Paphnutius who was counselling him, "After God you are my salvation." What Philip Rousseau calls a "hand-to-mouth spirituality" must also be recognized as mouth-to-mouth spirituality; that is, the passing on of the Spirit, in emulation of Christ (Jn 20:22).[30] An image of spiritual CPR (Cardio-Pulmonary Resuscitation) is not out of place here: we are all dying, the monastic texts suggest, and desperately

---

[26] Gould, 27-28. On the subject of master and disciple in early monasticism, see the excellent article by Jean-Claude Guy, "Educational Innovation in the Desert Fathers," *Eastern Churches Review* 6 (1974): 44-51.

[27] On renunciation, see Burton-Christie, 214-22.

[28] Coptic *Sayings* 11 (= Greek *Alphabetical Apophthegmata* 23). For other striking examples of obedience, see *Alphabetical Apophthegmata* Antony 20 and John Kolobos 1 and the tales about Abba John of Lycopolis, related by Cassian, *Institutes* 4.23-26.

[29] Jesus' final answer to the young man to give up everything and follow him (Mt 19:21) became the locus classicus for the understanding of the monastic calling.

[30] See Rousseau, 121.

require resuscitation in the Spirit. In the desert, those who ask
receive.

What virtues (practices, habits) were abbas like Macarius trying
to inculcate in their disciples in order to bring about a saving way of
life (*politeia*)? The list is long, and I can focus here only on a few that
are central. Perhaps the most important requirement of the ancient
monastic life was single-mindedness. Life in Christ is not easy. With
a wonderful metaphor, the Macarius of the *Virtues* teaches about
single-mindedness and its difficulties:

> If you pursue prayer, pay careful attention to yourself lest you
> place your pots in the hands of your enemies, for they desire to
> steal your pots, which are the thoughts of your soul. These are
> the precious pots with which you will serve God, for God does
> not look for you to glorify him only with your lips, while your
> thoughts wander to and fro and are scattered throughout the
> world, but requires that your soul and all its thoughts wait upon
> the sight of the Lord without distraction, for he is the great
> physician, the healer of souls and bodies, our Lord Jesus
> Christ.[31]

Waiting "upon the sight of the Lord without distraction" makes one
like the angels. In ancient sources the monastic life is often called
"the angelic life," but to truly appreciate what that means we need to
pry our minds free from cute and saccharine modern images of angels
and give ear to what Macarius is really saying: "The rank of monk is
like that of the angels. Just as the angels stand in the Lord's presence
at all times and no earthly thing hinders them from standing in his
presence, so too it is with the monk: it is fitting that he should be like
the angels his whole life."[32] The monk should always stand before
God and be in God's presence.

In early monasticism such an understanding lives (or fights) side
by side with Saint Paul's injunction to pray without ceasing (1 Thes

---

[31] *Virtues* 67. For the consequences of the theft of some non-metaphorical pots, see
Virtues 46.

[32] *Virtues* 55. See Karl Suso Frank, *Angelikos bios: begriffsanalytische und
begriffsgeschichtliche Untersuchung zum "engelgleichen Leben" im frühen Mönchtum*
(Beiträge zur Geschichte des alten Mönchtums und des Benediktinerordens, 26;
Münster, Westfalen: Aschendorff, 1964), and Agnes Lamy, "Monks and the Angelic
Life," *Monastic Studies* 1 (1963): 39-57.

5:17), one of the main goals, and fruits, of the monastic life. But Macarius then jarringly adds that by living like the angels the monk "will fulfill the word of our Savior who commands each of us to deny himself and take up his cross and follow him" [Mt 10:38//Lk 14:27]. One does not normally associate angels with the cross (unlike with the Annunciation, Nativity, and Resurrection of Christ, there are no angels at the Crucifixion), but Macarius does. By doing this he forcefully steers us away from our besetting sin—self-absorption, self-indulgence, narcissism, hyper-individualism, call it what we will—and returns our gaze, like the angels', to God.[33] Angels gaze but we human beings work with our backs, and our backs must bear the cross of Christ. In either case, gazing or groaning, we are worshipping God by working for Christ as he works his way to Calvary for us.

It should be no surprise, then, that the monastic life requires renunciation; in this it is only, and entirely, following the gospel (Mt 4:20, 19:21, 19:27; Acts 4:34-35). Macarius knew that gospel, and himself, well enough to know that even after years in the desert he could say "I have not yet become a monk, but I have seen monks." This seemingly astounding statement is in fact a common motif in early monastic literature. Macarius could say this because he had travelled from the relatively suburban security and comforts of Scetis out into the *real* desert; there he encountered two monks living naked on an island in a marshy lake where the wild animals came to drink.[34] When Macarius asks them how he can *become* a monk, they say to him, "If one does not renounce all worldly things, he can not become a monk." Macarius then laments, "I am weak; I can not be like you," to which they tersely reply, "If you can not be like us, sit in your cell and weep for your sins."[35] Perhaps Macarius was able later to "renounce all worldly things." In two sayings, when thieves are plundering his goods Macarius in fact helps them.[36]

Renunciation is not an end but rather the means, the path, to *hesychia*—silence, solitude, contemplative quiet—where the monk

---

[33] Abba Arsenius said (*Alphabetical Apophthegmata* Arsenius 13), "The thousands and myriads above have only one will, but people have many wills."

[34] On this theme see also "The Life of Onnophrius" in Tim Vivian, *Paphnutius: Histories of the Monks of Upper Egypt and the Life of Onnophrius*, rev. ed. (Kalamazoo: Cistercian, 2000), 143-66.

[35] Coptic *Sayings* 21 (= Greek *Alphabetical Apophthegmata* 2).

[36] *Alphabetical Apophthegmata* Macarius the Great 18 and 40.

can give all his or her attention to God.[37] Perhaps the best definition of *hesychia* is that by a poet, T.S. Eliot: "A condition of complete simplicity/(Costing not less than everything)."[38] The two hermits on the island mentioned above told Macarius to sit in his cell, and that was common monastic advice.[39] In the *Apophthegmata*, Macarius twice tells interlocutors to sit in their cells and weep for their sins.[40] Sitting in one's cell is not like being in one's apartment or room with the television on.[41] Nor is being solitary the same as being alone or lonely; one (seeming) paradox in early monastic literature is that the more one is solitary, the more one is with God—and with one's neighbor.[42] Solitude in prayer helps a person to cultivate relationship with God and purify the heart; voluntary poverty focuses one's attention where it should be, on the Creator instead of on what is created. Only then can the created world become "a 'reconciled space' because of the fraternity of all things in Christ." Now "there is no room for violence, contention, or rejection of the 'other.'"[43]

One of the early monks' favorite adjectives for God was *philanthrôpos*. *Philanthrôpia* may be translated as "God's loving compassion for humanity," and the monks at their best did their best to emulate God's love and compassion. Macarius was known for his compassion: he helped a widow in distress, went a great distance to find a treat for a sick monk, and healed the daughter of a government official.[44] One of the most delightful, and moving, stories about monastic compassion is that of Macarius and the healing of an

---

[37] As Gould observes, 172, *hesychia* "seems to imply one or both of two things: first, solitude considered in itself, and second, an inward disposition of freedom from disturbance." For a good discussion of *hesychia*, see Kallistos Ware, "Silence in Prayer: The Meaning of Hesychia," in Basil Pennington, ed., *One Yet Two: Monastic Practices East and West* (Kalamazoo: Cistercian, 1976), 22-47.

[38] T.S. Eliot, "Little Gidding," *The Four Quartets*, in T.S. Eliot, *The Complete Poems and Plays 1909-1950* (New York: Harcourt, Brace, 1952), 145.

[39] "Sit in your cell and your cell will teach you everything" (*Alphabetical Apophthegmata* Moses 6). See also *Alphabetical Apophthegmata* Evagrius 1; Paul of Tamma, "On the Cell," trans. Tim Vivian and Birger A. Pearson, "Saint Paul of Tamma: *On the Monastic Cell (De Cella)*," *Hallel* 23:2 (1998): 86-107, repr. in Vivian, *Words to Live By*; and Gould, 15-57.

[40] *Alphabetical Apophthegmata* Macarius the Great 27 and 41.

[41] For an interesting contemporary treatment of the cell, see Ramfos, 25-39.

[42] See Paul of Tamma, "On the Cell." On monastic relationships with neighbors, see Gould, 88-106.

[43] Philip Sheldrake, "Human Identity and the Particularity of Place," *Spiritus* 1.1 (Spring 2001): 43-64, at 59.

[44] *Alphabetical Apophthegmata* Macarius the Great 7, 8; Coptic *Sayings* 7.

antelope's young. An antelope comes to Macarius, "tearing out its fur, weeping as though it were a he-goat, its tears flowing to the ground," takes Macarius by the sleeve, and guides the old man back to where she lives. Macarius discovers that the antelope's young are deformed, with their chins on their backs. Macarius groans and petitions Christ: "You who care for all of creation, our Lord Jesus Christ, who have numerous treasuries of mercy, take pity on the creature you made." He then makes the sign of the cross over the young antelopes and heals them. With joy he marvels "at the goodness of God and the love for humanity of our Lord Jesus Christ as shown by his tender mercies for me and for the other beasts that he cares about."[45] This is not mere sentimentalism or ecological correctness; it demonstrates, rather, the incarnating of compassion, Christ's compassion, for all of God's creation, something we should take to heart.[46] In teaching about Christ's compassion, Macarius likens the Savior to a potter: just as the potter "prays for the precious and decorated vessels" made for emperors and priests, "he also prays for those that are ugly and inferior," those "used as chamber pots and for birthing stools," because both types of pots "are works of his hand," so too does Christ, "who possesses the treasuries of numerous mercies," rejoice over both saint and sinner.[47]

The soul friend of compassion is non-judgementalism, not judging our neighbor.[48] Early monastic literature abounds in stories teaching us not to judge. When Paphnutius, Macarius' disciple, asks the old man for a saving word, Macarius succinctly replies "Do not do anything evil and do not judge anyone, and you will be saved."[49] Perhaps the most striking thing said about Macarius in the ancient sources, something that was widely repeated, was that "he became a god upon earth."[50] Macarius' divinization (*theosis*) occurred because "just as God protects the world, so too did Abba Macarius cover

---

[45] *Virtues* 14.

[46] See Helen Waddell, *Beasts and Saints*, ed. Esther de Waal (London: DLT, 1995). The story also shares in the monastic theme of the return to paradise; see Vivian, trans., the *Life of Onnophrius*, in *Paphnutius*, 143-66.

[47] *Virtues* 38.

[48] For a fuller discussion, see Gould, 123-32. Ramfos, 132, pointedly observes that the desert fathers sense in judgementalism "a radical atheism, for when judgement and the will are made absolutes, God is no longer needed. The fathers therefore identify the censure of a person with the rejection of the judgement of God."

[49] Coptic *Sayings* 15 (= Greek *Alphabetical Apophthegmata* 28).

[50] For further discussion of this remarkable phrase, see Gould, 124 n. 78.

shortcomings: when he saw them it was as though he did not see them and when he heard them it was as though he did not hear them."[51] Non-judgementalism, of all the virtues, makes one most divine; this was something that the flinty Macarius of Alexandria had to learn from Macarius of Egypt.[52] When some brothers ask Macarius one time if feelings of pity are more important than works, he says yes and by way of illustration likens Christ to a street vendor:

> Look at the street vendor who sells to a customer. He says to him, "I've given you a good deal," but if he sees that the customer is unhappy, he gives him back a little of his money and the customer goes away happy. It's the same with acts also: if they stand unhappy before God, the giver of good things, the true judge, our Lord Jesus Christ, his numerous acts of compassion move him and the acts leave with joy and rejoicing and gladness.[53]

There is indeed judgement, Macarius teaches, but judgement belongs to God, and even in judgement Christ "is merciful and full of compassion."[54]

Compassion and non-judgementalism are the sweet fruits of humility, and Macarius both lived and taught humility. Macarius had an ascetic rule not to drink water if he had just drunk wine, but if other monks offered him wine he would humbly take it, not wishing to affront monastic hospitality. Thus he would deny himself of much-needed water in the scorching desert. Finally, Macarius' disciple, fearing for his master's health, had to rebuke the overly-generous monks: "For God's sake, do not give him any more wine. Isn't it

---

[51] Coptic *Sayings* 22 (= Greek *Alphabetical Apophthegmata* 32); see also *Virtues* 1, 32, and 74; the *Life of Macarius of Scetis* 34; and *Alphabetical Apophthegmata* Poemen 64. Coptic *hôbs* and Gk *skepazein* mean both "cover" and "protect"; an etymological echo of this in English may be heard in "protect," which derives from Latin *tegere*, to cover. The modern Coptic Liturgy of Saint Basil considers "covering" (*skepazein*) a divine attribute: God "has covered us, helped us, guarded us, accepted us, spared us, supported us, and has brought us [safely] to this hour."

[52] Coptic *Sayings* 27 (= Greek *Alphabetical Apophthegmata* 21).

[53] *Virtues* 25.

[54] *Virtues* 9. See Burton-Christie, 181-85, and Tim Vivian and Apostolos N. Athanassakis, "Spiritual Direction from the Early Monastic Mothers and Fathers on Observing a Holy Lent: Chapter Three of the Greek *Systematic Apophthegmata*, 'On Compunction,'" *Sewanee Theological Review* 44:1 (Christmas 2000): 60-78.

enough that he punishes himself in his cell?"[55] If a monk came to
Macarius "fearfully as though to a saint and great old man, he would
say nothing to him. But if one of the brothers heaped scorn on him,
saying, 'My father, when you were a camel-driver and stole nitre and
sold it, didn't the guards beat you?'," he would joyfully speak with
that person about whatever he wanted.[56] Perhaps the ultimate
compliment paid to Macarius' humility (one that he would not have
wanted) was when the Devil tried to cut the old man with a scythe but
was not able to. In shock the Devil cried out "You are powerful,
Macarius! I can't do anything against you! Look—what you can do, I
can do too: you fast and I don't eat anything at all; you keep vigil,
and I don't sleep at all. There is only one thing at which you're better
than me." When Macarius asked what that was, the Devil replied,
"It's your humility. On account of your humility, there is nothing I
can do to you."[57] The Devil can imitate exterior acts of asceticism but
cannot emulate interior virtues that come from the heart.

Defeating the Devil is not a simple thing and yet in a way it is.
Henry David Thoreau told his fellow citizens of Concord "Simplify!
Simplify! Let your affairs be two or three rather than numbering in
the thousands!"[58] What Thoreau preached and lived, the desert fathers
and mothers lived and taught centuries before: the fewer possessions
we have, whether material or psychic (that is, concerns about the past
and worries about the future), the fewer tools the Devil has to slice us
to shreds with. The ancient sources dare to suggest that Macarius had
become so simple (*haplous*), humble (*tapeinos*), and poor (*ptôchos*)
that he had stripped Satan of all his weapons; all that was left for the
Adversary was to helplessly evaporate: "when the saint stretched out
his hands, the demon disappeared and Abba Macarius continued on
his way, giving glory to God."[59] Simplicity, paradoxically, in the
hands (and heart) of the right person, is a very great spiritual weapon.
Simplicity allowed Macarius to radically simplify Christian living to
a few basic precepts; they could be written on the walls of the monk's
cell or inscribed on his heart. When Macarius was asked "How

---

[55] Coptic *Sayings* 5 (= Greek *Alphabetical Apophthegmata* 10).

[56] Coptic *Sayings* 12 (= Greek *Alphabetical Apophthegmata* 31).

[57] *Virtues* 2 (= Greek *Alphabetical Apophthegmata* 11). One of the most powerful
stories about humility in the Macarian corpus is that of the monk falsely accused of
theft; see *Virtues* 46. See also Burton-Christie, 236-58.

[58] Henry David Thoreau, *Walden*.

[59] *Virtues* 2 (= Greek *Alphabetical Apophthegmata* 11).

should one pray?" he told his questioner not to make long speeches: "It's enough to stretch out one's hands and say, 'Lord, as you will, and as you know, have mercy.' And if the conflict grows fiercer, say 'Lord, help!'"[60] One time when Paphnutius asked Macarius for a saving word, the old man replied, "Do no evil to anyone, and do not judge anyone. Observe this and you will be saved."[61] Someone like this, with such simple, yet profound, understanding and wisdom, deserved to be called "a god upon earth" and "the first shoot of this vine . . . that is Shiêt [Scetis]."[62]

II. SAINT ISAIAH OF SCETIS (d. 491)
Feast Day: 11 Abib (18 July)

Saint Macarius died some eighteen years before the first destruction of Scetis by barbarian invaders in 407-8.[63] At that time many monks were martyred (Moses and his companions) and many others left the desert community (John Kolobos). Scetis suffered a second devastation in 434.[64] About this time, perhaps because of marauders, Abba Isaiah left Scetis, becoming part of the Egyptian monastic diaspora, and journeyed to Sinai, where he took up residence near Gaza.[65] He died on August 11, 491, a hundred years after Macarius.[66] A miscellany of his sayings, instructions, homilies, and writings has

---

[60] Greek *Alphabetical Apophthegmata* 19.

[61] Greek *Alphabetical Apophthegmata* 28.

[62] *Life of Maximus and Domitius*, ed. Amélineau, ed., *Histoire des monastères de la Basse Égypte*, 263.

[63] On this destruction, see Evelyn White, 151-61. In one of the more poignant exclamations from late antique Christianity, at the first destruction of Scetis Abba Arsenius groaned "The world has lost Rome, the monks have lost Scetis" (*Alphabetical Apophthegmata* Arsenius 21).

[64] See Evelyn White, 162-64.

[65] Chitty, *The Desert a City*, 73; see Chitty, "Abba Isaiah," *Journal of Theological Studies*, N.S. 22:1 (April 1971): 47-72, at 66-68, for the identification of Isaiah of Scetis with Isaiah of Gaza. There are few fixed dates in Isaiah's life: about 431 he visited Paul of Thebes; he was in Palestine by 452-53 and visited Maiouma; in the autumn of 485 he was at Beit Daltha, four miles from Thavatha.

[66] On this date, see Lucien Regnault, "Isaïe de Scété ou de Gaza," *Dictionnaire de spiritualité, ascétique et mystique* (Paris, 1933-) 7.2, 2083-95, at 2084, citing P. Devos, *Analecta Bollandiana* 86 (1968): 350; and Regnault, "Isaiah of Scetis, Saint," *Coptic Encyclopedia*, ed Aziz N. Atiya (New York: Doubleday, 1992), 3.1305-6.

come down to us as the *Ascetic Discourses*.[67] As Lucien Regnault has
pointed out, Isaiah "presents us with a faithful echo of the teaching of
the great monks of Scetis"; he transmitted "to his disciples traditions
inherited from the old men of Scetis who shaped the monastic life."[68]
Isaiah's teachings, then, like Isaiah himself, became part of the wider
Egyptian diaspora and joined such eminent works as the *Life of
Antony*, the *Rules* of Pachomius, and the *Conferences* and *Institutes*
of Cassian that spread the gospel of early Egyptian monasticism to
Europe, Palestine, and Asia Minor.[69] Although most of what Isaiah
hands on belongs to the common heritage of early monastic teaching
(which is as he would have wanted it), his words nevertheless evince
"an original form and a personal flavor that reveal a faithful disciple
who has in turn become an eminent spiritual master."[70]

Isaiah's generation in the fifth century gathered and edited the
Apophthegmata Patrum and he himself faithfully handed on the
desert tradition to a new generation.[71] Isaiah has connections with a
number of prominent abbas from Scetis: Poemen, Sisoes, Arsenius,
Agathon, and Or, to name just a few; thus he represents a "bridge to
an earlier generation of elders," remembering conversations "held
between his own elders, or simply informants, and leading
personalities from the Egyptian generation of monastics in the
430s."[72] Isaiah's own writings, the *Ascetic Discourses*, most likely
owe their literary composition not to Isaiah but to his disciple Peter.[73]
This discipleship, in fact, helped shape (or not shape) the *Discourses*:
Peter collected and recorded "all that he could of the inherited

---

[67] There is still no critical edition. For the Greek text, see Augoustinos, *ΤΟΥ ΟΣΙΟΥ
ΠΑΤΡΟΣ ΗΜΩΝ ΑΒΒΑ ΗΣΑΙΟΥ ΛΟΓΟΙ ΚΘ* (Jersualem, 1911; 2nd ed., Volos:
Schoinas, 1962). For a French translation, see Hervé de Broc, *Abbé Isaïe, Recueil
ascétique* (Begrolles-en-Mauge: Bellefontaine, 1970). Citations below are from *Abba
Isaiah: Ascetic Discourses*, trans. John Chryssavgis and Pachomios (Robert) Penkett
(Kalamazoo: Cistercian Publications, 2002). I am indebted to John Chryssavgis and to
Rozanne Elder, editorial director at Cistercian Publications, for sending me a
manuscript of this work before publication.

[68] Regnault, DSp, 2088.

[69] On Isaiah's influence, see Regnault, DSp, 2093-95.

[70] Regnault, DSp, 2090; see Regnault, *CoptEncyc*, 1306.

[71] Chitty, JTS, 74; Regnault, CE, 1305; Chryssavgis, Introduction.

[72] Chryssavgis, Introduction; on the theme of remembering, see William Harmless,
SJ, "Remembering Poemen Remembering: The Desert Fathers and the Spirituiality of
Memory," *Church History* 69.3 (September 2000): 483-518. Scholars have spotted
Evagrian echoes in Isaiah's writings; see Regnault, DSp, 2092-93.

[73] Regnault, *CoptEncyc*, 1305; Regnault, DSp, 2086.

authentic teaching of the deserts, without presuming to impose on the material his own interpretation either by extensive rewriting or even by systematic ordering of the collected works."[74] The result is not "the systematic exposition of the mind of a single author. It is a collection, . . . expanded later, of a variety of occasional pieces— apophthegmata, monastic rule, homiletic—to ensure the recording for future generations of the authentic teaching of the desert fathers."[75] The *Discourses*, nevertheless, do have an overarching purpose, *praktikê*, inherited from Evagrius and the abbas of the *Apophthegmata*: *praktikê* is the spiritual method of cleansing the affective or "passionate" part of the soul,[76] which then allows the monk to reach concord with the nature of Jesus—τὸ κατὰ φύσιν τοῦ Ἰησοῦ.[77]

Underlying and informing Isaiah's *praktikê* is his understanding of the passions (*ta pathê*), those devices and desires that can rule and even tyrannize our hearts and minds and alienate us both from God and from our fellow human beings. Here Isaiah is more "theoretical" than Macarius or most of the abbas and ammas of the *Apophthegmata* (Evagrius excluded) in that he develops and expresses underlying theological principles for his ascetic beliefs and practices. (Although Isaiah, like Macarius, has a great deal to say about practical matters and practices—on thoughts, the cell, community, prayer, scripture—I will focus here on his overarching principles rather than on the bricks in the pavement beneath the arch.) At the fall, according to Isaiah, all of Adam's "senses were twisted towards that which is contrary to nature."[78] Christ, however, transforms what is contrary to nature (*para physin*) into what is in accordance with nature (*kata physin*). This struggle between the old Adam and the new (Rom 5) mirrors the battle that rages within each human being. Desire, for Isaiah, is not wicked or disordered: "Desire is the natural state of the intellect because without desire for God there is no love." But the Devil has "twisted" natural desire for God into "shameful desire" (AD 2).

The desert fathers and mothers of the fourth and fifth centuries gave a great deal of thought to the passions: if the passions are an

---

[74] Chitty, JTS, 68.

[75] Chitty, JTS, 69; see also Regnault, DSp, 2085.

[76] Evagrius, *Praktikos* 78. That is, the part of the soul with the passions. See below.

[77] See Chitty, JTS, 69. The Christological emphasis seems to be Isaiah's.

[78] *Ascetic Discourses* 2. Hereafter references to the *Discourses* will be given in the body of the essay with the abbreviation "AD" and the chapter number.

unbroken stallion, should the monk, with patience and hard work, break the stallion and, with bridle and bit, gain control over it (*damazein* in Greek), or should he acknowledge the incorrigibility of the stallion and destroy it?[79] Both approaches can be found among the early ammas and abbas. Kallistos Ware has observed that New Testament and Patristic thought on the whole views the desires or passions negatively but he believes that Isaiah considered the passions—desire, envy, jealousy, hatred, pride—to be in accordance with nature and therefore "a natural part of our personhood as created by God": "The ascetic seeks to redirect rather than to destroy."[80] It is true that Isaiah lists the passions and says that each "is in accordance with nature." But after each passion he immediately adds that it "has been changed within us" into what is now "contrary to nature" (AD 2). The reason for this change is the fall: "See, all these things were created together with man. But when he ate from the tree of disobedience, they were changed within him, into these shameful passions" (AD 2). For Isaiah, then, the passions were originally good but are now twisted and disordered.

Isaiah clearly develops a theology of nature and of the passions.[81] The passions, he unequivocally maintains, estrange us from God (AD 8). As Stelios Ramfos sharply puts it, the passions are atheistic, because they displace God.[82] Like some of the desert fathers of the fourth century, Isaiah maintains that destroying the passions is therefore a good thing (AD 17, 19). Destruction, though, probably means rectification rather than obliteration. In Cassian and Evagrius, *apatheia*, "passionlessness," "freedom from the passions," is not a state of emotionlessness but is rather a state of well-ordered emotions, as opposed to disordered emotions: the passions. For Isaiah, Moses is the archetype of the person who is "free from all passions" (AD 22). Moses legislated the Sabbath rest and Christ himself "will celebrate the true Sabbath." Christ could do this only by "ascending the Cross on the Day of Preparation" (AD 22). Isaiah celebrates this Sabbath with Christ but at the same time cries out "what a miserable wretch I am, sinning against the holy commandments! I, who carry heavy burdens on the Sabbath!" These burdens, Isaiah explicitly states, are

---

[79] See, for example, *Alphabetical Apophthegmata* John Kolobos 13.
[80] Kallistos T. Ware, "The meaning of 'Pathos' in Abba Isaias and Theodoret of Cyrus," *Studia Patristica* 20 (1989): 315-22, at 316, 319, 320.
[81] See AD 2, 16, 18, 25.
[82] Ramfos, 132.

the passions: "greed, vanity, sensual delight, lust, passion, and a loose heart" (AD 22).

The good news is that "all these and similar burdens the Lord Jesus wiped out in the body of saints and put to death in his holy body" (AD 22). Christ "came to put to death . . . the passions at work in us" (AD 23). Although Christ defeats the passions, he cannot do it alone. "Each day," Isaiah enjoins his disciples, "ponder which passion you have conquered before you proceed to make any requests to God" (AD 15). Such self-scrutiny and discipline shows that the monk progresses through *praktikê*, ascetic practices: "ascetic discipline protects us from the Enemy" (AD 4). Derwas Chitty thus rightly saw the *Ascetic Discourses* as "a practical guide."[83] "Force yourself to repeat many prayers," Isaiah teaches, "for prayer is the light of your soul. Every day ponder your mistakes. And, if you pray about them, God will forgive you" (AD 4). Isaiah buttresses such practical advice as this by allegorizing Rachael and Leah (Gen 29: 31-35). Leah is "a symbol of ascetic discipline" while Rachael symbolizes "genuine vision." Discernment brings ascetic discipline and humility leads one to genuine vision. Unless a person goes through the entire range of *praktikê*, he cannot acquire genuine vision (AD 4).

Through *praktikê* and getting control of themselves, the monks can return their bodily members to a natural state (AD 2). Thus Isaiah maintains and continues the early monastic vision and hope of restoration, whether one sees this as a Platonic return, as in Antony's letters, or in the more biblical understanding of paradise regained, a common belief of the early monks.[84] For Isaiah the intellect (*nous*) is the soul's battleground, with the gates of paradise shimmering within hailing distance. He quotes Mt 6:24, "You cannot serve God and Mammon," to show that "it is not possible for the intellect to care for two things . . . . Mammon represents all the works of this world and unless a person renounces this, he cannot serve God. Serving God means not having anything extraneous in our intellect while praying to him" (AD 25). Here Isaiah brings together the Evagrian practice of sloughing off all images that distract us from God and Macarius' single-mindedness, understood quite literally. Isaiah warns his disciples that "unless the intellect is restored from evil to health, a

---

[83] Chitty, JTS, 69.
[84] See Vivian, *Paphnutius*, 143-66.

person is not able to perceive the light of the Godhead" (AD 21), but he also assures them that "if the intellect stands diligently over its senses, it acquires immortality, and immortality brings it to such glory as God reveals to it" (AD 5).

For Isaiah, light and glory come for the monk, and for all of us, only by way of Calvary. The cross does not have a central place in fourth-century monastic thought, though by no means is it absent.[85] In the fifth century, however, Isaiah focuses more intently on the cross and his teaching on "the ascent of the cross" appears to be his original contribution to a theology and spirituality of the crucifixion (AD 16).[86] Isaiah says that the intellect cannot ascend the cross until it heals the senses of all desires and disease (AD 8). This is possible for human beings solely because of Christ: if Christ "had not first healed all the passions of humanity for which he came into the world, he would not have ascended the cross" (AD 8). Christ, therefore, is able to "resurrect" the intellect from carelessness. One may well ask Isaiah why the intellect must purge itself if Christ has already healed it. It seems that Isaiah understood Christ's healing and saving action as enabling (and ennobling) human efforts. Without Christ our efforts would be in vain and we would be standing in a wasteland without even a glimpse of the distant treetops of paradise.

Isaiah, like Evagrius, believes that there are different levels to the spiritual life. What is striking and original about Isaiah is that he uses the cross to explicate these different levels. Isaiah distinguishes "between bearing the cross, which signifies the preparatory stage of ascetic discipline," and mounting the cross, which represents a higher stage.[87] Ascending or mounting the cross requires *apatheia*, being freed from the passions that separate us from God. One "ascends the cross in stillness [*hesychia*]" only after enduring and laboring and being cleansed (AD 13). "The cross is a sign of future immortality" which one gains, Isaiah insists, only after "shutting the mouths of the

---

[85] *Alphabetical Apophthegmata* Poemen 144; see Harmless, 490-91. Cassian reflects more on the cross and crucifixion, although it is difficult to know how much of this reflects fourth-century desert tradition. See Cassian's retelling of a discourse by Pinufius in *Institutes* 4.34-35. Cassian mentions the crucificixion several times in the *Institutes*: with reference to monastic garb (1.4, 1.8) and to the canonical hours of prayer (3.3.3, 3.9.1).

[86] Regnault, DSp, 2091, says that the theme of mounting the cross belongs to the second stratum of the *Ascetic Discourses*, that is, not to Isaiah's words themselves but to what his disciple Peter or others remembered about his teaching.

[87] Chryssavgis, Introduction; AD 8.

Pharisees and Sadducees," which he interprets as faithlessness and hopelessness (Pharisees) and craftiness, hypocrisy, and vainglory (Sadducees) (AD 13). As Isaiah forcefully puts it, "If you wish to crucify the old person" with Christ (Eph 4:22), "you must remove those things that force you to descend from the cross" (AD 26). The version of this saying preserved in the Greek *Systematic Apophthegmata* puts it even more forcefully: "you must cut off from yourself until the day you die those who would bring you down from the cross." Isaiah then defines what being on the cross means: "And you must prepare yourself to bear humiliation, to bring peace to the hearts of those who do evil to you, to humble yourself before those who wish to rule over you, and to keep silent and not judge anyone in your heart."[88]

Christ bearing the cross shows the monk the necessity of ascetic toil and labor; Christ on the cross demonstrates the overcoming of hardship and opposition and the attainment of hesychia. For Isaiah, Christ remained calm throughout his suffering and passion, which tells us that "we too must overlook everything in this world before ascending the cross" (AD 13). When "the passions" have thus "been extinguished" and "the intellect is freed" and "when the intellect is liberated" from the passions "and reaches the Sabbath day of rest, it is in another, new age and considers new things, attending to matters not corruptible" (AD 13). Hesychia for Isaiah does not bring a person to some sort of drugged-out bliss or apathy but rather leads to greater understanding:

> Silence gives birth to ascetic discipline. Ascetic discipline gives birth to weeping. Weeping gives rise to fear of God. Godly fear begets humility. Humility begets foresight. Foresight begets love. Love renders the soul undiseased and free from the passions. Then, and only then, does a person know that he is far from God (AD 13).[89]

---

[88] *Systematic Apophthegmata* I.8; Jean-Claude Guy, ed., *Les Apophtegmes des pères: Collection systématique. Chapitres I-IX*. Sources chrétiennes 387 (Paris: Cerf, 1993). This differs slightly from what AD 26.1 has: Prepare your heart to bear the contempt of the evil ones. They will humiliate you in order to rule your heart. Impose silence so that you do not judge someone whom you know in your heart."

[89] Similar rhetorical "chains" may be found in Evagrius, *Praktikos*, Preface 9, trans. John Eudes Bamberger, *Evagrius Ponticus: The Praktikos and Chapters on Prayer* (Kalamazoo: Cistercian, 1981), 14, and Cassian, *Institutes* IV.43, trans. Boniface Ramsey, *John Cassian: The Institutes*, ACW 58 (Mahwah, NJ: Paulist Press, 2000),

The seeming paradox is that knowledge of our separation from God comes only *after* one is freed from the passions. Isaiah, again in a seeming paradox, calls this knowledge ascending the cross. On the cross we recognize our alienation. In early monastic spirituality, however, this is not a paradox but hard, truthful, reality. When we are caught up in our "atheistical" passions, we are too self-involved to be aware of God and thus of our separation from God. It is only in calmness, tranquility, and silence (*hesychia*) that we begin to discern the gulf that separates us from God, that is, as Thomas Merton put it, from our true self. This shows why humility is so important to the early monks in general and to Isaiah in particular.[90] This also shows why Isaiah's main concern is how to find and continuously maintain hesychia.[91] Hesychia requires manual work and austerities and fighting against thoughts, that is, the *praktikê* of the early monastic regimen. This may seem circular but is, rather, a coming full circle, a holistic way of viewing life where all activities are connected and interrelated, where no part of oneself is isolated from another. Within such an understanding and such a sanctuary, we are continuously in God's presence: "Become, in purity," Isaiah exhorts, "an altar of God, continually having the inner priest making sacrifices, both in the morning and in the evening, in order that the altar is never left without sacrifice" (AD 5). The monk's cell, on this understanding, becomes the holy of holies and the monk becomes the world's altar on which Christ continually offers himself, in love, for the whole world.

III. SAINT DANIEL OF SCETIS (6th c.)
Feast Day: 8 Bashans (16 May)

Macarius the Great and Isaiah of Scetis were holy men who, by word and example, taught others to live lives of holiness. One defacing of the modern western world has been the amputation of holiness from our common vocabulary and, more importantly, lived ethic. What is holiness? More importantly, what characteristics does a holy person

---

102. See the discussion in Owen Chadwick, *John Cassian: A Study in Primitive Monasticism* (2nd ed., Cambridge: Cambridge UP, 1968), 93.

[90] "Above everything we require humility" (AD 3).

[91] Regnault, DSp, 2088.

have? In other words, how does a holy person concretely manifest holiness in his or her life? The *Apophthegmata*, or *Sayings* of the desert fathers and mothers, like Jesus, do not explicitly define holiness (*hagiôsunê*, *hosiotês*) although one could entitle that collection "The Book of Holiness": most—perhaps all—of its sayings are concerned with what constitutes holy behavior.[92] Holiness gradually came to be seen more and more in the *person* of the holy man (and, more rarely, it seems, holy woman);[93] eventually, holiness resided less in the holy person and more in his or her relics.[94] Even in the earliest period of monasticism, however, holiness was often viewed, especially by outsiders, as the special provenance of the monks; hence the onslaught of pilgrims into the desert in the fourth century, both spiritual tourists and authentic pilgrims.[95] Abba Daniel of Scetis, 6th-century priest and monastic superior (*hêgoumenos*) of Scetis, was both a holy man *and* a witness to holiness.[96] The collection of tales surrounding his name offers the modern reader an important view of one perception of holiness in late antique Egypt.[97]

---

[92] Douglas Burton-Christie has recognized this by subtitling his excellent study of the *Apophthegmata, The Word in the Desert*, "Scripture and the Quest for Holiness in Early Christian Monasticism." For a general overview, see Burton-Christie, "Quest for Holiness in [the] Fourth Century: Pagan and Christian Approaches," in *The Word in the Desert*, 48-62.

[93] See Peter Brown, "The Rise and Function of the Holy Man in Late Antiquity," *Journal of Roman Studies* 61 (1971) 80-101 (repr. in Brown, *Society and the Holy in Late Antiquity* [Berkeley: University of California Press, 1982], 103-52) and "The Rise and Function of the Holy Man in Late Antiquity: 1971-1997," *Journal of Early Christian Studies* 6.3 (1998): 353-76.

[94] See Evelyn White, 2:292: "In the earlier period of the history of Nitria and Scetis, pilgrims made their way into the desert to be edified by the discourse of the fathers, to beg for their prayers, and to receive their blessing. . . . In the seventh century a change seems to have come over both pilgrims and monks. The former seek out holy places believing that prayer there will, through the mediation of some departed saint, lead to a cure or to some other benefit; the latter are drawn more and more to realize the advantages presented to them by such an attitude, and come to look upon relics as an attraction bringing renown and wealth to their monastery. In proportion, then, as the sanctity of the living grew less remarkable, the veneration of the dead increased."

[95] See Georgia Frank, *The Memory of the Eyes: Pilgrims to Living Saints in Christian Late Antiquity* (Berkeley: University of California Press, 2000).

[96] Daniel's life may be dated from 485 to 570-80; for a discussion of Daniel's life and dates, see Part III of the Introduction to Tim Vivian, ed., *Witness to Holiness: Abba Daniel of Scetis* (Kalamazoo: Cistercian Publications, forthcoming).

[97] For translations of this material, see Vivian, ed., *Witness to Holiness*. The Greek text, to which reference is made in this article, was published by Léon Clugnet, "Vie et Récits de L'Abbé Daniel, de Scété," *Revue de l'Orient Chrétien* 5 (1900): 49-73, 254-

The understanding of holiness in this collection is neither all-encompassing nor definitive. But the dossier does offer a different and unusual slant on holiness, one that may cause us to adjust our perceptions of holiness in late antiquity.

Douglas Burton Christie, like most scholars and readers of early Christian monasticism, has linked "the monks' pursuit of holiness" with a "dramatic act of withdrawal," the "separation and removal from the mainstream of society."[98] Antoine Guillaumont has urged further that "this movement of withdrawal, of 'anachoresis,' marks the movement from pre-monastic asceticism to monasticism properly called."[99] There can be no doubt that these scholars are right— properly understood. Monastic separation does not necessarily have to be spatial, into Antony's literal desert,[100] but some sort of withdrawal or distancing is necessary in order to gain perspective on the world and its values.[101] After his baptism, Jesus withdrew into the wilderness and found the Devil (Mt 4:1-11). Antony, as is famously known and pictured, confronted hordes of demons in the desert. So did later monks. In commenting on this phenomenon, so curious, and even repellent, to moderns, Vincent Desprez has observed that

these famous acts of the demons [*diableries*] reveal fundamentally the hard and difficult aspects [*dura et aspera*] of the monastic experience: the monk who has renounced certain of life's amenities must fight against "thoughts," against the attraction that these objects continue to exercise over him. The complete solitude of the desert exacerbates that formidable confrontation between a person and himself.[102]

271, 370-91. Translations of the Greek, Latin, Coptic, Syriac, Ethiopic, Armenian, and Old Church Slavonic texts will appear in *Witness to Holiness*.

[98] Burton Christie, *The Word in the Desert*, 54.

[99] Antoine Guillaumont, "La séparation du monde dans l'orient chrétien: ses formes et ses motifs," in Guillaumont, *Études sur la spiritualité de l'orient chrétien* (Spiritualité Orientale 66; Bégrolles-en-Mauges: Abbaye de Bellefontaine, 1996), 105-12, at 105.

[100] See Goehring, 13-25.

[101] On this theme, see the powerful meditation of Belden C. Lane, *The Solace of Fierce Landscapes: Exploring Desert and Mountain Spirituality* (New York: Oxford University Press, 1998).

[102] Vincent Desprez, *Le monachisme primitif: Des origines jusqu'au concile d'Éphèse*. Spiritualité orienatle 72 (Begrolles-en-Mauges: Abbaye de Bellefontaine, 1998), 184.

Withdrawal, then, does not mean flight and evasion but making the hard and difficult journey closer to one's true self, which is where God is.[103] Once one reaches this harbor, to use a favorite metaphor of the early monks, one has a secure and stable place from which to onload supplies and foodstuffs in order to sally out in search of those shipwrecked in the world. Abba Daniel, although certainly practicing separation or withdrawal in the desert of Scetis, was also very much engaged in the world, especially with travel from the desert *back into* "the world." This, in fact, is where he is most often pictured and where we, the audience-in-the-world, most often meet him: by our side—or up ahead, calling and waving to us to come look. Thus withdrawal is certainly an important and vital part of early monastic spirituality but, as the Daniel dossier shows, it needs to be balanced with *reaching out*. Monasticism, then, is as much centripetal as it is centrifugal. The monk flees one center, "the world," in search of his (or her) true center, God; once there, he can leave his monastic center (or, more accurately, embody it, take it with him) and seek out the world in a gesture of healing and salvation.

This tidal action offers at least one explanation for the numerous monastic tales recognizing holiness in the world. Just as the monk knows (or should know; that's why the stories exist) that he will not reach perfection in this world, he also comes to understand that holiness and goodness do not reside solely in the desert. The world has multiple spiritual centers radiating out from the one God; *topos* (locale) is not *tropos* (way of life):[104] "It was revealed to Abba Antony," the classic exemplar of withdrawal, "that there was one who was his equal in the city. He was a doctor by profession and whatever he had beyond his needs he gave to the poor, and every day he sang the Sanctus with the angels."[105] In another saying, Antony, like Daniel, goes to Alexandria and there learns about the virtue of a layperson who surpasses him and learns the nature of that person's virtue: each day this person affirms that the entire city will enter

---

[103] For a deep recent meditation on this theme, see Laurence Freeman, *Jesus: The Teacher Within* (New York & London: Continuum, 2000).

[104] See the *Life of Saint George of Choziba* 33: "Child, do not think that it is the place [*topos*] that makes you a monk; it's the way you live [*tropos*]"; Tim Vivian, *Journeying into God: Seven Early Monastic Lives* (Minneapolis: Fortress, 1996), 94.

[105] *Alphabetical Apophthegmata* Antony the Great 24; Ward, 6.

heaven because of their good works while he will suffer punishment for his sins.[106]

One of the most striking examples of this genre of "the return to the world" involves Abba Macarius the Great. One time "when he was praying in his cell," "a voice came to him, saying, 'Macarius, you have not yet reached the level of two women who live in such-and-such a village,'" so Macarius decided to search out the women. When he found them he asked for their way of life and they told him that they had left their husbands and had lived together for fifteen years. "We drew up a covenant," they said, "between ourselves and God that to the day of our death our mouths would not speak a worldly utterance but that we would direct our thoughts to God and his saints at all times and would devote ourselves unceasingly to prayers and fastings and acts of charity." When Abba Macarius heard these things he said, "Truly, it is not the name of 'monk' or 'lay person' or 'virgin' or 'wife and husband' but an upright disposition that God seeks, and he gives his Holy Spirit to all of these people."[107]

An "upright disposition" here seems to be understood as "prayers and fastings and acts of charity." The two women have indeed withdrawn, in this case from their husbands, but it is not their withdrawal per se that matters; it is the fruits of their *anachorêsis*. Edified, Macarius then returns to his cell, "clapping his hands and saying, 'I have not been at peace with my brothers like these lay women have with one another.'" There are striking parallels between what Macarius says here and what Peter proclaims in Acts 10:34-35; these women are "gentiles" like Cornelius and Macarius is a "Jew" like Peter who learns that God's bounty is not exclusive: "Thus Peter began to speak to them: 'I truly understand that God shows no partiality, but in every nation anyone who fears him and does what is right is acceptable to him.'" We see here being expanded right before us the boundaries of what defined the holy man—or woman. Holiness, the monks saw, almost in spite of themselves, was not the

---

[106] Lucien Regnault, *Les sentences des pères du désert: série des anonymes* (Solesmes: Bellefonatine, 1985), N 490.

[107] Coptic "Sayings of Saint Macarius the Great" 33. The text may be found in E. Amélineau, *Histoire des monastères de la Basse Égypte* (Annales de Musée Guimet 25; Paris, 1894), 203-4, and a translation in Tim Vivian, "The Coptic Sayings of Saint Macarius of Egypt," *Cistercian Studies Quarterly* 35:4 (2000): 499-524, 520, repr. in Vivian, *Saint Macarius the Spiritbearer* (Crestwood, NY: St. Vladimir's, 2004). Although this saying (story, really) is not found in the Greek Alphabetical Collection, it is in the Greek Systematic Collection XX.21.

exclusive possession of men domiciled in the desert.[108] As Claudia Rapp has noted, "Hagiographical texts play a significant and very particular role in the process that joins the author and his audience in their participation in the sanctity of the holy man or woman." Rapp calls this process "spiritual communication."[109] In the Daniel dossier, this "communication" is of persons *other than* the eponymous holy man. If the audience is monastic, then they are learning an important lesson in humility and equality; "the fact that it is possible for laity, living amid the pressures of the world, to attain such virtue heightens the sense of obligation which rests upon monks to rise to the same level."[110] If the audience is lay, that is, non-monastic, then they are learning the equally important lesson that holiness resides in their midst and not exclusively among the monastically garbed and gifted out in the desert.

The greatest confirmation of these understandings comes in the early monastic stories where the monks learn (and they do have to learn this) that the path to heaven is not as narrow as they might have imagined; in fact, sometimes the path seems to be a broad thoroughfare, with the double gates of heaven thrown wide open:

As Abba Silvanus sat one time with the brothers, he had a mystical experience (*en ekstasei*) and fell flat on his face. After a long time he got up and wept. The brothers entreated him, "What's wrong, father?" but he remained silent and continued weeping. When they forced him to speak, he said, "I was carried off to judgement and I saw numbers of people dressed like us in

---

[108] This can be seen at the conclusion of the story of Thomaïs in the Daniel dossier: when Abba Daniel orders her to be buried at the monastery, "some of [the monks] began to grumble because he was ordering a woman's corpse to be buried with the fathers, and she a victim of murder." But the old man says to them, "This young woman is my amma, and yours. Indeed, she died to protect her chastity." Afterwards, the story reports, "no one opposed the old man." Jerome came to define the "true" monk not as the ascetic living in town or city but as the anchorite; see Goehring, 53-72.

[109] Claudia Rapp, "Storytelling as Spiritual Communication in Early Greek Hagiography: The Use of *Diegesis*," *Journal of Early Christian Studies* 6.3 (1998): 431-48, 432.

[110] Graham Gould, "Lay Christians, Bishops, and Clergy in the Apophthegmata Patrum," *Studia Patristica* 25, ed. Elizabeth A. Livingstone (Leuven: Peeters, 1993), 399.

monastic habits going away to punishment and I saw numbers of people who were not monks going away into the kingdom."[111]

In our own day Flannery O'Connor vividly used this image to bulldoze the narrowly self-constructed gates of heaven that some Christians, in imitation of gated communities so popular now in suburbia, build for themselves and against others. In her story "Revelation," the self-righteous Mrs. Turpin sees

> a vast swinging bridge extending upward from the earth through a field of living fire. Upon it a vast horde of souls were rumbling toward heaven. There were whole companies of white-trash, clean for the first time in their lives, and bands of black niggers in white robes, and batallions of freaks and lunatics shouting and clapping and leaping like frogs.[112]

In another early monastic story, an old man "who served God for many years" is told by an angel that he does not please God like a certain gardener. The old man finds the gardener, who shows him great hospitality; like Macarius above, the old man questions the gardener about his way of life. The gardener tells the old man that he eats late in the evening and gives everything beyond his needs to the poor; in the morning before he goes to work and in the evening before going to bed he says, "This city, from the least to the greatest, will enter the kingdom because of their righteousness, but I alone will inherit punishment on account of my sins." When he hears this, the old man responds (rather smugly, we may imagine) that these practices are good but they do not surpass all his efforts in the desert. While the two are getting ready to eat, the old man hears people out in the street singing songs. He asks the gardener if he's not bothered by this and the gardener says no. "Brother," the old man responds, "wanting as you do to live according to God, how do you remain in this place and not be troubled when you hear them singing these [scandalous] songs." The gardener replies, "I tell you, abba, I have never been troubled or scandalized." When the old man hears this, he

[111] *Systematic Apophthegmata* III.33 (= Alph. Silvanus 2); Guy, ed., *Les Apophtegmes des pères*, 166-69.

[112] Flannery O'Connor, *Collected Works* (New York: Library of America, 1988), 654. O'Connor was probably thinking of Mt. 21.31, "Assuredly I say to you that tax collectors and harlots enter the kingdom of God before you."

asks the gardener what he conceives in his heart when he hears such songs. The gardener replies, "That they are all going to the kingdom." When the monk hears this he marvels and says, "This is the practice which surpasses my labour of all these years."[113] Amma Syncletica seems to have had such a person as this gardener in mind when she said, "Many of those living in a monastic community act like those living in cities and are lost while many of those living in cities do the works of the desert and are saved. Indeed, it is possible to live with a multitude and still be solitary in spirit just as it is possible to live as a solitary while one's thoughts are with the crowd."[114]

If the stories in the Daniel dossier, like the sayings cited above, expand the definition of holiness, they also contract it—or, in contracting it, empty part of it, leaving room for even greater expansion. One of the pronounced traits of later monastic hagiography is the wonderworking of the saints, the miracles in the desert.[115] The earliest strata of the monastic tradition, however, the *Apophthegmata*, do not give much emphasis to miracles and wonderworking; holiness resides in other, quotidian, activities like prayer and basket-making and living in community. The most noticeable—even astounding—thing about a later figure like Abba Daniel, contrary to one's hagiographical expectations, is that he does not perform a single miracle. It is true that in the Coptic *Life*, in the story of the repentant thief, a blind woman is healed by water that she believes has been used to wash Daniel's feet. (Although in a striking parallel in one story in the Greek dossier, Daniel orders similar water to be thrown on a nun who appears to be drunk and it has no effect on her. Apparently Daniel thought that the efficaciousness of the water lay in waking her up, not healing her.) Both she and the thief attribute this wonder to Daniel, but the miracle appears to have taken place because of the blind woman's faith in God and Abba Daniel.[116] Often in ancient story-telling "the author steps out of the mimetic narrative

[113] Columba Stewart, *The World of the Desert Fathers* (Fairacres, Oxford: SLG Press, 1986), 12-13.

[114] *Alphabetical Apophthegmata* Syncletica 19; *Life of Syncletica* 97 (PG 28.1438A).

[115] See, for example, the *Historia Monachorum*; see Benedicta Ward's excursus in *The Lives of the Desert Fathers: The Historia Monachorum in Aegypto*, trans. Norman Russell (Kalamazoo: Cistercian, 1980), 39-45.

[116] Her exclamation "May God and your name have mercy on me!" is reminiscent of the response to the holy man Paphnutius; see Tim Vivian, trans., *Paphnutius: History of the Monks of Upper Egypt and The Life of Onnophrius* (Kalamazoo: Cistercian, rev. ed., 2000), 30-37.

to guarantee . . . that what will seem unbelievable to the reader actually took place."[117] There is no "stepping out" in the Daniel dossier because there are, really, no miracles, no steps to take. Daniel, therefore, by the standards both of hagiography and classical historiography, is an unusual holy man: he is not a thaumaturge.[118] His charism, at least as understood by his disciple, the narrator of the tales, lies in discerning holiness, bearing witness to it, and summoning others to bear witness *and* to benefit from it.

In the story of Mark the Fool, Daniel tells the people and clergy of Alexandria that Mark, the holy fool, is a chosen vessel and that there is no one in the city as righteous as he; Daniel's declaration prompts the pope to beg Mark to tell them who he is which in turn causes Mark to tell his story. After Mark's death, Daniel summons all the monks of Scetis to come receive the old man's blessing. In the story of the Holy Mendicant, Daniel in similar fashion sees that a blind beggar is in truth doing great things; he and his disciple follow the beggar home and become the recipients of his generosity and hospitality. In the story of the Woman Who Pretended to be Drunk, Daniel discerns that the drunken nun, like Mark, is really a holy fool, and so he devises a plan to discover her hidden sanctity. After her holiness is revealed to the nuns, which brings about their repentance for their ill-treatment of her, Daniel declares that it was "for this reason" that he came there, "for God loves such drunkards as these." The Syriac version of this story makes Daniel's point even more explicit: "You have seen this mad girl; in truth God loves mad people such as these, who are drunkenly mad with ardent love for him."

One scholar has commented that "the people always were eager to see sanctity in the eccentric."[119] But perhaps that is putting the emphasis in the wrong place. Yes, there are "eccentrics" aplenty in the Daniel dossier, but the emphasis is not on eccentricities of madness and feigned drunkenness but rather on holiness. In the dossier, madness sometimes points to holiness, but it is not the only

---

[117] John Marincola, *Authority and Tradition in Ancient Historiography* (Cambridge: Cambridge UP, 1997), 82. For a Christian example, see the Preface to the *Life of Antony*.

[118] By contrast, see the stories about Abba Aaron in Vivian, trans., *Paphnutius*, 114-41.

[119] Charles A. Frazee, "Late Roman and Byzantine Legislation on the Monastic Life from the Fourth to the Eighth Centuries," *Church History* 51.3 (September 1982): 263-279, at 265.

indicator; Andronicus, Athanasia, and Eulogius, in their acts of charity, are far from mad (except, of course, that "the world" may regard them as mad for giving away all their money). "Eccentricity," however, is a signal: the stories in the Daniel collection, like the Gospels (e.g., the Good Samaritan), do demonstrate that holiness may reside where we least suspect it. Daniel's role as monastic authority is to lend weight to this gospel witness. As priest and superior of Scetis, he has the power, apparently, to summon the monks of Scetis to come to Alexandria. This authority, according to the stories in the collection, was widely recognized: when Daniel goes to the Upper Thebaid, "the fathers for about seven miles went out to greet him . . . . some were spreading their clothing before him while others were laying down their cowls and tears could be seen pouring forth like gushing fountains. . . . The archimandrite came out and venerated him seven times." When he goes on to the women's monastery, the whole community comes running out "and they spread their veils from the gate out to where the old man was."

Although Daniel had great authority, as these stories indicate, the narrator takes pains, quietly to be sure, to show his readers that Daniel's power really lay elsewhere: in the stories of Anastasia and Eulogius, Daniel appears to be holy precisely because he has the humility and discernment to see holiness *in others*. He recognizes the saintliness of the "eunuch" Anastasia, finds a cell for her, protects her identity, and counsels her. When she is dying Daniel asks for her blessing and prayers for himself and his disciple. In the story of Eulogius, Daniel recognizes the grace-filled charism of Eulogius' hospitality and care for strangers.[120] Thus Daniel confirms the spiritual truth that monks had long known and that the *Apophthegmata* affirm: holy persons do not reside only in the desert; they live also, and perhaps with even more difficulty and sanctity, in the towns, villages, and cities of this fallen world: "The qualities for which these lay people are commended are the same qualities that the monks themselves wished to cultivate: not only charity, hospitality, and chastity, but humility, detachment, freedom from anger, and the possession of a 'good will' in whatever state of life, lay or secular, married or unmarried, someone lives."[121]

---

[120] Interestingly, in his zeal to intercede for Eulogius, he oversteps his bounds, gets himself into trouble, and is reproved for his hubris by an angelic being in a vision.

[121] Gould, "Lay Christians," 399.

As part of its expansive nature, the Daniel dossier presented the ancient monk with a number of different types of asceticism, not just withdrawal into the desert, which became the norm in the fourth century. Celibacy, testified to by the New Testament, was the first form of *anachorêsis* in the Church and "was already a manifestation of separation from the world."[122] Eulogius in his ministry is presumably celibate and Andronicus and Athanasia, though married, live celibately. Despite the fact that *anachorêsis* or separation later came to be identified almost solely with withdrawal into the desert, the Daniel dossier shows that separation from the world could continue to take diverse forms: in the "fool for Christ";[123] in *xeniteia*, or loss of one's homeland;[124] and in monastic transvestism,[125] all forms of withdrawal from the norms of society. The fool forsook his rational self; the expatriate pulled up deeply set roots; the monastic transvestite gave up sexual and social identity. These different *anchorites* (with the original sense of *anachorêsis*), with their different ascetic disciplines and renunciations of the world's priorities, illustrate monasticism's deep and abiding need to return to its roots and sources, thus reforming itself. Precisely because they stand *outside* the main monastic tradition (as later configured) while remaining part of the ascetic critique, the fool, expatriate, and transvestite confront and challenge the tradition, which is what they do in the Daniel dossier. Later figures like Saints Benedict, Francis, and Bernard are commonly seen as the great monastic reformers, but already in the fifth century Isaiah of Scetis, in his withdrawal from Egypt to Sinai, can be seen as representing the spirit of renewal, both individual and corporate, that monasticism needs:

> After many years spent in a monastery, the monk can feel
> resurfacing that which he had wanted to flee by leaving the

---

[122] Guillaumont, "La séparation," 105. Guillaumont's essays, cited here and below, have greatly influenced the discussion in this paragraph and the next.

[123] See Antoine Guillumont, "La folie simulée, une forme d'anachorèse," in *Études sur la spiritualité de l'orient chrétien*. Spiritualité Orientale 66 (Bégrolles-en-Mauges: Abbaye de Bellefontaine, 1996), 125-30.

[124] See Antoine Guillaumont, "Le depaysement comme form d'ascese, dans le monachisme ancien," in Guillaumont, *Aux origines du monachisme chrétien: Pour une phénoménologie du monachisme* (Spiritualité Orientale 30; Bégrolles-en-Mauges: Bellefontaine, 1979), 89-116.

[125] See "A Woman in the Desert: Syncletica of Palestine," in Tim Vivian, *Journeying into God*, 37-52.

world, that is, the weight of habits, comforts, the considerations of his circle of friends, and he then feels the need—in order to remain loyal to his ideal—for a new break, which he will realise through the anchoretic life, through *xeniteia*, and by leading a reclusive life.[126]

By the sixth century monasticism had become a generally accepted perversion; it was also ecclesiastically sanctioned and politically regulated, which meant that it had lost some of its countercultural nature and reason for being. Many of the figures in the Daniel dossier, by contrast, retain some of monasticism's—and Christianity's—original jaggedness: the holy mendicant, anticipating the evangelical fervor of Saint Francis, lives out true self-giving poverty; Andronicus and Athanasia abandon home, property, and country; Anastasia not only renounces great wealth but also gives up completely her social identity. The foolishness of someone like Mark or the drunken nun, whose madness, as Antoine Guillaumont has pointed out, is "essentially a form of separation from the world," might just knock the ascetic reader back against the original sharp corners of his or her monastic and gospel vocation.[127] At a time when monasticism had pretty much settled down into Basilian, Saban, Pachomian, or Antonian patterns, the main figures of the Daniel dossier are barbarians at the monastery gates—or *within* the gates. Daniel, as it were, instead of merely performing the duties of law-abiding abbot, goes outside the enclosure to welcome these atypical ascetics inside, knowing full well that their presence within will initially provoke consternation and resistance but that such friction will eventually wear at the accumulated rusts of lazy habits and comfortable traditions.

In post-modern terms, Daniel's greatest authority may be precisely that of witness and storyteller, communicator of holiness, for it is he who tells his disciple the stories of Anastasia and Eulogius. It is he who causes Mark to tell his story and it is he who discovers the blind man's story and that of the "drunken" female monastic. In a sense, this narrative strategy only confirms Daniel's humility: it points the reader's attention *away* from the holy man and *towards* the virtues and holiness of the saints whose stories he tells—that is,

---

[126] Guillaumont, "Le dépaysement," 100, speaking of Isaiah.
[127] Guillaumont, "La séparation," 107.

towards the reader himself. Thus Daniel becomes a narrator within the narrative, and his position as monastic superior and status as holy man lend weight and credence to the disciple's tales. Unlike most hagiographical narratives, in these stories Daniel disappears from the narrative. It's as though the narrator had Daniel saying, in the words of Saint Macarius the Great, "That is why I said that I have not yet become a monk, but I have seen monks."[128] Daniel, Macarius, and Isaiah, and the early desert ammas and abbas in general, thus point beyond themselves and by doing so "confront us with our own responsibilities, since they invite us urgently to cherish the monastic original for existential reasons, rather than study the past for its own sake, and to extend its meaning into our own lives."[129]

Bibliography

Amélineau, Emile. *Histoire des moines de la Basse-Égypte*. Annales de Musée Guimet 25; Paris, 1894.

Augoustinos, *ΤΟΥ ΟΣΙΟΥ ΠΑΤΡΟΣ ΗΜΩΝ ΑΒΒΑ ΗΣΑΙΟΥ ΛΟΓΟΙ ΚΘ*. Jersualem, 1911; 2nd ed., Volos: Schoinas, 1962.

Broc, Hervé de. *Abbé Isaïe, Recueil ascétique*. Begrolles-en-Mauge: Bellefontaine, 1970.

Brown, Peter. "The Rise and Function of the Holy Man in Late Antiquity." *Journal of Roman Studies* 61 (1971) 80-101. Repr. in Brown, *Society and the Holy in Late Antiquity*, 103-52. Berkeley: University of California Press, 1982.

___. "The Rise and Function of the Holy Man in Late Antiquity: 1971-1997." *Journal of Early Christian Studies* 6:3 (1998): 353-76.

Bunge, Gabriel. *Geistliche Vaterschaft: Christliche Gnosis bei Evagrios Pontikos*. Regensburg: Friedrich Pustet, 1988.

Burton-Christie, Douglas. *The Word in the Desert: Scripture and the Quest for Holiness in Early Christian Monasticism*. New York & Oxford: Oxford UP, 1993.

Cassian, John. *The Institutes*, trans. Boniface Ramsey. ACW 58; Mahwah, NJ: Paulist Press, 2000.

Chadwick, Owen. *John Cassian: A Study in Primitive Monasticism*. 2nd ed., Cambridge: Cambridge UP, 1968.

Chitty, Derwas. "Abba Isaiah." *Journal of Theological Studies*, N.S. 22:1 (April 1971): 47-72.

---

[128] *Alphabetical Apophthegmata* Macarius the Great 2; PG 65:261A.
[129] Ramfos, 62, speaking about Antony the Great.

___. *The Desert a City*. Crestwood, NY: St. Vladimir's, 1966.

Chryssavgis, John, and Pachomios (Robert) Penkett, trans. *Abba Isaiah: Ascetic Discourses*. Kalamazoo: Cistercian Publications, 2002.

Collins, Kenneth J. ed., *Exploring Christian Spirituality: An Ecumenical Reader*. Grand Rapids, MI: Baker Books, 2000.

Clugnet, Léon. "Vie et Récits de L'Abbé Daniel, de Scété." *Revue de l'Orient Chrétien* 5 (1900): 49-73, 254-271, 370-91.

Desprez, Vincent. *Le monachisme primitif: Des origines jusqu'au concile d'Éphèse*. Spiritualité orientale 72; Begrolles-en-Mauges: Abbaye de Bellefontaine, 1998.

Donahue, Cecil. "The ΑΓΑΠΗ of the Hermits of Scetis." *Studia Monastica* 1 (1959): 97-114.

Eliot, T.S. "Little Gidding," *The Four Quartets*, in T.S. Eliot, *The Complete Poems and   Plays 1909-1950*. New York: Harcourt, Brace, 1952.

Evagrius Ponticus. *The Praktikos and Chapters on Prayer*, trans. John Eudes Bamberger. Kalamazoo: Cistercian Publications, 1981.

Evelyn White, Hugh G., ed. Walter Hauser. *The Monasteries of the Wâdi 'N Natrûn*, vol. 2, *The History of the Monasteries of Nitria and of Scetis*. New York: Metropolitan Museum of Art, 1932; repr. Arno Press, 1973.

Frank, Georgia. *The Memory of the Eyes: Pilgrims to Living Saints in Christian Late Antiquity*. Berkeley: University of California Press, 2000.

Frank,   Karl   Suso.   *Angelikos   bios: begriffsanalytische   und begriffsgeschichtliche Untersuchung zum "engelgleichen Leben" im frühen Mönchtum*. Beiträge zur Geschichte des alten Mönchtums und des Benediktinerordens, 26; Münster, Westfalen: Aschendorff, 1964.

Frazee, Charles A. "Late Roman and Byzantine Legislation on the Monastic Life from the Fourth to the Eighth Centuries." *Church History* 51.3 (September 1982): 263-279.

Freeman, Laurence. *Jesus: The Teacher Within*. New York & London: Continuum, 2000.

Goehring, James E. *Ascetics, Society, and the Desert: Studies in Early Egyptian Monasticism*. Studies in Antiquity and Christianity; Harrisburg, PA: Trinity, 1999.

Gould, Graham. *The Desert Fathers on Monastic Community*. Oxford: Clarendon, 1993.

___. "Lay Christians, Bishops, and Clergy in the Apophthegmata Patrum," *Studia Patristica* 25, ed. Elizabeth A. Livingstone. Leuven: Peeters, 1993.

Guillaumont, Antoine. "Histoire des moines aux Kellia." *Orientalia Lovaniensia Periodica* 8 (1977): 187-203.

___. "La folie simulée, une forme d'anachorèse," in *Études sur la spiritualité   de   l'orient chrétien*, 125-30. Spiritualité Orientale 66; Bégrolles-en-Mauges: Abbaye de Bellefontaine, 1996.

___. "La séparation du monde dans l'orient chrétien: ses formes et ses motifs," in Guillaumont, *Études sur la spiritualité de l'orient chrétien*,

104   TIM VIVIAN

105-12. Spiritualité Orientale 66; Bégrolles-en-Mauges: Abbaye de
   Bellefontaine, 1996.

___. "Le depaysement comme form d'ascese, dans le monachisme ancien," in
   Guillaumont, *Aux origines du monachisme chrétien: Pour une
   phénoménologie du monachisme*, 89-116. Spiritualité Orientale 30;
   Bégrolles-en-Mauges: Bellefontaine, 1979.

Guy, Jean-Claude. "Educational Innovation in the Desert Fathers." *Eastern
   Churches Review* 6 (1974): 44-51.

___. *Les Apophtegmes des pères: Collection systématique. Chapitres I-IX.*
   Sources chrétiennes 387; Paris: Cerf, 1993.

Harmless, William, SJ. "Remembering Poemen Remembering: The Desert
   Fathers and the Spirituality of Memory." *Church History* 69.3
   (September 2000): 483-518.

Lamy, Agnes. "Monks and the Angelic Life." *Monastic Studies* 1 (1963): 39-
   57.

Lane, Belden C. *The Solace of Fierce Landscapes: Exploring Desert and
   Mountain Spirituality.* New York: Oxford UP, 1998.

Marincola, John. *Authority and Tradition in Ancient Historiography.*
   Cambridge: Cambridge UP, 1997.

O'Connor, Flannery. *Collected Works.* New York: Library of America, 1988.

Ramfos, Stelios. *Like a Pelican in the Wilderness: Reflections on the Sayings
   of the Desert Fathers*, trans. and abridged by Norman Russell.
   Brookline, MA: Holy Cross Orthodox Press, 2000.

Rapp, Claudia. "Storytelling as Spiritual Communication in Early Greek
   Hagiography: The Use of *Diegesis*." *Journal of Early Christian Studies*
   6.3 (1998): 431-48.

Regnault, Lucien. "Isaiah of Scetis, Saint," *Coptic Encyclopedia*, ed Aziz S.
   Atiya, 3.1305-6. New York: Doubleday, 1992.

___. "Isaïe de Scété ou de Gaza." *Dictionnaire de spiritualité, ascétique et
   mystique* (Paris, 1933-), 7.2, 2083-95.

___. *La vie quotidienne des pères du désert en Égypte au IVe siècle.* Paris:
   Hachette, 1990. Engl. trans. Étienne Poirier, Jr., *The Day-to-Day Life of
   the Desert Fathers in Fourth-Century Egypt.* Petersham, MA: St. Bede's
   Publications, 1999.

___. *Les sentences des pères du désert: série des anonymes.* Solesmes:
   Bellefonatine, 1985.

Sheldrake, Philip. "Human Identity and the Particularity of Place." *Spiritus*
   1.1 (Spring 2001): 43-64.

Rousseau, Philip. "The Desert Fathers, Antony and Pachomius," in Cheslyn
   Jones, et al., eds., *The Study of Spirituality*, 119-30. London: SPCK,
   1992.

Russell, Norman, trans. *The Lives of the Desert Fathers: The Historia
   Monachorum in Aegypto.* Kalamazoo: Cistercian, 1980.

Stewart, Columba. *Cassian the Monk.* New York and Oxford: Oxford UP,
   1998.

___. "Radical Honesty about the Self: the Practice of the Desert Fathers." *Sobornost* 12 (1990): 25-39.

___. "'We'? Reflections on Affinity and Dissonance in Reading Early Monastic Literature." *Spiritus* 1.1 (Spring 2001): 93-102.

___. *The World of the Desert Fathers*. Fairacres, Oxford: SLG Press, 1986.

Mark Sheridan. "The Spiritual and Intellectual World of Early Egyptian Monasticism," *Coptica* 1 (2002): 1-51.

Vivian, Tim. "The Coptic Sayings of Saint Macarius of Egypt." *Cistercian Studies Quarterly* 35.4 (2000): 499-523.

___. *Paphnutius: Histories of the Monks of Upper Egypt and the Life of Onnophrius*, rev. ed. Kalamazoo: Cistercian, 2000.

___. *Saint Macarius the Spiritbearer: Coptic Texts Relating to Saint Macarius the Great*. Crestwood, NY: St. Vladimir's Seminary Press, 2004.

___."The Coptic Sayings of Saint Macarius of Egypt." *Cistercian Studies Quarterly* 35.4 (2000): 499-524.

___."Words to Live By: 'A Conversation that the Elders Had with One Another Concerning Thoughts (ΠΕΡΙ ΛΟΓΙΣΜΩΝ).'" *St. Vladimir's Theological Quarterly* 39.2 (1995).

___. *Words to Live By: Journeys in Ancient and Modern Monasticism*. Kalamazoo: Cistercian, forthcoming.

___. and Apostolos N. Athanassakis, trans. *The Life of Antony*. Kalamazoo: Cistercian Publications, 2003.

___. "Spiritual Direction from the Early Monastic Mothers and Fathers on Observing a Holy Lent: Chapter Three of the Greek *Systematic Apophthegmata*, 'On Compunction.' *Sewanee Theological Review* 44.1 (Christmas 2000): 60-78.

___. and Birger A. Pearson. "Saint Paul of Tamma: *On the Monastic Cell (De Cella)*." *Hallel* 23.2 (1998): 86-107.

Ware, Kallistos. "Silence in Prayer: The Meaning of Hesychia," in Basil Pennington, ed., *One Yet Two: Monastic Practices East and West*, 22-47. Kalamazoo: Cistercian, 1976.

___. "The meaning of 'Pathos' in Abba Isaias and Theodoret of Cyrus." *Studia Patristica* 20 (1989): 315-22.

Consecration of the Myron
At Saint Macarius Monastery
(MS 106 Lit.)

Youhanna Nessim Youssef*

I have concentrated my investigation of the Myron in Wadi al-Natrun to the ceremony which took place in 1374 AD in the monastery of Saint Macarius under Pope Gabriel IV, of which I am preparing the edition of the whole text. The importance of this manuscript is not only because of the rarity of the published manuscripts[1] concerning the Myron[2] but also it reflects some local tradition from Upper-Egypt which I will highlight in this paper.

---

[*] It was a great pleasure to present this paper to the Symposium of Wadi Natrun; I would like first to thank H.H. Pope Shenoudah the third for his kind invitation and for allowing me to study the Manuscript 106 Liturgy from the patriarchal library in Cairo. I would like to thank those who helped me in this study especially Mr Nabih Kamel Daoud. I am grateful to the organisers of this Symposium Dr Fawzi Estefanous and Mr Hany Takla.

[1] A. Van Lantschoot, "Le manuscrit Vatican Copte 44 et le Livre du Chême ms Paris arabe 100," *Le Muséon* 45 (1932), 181-234; L. Villecourt, "Le livre du chrême (ms arabe 100)," *Le Muséon* 41 (1928), 49-80; O.H.E. Burmester; "A Folio of a XIV Century MS of the Rite of the Consecration the Chrism and the Kallielaion from the Monastery of Saint Macarius in Scetis," *SOCC* 9 (1964), 225-231; idem, "Three Folios From the Service for the Consecration of the Chrism and the Kallielaion," *SOCC* 10 (1965), 239-248; L. Störk, *Koptische Handschriften 2, die Handschriften der Staats- und Universitätsbibliothek Hamburg*, Teil 2, *Die Handschriften aus Dair Anba Maqar; Verzeichnis der Orientalischen Handschriften in Deutschland*, Band XXI.2 (Stuttgart, 1995), n° 146 p. 310-311; Shams al-Riasah Abūl Barakāt Ibn Kabar, مصباح الظلمة فى إيضاح الخدمة, [*The Lamp of darkness for the explanation of the Service*], Samir Khalil, ed. (Cairo 1971), p. 350-376; L. Depuydt, *Catalogue of Coptic Manuscripts in the Pierpont Morgan Library, Corpus of Illuminated Manuscripts* (Leuven 1993), p. 121-122 n°60.

[2] For specific studies on this subject cf. O.H.E. Burmester, "A Coptic tradition concerning the holy Myron (Chrism)," *Publications de l'Institut d'Etudes Orientales de la Bibliothèque Patriarcale d'Alexandrie* 3 (1954), 52-58; L. Villecourt, "Un manuscrit arabe sur le saint-chrême dans l'Eglise Copte," *Revue d'Histoire Ecclésiastique* 17 (1921), 501-514; 18 (1922), 5-19; O. Meinardus, "About the Coction and Consecration of the Holy Myron in the Coptic Church," *Coptic Church Review* 12 (1991), 78-86; idem, "The holy Myron in 1993," *Coptologia* 14 (1994), 65-72.

Introduction

Manuscript 106 Liturgy is thus described in the Catalogue of Simaïka:

(1) The history of the Preparation of the Myron (Chrism) together with the manner of preparing it in detail by Anba Ghabryal (Gabriel IV th) the 86th patriarch. Contains Greek and Coptic (Bohairic and Sa'idic) sections by Anba Athanasius of Qus. Notes at the beginning. (2) The Martyrdom of Yūhannā, a monk of the Monastery of Anba Pishoi (Bishui) and his interment in the church of Sitt Barbara on the 30th of Hathur, A.M. 1298 (A.D. 1581); (3) The Martyrdom of St. Salib, a native of Hur on the 3rd Kyahk, A.M. 1229 (A.D. 1512); Arabic 154 folios, 25 lines, 26x17cm. Dated on folio 56(v) 4 Tubeh, AM 1093 (A.D. 1377). For Anba Ghabryal (Gabriel IVth), the 86th Patriarch. Dedicated by Anba Yu'annis (John XIIIth), the 94th Patriarch (A.D. 1484-1525) to the Church al-Mu'allaqah in A.M. 1213 (A.D. 1496-1497).[3]

As we can see from this description our manuscript is in fact three manuscripts bounded together.

The Author and Compiler of this Rite

The author and compiler of this rite is Athanasius of Qūs,[4] who is known for his literary activities. He is the author of a Coptic *Scala* in Sahidic and a grammar book,[5] he is the author of a treaty (*arguzah*) extracted from the Apostolic Canons,[6] and another on Baptism and one hundred questions and answer on the same subject.[7] In 1371

---

[3] M. Simaika and Y. 'Abd al-Masih, *Catalogue of the Coptic and Arabic Manuscripts in the Coptic Museum, the Patriarchate, the Principal Churches of Cairo and Alexandria and the Monasteries of Egypt*, Vol.II, Fasc.I (Cairo 1942), p. 331 Serial No. 723, Call No. Lit. 106.

[4] G. Graf, *Geschichte der christlichen-arabischen Literatur.* Studi e Testi 133 (Cité del Vatican), p. 455.

[5] G Bauer, *Athanasius von Qus Qiladat at-tahrir fi 'ilm at-tafsir. Eine Koptische Grammatik in arabischer Sprache aus dem 13/14 Jahrhundert,* IU 17 (1972) p. 1-48; book review Adel Sidarus *BiOr* 34 (1977), 142-146.

[6] Simaika, *op. cit.*, p. 128 N°302 Call N°298 Theol; p. 341 N°747 Call N° 367 Lit.

[7] Simaika, *op. cit.*, p. 144 N° 340 Call N°300 Theol; p 242 N° 545 Call N° 303 Theol.

A.D., he took part in the enthronement of Timothy, consecrated bishop of Qasr Ibrim.[8] In 1374 A.D., he participated in the concoction of Myron. Bishop Athanasius was a bishop of a great center of Islam, but which kept an ancient tradition of Christianity.[9]

Although the conditions of life for the Copts during the Mamluk epoch were very hard, as we can see from the persecutions which happened only a few years before this rite (such as in 1354 A.D.),[10] we may notice that the Coptic community was active.[11]

It is noteworthy to mention that the list of bishops provided by this manuscript is not complete, hence bishop Mark of Qift, who attended the enthronement of Timothy, bishop of Qasr Ibrim, is absent, as well as Timothy himself.[12]

The Importance of this Manuscript for the Study of the Development of the Coptic Liturgy

About half a century ago, Father Muyser, while editing a Coptic Psali, stated that the Coptic liturgical texts[13] are not well known.[14] In this paper we will highlight the development of three hymns from the Ms 106 lit.

---

[8] M. Plumley, *The Scrolls of Bishop Timotheos. Two Documents from Medieval Nubia, Texts from Excavations, First Memoir* (London 1975), book review R.-G. Coquin, *BiOr* 34 (1977), 142-147.

[9] J.C. Garcin, *Un centre musulman de la Haute-Egypte médiévale Qus* (Le Caire 1974), p. 30-35 p. 96-97; 120-121 and p 250-252.

[10] U. Vermeulen, "The Rescript of al-Malik as-Salih Salih against Dimmis (755A.H./1354A.D)," *OLP* 9 (1978), 175-184.

[11] We can mention as example the production of manuscripts such as the twelve prophets and Daniel, cf. W.E. Crum, *Catalogue of the Coptic Manuscripts in the British Museum* (London 1905), p. 320-321 n°729.

[12] Plumley, *op.cit.*, p. 36.

[13] For these books see Hanna Malak, "Les Livres Liturgiques de l'Eglise Copte," *Mélanges Eugène Tisserant* III, Studi e Testi 233 (Vatican 1964), p. 1-35; U. Zanetti, "Bohairic Liturgical Manuscripts," *OCP* 60 (1995), 65-94. It is noteworthy that many of these liturgical hymns are not yet printed or published. See for example L. Störk, *Koptische Handschriften 2, die Handschriften der Staats- und Universitätsbibliothek Hamburg, Teil 2, Die Handschriften aus Dair Anba Maqar; Verzeichnis der Orientalischen Handschriften in Deutschland*, Band XXI.2 (Stuttgart, 1995), p. 402-405; H. G. Evelyn Whiten *The Monasteries of Wadi n'Natrun, Part I New Coptic Texts from the Monastery of Saint Macarius* (New York 1926), p. 135-141, p. 216-222.

[14] J. Muyser, "Un 'Psali' acrostiche Copte 'corum Patriarcha et Episcopi," *Le Muséon* 66 (1953), 31-40.

1- *"Bohairicization"*

R.F. Professor T. Lefort, while speaking about the Bohairic Literature, more than half century ago, used the term *"Bohairicization"* and *"Nitriacization"*[15] giving some examples from the life of Saint Pachom.[16]

This phenomenon of *Bohairicization* occurred also in Coptic liturgical books. Burmester provided some examples from the pericopae of the book of Proverbs in the Lectionary of the Holy Week.[17]

While studying the book of the glorification,[18] I was intrigued by an uncommon form of the verb "resemble." The edited text is thus:

ερε πτλιο ʼⲧⲉⲕⲕⲗ̅ⲏⲥⲓⲁ ⲧⲟⲛⲑⲉⲛ ⲟⲩⲥⲟⲃ̅ⲧ ⲉϥⲕⲏⲧ ⲕⲁⲗⲱⲥ[19]
The honour of the Church resembles a fortress well built.

Crum's dictionary does not give the form ⲧⲟⲛⲑⲉⲛ for the verb ⲑⲟⲛⲧⲉⲛ.[20] *Le Complément* of Professor Kasser did also the same.[21]

This hymn occurs in the Manuscript Vatican Copte 23[22] and the Manuscript Vatican Copte 39 both from the 14th century.[23] This book is identified as Psalmodia by Hebbelynck,[24] I would prefer to call it

---

[15] Meaning "Wadi Natrun," for at this time this site identified as Nitrie. Before the discovery of the Site of Kellia and Nitria cf. F. Daumas et A. Guillaumont, *Kellia I, Kôm 219, Fouilles exécutées en 1964 et 1965* (Le Caire 1969), p. 1-30. It would be better to speak now about the "Natrunization."

[16] T. Lefort, "La littérature Bohaïrique," *Le Muséon* 44 (1931), 115-135.

[17] O.H.E. Burmester, "The Bohairic Pericopae of Wisdom and Sirach," *Biblica* 15 (1934), 451-465.

[18] For this book see Youhanna Nessim Youssef, "Un témoin méconnu de la littérature copte," *BSAC* 32 (1993), 139-147; idem, "Une relecture des glorifications coptes," *BSAC* 34 (1995), 77-83.

[19] 'Attalla Arsinius al-Muharraqi, ⲡⲭⲱⲙ ⲛⲧⲉ ⲛⲓⲝⲓⲛϯⲱⲟⲩ ⲉⲑⲩ ⲛϯⲡⲁⲣⲑⲉⲛⲟⲥ ⲛⲓⲁⲅⲅⲉⲗⲟⲥ ⲛⲓⲁⲡⲟⲥⲧⲟⲗⲟⲥ ⲛⲓⲁ̅ ⲛⲉⲙ ⲛⲏⲉⲑⲩ [*The Book of the Holy Glorifications for the Virgin, the Angels, the Apostles and the Saints*] (Cairo 1972), p. 38.

[20] W.E. Crum, *A Coptic Dictionary* (Oxford 1939), p. 420a.

[21] R. Kasser, *Compléments au Dictionnaire Copte de Crum*, BEC 7 (Le Caire 1964), p. 66.

[22] For a detail description of this Manuscript cf. A. Hebbelynck et A. Van Lantschoot, *Bibliothecae Apostolicae Vaticanae codices manuscripti recensiti iussu Pii XI ...Codices Coptici Vaticani, Barberiniani, Borgiani, Rossiani, Tomus I* (Vatican 1937), p. 80-82; and especially p. 80-81.

[23] A. Hebbelynck, "Un fragment de Psalmodie du manuscrit Vatican Copte 23, en dialecte bohairique," *Le Muséon* 44 (1931), 153-168.

[24] A. Hebbelynck, *op.cit.*, p.153-168.

"the book of Glorification."

Vatican 23 fol. 13r reads this hymns thus
ερε πτλιο ñ†εκκ⳿ληcιλ *εηθηη* ογcoßτ εϥκητ κλⲗωc

Vatican 39 fol. 206r
ερε   πτλιο   ñτλιπλρθεηοc   *τεηθωητ* εογπγρгοc   εϥκητ
κλⲗωc

While preparing the edition of Manuscript 106 liturgy[25] of the Patriarchal Library in Cairo,[26] I was fortunate enough to find this text, in Sahidic dialect in fol. λ̄λ̄r. written thus:

ερε   πτλειο   ñ†εκκⲗηcιλ   o   ηθε   ηoγcωßτε   εϥκητ
κλⲗωc

It is easy now to follow the steps of the evolution of the *Bohairicization* of this hymn and this term thus:

1- †εκκⲗηcιλ *o ηθε* ηoγcωßτ   Cairo 106 Lit., 1374 AD
2- †εκκⲗηcιλ *εηθηη* oγcoßτ   Vat. Copt. 23, 14th c.
3- †εκκⲗηcιλ *τoηθεη* oγcoßτ   Eds. Domadius and Attala.
4- τλιπλρθεηoc *τεηθωητ* εoγπγргoc Vat. Copt. 39, 14th c.

The *Bohairicizer* did not use the Bohairic synonyms such as ερε   πτλιο   ñ†εκκⲗηcιλ   oι   ⲙϕρη†   ηoγcoßτ...for he preferred to keep the rhymes and rhythm, as it is a sung hymn. It is not easy to add more syllables, and at the same time respect tunes and the melodies.

This example illustrates the process of *Bohairicization*. It highlights once more the interest of liturgical studies for the development of the Coptic language. We hope that the editors of late Bohairic texts will have in mind the Sahidic Substratum.

---

[25] M. Simaika & Yassa 'Abd Al-Masih, *op.cit*, p. 331 MS 723, 106 Liturgie.
[26] For the other Sahidic texts of this manuscript, cf. Youhanna Nessim Youssef, "Les textes en dialecte sahidique: du MS 106 Lit. Bibliothèque Patriarcale-au Caire (La coction myron)," *BSAC* 37 (1998), 121-134, and especially p. 132.

2- The Celebration of the Prayer of the Lamp

The prayer of the Lamp[27] (or the anointment of the sick) is mentioned in the Ms 106 Lit. thus:

fol. 9v (96 restoration)

و لما كان ليلة الاحد المقدس الذى هو الاحد السادس من الصيام
المقدس وهو احد العماد المقدس ثالث عشرين شهر برمهات
سنة تاريخه حضر الاب السيد البطريرك الكنيسه بكنيسة
المعلقه . . . وسحر الاحد . الاحد (sic) المقدس المذكور حضر
الاب السيد البطريرك الكنيسه وعمل خدمه القنديل بالاساقفه
المذكورين

And when it was the eve of the holy Sunday, which is the sixth Sunday of the holy Lent, which is the Sunday of the holy Baptism, the 23rd of Baramhāt of this year, the lord, father, the patriarch attended the celebration in the church of Muʿallaqah... and in the dawn of the above mentioned holy Sunday, the lord, father, the patriarch came to the church and celebrated the Candle with the above mentioned bishops...

fol. 14v (101 restoration)

و في سحر الاحد جدا توجه ناظمها اتناسيوس القوصي الي
الكنيسه وعمل القنديل علي جارى عادته و بعد فراغ القنديل
حضر الاب السيد البطريرك وصحبته الاساقفه كلهم الي
الكنيسه صبيحه نهار احد الشعانين المقدس. و هو اخر شهر
برمهات. وقريت مزامير صلوه ...

And very early in the morning of Sunday, his compiler Athanasius of Qūs went to the church and celebrated the Candle, as it was his custom, and after the (prayer of the) Candle, the lord, father the patriarch came with the all the

---

[27] Alfonso ʿAbdallah, *L'Ordinamento Liturgico di Gabriele V) 88° Patriarca Copto*. Studio Orientalia Christiana Aegyptiaca (Cairo 1962), p. 149-151 (text), p. 345-347 (translation).

bishops to the church in the morning of the holy Palm Sunday which is the last day of the month of Baramhāt...

From these two quotations we find that there were two traditions:

a- The Lower Egyptian tradition celebrating this rite before the liturgy of the Sixth Sunday of Lent. It is amazing that Ibn Kabar, did not mention this rite while speaking about the sixth Sunday of Lent.[28]

b- The Upper Egyptian tradition celebrating this rite before the liturgy of Palm Sunday.[29]

It is known that during Lent, in the Coptic Church, there are special tunes and hymns[30] for Saturdays and Sundays, while there are other tunes for the rest of the week. Actually this rite is used in *Friday* called the end of Lent,[31] but using the tunes and the hymns of the *Sundays*. We may suspect that a compromise had taken place later between the two traditions but keeping some features of the Sundays.

3- *The Hymn of the Virtues According to Ms 106 lit.*

The Coptic hymn used for welcoming bishops and the patriarch,[32] is published in the Book of the Diaconal as follows:[33]

---

[28] L. Villecourt, "Les observances liturgiques et la discipline du jeûne dans l'Eglise Copte," *Le Muséon* 38 (1925), 268-269; A. Wadi, "Abū al-Barakāt Ibn Kabar, Miṣbāḥ al-Ẓulmah (cap.18: il digiuno e la settimana santa)," *SOC Collectanea* 34 (2001), 253-255.

[29] It goes without saying that the earliest lectionaries of the Holy Week except few manuscripts are all from the Lower Egyptian tradition and hence did not include this rite for the Holy Week, cf. O.H.E. Burmester, *Le Lectionnaire de la Semaine Sainte*, *PO* 24/2 N°117 (Brepols, Turnhout 1985), p. 174.

[30] 'Abd-Masih Salib, ⲡⲓⲭⲱⲙ ⲛⲧⲉ ⲡⲓⲉⲩⲭⲟⲗⲟⲅⲓⲟⲛ ⲉⲑⲟⲩⲁⲃ [*The Book of the Holy Euchologion*] (Cairo 1902), p. 216-217. For this edition cf. U. Zanetti, "Esquise d'une typologie des Euchologes Coptes," *Le Muséon* 100 (1987), 407-418.

[31] 'Attalla Arsinius al-Muharraqi, ⲡⲓⲭⲱⲙ ⲛⲧⲙⲉⲧⲣⲉϥϣⲉⲙϣⲓ ⲛⲧⲉ ⲡⲓⲇⲓⲁⲕⲱⲛ ⲛⲉⲙ ⲛⲓⲃⲱⲅⲉⲙ [*The Book of the Service of the Deacon and the Hymns*] (Cairo 1970), p. 10.

[32] There are several hymns for this occasion, cf. Muyser, *op. cit.*, 35-40; O.H.E. Burmester, "The liturgy *Coram Patriarcha aut Episcopo* in the Coptic Church," *Le Muséon* 49 (1936), 79-84.

ϯⲙⲏϯ ⲥⲛⲟⲩϯ ⲛⲁⲣⲉⲧⲏ ⲙ̄ⲡⲓⲡⲛⲁ̄	The twelve virtues of the Holy
ⲉⲩⲑ ⲉⲧⲥϧⲏⲟⲩⲧ	Spirit written in
ϧⲉⲛ ⲛⲓⲅⲣⲁⲫⲏ ⲉⲑⲩ̄ ⲉⲧⲉ ⲛⲁⲓ ⲛⲉ	the Holy Books,[34] whose
ⲛⲟⲩⲣⲁⲛ	names are...

The Response of the second group to be chanted twice

ⲉⲩⲉϣⲱⲡⲓ ⲉϫⲉⲛ ⲧⲁⲫⲉ ⲙ̄ⲡⲉⲛⲓⲱⲧ	Come upon the head of our
ⲉⲩⲑ ⲛⲁⲣⲭⲏⲉⲣⲉⲩⲥ ⲡⲁⲡⲁ ⲁⲃⲃⲁ	holy father, the high priest
(...)	Pope Abba (...)
ϯϩⲟⲩⲓϯ ⲧⲉ ϯⲁⲅⲁⲡⲏ	First is love
ϯⲙⲁϩⲃ̄ϯ ⲧⲉ ϯϩⲉⲗⲡⲓⲥ	Second is hope
ϯⲙⲁϩⲅ̄ϯ ⲧⲉ ϯⲡⲓⲥⲧⲓⲥ	Third is faith

Second group chants "Come upon ..."

ϯⲙⲁϩⲇ̄ ⲧⲉ ⲡⲓⲧⲟⲩⲃⲟ	Fourth is purity
ϯⲙⲁϩⲉ̄ ⲧⲉ ϯⲡⲁⲣⲑⲉⲛⲓⲁ	Fifth is chastity
ϯⲙⲁϩⲋ̄ ⲧⲉ ϯϩⲓⲣⲏⲛⲏ	Sixth is peace

Second group chants "Come upon ..."

ϯⲙⲁϩⲍ̄ ⲧⲉ ϯⲥⲟⲫⲓⲁ	Seventh is wisdom
ϯⲙⲁϩ ⲏ̄ ⲧⲉ ϯⲇⲓⲕⲉⲟⲥⲩⲛⲏ	Eighth is righteousness
ϯⲙⲁϩⲑ̄ϯ ⲧⲉ ϯⲙⲉⲧⲣⲉⲙⲣⲁⲩϣ	Ninth is gentleness

Second group chants "Come upon ..."

ϯⲙⲁϩⲓ̄ϯ ⲧⲉ ϯϩⲩⲡⲟⲙⲟⲛⲏ	Tenth is endurance
ϯⲙⲁϩⲓⲁ ⲧⲉ ϯⲙⲉⲧⲣⲉϥⲱⲟⲩⲛ̄ϩⲏⲧ	Eleventh is patience
ϯⲙⲁϩⲓⲃ̄ϯ ⲧⲉ ϯⲉⲅⲕⲣⲁⲧⲓⲁ	Twelfth is self-control

The Ordo of Patriarch Gabriel V (1409-1427 A.D.) gives another version of this hymn:[35]

ϯϩⲟⲩⲓϯ ⲧⲉ ϯⲁⲅⲁⲡⲓ(sic) :	First is love,
ϯⲙⲁϩⲃ̄ ⲛ̄ⲧⲉ ϯϩⲉⲗⲡⲓⲥ :	Second is hope,
ϯⲙⲁϩⲅ̄ ⲛ̄ⲧⲉ ϯⲡⲓⲥⲧⲓⲥ :	Third is faith.
ϯⲙⲁϩⲇ̄ ⲡⲉ ⲡⲓⲧⲟⲩⲃⲟ :	Fourth is purity,
ϯⲙⲁϩⲉ̄ ⲧⲉ ϯⲡⲁⲣⲑⲉⲛⲓⲁ :	Fifth is chastity,
ϯⲙⲁϩⲋ̄ ⲧⲉ ϯϩⲓⲣⲏⲛⲓ(sic) :	Sixth is peace.
ϯⲙⲁϩⲍ̄ ⲧⲉ ϯⲥⲟⲫⲓⲁ :	Seventh is wisdom,

---

[33] 'Attalla Arsinius al-Muharraqi, ⲡⲭⲱⲙ ⲛ̄ϯⲙⲉⲧⲣⲉϥϣⲉⲙϣⲓ ⲛ̄ⲧⲉ ⲡⲓⲇⲓⲁⲕⲱⲛ ⲛⲉⲙ ⲛⲓⲃⲱϩⲉⲙ [*The Book of the Ministry of the Deacon and the Hymns*] (Cairo 1973), p. 469-471.

[34] We prefer to translate the word ⲅⲣⲁⲫⲏ as "books" rather than "Scriptures," for it is clear from our demonstration that it is not referring to the Bible.

[35] Alfonso 'Abdallah, o.f.m., *op.cit.*, p. 209 (text), p. 390 (translation).

ϯⲙⲁϩ ⲏ̄ ⲧⲉ ϯⲇⲓⲕⲉⲟⲥⲩⲛⲏ :	Eighth is righteousness,
ϯⲙⲁϩⲑ̄ ⲇⲉ ϯⲁⲅⲛⲓⲁ:	Ninth is unsullied.
ϯⲙⲁϩⲓ̄ ⲇⲉ ϯⲉⲅⲕⲣⲁⲧⲓⲁ :	Tenth is self control,
ϯⲙⲁϩⲓⲁ̄ ⲇⲉ ϯⲙⲉⲧⲣⲉϥϣⲟⲩⲛϩⲏⲧ:	Eleventh patience,
ϯⲙⲁϩⲓⲃ̄ ⲁⲥⲕⲏⲥⲓⲥ:	Twelfth is ascesis.

In Manuscript 106 Lit, the hymn is written differently. The list of these virtues occurs in fol 37r (124 of the restoration)

ϯⲓⲃ̄ ⲛⲁⲣⲉⲧⲏ ⲛⲧⲉ ⲡⲓⲡⲛⲁ ⲉⲑⲟⲩⲁⲃ ⲉⲧⲥϧⲏⲟⲩⲧ ϧⲉⲛ ⲛⲓⲅⲣⲁⲫⲏ ⲉⲑⲃ̄. ⲉⲧⲉ ⲛⲁⲓ ⲛⲉ ⲛⲟⲩⲣⲁⲛ.	The twelve virtues of the Holy Spirit written in the Holy Books, whose names are
ⲉⲩⲉϣⲱⲡⲓ ⲉϫⲉⲛ ⲡⲉⲛⲓⲱⲧ ⲙⲡⲁⲧⲣⲓⲁⲣⲭⲏⲥ ⲁⲃⲃⲁ ⲅⲁⲃⲣⲏⲓⲗ .	Come upon the head of our father, the patriarch Abba Gabriel
ⲡⲓϩⲟⲩⲓⲧ ⲡⲉ ϯⲡⲓⲥⲧⲓⲥ: ϯⲙⲁϩⲃ̄ ⲡⲉ ϯⲙⲉⲑⲙⲏⲓ: ϯⲙⲁϩⲅ̄ ⲡⲉ ϯϩⲏⲣⲓⲛⲏ ⲉⲥⲉϣⲱⲡⲓ ⲉϫⲉⲛ ⲡⲉⲛⲉⲓⲱⲧ ⲙⲡⲁⲧⲣⲓⲁⲣⲭⲏⲥ ⲁⲃⲃⲁ ⲅⲁⲃⲣⲓⲏⲗ	First is faith, second is righteousness, third is peace Come upon the head of our father, the patriarch Abba Gabriel
ϯⲙⲁϩⲇ̄ ⲡⲉ ϯⲉⲅⲕⲣⲁⲧⲓⲁ: ϯⲙⲁϩ ⲉ̄ ⲡⲉ ϯⲡⲁⲣⲑⲉⲛⲓⲁ: ϯⲙⲁϩ ⲋ̄ ⲧⲉ ϯⲁⲅⲁⲡⲏ. ⲉⲩⲉϣⲱⲡⲓ ⲉϫⲉⲛ ⲡⲉⲛⲓⲱⲧ ⲙⲡⲁⲧⲣⲓⲁⲣⲭⲏⲥ ⲁⲃⲃⲁ ⲅⲁⲃⲣⲓⲏⲗ	fourth is self control, fifth is chastity, sixth is love Come upon the head of our father, the patriarch Abba Gabriel
ϯⲙⲁϩⲍ̄ ⲡⲉ ϯϩⲩⲡⲟⲙⲟⲛⲏ: ϯⲙⲁϩⲏ̄ ⲡⲉ ϯⲥⲟⲫⲓⲁ: ϯⲙⲁϩⲑ̄ϯ ϯⲙⲉⲧⲣⲉⲙⲣⲁⲩϣ ⲉⲩⲉϣⲱⲡⲓ ⲉϫⲉⲛ ⲡⲉⲛⲓⲱⲧ ⲙⲡⲁⲧⲣⲓⲁⲣⲭⲏⲥ ⲁⲃⲃⲁ ⲅⲁⲃⲣⲓⲏⲗ	Seventh is endurance, eighth is wisdom, ninth is gentleness Come upon the head of our father, the patriarch Abba Gabriel
ϯⲙⲁϩⲓ̄ ⲡⲉ ⲡⲓⲧⲟⲩⲃⲟ: ϯⲙⲁϩⲓⲁ̄ ϯⲙⲉⲧⲣⲉⲱⲟⲩⲛϩⲏⲧ: ϯⲙⲁϩⲓⲃ̄ ϯⲙⲉⲧⲁⲅⲁⲑⲟⲥ ⲉⲩⲉϣⲱⲡⲓ ⲉϫⲉⲛ ⲡⲉⲛⲓⲱⲧ ⲙⲡⲁⲧⲣⲓⲁⲣⲭⲏⲥ ⲁⲃⲃⲁ ⲅⲁⲃⲣⲏⲓⲗ	Tenth is purity, eleventh patience, twelfth is goodness. Come upon the head of our father, the patriarch Abba Gabriel

The Manuscript of the Enthronement of a new Bishop in the Coptic Patriarchal Library (Lit 91),[36] and dated 1052 AM (=1335 AD), mentions only ten virtues thus:

ϯ̄ ⲛⲁⲣⲉⲧⲏ ⲛ̄ⲧⲉ ⲡⲓⲡ̄ⲛ̄ⲁ̄ ⲉⲑⲟⲩⲁⲃ	The ten virtues of the Holy Spirit
ⲉⲧⲉ ⲛⲁⲓ ⲛⲉ	whose are
ϯⲡⲓⲥⲧⲓⲥ: ϯⲙⲉⲑⲙⲏⲓ: ϯϩⲓⲣⲏⲛⲏ	faith, righteousness, peace
ϯⲉⲅⲕⲣⲁⲧⲓⲁ: ϯⲡⲁⲣⲑⲉⲛⲓⲁ: ϯⲁⲅⲁⲡⲏ	self-control, chastity, love
ϯϩⲩⲡⲟⲙⲟⲛⲏ: ϯⲥⲟⲫⲓⲁ:	endurance, wisdom,
ϯⲙⲉⲧⲣⲉⲙⲣⲁⲩϣ: ⲡⲓⲧⲟⲩⲃⲟ:	gentleness, purity. [37]

Ibn Kabar (d. 1324 AD)[38] in his encyclopedia *The Lamp of Darkness of the Explanation of the (Liturgical) Service*,[39] includes this hymn in the rite of the enthronement of the bishop:

The number of virtues is only ten:

ϯⲡⲓⲥⲧⲟⲥ[(sic)]: ϯⲙⲉⲑⲙⲏⲓ: ϯϩⲓⲣⲏⲛ	faith, righteousness, peace
ϯⲉⲅⲕⲣⲁⲧⲓⲁ: ϯⲡⲁⲣⲑⲉⲛⲓⲁ: ϯⲁⲅⲁⲡⲓ[(sic)]	self-control, chastity, love
ϯⲥⲟⲩⲫⲓⲁ[(sic)]: ϯⲙⲉⲧⲣⲉⲙⲣⲁⲩϣ	wisdom, gentleness
ⲡⲓⲧⲟⲩⲃⲟ: ϯϩⲩⲡⲟⲙⲟⲛⲓ[(sic)]	purity, endurance

Comments

- It is important to note that our text shows clearly that these ⲁⲣⲉⲧⲏ[40] (Greek loan word)[41] are not mentioned in the Holy Books. The

---

[36] M. Simaika and Yassa ʿAbd al-Masih, *op.cit.*, p. 325.

[37] Ibid., pl. XLVII.

[38] For this author, cf. R-G Coquin "Ibn Kabar (Shams ar-Riʾasa Abū ʾl-Barakat)," *Ca* 6 (1966), col.1349-1351; Samir Khalil, "Un manuscrit arabe d'Alep reconnu, le Sbath 1125," *Muséon* 91 (1978), 179-188; "Ibn Kabar," *CoptEncyc* 4: 1267-1268.

[39] Samir Khalil, p. 417. For this edition, cf. Ugo Zanetti, "Abū-l-Barakat et les lectionnaires de Haute-Egypte," *Actes du IVᵉ Congrès Copte*, édités par M. Rassart-Debergh et J. Ries, PIOL 41 (Louvain 1992), p. 450-462.

[40] Cf. J.-M. Aubert, "Vertus," *Dictionnaire de Spiritualité* (Paris Beauchesne 1994), Vol. 30, Col. 485-497.

[41] For these words cf. W.A. Girgis, "Greek Loan words in Coptic," *BSAC* 17 (1963-1964), 63-73; 18 (1965-1966), 71-96; 19 (1967-1968), 57-87; 20 (1969-1970), 27-32; 21 (1971-1971), 33-53; 23 (1976-1978), 199-222; 30 (1991), 77-92.

New Testament while using this word in Philippians 4:8, I Peter 2:9, II Peter 1:3, 5. does not include this enumeration of virtues.

- Moreover, we did not have such enumeration in the Greek pseudepigraphic books of the Old Testament,[42] or in the Gnostic library of Nag-Hammadi.[43]
- We may notice the influence of monastic teaching. In fact, each Desert Father has his own list of virtues.[44]
- The twelve virtues seems to be a monastic tradition from Upper Egypt. The niche of Bawit (Chapel 6) enumerates the virtues thus:

ⲦⲘⲚⲦⲢⲱϩⲏⲦ – ⲦⲢⲏⲚⲏ – ⲦⲘⲚⲦⲢⲘⲢⲀⲱ – ⲦⲀⲄⲀⲠⲎ – ⲐⲈⲖⲠⲓⲥ – ⲦⲠⲓⲥⲦⲓⲥ – Lacuna – ⲦⲘⲚⲦⲬ̅Ⲣ̅Ⲥ̅ – ⲦⲠⲀⲣⲐⲈⲚⲓⲀ – ⲐⲨⲠⲟⲘⲟⲚⲎ – ⲦⲘⲚⲦⲢⲘⲚϩⲏⲦ – ⲐⲀⲄⲚⲓⲀ.[45]

- Chapel XLII contains another inscription mentioning the twelve virtues of the Holy Spirit "ⲦⲘⲚⲦⲤⲚⲟ]ⲞⲨⲤ Ⲛ[ⲀⲠⲈⲦⲎ Ⲙ̅Ⲡ̅Ⲡ̅Ⲛ̅]Ⲁ̅ ⲈⲦⲞⲨⲀⲀⲂ."[46]
- The book of ordinations mentioned that the bishop says inaudibly:
...ⲀⲚⲟⲔ ϧⲀ ⲠⲓⲬⲱⲂ ⲚⲣⲉϥⲉⲣⲚⲟⲂⲓ (ⲚⲘ) Ⲭⲱⲱ ⲈϩⲢⲎⲓ ⲈⲬⲱⲓ Ⲛ̅Ⲧ̅ⲓ̅Ⲃ̅ ⲚⲀⲢⲈⲦⲎ ⲚⲦⲈ ⲦⲈⲔⲘⲈⲦⲬ̅Ⲥ̅... Me, the poor sinner (so and so), pour forth on me the *twelve virtues* of Your Goodness.[47]

---

[42] A.-M. Denis et Y. Yanssens, *Concordance Grecque des Pseudépigraphies d'Ancien Testament* (Louvain-la-Neuve: Institut Orientaliste, 1987), p. 180-181.

[43] Folker Siegert, *Nag-Hammadi-Register*. Wissenschaftliche Untersuch-ungen zum Neuen Testament 26 (Tübingen 1982), p. 219.

[44] For some examples see D. Burton-Christie, *The Word in the Desert- Scripture and the Quest for Holiness in Early Christian Monasticism* (Oxford: Oxford University Press, 1993), p. 217. Most of the Monastic writing have another arrangement of Virtues and vices cf. J.-C. Guy, *Recherches sur la tradition Grecque des Apophthegmata Patrum*. Subsidia Hagiographica 36 (Bruxelles: Société des Bollandistes, 1984), p. 120-188. Palladius, *The Lausiac History,* edited by Robert Meyer. Ancient Christian Writers (London: Newman Press, 1965), p. 263. John Climacus, *The Ladder of Divine Ascent*. Edited by Com Luibheid, Norman Russel, Kallistos Ware. The Classics of Western Spirituality (New York: Paulist press, 1982), p. 222, 232, 237-238, 266.

[45] J. Maspero, *Fouilles exécutées à Baouit, MIFAO* 35 (Le Caire 1931), p. 146. For this niche cf. C. Ihm, *Die Programme der christlichen Apsismalerei vom vierten Jahrhundret bis zur Mitte des achten Jahrhunderts* (Wiesbaden 1960), p. 200-202; G. Deneuve, *L'Arte Copta*. Forma e colore 57 (Florence 1970), p. 19-22.

[46] J. Clédat, *Le monastère et la nécrople de Baouit, MIFAO* 111 (Le Caire 1999), p.41. Cf. also R.-G. Coquin, "Les vertus (APETAI) de l'Esprit en Egypte," *Mélanges H.-Ch. Puech* (Paris 1974), p. 447-457.

[47] Athanasius, ⲠⲓⲬⲱⲘ ⲚⲦⲈ ⲦⲀⲔⲟⲖⲞⲨⲐⲓⲀ ⲚⲦⲈ ⲠⲓⲬⲓⲚϥⲱⲱ ⲚⲚⲓⲦⲀϩⲓⲤ Ⲛ†ⲘⲈⲦⲞⲨⲎⲂ ⲈⲂⲟⲖϧⲉⲚ ⲞⲨⲀⲚⲀⲄⲚⲱⲤⲦⲎⲤ ⲱⲀ ⲠⲓϩⲎⲄⲞⲨⲘⲈⲚⲟⲤ ⲚⲈⲘ ⲈⲠⲬⲓⲚⲉⲢⲀⲄⲓⲀⲌⲓⲚ ⲚⲚⲓⲤⲔⲈⲨⲟⲤ ⲦⲎⲢⲞⲨ ⲚⲦⲈ ⲠⲓⲘⲀⲚⲉⲢⲱⲟⲩⲱⲱⲓ [*The Book of*

The table given in Appendix II summarises the development of this hymn through the five versions. The next table shows the frequency and the order of each virtue; the Arabic numeral refers to the order of each virtue in the text.

1	ϯⲁⲅⲁⲡⲏ/ love	I,1; II,1, III,6; IV,6; V,6 B4
2	ϯⲁⲅⲛⲓⲁ/ unsullied	II,9; [12
3	ϯⲁⲥⲕⲏⲥⲓⲥ/ ascesis	II,12;
4	ϯⲇⲓⲕⲉⲟⲥⲩⲛⲏ/ righteousness	I,8; II,8;
5	ϯⲉⲅⲕⲣⲁⲧⲓⲁ/ self-control	I,12; II,10; III,4; IV,4; V,4
6	ϯϩⲉⲗⲡⲓⲥ/ hope	I,2; II,2, [5
7	ϯϩⲓⲣⲏⲛⲏ/ peace	I,6; II,6; III,3; IV,3; V,3, B2
8	ϯⲙⲉⲑⲙⲏⲓ/ righteousness	III,2; IV,2, V,2
9	ϯⲙⲉⲧⲁⲅⲁⲑⲟⲥ/ goodness	III,12;
10	ϯⲙⲉⲧⲣⲉⲙⲣⲁⲩϣ/ gentleness	I,9; III,9; IV,9, V,8, [3
11	ϯⲙⲉⲧⲣⲉϥⲱⲟⲩⲛϩⲏⲧ/patience	I,11; II,11; III,11; [11
12	ϯⲡⲁⲣⲑⲉⲛⲓⲁ/ chastity	I,5; II,5; III,5; IV,5; V,5, B10
13	ϯⲡⲓⲥⲧⲓⲥ/ faith	I,3; II,3; III,1; IV,1; V,1, B6
14	ⲡⲓⲧⲟⲩⲃⲟ/ purity	I,4; II,4; III, 10; IV,10; V,9
15	ϯⲥⲟⲫⲓⲁ/ wisdom	I,7; II,7; III,8; IV,8; V,7
16	ϯϩⲩⲡⲟⲙⲟⲛⲏ/ endurance	I,10; III,7; IV, 7; V,10, [11
17	ϯⲙⲛⲧⲣⲙⲣⲁⲩϩⲏⲧ	[1
18	ϯⲙⲛⲧⲭ̅ⲣ̅ⲥ̅	[9

Diaconal = I   Myron = III   Ibn Kabar = V
Gabriel V = II   Ms 91 = IV   [awit =[

The total number of the virtues in all editions are eighteen.

We may conclude that the number and the names of the virtues had evoluted. This hymn has a monastic origin, hence the word Holy [ooks refers to some monastic rules. The study of this hymn will

---

Rite of Ordination of the Ranks of Priesthood from the Reader to the Hegumenos and the Consecration of All the Vessels of the Altar], 2nd ed. (Cairo 1992), p. 6. It is amazing that this prayer is not included in the Ms 253 Liturgy in the collection of the Coptic Museum in Cairo dated to 1364 AD and edited by O.H.E. [urmester, *The Ordination Rites of the Coptic Church: Coptic text, translation and annotation.* Textes et Documents (Cairo 1985).

contribute to our understanding of early monasticism and the Coptic liturgy.[48]

These three examples highlight the importance of the study of the manuscript of the Concoction of the Myron 106 Lit. The publication of this manuscript which we are preparing, will contribute to the study of the development of the Coptic liturgy.

In addition, this manuscript is important for the study of the development of monasticism in Wadi n'Natrun by the end of the 14th century. It will contribute positively to the study of the architectural development of the monastery of Saint Macarius. The Sahidic and Greek texts of this manuscript are very important for the language and the liturgy. This manuscript contains a detailed description of the journey from Old Cairo to the Monastery of Saint Macarius, which will be very benificial for the study of the geography of Egypt at this time.

---

[48] It is not known when or why these virtues shift from monastic use to a prayer for the bishop.

Appendix I

Other example of Bohairicization from Coptic liturgical books

The Hymn of the Ascension

Manuscript 23 Vatican Copte mentions Ps. 17:9-10 in fol. 12r:

ⲁϥⲣⲉⲕ   ⲧϥⲉ   ⲁϥⲓ   ⲉⲡⲉⲥⲏⲧ   ⲉⲣⲉ   ⲟⲩⲭⲟⲥⲉⲙ   ϧⲁ
ⲛⲉϥⲟⲩ[ⲟⲩⲉ]ⲣⲉⲧⲏ   ⲁϥⲁⲗⲉ   ϩⲉⲣⲏⲓ   ⲉⲭⲉⲛ   ⲛⲉⲛⲭⲉⲣⲟⲩⲃⲓⲙ
ⲁϥϩⲱⲗ   ⲁϥϩⲱⲗ   ⲉⲭⲉⲛ   ⲛⲓⲧⲉⲛϩ   ⲛⲧⲉ   ⲛⲓⲑⲏⲟⲩ.[49]

While the actual edition of this hymn replaced this quotation by the same Psalm taken from the bohairic version of the Psalms,

ⲁϥⲣⲉⲕ   ⲧϥⲉ   ⲁϥⲓ   ⲉⲡⲉⲥⲏⲧ   ⲟⲩⲟϩ   ⲟⲩⲅⲛⲟⲫⲟⲥ   ⲁϥϣⲱⲡⲓ
ϧⲁ   ⲛⲉϥϭⲁⲗⲁⲩⲭ   ⲁϥⲟⲗϥ   ⲉⲭⲉⲛ   ⲛⲓⲭⲉⲣⲟⲩⲃⲓⲙ   ⲁϥϩⲁⲗⲁⲓ
ⲁϥϩⲁⲗⲁⲓ   ⲉⲭⲉⲛ   ⲛⲓⲧⲉⲛϩ   ⲛⲧⲉ   ⲛⲓⲑⲏⲟⲩ.[50]

it is clear that Vat Copt 23 is a *Bohairicization* of the Sahidic version of the same Psalm.

ⲁϥⲣⲉⲕⲧ   ⲧⲡⲉ   ⲁϥⲉⲓ   ⲉⲡⲉⲥⲏⲧ   ⲉⲣⲉ   ⲟⲩϭⲟⲥⲙ   ϩⲁ
ⲛⲉϥⲟⲩⲉⲣⲏⲧⲉ   ⲁϥⲁⲗⲉ   ⲉϩⲣⲁⲓ   ⲉⲭⲛ   ⲛⲉⲭⲉⲣⲟⲩⲃⲓⲙ   ⲁϥϩⲱⲗ
ⲁϥϩⲱⲗ   ⲉⲭⲛ   ⲛⲧⲛϩ   ⲛⲛⲧⲏⲩ[51]

Mgr Samuel, while editing the book of *Tartīb al-bay'ah* [*The Ordre of the Church*], referring to five manuscripts, mentioned this:

---

[49] A. Hebbelynck, "Un fragment de Psalmodie du manuscrit Vatican Copte 23, en Dialecte Bohairique," *Le Muséon* 44 (1931), 157.

[50] 'Attala Arsinius al-Muharraqi, ⲡⲭⲱⲙ ⲛⲧⲙⲉⲧⲣⲉϥϣⲉⲙϣⲓ ⲛⲧⲉ ⲡⲓⲇⲓⲁⲕⲱⲛ ⲛⲉⲙ ⲛⲓⲃⲱϩⲉⲙ [*The Book of the Ministry of the Deacon and the Hymns*] (Cairo 1973), p. 390. For the Psalms cf. C. Labib, ⲡⲭⲱⲙ ⲛⲧⲉ ⲛⲓⲯⲁⲗⲙⲟⲥ ⲛⲧⲉ ⲇⲁⲩⲓⲇ ⲡⲓⲡⲣⲟⲫⲏⲧⲏⲥ ⲟⲩⲟϩ ⲡⲓⲟⲩⲣⲟ ⲛⲉⲙ ⲛⲓϩⲱⲇⲏ [*The Book of the Psalms of the Prophet and King David and the Odes*] (Cairo 1897), p. 29-30.

[51] E.A. Wallis Budge, *The Earliest Known Coptic Psalter* (London 1898), p. 16. See also W. Worrell, T*he Coptic Manuscripts in The Freer Collection* (New York 1923); A Rahlfs, *Die Berliner Handschrift des sahidischen Psalters, Abhandlungen der Akademie der Wissenschaften in Göttingen,* (Göttingen 1970).

ⲁϥⲣⲉⲕⲧϥⲉ ⲁϥⲓ ⲉⲡⲉⲥⲏⲧ   ان كانوا يحفظوا لحن الصعود

And if they known the hymn of the Ascension.[52]

This remark shows clearly that this hymn was not known at the time of copying this manuscript, which is conserved in the collection of the Patriarchale Library (Lit. 73). It is dated in 1444 A.D.[53] This means that the *Bohairicization* took place between the XIV and the XV centuries.

---

[52] Mgr Samuel,   ترتيب البيعة عن مخطوطات البطريركية بمصر
والأسكندرية ومخطوطات الأديرة والكنائس, Vol. 3, 2 ed. (Cairo 2000), p. 87.

[53] M. Simaika and Y. ʿAbd al-Masih, *Catalogue of the Coptic and Arabic Manuscripts in the Coptic Museum, the Patriarchate, the Principal Churches of Cairo and Alexandria and the Monasteries of Egypt*, Vol.II, Fasc.I (Cairo 1942), p. 339 N°742 (not in the catalogue of Graf).

Appendix II

	Diaconal	Gabriel V (1409-27)	Myron, 1374	Ms 91 Lit., 1335	Ibn Kabar, 1324
First	†ⲁⲅⲁⲡⲏ/love	†ⲁⲅⲁⲡⲓ/love	†ⲡⲓⲥⲧⲓⲥ/faith	†ⲡⲓⲥⲧⲓⲥ/faith	†ⲡⲓⲥⲧⲟⲥ/faith
Second	†ϩⲉⲗⲡⲓⲥ hope	†ϩⲉⲗⲡⲓⲥ hope	†ⲙⲉⲑⲙⲏⲓ righteousness	†ⲙⲉⲑⲙⲏⲓ righteousness	†ⲙⲉⲑⲙⲏⲓ righteousness
Third	†ⲡⲓⲥⲧⲓⲥ/faith	†ⲡⲓⲥⲧⲓⲥ/faith	†ϩⲓⲣⲏⲛⲏ/peace	†ϩⲓⲣⲏⲛⲏ/peace	†ϩⲓⲣⲏⲛⲏ/peace
Fourth	ⲡⲓⲧⲟⲩⲃⲟ purity	ⲡⲓⲧⲟⲩⲃⲟ purity	†ⲉⲅⲕⲣⲁⲧⲓⲁ self-control	†ⲉⲅⲕⲣⲁⲧⲓⲁ self-control	†ⲉⲅⲕⲣⲁⲧⲓⲁ self-control
Fifth	†ⲡⲁⲣⲑⲉⲛⲓⲁ/chastity	†ⲡⲁⲣⲑⲉⲛⲓⲁ/chastity	†ⲡⲁⲣⲑⲉⲛⲓⲁ/chastity	†ⲡⲁⲣⲑⲉⲛⲓⲁ/chastity	†ⲡⲁⲣⲑⲉⲛⲓⲁ/chastity
Sixth	†ϩⲓⲣⲏⲛⲏ/peace	†ϩⲓⲣⲏⲛⲏ/peace	†ⲁⲅⲁⲡⲏ/love	†ⲁⲅⲁⲡⲏ/love	†ⲁⲅⲁⲡⲓ/love
Seventh	†ⲥⲟⲫⲓⲁ wisdom	†ⲥⲟⲫⲓⲁ wisdom	†ⲥⲟⲫⲓⲁ wisdom	†ϩⲩⲡⲟⲙⲟⲛⲏ endurance	†ⲥⲟⲩⲫⲓⲁ wisdom
Eighth	†ⲇⲓⲕⲉⲟⲥⲩⲛⲏ righteousness	†ⲇⲓⲕⲉⲟⲥⲩⲛⲏ righteousness	†ⲥⲟⲫⲓⲁ wisdom	†ⲥⲟⲫⲓⲁ wisdom	†ⲙⲉⲧⲣⲉⲙⲣⲁⲩϣ gentleness
Ninth	†ⲙⲉⲧⲣⲉⲙⲣⲁⲩϣ gentleness	†ⲁⲩⲛⲁ unsullied	†ⲙⲉⲧⲣⲉⲙⲣⲁⲩϣ gentleness	†ⲙⲉⲧⲣⲉⲙⲣⲁⲩϣ gentleness	ⲡⲓⲧⲟⲩⲃⲟ purity
Tenth	†ϩⲩⲡⲟⲙⲟⲛⲏ endurance	†ⲉⲅⲕⲣⲁⲧⲓⲁ self-control	ⲡⲓⲧⲟⲩⲃⲟ purity	ⲡⲓⲧⲟⲩⲃⲟ purity	†ϩⲩⲡⲟⲙⲟⲛⲓ endurance
Eleventh	†ⲙⲉⲧⲣⲉϥϣⲟⲩ ⲛϩⲏⲧ/ patience	†ⲙⲉⲧⲣⲉϥϣⲟⲩ ⲛϩⲏⲧ/ patience	†ⲙⲉⲧⲣⲉϥϣⲟⲩ ⲛϩⲏⲧ/ patience	///////////	///////////
Twelfth	†ⲉⲅⲕⲣⲁⲧⲓⲁ self-control	†ⲁⲥⲕⲏⲥⲓⲥ ascesis	†ⲙⲉⲧⲁⲅⲁⲑⲟⲥ goodness	///////////	///////////

Liturgy at Wadi al-Natrun

Ugo Zanetti[*]

The title which the organisers of our symposium have proposed for my paper, "Liturgy and Wadi al-Natrun," immediately evokes a reference to the history of the liturgy of the Coptic Church.

It is well known that the monasteries of Wadi al-Natrun played an important role in unifying the Coptic liturgy and endowing it with the ritual which is in use today. The wide diversity which subsisted in ancient times was slowly reduced either by particular events, such as the gradual disappearance of monasticism in Upper Egypt, or through the decisions of patriarchs who encouraged unification (in Egypt just as in other parts of ancient Christendom). Unfortunately, the oldest documentary witnesses to that liturgy go back no further than the 12th or 13th century, a period at which the liturgy had already taken on its present form;[1] it would therefore be very difficult for us to establish its history.[2] There is also a great temptation to suppose that the services celebrated today have scarcely evolved at all. But this is only a temptation, which can be overcome to some extent, even without liturgical manuscripts older than the year 1000, through the study of texts and comparative liturgy.[3]

---

[*] The present paper owes much to the remarks of Heinzgerd Brakmann who not only made available to us the text and bibliography of the *Neue Funde 1996-2000* (currently being printed), but also drew our attention to a number of complementary data, primarily of a bibliographical nature. I have made use of this material with his permission. The most important elements are mentioned explicitly.

[1] "Die Liturgie, die uns aus den Quellen entgegentritt, hat ihre Jugend erkennbar bereits hinter sich, wirkt weithin verfestigt, in manchem schon dekadent" Brakmann, "Neue Funde 1992-1996," p. 457.

[2] "L'Ordo missae copte... est le résultat d'un développement historique dont la phase décisive, la fusion de l'héritage alexandrino-égyptien avec un cérémonial syrien et divers textes importés (dont l'anaphore dite alexandrine de saint Basile), nous échappe par manque de documents coptes contemporains" H. Brakmann, *Le déroulement de la messe copte*. Structure et histoire, in A.M. Triacca et A. Pistoia (ed.), *L'eucharistie: célébrations rites, piétés*. Conférences Saint-Serge. XLIe semaine d'études liturgiques, Paris, 28 Juin – 1 Juillet 1994 (= *Bibliotheca "Ephemerides Liturgicae."* Subsidia, 79), Rome, 1995, p. 107-132 (see p. 107).

[3] This has been the case for the liturgy of Scetis by H. Quecke, *Gebet und Gottesdienst der Mönche nach den Texten*, in *Le site monastique copte des Kellia*.

Still another path can be explored: although the extant liturgical manuscripts are of recent date, they can offer us some data (sadly, at times only fragmentary) concerning the services which were in use during the Middle Ages and have since disappeared, or on the ways in which these were celebrated. The monasteries, as well as the various libraries which have come to hold manuscripts of monastic origin, can offer quite an abundant documentation on this issue.

Moreover, one can enrich the material by comparing it with data found in medieval literature, among the Coptic encyclopedists of the "Golden Era," whose remarks can reinforce the data which the liturgical manuscripts and the lives of saints may yield.

1. Evidence from the manuscripts

We shall thus begin with the manuscripts, as a philologist ought to do!

a) *Evidence drawn from monastic manuscripts*

The analysis of the library of Saint Macarius' monastery, which I have unfortunately not yet published in detail, and a study of various other collections, shows that monastic liturgical manuscripts basically differ very little from other liturgical manuscripts on the subject of ordinary services, with the predictable exception of a few elements, such as their greater numbers, since they constitute the core of monastic libraries, and the simplicity of the volumes, since monks seek instruments to help them pray, rather than luxury items;[4] Liturgical manuscripts of monastic origin also include their own peculiar annexes, such as the "prayer of the veil" (*ṣalāt al-sitār*) in

---

Sources historiques et explorations archéologiques. Actes du Colloque de Genève (13 au 15 août 1984), Geneva, 1986, p. 93-103. — Taft, *Lit. Hours,* p. 249-259, also, in the space of only a few pages, managed to piece together the essentials of the Coptic divine office, by comparing data from antiquity, parallel documentation, and contemporary usage.

[4] I have pointed out: " La bibliothèque du monastère de Saint-Macaire est typiquement "monastique", c'est-à-dire essentiellement composée de livres religieux (parmi lesquels plus de la moitié sont des ouvrages liturgiques), et pauvre en manuscrits de luxe; en particulier, l'ornementation — quand il y en a — est simple, le plus souvent limitée à des croix en pleine page ou des frontispices, et on n'y trouve qu'un tout petit nombre de mss richement enluminés; de même, les reliures sont utilitaires, et non pas luxueuses " (in *Les manuscrits de Saint-Macaire: Observations codicologiques,* in Ph. Hoffmann and Chr. Hunzinger [ed.], *Recherches de codicologie comparée. La composition du codex au Moyen Âge, en Orient et en Occident* (Paris, Presses de l'École Normale Supérieure, 1998), p. 171-182 [see p. 172]).

the horologia, or the inclusion of numerous holy monks in the doxologies and other collections of hymns, etc. With the exception of these particularities, the manuscripts of Wadi al-Natrun or elsewhere conform most often to the common model. They can therefore help us to trace its history.

Their very numbers much increase the chances of finding basic evidence of remnants of services or rites which have been dropped, to which, in the most favourable of cases, an ancient author might allude, usually without offering sufficient detail to satisfy our curiosity. In such a case, the liturgist will be very grateful for a few pages, often in poor condition, which offer a clue to a vanished reality. This has been the case with the manuscripts of Saint Macarius, which have yielded some interesting details, which we shall come back to below (c).

But in the library of Saint Macarius' monastery I described only complete manuscripts, leaving fragments for a better day, when myself or some other scholar will have the leisure to deal with them;[5]

---

[5] I would like to take this occasion to rectify a misunderstanding based on a totally unfounded hypothesis. Contrary to what L. Störk (*Hamburg 2*, p. 86), wrote, no doubt with the best of intentions, it is not true that Father Mattā-l-Maskīn or anyone else at Saint Macarius tried to deny me access to the fragments of manuscripts kept in boxes in the monastery keep. I was offered the chance to examine them and describe them, but chose not to pursue that line of activity for lack of time. The task of describing the 490 complete manuscripts had already obliged me to prolong my stay in Egypt by six months, and it was quite impossible to stay on any longer. I have never had to regret making the "strategic choice" of describing the complete manuscripts rather than the fragments, although I am aware that it did not correspond to the custom of certain Coptic scholars. As I have more than once pointed out elsewhere, the complete manuscripts, although relatively recent and/or in Arabic translation, can furnish the "map" of the puzzle which allows one to fit together with some certainty the various fragments of older documents, and to avoid working with hypotheses, which, however brilliant they may be, are never as good as a solid demonstration.

To answer fully the question raised by Störk, *loc.cit.*, I would point out that, in the sentence "le reste est demeuré enfermé dans ses boîtes, et nous ne l'avons pas vue" ("the rest remained it its boxes, and I did not examine it"), the word "ses" refers to "reste", not to Father Mattā-l-Maskīn, as Störk appears to have understood.

Finally, contrary to Störk's statement, I did not attempt to investigate whether those fragments did or did not come from the monastery keep. I only repeated the information which the monks of the monastery had given me. I saw no ground then, nor do I now, to cast any doubt on the validity of that information. My only concern was to cooperate with Coptic Christians in trying the better to understand and appreciate their traditions, and that lead me systematically to prefer to trust them ; on no occasion did I ever have reason to call that trust into question.

Addendum (21.02.2002) After the symposium, I stayed on in Egypt for a few days, and saw the boxes containing the fragments in the library of Saint Macarius'

that is why I handled almost no material older than the 13th century
(with the exception of two literary fragments, both of which are
foreign to the subject discussed here). The recent description of
fragments originating at Saint Macarius and presently held at
Hamburg (Störk, *Hamburg 2*) has furnished an abundance of ancient
material, which, though fragmentary, either confirms several
hypotheses, or gives, for a service we have discovered, an attestation
which is a century and half older than what had been previously
found.

b) *The ordinary services*

As for the "ordinary services" – by this we mean those which
correspond to the present liturgical norm –, manuscripts of monastic
origin furnish a large number of witnesses, generally in conformity
with current usage, which had already been established when the
oldest among them were copied. The only variants to be found in
monastic manuscripts are also known through liturgical books of
secular origin, but this by no means diminishes their interest.

   Euchologia, for example, do not deviate from present usage,
although one can find in them examples of the "prayer of the
fraction" (*ṣalāt al-qisma*), absent from the current liturgical editions.
Other minor variants can also be found, but these are also found in
euchologia belonging to diocesan clergy.[6] Likewise, while it is quite
normal to find in monasteries abundant manuscripts of the **Annual
Psalmody**, no variants appear to allow one to enrich the history of
that service. The copies held at Saint Macarius yielded only seven
relatively insignificant variants, which are also to be found in copies
meant for parish use.[7] We have little doubt that this will also prove to
be the case for the **antiphonary** (*difnār*), a very rare book (no more
than 3 copies at Saint Macarius), though one can expect the selection

---

monastery. There must have been about twenty boxes, and it would take quite some
time to carry out describing them. The monastery has taken steps to have the fragments
stored in transparent plastic envelopes, to insure their proper conservation and to
facilitate their being consulted, without separating fragments which might have to be
kept together. Under present circumstances, it is not possible to do research on these
fragments, as it would first be necessary to provide at least a summary description and
to attribute an inventory code to each of them.
   [6] Cf. Ugo Zanetti, "Esquisse d'une typologie des euchologes coptes bohaïriques,"
Muséon 100 (1987), p. 407-418.
   [7] Cf. *Boh. Lit. MSS*, p. 88.

of pieces dedicated to holy monks to be more voluminous than elsewhere.[8] **Rituals** of ancient date are no longer present;[9] upon examination, they prove to conform to general usage. **Pontificals** are necessary, at least for priestly and monastic ordinations. At Saint Macarius, which for centuries was the residence of the patriarch, there are old and valuable copies (14th century) which are predictably without originality compared with those of the patriarchal library. Finally, the manuscripts containing special services celebrated every year in each church, such as the *laqān* (blessing of holy water celebrated on the Feast of the Epiphany, on Maundy Thursday and at the Feast of Saints Peter and Paul) and the *sajda* (service of genuflection, celebrated at vespers on Whitsunday), are naturally also found in monasteries, but they do not appear to present any notable peculiarities; however, they could still yield useful topographic information. The "rite of the jar," for the purpose of reconciling apostates (in the strict sense as well as in a broader sense) to the Church, is rare, but is attested in at least one 14th century manuscript.[10] The **lectionaries** are a special case which we shall come back to later (in point c).

A final remark of a linguistic nature: the monasteries of Wadi al-Natrun have always been considered the "last refuge" of the Coptic (Bohairic) language, and one would have expected to find more Coptic than Arabic manuscripts there. This does not appear to be the case. A number of old fragments are only in Coptic, but most of their

---

[8] Cf. Gawdat Gabra, "Untersuchungen zum Difnar der koptischen Kirche. 1. Quellenlage, Forschungsgeschichte und künftige Aufgaben," *BSAC* 35 (1996), 37-52; "2. Zur Kompilation," *BSAC* 37 (1998) 49-68.

[9] The rituals held at Saint Macarius library are almost all of recent date. Many copies must have suffered wear and tear before disintegrating, while older copies found other homes. Thus Burmester, *Hamburg,* and Störk, *Hamburg 2,* mention a number of rituals (most often fragmentary) which can be dated from the 11th to the 14th centuries, containing all the ceremonies found elsewhere (baptism, marriage, anointing of the sick, funeral services for the various categories of the faithful, from little girls to patriarchs, etc.).

[10] Cf. *Boh. Lit. MSS.,* p. 82; all four copies of this found at Saint Macarius are from the 19th century, as are also the two copies mentioned by Burmester, but the Coptic Museum holds one 14th century copy. Two recent publications of the rite are: G. Viaud, "Le quidra dans la tradition égyptienne," *BSAC* 37 (1998) 117-20, and Leslie S.B. MacCoull, "The Rite of the Jar: Apostasy and Reconciliation in the Medieval Coptic Orthodox Church," in D. Wolfthal (ed.), *Peace and Negotiation: Strategies for Coexistence in the Middle Ages and the Renaissance* (Turnhout 2000), p. 145-162.

contemporaries have disappeared,[11] and almost all the 14th century copies are bilingual (with only a few exceptions, they give the rubrics only in Arabic!); all of these come from the monasteries or from rich Cairo churches. The psalmodies are free of this tendency, since the divine office was always sung in Coptic (note that this is only partly true of the Psalters and of the Horologia, which gradually change to Arabic); lectionaries are also exempt, because even parish churches managed to keep alive the custom of reading at least part of the readings in Coptic.[12]

From the linguistic point of view, the question of the survival of Greek in the Scetis liturgy arises. We shall not examine that question here for the simple reason that H. Brakmann has given it ample treatment in the paper he gave at the last Congress of Coptic Studies; his discussion of the subject can be found especially at the beginning of § 6 (Nordägypten) with all the necessary information.[13]

c) *Witnesses to non-extant services*

If the "ordinary" celebrations contained in manuscripts of monastic origin offer few new variants, it is no less true, on the other hand, that, due to the conservative character of monastic circles, one can find services and types of devotional prayer which have disappeared elsewhere. Thus a few rare examples have been conserved of the **"Prayer of the 11th Hour according to the Cairene usage"**, the structure of which is reminiscent of the Byzantine prayer at vespers, of Sabaite origin. Although they are isolated examples, they hold evidence which leads one to conclude that the service was truly celebrated in the Scetis monasteries in the 14th century, and probably

---

[11] With some exceptions, such as ms. Vatican Coptic 5 (13th century, psalms and canticles exclusively in Bohairic Coptic), and the Hamburg *Horologion* 11 (12th or 13th century; cf. Störk, *Hamburg 2*, p. 280), which formerly belonged both to Saint-Macarius.

[12] Abū l-Barakāt († 1324 A.D.) points out that in his time the monks of Saint Macarius read the gospel in the Coptic language, without repeating it in Arabic, as was done elsewhere (cf. Villecourt, *Observances 2*, p. 252, *ut infra*, note 47). This information was almost outdated at the time it was written, since the monasteries of Scetis had lectionaries written only in Arabic (each corresponding to a single Coptic volume) from the second third of the 14th century: cf. *Lect. copt. ann.*, p. 318-319 (see, in chronological order: S 113, S 100 et S 109, S 114, S 112).

[13] H. Brakmann, "Neue Funde (1996-2000)" [being printed].

up to the 17th century.[14] Other evidence has also been brought to light. The catalogues of L. Störk, describing the damaged manuscripts coming from Saint Macarius and held at Hamburg revealed three hitherto unknown fragments of the same service (none of the three gives the complete series of psalms in question); it is found in two psalmodies for the month of Kyahk (Hymnology 7 and Hymnology 27) as well as a fragment which we would not venture to classify on the basis of the information given in the catalogue, but which might come from an Annual Psalmody (Hymnology 119).[15] Moreover, it is now known that the Hamburg fragment described by Burmester as Horologion 1 (to which I referred in 1989) should be classified with Liturgy fragment 22 and Psalmody 82 of the same collection.[16]

Furthermore, describing the manuscripts of Saint Macarius drew our attention to the various ways of **subdividing the Psalter** for the divine office.[17] Surely, the various copies used to support the four categories in question did not all come from Wadi al-Natrun, and not all of them were of monastic origin, since various literary works (written in secular context) were included in the witnesses I used: the services discovered were not limited to Scetis! This fact appears to us as a characteristic which can shed light on the role played by the Scetis monasteries as a forum of cultural exchange, especially as far as the liturgy is concerned.

Horologion 5,[18] a fragment dating from the 12th or 13th century, clearly belongs to the category which we have called the "ordo of the full Psalter." At compline it prescribes the recitation of Psalms "71 to 76, 78 to 82, 87 to 89, 104 to 106."[19] At the office of midnight, Psalms "119 to 134" at the second nocturne, and "137 to 147 and

---

[14] Cf. U. Zanetti, "Horologion copte et vêpres byzantines," *Muséon* 102 (1989), p. 237-254: see p. 244-248 and 250.

[15] Cf. Störk, *Hamburg 2,* respectively p. 358, 387 and 572.

[16] Cf. Störk, *Hamburg 3* (= additions and corrections to Burmester, *Hamburg!*), p. 55: *Psalmod. 115.*

[17] Cf. U. Zanetti, "La distribution des psaumes dans l'horologion copte," in *OCP* 56 (1990), 323-369.

[18] Störk, *Hamburg 2,* p. 269-273.

[19] Cf. *Distribution,* p. 359 and 360 (ms. Barberini Or. 2 and monastery of Saint George at Sadamant), at compline. Recognizing the series allows one to fill in Störk's reading in places where the manuscript is damaged. Notice that the psalms are among those which never appear in present Horologion (cf. *ibid.,* p. 342: *psaumes exclus de l'ajbīya*).

151" at the third nocturne.[20] It further offers many precious rubrics not found in the indexes from which we had drawn the description of this distribution, and deserves closer examination.

As for the **lectionaries**, a study of nearly 250 witnesses showed, some time ago, that the series of readings (epistles and gospels) presently used by the Coptic Church very likely represents an ancient tradition, and has (with a number of variations of detail) been in constant use in the parishes; but in the monasteries of Scetis, over the centuries, it was often supplanted by a lectionary of a different type, much more voluminous, no doubt responding better to the needs of the daily celebration of the Eucharist. We have called that lectionary "the Lectionary of Samuel," after the name of the scribe who wrote the most noteworthy copy, the monk Samuel of the Hermitage of the Forty-Nine Martyrs of Scetis (which belonged to Saint Macarius' monastery).[21] The reason for its falling into desuetude is probably the fact that printed editions became the norm, and perhaps also because it no longer answered a need, since the Eucharist was no longer celebrated every day.[22]

Today, thanks to the catalogues of L. Störk, describing the fragments coming from Saint Macarius and held at Hamburg, it is possible to make notable progress in describing this lectionary, and to draw conclusions on the structure of the liturgical books. Indeed, there are fractions of Coptic lectionaries apparently copied in the 12th or 13th century, which correspond perfectly (though not without some variants) to our "Lectionary of Samuel,"[23] thus proving that around the year 1200 this type of lectionary was already in existence. Moreover, these fragments oblige us to go a very important step further, because Lectionary 21 includes only the readings proper to the Mass ("Liturgy": probably "Synaxis" in the Coptic text), while Lectionaries 23 and 24 have only the readings for the evening and morning offering of incense. This takes back to a stage in the formation of complete lectionaries (a stage attested in Sahidic), where

---

[20] This corresponds only partially to the services indicated in the previous note, but we are surprised to find no psalm indicated for the first nocturne: one might conjecture that the rubric prescribing psalms 118 and 135 might have escaped the attention of the redactor because of the poor condition of the fragment.

[21] Cf. *Lect. copt. ann.*, p. 196-213 (description of the main manuscript: p. 199).

[22] Cf. *Lect. copt. ann.*, p. 213-217.

[23] These are Lectionaries 21, 23 and 24 at least (Störk, *Hamburg 2,* p. 163-166 and 171-179). There are probably others, as we shall see.

"cathedral services" of offering incense are distinguished from the celebration of the Eucharist.[24] The Hamburg library holds various other fragments of lectionaries from the same period which were meant only for the offering of incense or only for the Eucharist. To analyse them will require some research, due to the (total or near total) lack of indication of the date of the feasts (or ferias) for which the readings are meant.

Concerning the "Lectionary of Samuel," notice that if the hypothesis formulated some twenty years ago[25] can be confirmed, that is, that this is the lectionary which Mark ibn al-Qunbar[26] took for pastoral use in his parish, we would be in the presence of a case of direct influence of the monastic rite on cathedral usage.[27] Still, the fact, mentioned above, that the lectionary had been handed down in distinct volumes meant either for the offering of incense or for the celebration of the Eucharist, should urge us to the inverse supposition, namely, that it is not Mark who borrowed for his parish a monastic lectionary, but that, being a man of great culture, he knew, and used in his church, an old cathedral lectionary which had already ceased to be used anywhere except in the monasteries of Scetis, where ancient traditions were always held in high esteem. In that case, it would be rather a question of the monasteries preserving a lectionary inherited from cathedral usage.

Notice that the Hamburg fragments from Saint Macarius offer three ancient indexes to the psalms, a rare kind of document, which unfortunately is found almost always in fragmentary form.[28] As they

---

[24] Cf. *Lect. copt. ann.*, p. 8 (and the reference to Quecke, *Untersuchungen*, p. 2-13).

[25] That hypothesis, which no material element has so far been able to confirm or invalidate for lack of new documentary proof, was formulated by U. Zanetti, "Premières recherches sur les lectionnaires coptes," *Ephemerides Liturgicae* 98 (1984), p. 3-34 (cf. p. 13-25). It was reiterated and discussed in *Lect. copt. ann.*, p. 196-198.

[26] Following the transcription of the name proposed by Father Samir, "Vie et œuvre de Marc Ibn al-Qunbar," in *Christianisme d'Égypte* [= *Cahiers de la Bibliothèque Copte, 9*] (Paris-Louvain, 1994), p. 123-158. Until then, the transcription "ibn Qanbar", following Graf, was used.

[27] Notice that all manuscripts containing this lectionary originate, until proven otherwise, from the Scetis monasteries (cf. *Lect. copt. ann.*, p. 199-207). The copies held at Hamburg also conform to this rule, as they come from Amba Bishoï (Burmester, *Hamburg*) or from Saint Macarius (Störk, *Hamburg 2*).

[28] Cf. *Lect. copt. ann.*, p. 84-87; cf. Störk, *Hamburg 2, Lectionaries 7* through 9 (p. 135-140).

too are very incomplete, they offer no conclusive evidence, but must be borne in mind.[29]

The Scetis monasteries also knew the use of "monthly lectionaries," composed of selections from the services of the sanctoral (probably) covering the thirty days of the month, allowing for the daily celebration of the Mass without having to encumber oneself with heavy books.[30] This system, which has deep roots in the Coptic Church (where three feasts return each month on the same day of the month), was to prove very successful in Ethiopia.[31]

The **Holy Week Lectionary** presents us with a rather different situation.[32] The Codex Scaligeri is a bilingual Greek-Arabic manuscript copied in 1265 in a Scetis monastery, which presents a rather less voluminous (as it is a more archaic) service than that which Patriarch Gabriel ibn Turaik (1131-1145) imposed a century earlier. Notice that the colophon attributing the reform to Patriarch Gabriel mentions that Patriarch Gabriel had noticed that lay people were no longer able to take part in the long services of Holy Week, and entrusted to a commission of scholars the task of sizing the services down to a more reasonable length[33] (nevertheless, roughly one hundred years later, Bishop Peter of Behnesā lengthened them

---

[29] The same is true of the Greek documents coming from Upper Egypt (the White Monastery) mentioned by Henner, *Fragm. Lit. Copt.,* p. 112, notes 74 and 75.

[30] Cf. *Lect. copt. ann.,* p. 254 (summary).

[31] The monthly celebration of saints' days occurs frequently there (though this is not the only possibility). Cf. E. Fritsch, CSSp., *The Liturgical Year of the Ethiopian Church.* (*Ethiopian Review of Cultures,* Special Issue, IX-X (Addis Abeba, 2001), see p. 70-72; and E. Fritsch, CSSp., "Les lectionnaires éthiopiens," in Chr.-B. Amphoux et J.-P. Bouhot (ed.), *La lecture liturgique des Épîtres catholiques dans l'Église ancienne.* Histoire du texte biblique 1 (Lausanne, 1996) p. 197-219, esp. 204-205.

[32] Considering only liturgical manuscripts from Scetis. It is well known, indeed, that other documents give information on the transition from the patriarcal Liturgy, celebrated in the Cathedral of Alexandria, with the consecration of the *Myron* (Holy Chrism) and baptisms, to a more discrete celebration at Saint-Macarius' monastery, with no catechumens to baptize, and at which the consecration of the *Myron* occurs more rarely: cf. H. Brakmann, "La "Mystagogie" de la liturgie alexandrine et copte," in A.M. Triacca and A. Pistoia (ed.), *Mystagogie: Pensée liturgique d'aujourd'hui et liturgie ancienne.* Conférences Saint-Serge. 39e Semaine d'études liturgiques. Bibliotheca Ephemerides Liturgicae. Subsidia, 70 (Rome, 1993), p. 55-65 (with bibliography; cf. p. 61 ff.).

[33] Cf. *Ethiopian Holy Week,* p. 765 f., with the earlier bibliography (the detail of the colophon, the translation of which can be found in the catalogue of London Ethiopian manuscripts compiled by Dillmann [n° 27, p. 30-31, = ms. *Add. 16.250*], is given explicitly in a 17th century poem: O. H. E. Burmester, "A Coptic Lectionary Poem," *Muséon* 43 [1930], p. 373-385: see p. 381).

again…). This is not to suggest that the monks feared spending long hours in church during Holy Week, as can be seen from the collection of homilies written to fill out the canonical hours of the "Great Week" (except vespers, which are dropped on fast days, since Mass is celebrated at the end of the day), a collection which fills around a hundred very large folios.[34]

There are also a number of **devotional prayers** and paraliturgical services, which are not necessarily the exclusive property of the monks. If the songs of welcome to Scetis which I took from two manuscripts from Saint Macarius were clearly composed for use at Wadi al-Natrun,[35] the "Book of seven prayers" or "*Kitāb al-mukhtār min ṭalabāt al-abrār*" ("Chosen <book> made from the biddings of the just") can be found in secular manuscripts, and has a history which, to my knowledge, has not yet been written.[36] For lack of time, I was not able to describe the "Book of biddings to Our Lady" or *Kitāb ṭalabāt li-l-Sayyida al-'adhra'*, which I encountered among the various manuscripts at Saint Macarius, the title of which might be artificial; only a detailed analysis can allow us to situate it.

Indeed, the description of monastic manuscripts taught us not to give too much trust to inscriptions. Thus, the Saint Macarius manuscript Liturg. 160 (= *Inventaire DAM*, n° 204, p. 32) simply presents the collected secret prayers recited by the priest, taken from the Euchologion, but contrived a title as pompous as the "Book of the Mysteries for the Service of the Just" or *Kitāb al-asrār fī khidmati al-abrār*!

---

[34] Cf. Ugo Zanetti, "Homélies copto-arabes pour la Semaine Sainte," *Augustinianum* 23 (1983), p. 517-522 (+ 1 inset): we refer to ms. Saint-Macarius, Homilies 46 (= *Inventaire DAM*, Nr. 472), which measures 440 x 305 mm. — More precisely, we must admit that none of the manuscripts which we identified (nor the three from Saint Macarius, nor the three from the Coptic Museum quoted on p. 522 of that article) bears any colophon proving their monastic origin, though we have no doubt about this latter.

[35] Cf. U. Zanetti, "Deux chants de bienvenue à Scété," in *EYΛΟΓΗΜΑ. Studies in Honor of Robert TAFT S.J.* Studia Anselmiana 110 (Rome, 1993), p. 593-611. Let us take this occasion to correct a mistake which I committed in translating the second piece. This latter is meant for the "new priests" (*mustajiddīn*) and not for the "priests on pilgrimage" (*mustajidīn*: form VIII [*istajada*] from *sajada* seems not to exist!)

[36] Cf. *Boh. Lit. MSS.*, p. 92 and n. 95, in which I mention the presence of this text in a Syriac Carshuni manuscript as well as its "descendance" in Ethiopian (under the name of *Weddāsē Amlāk* = "The praise of God").

2. The literary works

The works to which I have just referred lead us to the borderline between liturgy and literature. Some literary works, in fact, whether found amongst the manuscripts of Wadi al-Natrun or not, can shed some light on the way the liturgy was celebrated.

A few years ago, Father Ṣamū'īl al-Suryānī, who is now a bishop, made **Abū l-Makārim** better known. A portion of Abū l-Makārim's *Description of [Egyptian] Churches and Monasteries* was already known for the last hundred years under the name of Abū Ṣāliḥ, and Jirjis Fīlūthā'ūs 'Awaḍ had procured a little known edition in 1931.[37] I have looked through the part of the work which describes the monasteries of Wadi al-Natrun,[38] and discovered some interesting details. Beside the fact that the monasteries were places of refuge – and that even during the worse times of the persecution of caliph Al-Ḥākim, the liturgy never ceased to be celebrated there, for God saw to it that those churches would at least not be destroyed (f. 64, ed. p. 113) – the work mentions various miracles which we shall not discuss here, because they are scarcely informative on the subject of the liturgical rubrics. But the account does tell that in the cell of Dorotheus the monks could not say the Alleluia (that is, they were not able to participate in the divine service!) without knowing all of the psalms by heart (f. 6, ed. p. 117) – this confirms the well known fact that the first thing a novice had to do was to memorise the Psalter. Reading Abū l-Makārim afforded us one very valuable piece of information which can shed light on an obscure episode in the life of Saint John of Scetis (who was hegumen of Scetis in the 7th century):[39]

---

[37] *Ta'rīkh al-kanā'is wa-l-adyura fī l-qarn al-thānī 'ashar al-mīlādī li-'Abī al-Makārim, alladhī nusiba khaṭa'an ilā 'Abī Ṣāliḥ al-Armanī, i'dād wa-ta'līq al-rāhib Ṣamū'īl al-Suryānī.* 4 vols. (Cairo, 1984). — *Kitāb al-kanā'is wa-l-adyura fī al-quṭr al-miṣrī wa-Afrīqīyā wa-Āsyā wa-Ūrūbā, ta'līf al-shaikh al-mu'taman Abī al-Makārim Sa'ad Allāh ibn Jirjis ibn Mas'ūd, al-mutawaffā ba'd sana 925 sh. – 1209 m.* (etc.), bi-qalam … Jirjis Fīlūthā'ūs 'Awaḍ (Cairo, 1647 AM- 1931 AD). (It is through Enzo Lucchesi that I have come to be acquainted with this latter edition, and I wish to thank him very warmly).

[38] Edition by Amba Ṣamū'īl, vol. I, p. 113 to 129, corresponding to f. 64 to 74 of the manuscript.

[39] Cf. U. Zanetti, "Vie de S. Jean, higoumène de Scété au VIIe siècle," *Analecta Bollandiana* 114 (1996), p. 273-405.

in order to blame a group of people who are here called Sarakote,[40]
who used to communicate without respecting the eucharistic fast, a
story is told of a priest who – apparently without there initially being
any violation of a religious prohibition – had drunk wine the night
before the paschal celebration (at the dawn of Easter day), and that an
angel would have struck him with a sword if God himself had not
protected him.[41] Abū l-Makārim mentions (f. 69ᵛ, ed. p. 121-122) that
Damian, the 35th Patriarch of Alexandria (578-605), "banned people
known as the *baṭṭālīn* (good-for-nothings)[42] who during the night
drank many times from the cup before going to church, (even) in
these monasteries (of Wadi al-Natrun)."[43] It seems difficult not to

---

[40] The Arabic text writes *sarākūdā*, which I at first found difficult to read. Father
Hans Quecke pointed out that it is the transcription of the Coptic *sarakôte* (cf. U.
Zanetti, "Arabe Serākūdā = copte Sarakote = "gyrovagues" dans la Vie de Jean de
Scété," *Analecta Bollandiana* 115 (1997), p. 280). Later, L. MacCoull and E. Lucchesi
both, in private correspondence drew my attention to the fact that the term probably
designated Meletian monks. Recently, Chr. Cannuyer revived a suggestion made by
Crum (but independently of him) and proposed that the Coptic word is the origin of the
word *sarabaita* used by John Cassian ("L'identité des sarabaïtes, ces moines d'Égypte
que méprisait Jean Cassien," in *Mélanges de Science Religieuse* [Université de Lille],
58/2, April-June 2001, p. 7-19). This need not exclude the possibility that within Egypt
the word might have been applied to the Meletians.

[41] Cf. "Vie de Jean de Scété," chap. 7, § 58-67, p. 306-309, and the commentary, p.
369-374.

[42] Might this be a translation of *sarakote*? In the examples given by Crum, *Coptic
Dictionary,* 354 b, the word *sarakote* is found twice in connection with *parasitos* (loan
word from the Greek, obviously meaning "parasite").

[43] This situation was examined by H. Brakmann, "Zur Geschichte der
eucharistischen Nüchternheit in Ägypten," *Muséon* 84 (1971), p. 197-211. Most kindly,
the author presented us with an updated version of what he had written. Given the
interest of the text, we offer it here for the use of our readers:
    "Der alexandrinische Patriarch Damian († 606), ein gewesener Sketis-Mönch
syrischer Herkunft, bekämpfte Meletianer aus der Sketis, die nachts vor der Kommunion mehrmals Wein tranken, da auch Jesus seinen Jüngern beim Abendmahl zwei
Becher gereicht habe. Damian belehrte sie, daß der erste Becher Jesu habe dem alten
Pascha entsprochen, nunmehr aber verböten die Kanones, irgendetwas vor dem
Empfang der Eucharistie zu genießen. Wer sich daraufhin von seinem Irrtum noch
nicht löste, verfiel der Verbannung (*Synaxaire arabe jacobite. Rédaction copte,* 17.
Baounah = *PO* 17, 376 Basset). Eine ähnliche Episode wird von Damians
Zeitgenossen Johannes, Bischof des hoch im Norden am gleichnamigen See gelegenen
Paralos, berichtet. Als "großer Ketzerhammer" exkommunizierte er unter anderem
Sektierer, "die zwanzigmal täglich kommunizierten und nicht nüchtern waren," und
verbot ihnen, ihre sündige Praxis fortzuführen (*Synaxaire arabe jacobite, Rédaction
copte,* 19. Khiak = *PO* 3, 388 Basset); zur Übersetzung vgl. J. Muyser, "Notes sur la
discipline eucharistique dans l'Église copte," *XXXV Congreso Eucharistico
Internacional.* Sesiones de Estudio 2 (Barcelona 1952) 727. Johannes greift dabei

recognise here a situation identical to the one described in the Life of
Saint John of Scetis. Other details given by that author have been
published elsewhere.[44]

We shall not discuss the **Book of the Chrism** here, as another
speaker has been asked to treat that topic.[45] It would nevertheless be
useful to point out that the work is almost as interesting for its
chronicle as for the liturgical indications which it contains, and that it
emphasises one of the roles played by the monasteries of Wadi al-
Natrun during the Middle Ages, that is, that of the rallying point for
the Coptic clergy. There, indeed, far from the civil authorities, it was
possible to give liturgical expression to a communion that in daily life
was very real in the hearts of Christians, but was impossible to
manifest in social life, except with great prudence, for fear of setting
off the ire of fanatics who regularly destroyed churches or sought to
obtain forced conversions.

Most of the other works of the great Coptic authors of the Golden
Age can be found in the monastic libraries of Scetis, but they have
little to do with our subject, since they deal more with dogmatics than
with the liturgy. That is at least what one can conclude from a rapid
survey of the works at hand.

On the other hand, the **Lamp of Darkness** (*Kitāb miṣbāḥ al-
ẓulma fī īḍāḥ al-khidma*) by Abū l-Barakāt ibn Kabar,[46] which
devotes a number of chapters to the liturgy, could hardly avoid
referring to the monasteries of Wadi al-Natrun. This eminent liturgist
quotes all the liturgical particularities of which he is aware, those of
Cairo (*Miṣr*), those of the Christians of Upper Egypt and those of the
monasteries, Saint Macarius' as well as the others (for example the
monastery of Saint Mercurius at Shahrān, that of Saint George at
Sadamant, etc.). These details enrich our knowledge of the history of

---

offenbar eine Schenute-Polemik (H. Guerin, *Sermons inédits de Senouti*, in: *Rev.
Égyptologique* 11 [1904] 18) auf. Ähnliches wird von Mönchen im Gebiet von Pyrrha
berichtet (*Chron. anonymum Ps-Dionysianum a. 509/10* [= *CSCO* 507/*Syr.* 213, 7f])."

[44] Both of these pieces of information concern the monastery of Saint Macarius, that
is, that no one entered the sanctuary (σκήνη), except the patriarch and the priests of the
monastery (f. 65, ed. p. 114); and that it was only in that monastery that the
consecration of the Holy Chrism or Myron took place (f. 67v, ed. p. 118).

[45] Nevertheless, see the reference to Brakmann (note 32 *supra*).

[46] Cf. K. Samir, "L'encyclopédie liturgique d'Ibn Kabar († 1324) et son apologie
d'usages coptes," in H.J. Feulner & E. Velkovska & R.F. Taft (eds.), *Crossroads of
Cultures. Studies in Liturgy and Patristics in Honor of Gabriele Winkler*. Orientalia
christiana Analecta 260 (Rome, 2000), p. 619-655.

the liturgy, but I do not think it useful to dwell on them here, because such technicalities could scarcely lead to a synthesis of wider interest.[47]

The same goes for the **Liturgical ritual** (*Al-Tartīb al-ṭaqsī*) of Patriarch Gabriel V (1409-1427). It contains one allusion to Scetis, that is, the detail that the rite of "filling the chalice" (*ta'mīr al-ka's*) was taken from a manuscript of Saint Macarius.[48] This is well worth mentioning in the framework of this paper, but only to the end of being as complete as possible.

In the work entitled "The Order of the Priesthood" (**Tartīb al-kahanūt**), I found only one mention of the monasteries of Scetis, that is, where it is stated that, after his ordination, the new patriarch will go "to the holy desert, the monastery of Saint Macarius, and will celebrate in the sanctuary of Abba Benjamin, then in the other monasteries..."[49] But this remains beyond the bonds of our subject.

The mention of the "sanctuary of Abba Benjamin" recalls a much more ancient work telling of the consecration of that place by Patriarch Benjamin, which was published R.-G. Coquin.[50] It will nevertheless be noticed that this text, like so many others, is poor in concrete liturgical details, since the rubrics were self-evident for the author.

---

[47] Here are some examples taken from Villecourt, *Observances II* : p. 248 (= p. 92 in the offprint; = ms. P, f. 205; ms. U, f. 183ᵛ): "Les prêtres du monastère d'Abū Macaire ne revêtent pas le burnous au temps du service de la messe, mais ils le revêtent pendant la prière, conformément à leur règle;" *ibid.*, p. 251 (= p. 95; ms. P, f. 206; ms. U, f. 185): "Au monastère d'Abū Macaire: les psalmodistes le *[= le psaume]* chantent au milieu de l'église, et à cela personne ne leur répond;" *ibid.*, p. 252 (= p. 96; ms. P, f. 206; ms. U, f. 185): "Et on interprète *[l'évangile]* en arabe, excepté au monastère d'Abū Macaire, car ils n'interprètent nullement en arabe jusqu'à ce jour où nous sommes."

[48] A. 'Abdallah, *L'ordinamento liturgico di Gabriele V, 88° Patriarca copto (1409-1427)* [= *Studia orientalia christiana.* Aegyptiaca] (Cairo, 1962); the text is found in f. 120-126ᵛ of the manuscript, p. 260 ff. and translation p. 430 ff. — Heinzgerd Brakmann suggests that there might be a link between this ritual and the *Liturgie des Présanctifiés de S. Marc* referred to in ms. Paris grec 325.

[49] J. Assfalg, *Die Ordnung des Priestertums...* (*Publications du Centre d'Études Orientales de la Custodie Franciscaine de Terre-Sainte.* Coptica 1 (Cairo, 1955): f. 143ᵛ of ms., see p. 27 et 101. — Heinzgerd Brakmann points out that more information can be found on the ritual of the "Joyful Entry" of the new patriarch into Scetis, in E. Renaudot, *Liturgiarum orientalium collectio* (ed. Frankfurt, 1847), I, p. 404-407, according to "Ebnassalus."

[50] R.-G. Coquin, *Livre de la consécration du sanctuaire de Benjamin.* Bibliothèque d'études coptes 13 (Cairo : IFAO, 1975).

Finally, let us list the various peculiarities of the Scetis monasteries which were observed from the different literary sources.[51] At times these are corroborated by evidence yielded by liturgical manuscripts. For example, the discussion concerning whether or not the Body and Blood of Christ were kept after the eucharistic celebration at Saint Macarius' monastery was studied by O. Nußbaum;[52] the modification of the confession of faith recited by the priest before the communion, introduced by Patriarch Gabriel II ibn Turaik (1131-1145), and the controversy with monks of Saint Macarius which was connected with that modification;[53] the mention of Saint Macarius before Saint Anthony in the *majma'* or commemoration of all holy fathers, which is made near the end of the eucharistic anaphora, in conformity with an ancient rubric proper to Northern Egypt but contrary to the usage attested to by the majority of manuscripts.[54]

3. The Influence of the Monasteries

But is the interest of the Wadi al-Natrun monasteries for the liturgy of the Coptic Church limited to this rich material documentation? Certainly not! These monasteries have always been an indisputable point of reference in the liturgical life of the Coptic Church. It is there that the very "heart" of Coptic spirituality is to be found (with no play on words with the incorrect but widespread etymology, ϣⲓϩⲏⲧ/*shihēt*, "heart scales," or in Arabic, *mīzān al-qulūb*, "the balance of hearts"). That heart is prayer itself, and prayer never ceased at Wadi al-Natrun, even at the worst of times.

It is therefore quite natural that the influence of the Scetis monasteries on the Coptic liturgy should become apparent first of all

---

[51] I owe this list to Heinzgerd Brakmann, and include it here for the convenience of the reader.

[52] O. Nussbaum, *Die Aufbewahrung der Eucharistie* (= *Theophaneia*, 29), (Bonn, 1979), p. 25 ff.

[53] H. Brakmann, "Zur Stellung des Parisinus graecus 325 in der Geschichte der alexandrinisch-ägyptischen Liturgie," *Studi sull'Oriente Cristiano* 3.1 (1999), p. 97-110 et H. Engberding, "Ein Problem in der Homologia vor der hl. Kommunion in der ägyptischen Liturgie," *OCP* 2 (1936), p. 145-154.

[54] G. Graf, "Die Rangordnung der Bischöfe Ägyptens nach einem protokollarischen Bericht des Patriarchen Kyrillos ibn Laklak," *OC* 24 (1927), p. 299-337 (see p. 317). Macarius is found before Anthony, for example, in Paris. gr. 325, fol. 27^r (a later addition), and in the fragment published by Mgr Lefort: *Coptica Lovaniensia, 31 = Muséon* 53 (1940), p. 32.

in prayer. It is no accident that the Coptic Horologion is of a thoroughly monastic type,[55] although it competed, during Antiquity and the High Middle Ages, with services of the cathedral type such as the "Prayer of the 11th Hour according to the Custom of the Cairenes," to which I have referred above, the ancient cathedral services of the evening and morning Offering of incense, and the present Psalmody.[56] As for the latter, one will note that it conserves a series of *psalies* which invoke the Name of Jesus, the fruit of a kind of prayer which goes back to the Desert Fathers of Scetis, and further still, to the insights of Origen, one of the most brilliant sons of the metropolis of Alexandria.[57]

As places of unceasing prayer, the monasteries of Wadi al-Natrun have been – as I mentioned earlier when reading Abū l-Makārim – a "garden" meant to preserve the liturgy. Even the most ordinary services, such as the Eucharist and the offering of incense, were always kept alive, at times when circumstances had forced them to become rare in other places. This is the reason for the considerable proportion of the manuscripts of monastic origin among those which are older than the 18th century (later, manuscripts of parochial origin grew more numerous).

It is also for this reason that, in every period, the monasteries were always a place of pilgrimage, where pilgrims sought spiritual refreshment, the blessing of the holy men who lie buried there. They sought there to learn to celebrate the liturgy (for example, during a retreat at a monastery, following one's ordination), and they hoped simply to find their own Coptic Christian identity, in a place where that identity reigned supreme. Numerous marks were left in the manuscripts, signatures and reminders of donors (*waqf*), colophons evoking the dispositions of one come to Scetis to beg God's forgiveness for his sins and to leave a copy of a liturgical book so that the monks might regularly pray to God for him … all this reminds us

---

[55] Cf. Taft, *Lit. Hours*, p. 249: "As one would expect, the Eastern office that has retained the purest monastic form is that of the Coptic Church of Egypt."

[56] Cf. Taft, *Lit. Hours*, p. 256.

[57] Cf. E. Lanne, "La "prière de Jésus" dans la tradition égyptienne. Témoignage des psalies et des inscriptions," *Irénikon* 50.2 (1977), p. 163-203; A. Grillmeier, "Das "Gebet zu Jesus" und das "Jesu-Gebet." Eine neue Quelle zum "Jesus-Gebet" aus dem Weißen Kloster," in C. Laga (ed.), *After Chalcedon. Studies... offered to Prof. Albert van Roey*. Orientalia Lovaniensia Analecta 18 (Leuven, 1985), p. 187-202.

of the "pedagogical" role played by Wadi al-Natrun throughout the history of the Coptic Church.

Around the beginning of the 20th century, 'Abd-al-Masīḥ Ṣalīb al-Mas'ūdī al-Baramūsī (nephew of the monk 'Abd-al-Masīḥ Jirjis al-Mas'ūdī al-Baramūsī, who wrote books on dogmatics) began an intellectual endeavour and gave his Church, among other things, valuable liturgical editions. He foretold, several decades in advance, the current favourable period, in which the monasteries of Wadi al-Natrun (as well, thank God, as the other Coptic monasteries) publish all kinds of material, from printing ancient texts to pastoral magazines, from historical syntheses to brochures for tourists, ever hoping to share with all their knowledge and the love of their Church and its spiritual tradition, especially its monastic tradition.

It is not my task to say the direction in which the monasteries ought to develop. Should the accent be laid on study of tradition and the sharing of knowledge – or, in other words, on sharing the spiritual experience which comes of spending long years in monastic life and prayer? Or, on the other hand, should they seek to return to a more eremitic line, recognising that prayer is enough to fill the life of a monk, and to "justify" his existence? It is clear that both these ways of life are necessary for the Church, and that each has richly contributed to the renewal of the Coptic Church. Both should probably coexist in everyone according to his capacity, in function of what God asks of him through the intermediary of his superiors and the blessing of his spiritual father. For God gives generously; He always gives what is necessary for today. We must not give in to the temptation to "eat of the tree of the knowledge of good and evil" by trying to decide what to do all by ourselves, without referring to Divine Providence. No more give in to the temptation to "build up reserves" for the future, for, just like manna in the desert, the gift of God cannot be preserved to another day. We must be attentive to the call of the Holy Spirit, in prayer, and the liturgy is an expression of prayer. Today, like yesterday, the monks of Wadi al-Natrun are called, by their prayer, in particular by their liturgical prayer, to keep alive that attention to the Holy Spirit, in their country, in their Church, and for the whole world.

List of Abbreviations

Boh. Lit. MSS = U. Zanetti, "Bohairic Liturgical Manuscripts," *OCP* 61 (1995), p. 65-94.

Brakmann, "Neue Funde 1992-1996" = H. Brakmann, "Neue Funde und Forschungen zur Liturgie der Kopten (1992-1996)," in *Ägypten und Nubien in spätantiker und christlicher Zeit.* Akten des 6. Internationalen Koptologenkongresses in Münster, 20.-26. Juli 1996, 1 (= *Sprachen und Kulturen des christlichen Orients*, 6, 1), Wiesbaden, 1999, p. 451-464.

Brakmann, "Neue Funde 1996-2000" = H. Brakmann, "Neue Funde und Forschungen zur Liturgie der Kopten (1996-2000)" [paper read at the *7th International Congress of Coptic Studies*, Leiden, August 2000; currently being printed].

BSAC = *Bulletin de la Société d'Archéologie copte*, Cairo.

Burmester, *Hamburg* = O.H.E. KHS-Burmester, *Die Handschriftenfragmente der Staats- und Universitätsbibliothek Hamburg. Teil 1.*, (= *Verzeichnis der orientalischen Handschriften in Deutschland*, XXI, 1), Wiesbaden, 1975.

Distribution = U. Zanetti, "La distribution des psaumes dans l'horologion copte," *OCP* 56 (1990), 323-369.

Ethiopian Holy Week = U. Zanetti, "Is the Ethiopian Holy Week service translated from Sahidic? Towards a study of the *Gebra Ḥemāmāt*," in *Proceedings of the Eleventh International Conference of Ethiopian Studies,* Addis Ababa, April 1-6 1991. Vol. I, edited by Bahru Zewde, Richard Pankhurst, Tadesse Beyene, Addis-Abeba, 1994, p. 765-783.

Henner, *Fragm. Lit. Copt.* = J. Henner, *Fragmenta Liturgica Coptica.* Editionen und Kommentar liturgischer Texte der Koptischen Kirche des ersten Jahrtausends (= *Studien und Texte zu Antike und Christentum*, 5), Tübingen, 2000.

Inventaire DAM = U. Zanetti, *Les manuscrits de Dair Abû Maqâr.* Inventaire, (= *Cahiers d'Orientalisme,* 11), Geneva (Patrick Cramer), 1986, 102 p.

Lect. copt. ann. = U. Zanetti, *Les lectionnaires coptes annuels: Basse-Égypte,* (= *Publications de l'Institut Orientaliste de Louvain,* 33), Louvain-la-Neuve, 1985, XXIII + 383 pages.

Muséon = *Le Muséon*. Revue d'études orientales, Louvain.

OC = *Oriens christianus*.

OCP = *Orientalia Christiana Periodica*, Rome.

Störk, *Hamburg* 2 = L. Störk, *Die Handschriften der Staats- und Universitätsbibliothek Hamburg.* Teil 2: Die Hanschriften aus Dair Anbā Maqār, (= *Verzeichnis der orientalischen Handschriften in Deutschland,* XXI, 2), Wiesbaden, 1995.

Störk, *Hamburg* 3 = L. Störk, *Die Handschriften der Staats- und Universitätsbibliothek Hamburg.* Teil 3: Addenda und Corrigenda zu Teil

1, (= *Verzeichnis der orientalischen Handschriften in Deutschland,* XXI, 3), Wiesbaden, 1996.

Taft, *Lit. Hours* = R. Taft, *The Liturgy of the Hours, East and West.* Collegeville, MN, 1985.

Villecourt, *Observances* = L. Villecourt, "Les Observances liturgiques et la discipline du jeûne dans l'Église Copte. (Ch. XVI-XIX de la Lampe des Ténèbres)," *Le Muséon* 36 (1923), p. 249-292; 37 (1924), p. 201-280; and 38 (1925), p. 261-320.

Scetis at the Red Sea:
Depictions of Monastic Genealogy in the
Monastery of St. Antony

Elizabeth S. Bolman[*]

An alliterative trio of words captures the thematic content of this paper: *mimesis*, martyrdom, and monasticism. All three are ritualistic modes of being and acting. The visual subjects of my paper today are the paintings in the nave of the Church of St. Antony, located in the Monastery of the same name, near the Red Sea coast. My intention is to explain the rationale for the existence of the nave paintings. *Mimesis*, martyrdom, and monasticism are connected in this program genealogically. The genealogy in question is a spiritual one, and establishes ties between Scetis and the Red Sea coast.

These *secco* wall paintings date to 1232/1233 CE, and were painted by a team of Coptic artists led by a master named Theodore (Figure 1). They are not the earliest layer of paintings in the church, but cover at least one, and possibly more, earlier painted programs. The church itself dates to the sixth century, or thereabouts, and was renovated at least once prior to the 1232/1233 campaign. It is embedded within the core of the monastery. The early thirteenth-century painted program covers almost the entire church interior, and constitutes the best preserved and most complete group of paintings from a medieval Coptic church.

Until recently, the paintings were barely visible, covered under layers of soot and unappealing overpainting. Insects had burrowed

---

[*] This paper is based on a talk that was written before the publication of E.S. Bolman, ed., *Monastic Visions: Wall Paintings in the Monastery of St. Antony at the Red Sea* (New Haven: Yale University Press and the American Research Center in Egypt, 2002). Some of the material in the current paper is drawn from work on that book. Many thanks to Robert K. Vincent, Jr. for permission to use this material and one of the illustrations from the volume in this article. Also, thanks to the American Research Center in Egypt for administering work on the Monastery of St. Antony, to the United States Agency for International Development for funding it, to the Coptic Church and the community at the Monastery of St. Antony for their support and hospitality, and to the Egyptian Supreme Council of Antiquities for their collaboration.

into the mud brick of the church, and large sections of painted plaster were but loosely attached to the walls. With the permission of His Holiness Pope Shenouda, and at the invitation of the Monastery of St. Antony, the American Research Center in Egypt undertook the challenging task of cleaning and conserving the paintings. All work was done in collaboration with the Egyptian Supreme Council of Antiquities. This massive project was funded by the United States Agency for International Development. Adriano Luzi and Luigi de Cesaris, and their assistants, performed the delicate work of conservation.

The Church of St. Antony consists of a two-part nave, a *khurus*, and a sanctuary, with three altars (Figure 2). A small side chapel is located off of an annex, at the western end of the church. Each half of the nave is covered by a dome. The nave lacks aisles. A broad archway and a low wall divide its western and eastern halves. This architectural segmentation predates the 1232/1233 paintings. A horizontal band of paintings encircles the viewer in the nave. It begins just under six feet from the current floor level (Figure 1). Most, but not all, of the subjects in the western end are equestrians (Figure 3). A few, positioned frontally, are standing figures (Figure 4). All of them are men, and they are set within rectangular framed spaces, against a tripartite colored background. The lowest register is yellow-ocher, the middle register is olive green, and the upper zone is usually, but not always, gray blue.

The eastern half of the nave is filled with upright figures, framed variously, usually with some sort of arcade (Figure 5). All are standing men, dressed in monastic or episcopal garb, with the single exception of the enthroned Virgin and Child. The segmentation of the background into three colored registers is generally followed here as well. Considering pose alone, the nave program appears to lack balance. The equestrian riders have been identified as martyrs, and the standing figures as monks. The band of equestrians fills only three-quarters of the western end of the nave. All of the rest of the principal subjects stand frontally.

The answer to the question concerning the visually uneven nave program is to be found in the four extant standing figures of the western end (Figure 4). They are: Pakaou, seen at the far left, holding a short devil by the hair; Noua; and the pair under a single arch, Piroou and Athom. These two at the far right are shown within the same arch because they were brothers. They were peasants, and

Coptic accounts tell us that they lived in Egypt during the "era of the martyrs." One day, they encountered soldiers who were preparing to throw the body of a recently killed Christian martyr into the sea. Piroou and Athom bribed the soldiers to hand over the body, which they buried properly. After arranging for the ongoing care of the grave, and inspired by the martyr's model, they went off to embrace martyrdom themselves. The man whose body they rescued, and buried, was Noua. He is painted next to them in the nave. While they never met in life, their painted proximity suggests that they all stand together in the kingdom of heaven. Noua was not a peasant, but a physician, and possibly also a priest. Pakaou, shown here holding a devil named Soufounesar, was an ascetic, who also lived in the era of martyrs. He was called by the Archangel Gabriel to become one himself.

The equestrians whose images so compellingly fill the rest of the western end of the nave were all originally either soldiers, or aristocrats, or both. The horses and armor convey their military status, first as soldiers of the emperor, and then as soldiers of Christ. St. George and St. Theodore wear familiar Roman military garb, a cuirass and tunic (Figure 3). They are equipped with shields, spears, swords, and a bow. Coptic martyrdom accounts tell us that Victor was the son of a caesar, and was expected to follow his father in a military career. Victor caused trouble for his family first by refusing to join the army, and then by converting to Christianity and embracing martyrdom. Uniquely in this painted program, Victor is shown wearing delicate slippers and loose pants, and sitting on an elaborately tattooed horse, conveying his high social status and his pacific nature. These paintings of equestrians, in the lower zone, usually show the martyr killing some evil creature. Here, Victor is depicted suffering the tortures of martyrdom, in the furnace of a bath house.[1]

While at first appearing to be unbalanced, the western half of the nave can now be understood to form a coherent whole thematically, if not visually. All of the figures depicted here were martyrs. Pakaou, shown in the pose of the standing monks in the eastern end, provides a kind of bridge between the two groups of martyrs and monks. He was an ascetic holy man who was also a martyr.

---

[1] Cf. E.A.W. Budge, *Coptic Martyrdoms in the Dialect of Upper Egypt* (London: British Museum, 1914), 266-267 and 276; cf. BMO 7022, fols. 8a, 14a.

With the exception of the Virgin Mary and Christ child, as I said earlier, all of the figures in the eastern end lived as hermits or as members of monastic communities. Within this eastern end, the eastern wall is the place of greatest prominence, being closest to the sanctuary and its three altars. Facing east, the nave wall at the left depicts the Virgin Mary and Christ. At the right, we see Antony the Great and the senior ascetic Paul (Figure 5). As the founder of the monastery, Antony's position is appropriate. More even than this, his designation as the "Father of Monasticism" makes this location the only proper one for him. On the walls stand such eminent figures as Macarius the Great (Figure 6), Moses the Black, Pishoi, and John the Little, all of whom shaped monasticism at Scetis (Figure 7).

Two prominent monastic leaders fill the archway between the two halves of the nave. Shenoute and Pachomius bend over everyone moving from the western to the eastern end. The obvious exception to these groups of martyrs (at the west) and monks (at the east) is the pair of the Virgin and Child, to which I will return at the end of this paper. I will now propose an interpretation of the rationale for the juxtaposition of martyrs and monks in the nave program.

Pachomius' biographer addressed the subject of the construction of monasticism. Pachomius and his brethren "offered their souls and bodies to God in strict ascesis and with a befitting reverence, not only because they looked day and night to the holy Cross, but also because they saw the martyrs take up their struggles. They saw them and imitated them."[2] Monks are here described as modeling themselves on Christ and also on the martyrs. The method used is *mimesis*, or imitation, a subject which has been explored with respect to pilgrimage by Gary Vikan and Georgia Frank, and on which I have been working for several years now, in the context of Coptic monastic painting.

Martyrs are the original soldiers of Christ, and those who were in the military are often described as having transferred their allegiance from Caesar to Christ. Their role as combatants is maintained, but their enemy is now evil. The symbolic shift even applies to their clothing and weaponry, as the following passage from the martyrdom of St. Mercurius tells us. The saint is addressing the Roman emperor Decius, and says: "I have upon me the whole armor of God, and the

[2] Bohairic *Life of Pachomius*, 1; cf. A. Veilleux, trans., *Pachomian Koinonia* (Kalamazoo, Mich.: Cistercian Press, 1980), 1:24.

breastplate of faith, by means of which things I shall overcome all thy designs and all thy crafty arts."[3] That which had been physical and material is now spiritual. This shift to a spiritual realm is significant.

The monastic life surely counts among the most carefully and artificially created patterns for living in human history. Basic human needs such as speech, sleep, food, shelter, and the physical passions, are controlled and either limited or completely denied. This ritualized form of existence is intensely symbolic. The passage I read a moment ago about Pachomius and his fellow monks describes the application of *mimesis*, a practice which is central to the monastic life. The ultimate goal, of course, is the imitation of Christ, but progress towards that aim could be made by patterning oneself after other, significant exemplars. Pachomius' biographer tells us explicitly that "they saw the martyrs take up their struggles. They saw them and imitated them."

The sources tell us that a cherub addressed Macarius the Great (Figure 6), and told him:

> You will be crucified with Christ and you will join him on the cross with the virtues adorning you with their perfume, and your ascetic practices will spread to the four corners of the earth and will raise up a multitude sunk in the mire of sin and they will become warriors and soldiers in Christ's army.

This multitude consists of the men who joined Macarius and lived in Scetis as soldiers of Christ. Elsewhere, the cherub described these men as Macarius' "spiritual sons."[4]

In spiritual terms, the program of paintings in the nave of the Church of St. Antony is a genealogy. It begins with the martyrs, both equestrian and standing, at the western end. It is completed to the east, with the rows of standing monastic saints, several of whom are the spiritual descendants not only of the martyrs, but of the more

---

[3] *The Martyrdom of Saint Mercurius the General*, in E.A.W. Budge, ed. and trans., *Miscellaneous Coptic Texts in the Dialect of Upper Egypt* (London: British Museum, 1915), 817; cf. BMO 6801, fol. 10b.

[4] Edward Malone, *The Monk and the Martyr* (Washington, DC: Catholic University of America Press, 1956), 211, has the following to say on this subject: "Monastic life becomes a *militia spiritualis*, a spiritual warfare, or spiritual military service; the monk is now the soldier of Christ who goes forth to give battle for Christ against the evil spirits and the enemies of Christ in the world."

senior among the monks. Antony the Great is called the "father of monasticism," and recalling the cherub's words to Macarius the Great, that he would be the father of Scetis, a significant center of monasticism.[5] Also, according to the *Life of Macarius*, shortly before Antony's death Macarius visited him. At this time, Antony "clothed Abba Macarius in the monastic habit and this is the reason he is called the disciple of Abba Antony."[6] Macarius is one of Antony's "spiritual sons."

Several of Macarius' own spiritual progeny are included in the eastern end of the nave program, including Pishoi the Great, John the Little (Figure 7), Maximous and Domitius, and Moses the Black. Tradition tells us that all of them founded monasteries in Scetis after Macarius settled there.   These bonds of spiritual kinship, and monastic leadership, can be seen as ties connecting the figures across the three dimensional space of the nave. Antony looks out over the entire program from his privileged position on the eastern wall. Directly opposite him, on the narrow extension of wall at the middle of the nave, stands Barsum the Syrian, who is known as the "father of Syrian monks."[7] Macarius and the cherub mark the center of the northern wall, opposite his spiritual sons, Pishoi and John the Little.

Pishoi the Great and John the Little are located next to each other on the south wall (Figure 7), and provide an interesting example of the subtle character of the narrative elements embedded in these paintings. Pishoi and John lived in the fourth and early fifth centuries, and were contemporaries of Macarius the Great. They were bound to each other in spiritual friendship,[8] and so are shown side by side, and across the nave from the other monastic founders of Scetis. Pishoi stands facing straight ahead, with his hands in the attitude of prayer. He is distinguished from the monks flanking him by a bust-length figure of Christ, who appears from between two arches at the top of the arcade, and points to Pishoi. This gesture immediately conveys the idea that Christ has singled Pishoi out for greatness, but it also

[5] A. Cody, "Scetis," in *The Coptic Encyclopedia*, ed. Aziz S. Atiya (New York: Macmillan, 1991), 7:2103.

[6] T. Vivian, "Virtues of St. Macarius," in idem, trans., *Disciples of the Soul's Beloved: St. Macarius the Spirit Bearer* (vol. 2) (Louvain: Peeters, forthcoming).

[7] D. O'Leary, *The Saints of Egypt* (New York: Macmillan, 1937), 99.

[8] R.-G. Coquin, "Pishoi of Scetis," in *The Coptic Encyclopedia*, ed. Aziz S. Atiya (New York: Macmillan, 1991), 6:2029.

refers to the fact that Christ appeared to Pishoi several times, even permitting the saint to wash his feet.[9]

Prior to the cleaning of the paintings in the nave, the image now known to us as John the Little was unidentified.[10] Pishoi and John stand within a four-part arcade, with two other saints, Sisoes/Shishoi, and Arsenius. Their heads reach a roughly even height within the arches. John's significantly shorter figure manages to reach the same general height of the other three because he is standing on a small hill! His short stature is an identifying element. Other features in this painting of John the Little are encoded with meaning. The small flowering tree adjacent to his left foot refers to the decisive moment when what may well be John's most famous miracle occurred. John's spiritual advisor, Father Amoi, tested him by placing a dry stick of wood about twelve miles from his cell, and instructing John to water it daily.

> Now the water was a long way from the place where the tree was planted, but Abba John would leave with the water basin at night and he would return in the morning. He did this for three years, and the tree lived, blossomed, and brought forth fruit. The elder Abba Amoi took the fruit of the tree and brought it to the church and gave it to the elders, saying, "Take, eat from the fruit of obedience."[11]

Hopefully, I have presented enough evidence for you to see the significance of my alliterative group for this painted program: *mimesis*, martyrdom, and monasticism.   Martyrs are the spiritual forerunners of the monks.   The monks model themselves on the martyrs.   These ascetics in turn establish a spiritual genealogy as monasticism grows, following the model of the father of monasticism, Antony the Great, and becoming his spiritual sons. Most of the monks shown in this program were Egyptians, which seems fitting, in this church established where Antony is believed to have lived out the last days of his life.   The martyrs were either

---

[9] Coquin, "Pishoi," 2029–2030.

[10] P. Van Moorsel, *Les Peintures du Monastère de Saint-Antoine près de la Mer Rouge* (Cairo: Institut Français d'Archéologie Orientale, 1995), 1:133–134.

[11] Zacharias of Sakhâ, *Encomium on the Life of John the Little*, §§25 and 31, in M.S. Mikhail and T. Vivian, "Zacharias of Sakhâ: An Encomium on the Life of John the Little," *Coptic Church Review* 18 (1997), 1-64, at 31 and 33.

Egyptian, or were buried or particularly venerated in Egypt. A
prominent example is Menas, whose pilgrimage site in the desert to
the west of Alexandria was for centuries, and is again, drawing
countless pilgrims. All of the martyrs and monks included in the
program are men. This seems to be typical of Coptic paintings after
about the sixth or seventh century, and is in contrast to the common
practice in the Byzantine realm of depicting holy women. Martyrdom
and monasticism, at least in the context of Antony's monastery, is
gendered exclusively male.

Mimesis can be understood as the material that forges the
genealogical chain. This chain links those now living in Christ, in
other words the martyrs and deceased monks, to those who in the
thirteenth century were living in the flesh, and following in Antony's
footsteps – physically, at this site, and spiritually. The patterns of
their way of life reiterate its mimetic ties to Christ, the martyrs, and
senior monks. The accounts of the *Apophthegmata Patrum* and
martyrdoms were read and copied through the centuries, and
informed the selection of these paintings. The prominence of the
founding fathers of Scetis in this program is a thirteenth-century
visual assertion of their significance in the development of Coptic
monasticism.

Within this physical, ritual, and textual setting for *mimesis*, I
would like to briefly expand on the significant role of the paintings, to
their original audience. Too often scholars privilege texts over
images, a practice which I, as an art historian, understandably find
limiting. Two thirteenth-century Coptic authors address the function
of images in churches. Abu al-Hair ibn al-Tayyib describes the effect
on the Christian viewer of seeing paintings of the martyrs. These
models strengthen their faith, and prepare them to hold fast to it, even
to the point of death, should anyone attempt to persuade them to
convert.[12] Al-Mu'taman abu Ishaq al-'Assal devotes a whole chapter
of his *Treatise on Religion* to "the paintings of images in churches,
models of those they represent, in order that one [in other words, the
viewer] remembers them and asks them for their intercession with
God."[13] The paintings illustrate the lives of the holy exemplars

[12] Abu l-Hair ibn al-Tayyib, *Le Remède de l'Intelligence*, in U. Zanetti, "Les Icones
chez les Théologiens de l'Église Copte," *Le Monde Copte* 19 (1991), 78–79.
[13] Al-Mu'taman abu Ishaq al-'Assal, *Somme des Aspects de la Religion*, in Zanetti,
"Les Icones," 79–80.

depicted, and have as primary a role in presenting them for imitation as do the textual accounts of their lives.

I will end this paper with a very brief mention of the role of the Virgin Mary in this painted program (Figure 5), and in the network of *mimesis*, martyrs, and monks. While a very small number of women are included in the diminutive narrative events taking place under the hooves of the martyrs' horses, Mary is the only woman to be depicted in the larger size. Her position is significant on the eastern nave wall, balancing that of Antony. She too is an exemplar for martyrs and monks, as the one who bore Christ, and who was both obedient and a virgin.[14] Additionally, Cyril of Alexandria describes her as filling a role that accounts perfectly for her position here in this visual genealogy, balancing that of the father of monasticism. Cyril states that she is "the mother of all the monks and all the nuns."[15]

---

[14] G. Ladner, "Anthropology of Gregory of Nyssa," *Dumbarton Oaks Papers* 12 (1958), 88-94.
[15] Cyril of Alexandria, "Discourse on the Virgin Mary," in Budge, *Miscellaneous Coptic Texts*, 720; cf. BMO 6782, fols.32b1–32b2.

Figure 1: General view of the nave, western end (photo by Elizabeth S. Bolman)

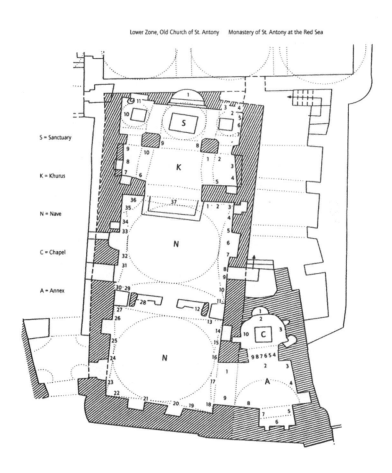

Figure 2: Plan, Church of St. Antony, by Peter Sheehan, from a survey conducted by
Mallinson Architects, © The American Research Center in Egypt

Figure 3: Theodore Stratelates (photo by Elizabeth S. Bolman)

Figure 4: Western end of nave, standing figures on southern wall
(photo by Elizabeth S. Bolman)

Figure 5: Eastern end of nave, with Virgin Mary and Antony
(photo by Elizabeth S. Bolman)

Figure 6: Macarius the Great with the cherub (photo by Elizabeth S. Bolman)

Figure 7: Pishoi and John the Little (photo by Elizabeth S. Bolman)

On the Architecture at Wādī al-Naṭrūn

Peter Grossmann

About the architectural characteristics of the monasteries of Scetis (Wādī al-Naṭrūn) is at present not much to say. Contrary to the conditions of the *lauras* in Kellia, the known dwellings of the monks of Scetis are until now not seriously studied. Among the completely or partly excavated examples only one *kellion*, or МА Ṅ(Ṣ)ШШПЄ,[1] as it is called in the Coptic language, has been accurately surveyed. This is the so-called "Monastery of the Armenians." It is dated to the ninth century, based on pottery evidence,[2] and thus not very informative for the earlier examples. Some other houses traceable in the neighborhood of the Syrian Monastery and Dayr al-Baramūs were only superficially studied, and the dates are not known at all.

However, at least some information about them can be gained from the written sources. It appears that already, from the beginning, the cells of the individual monks were composed of several rooms, a fact that was valid all over Egypt.[3] According to the *Life of Makarios* 76, erroneously ascribed to Sarapion of Thmuis (fourth century), already the first cell of Makarios in Scetis was composed of two rooms, of which one served for living and sleeping, while the other was a little chapel where he – as it is expressed in the text – "received the benediction,"[4] an obvious indication that it served for the celebration of the eucharist and – since he was at that time the only inhabitant of the region – makes it clear that he had already by that

---

[1] By modern Copts usually used in the Arabic version *manshubiyya*. See M. al-Miskîn, "Dayr Anbā Maqār," in *The Coptic Encyclopedia*, ed. Aziz S. Atiya (New York: Macmillan, 1991), 3:749.

[2] As suggested by Darlene Brooks Hedstrom, who examined the pottery in the field.

[3] P. Grossmann, *Christliche Architektur in Agypten* (Leiden: Brill, 2002), 261f.

[4] *Life of Makarios*, ed. and trans. E. Amélineau, *Monuments pour servir à l'histoire de l'Égypte chrétienne* (Paris, Ernest Leroux, 1894), 46-117, at 76. According to the French translation of Amélineau, "...il creusa deux cavernes dans le rocher; en l'une d'elles il fit un tabernacle, du côté de l'est, afin d'y prendre la bénédiction."

time achieved the status of a priest.[5]   The size of the chapel is
described as so small that apart of him hardly anybody else could
have found a place in it. Also from what was written about the cell of
Isidor, the famous priest of the *laura* of Baramūs, we can understand
that it had several rooms. The *apophthegma* 415 (Isidor 7) informs us
that he used to hide himself in the most interior corner of his cell
when certain visitors were looking for him – a flight which would not
have made sense if his cell had consisted of only one room.
Concerning the architectural performance of the kellia in Scetis we
learn from *apophthegma* 486 (Makarios 34) that they were – at least
in the early period – built of stone rubble (instead of crude bricks as
in Kellia) with ceilings supported by wooden beams, a material which
was not available in Kellia.   The distribution of the houses form
widely spread *laures*, as they are to be met also in other regions.
When the large monastic settlement of Kellia was founded, the two
founders Ammon and Antony took care that the houses of the
brethrens stood far enough from the others that they could not hear
them (*Apophthegmata Patrum* [*AP*] 34; [Antony 34]), a rule which
was considered also elsewhere.   However, somewhat unique is the
development in medieval times when the inhabitants of several *laures*
in Wādī al-Naṭrūn decided to reduce their extension and surrounded
the remaining rest with tall fortification walls. The advice to do so
was at first given by the Patriarch Šinūdā I (859-880) to the
inhabitants of the *laura* of St. Makarios.   But other monk
communities copied this idea. This was an essential decision and the
laures who did not follow this example, as the ones of Kellia and
Nitria, perished.

On the other hand, some of the churches in Wādī al-Naṭrūn
belong to the earliest churches in Egypt still in use. The 'Adhrā'
church of the Baramūs Monastery is a building of the time of
Patriarch Damianos (577/8-606/7), as it appears also by its name
devoted to the Holy Virgin, and the 'Adhrā' church of the Syrian
Monastery is, according to al-Maqrīzī (d. 1441), a building of the
time of the Patriarch Benjamin (627-665). The latter church is also
the earliest example with a fully integrated *khūrus*.   With all

---

[5] Cf. P. Grossmann, "Zur Datierung der ersten Kirchenbauten in der Sketis,"
Byzantinische Zeitschrift 90 (1997), 367-395, especially 369f and nn. 22 and 33; a
different view holds H. G. Evelyn White, *The Monasteries of the Wâdi 'n Natrûn*, 3
vols. (New York: Metropolitan Museum of Art, 1926-1933), 2:66 n. 5 and 2:69.

probability the idea of its introduction originates from the same Patriarch Benjamin.

But before entering into the descriptions of other monk cells, some geographical facts of the Wādī al-Naṭrūn have to be made clear. Contrary to the impression of every modern visitor who sees the area of Wādī al-Naṭrūn today, supporting as it does intensively cultivated and green areas situated roughly halfway between Alexandria and Cairo, the area in antiquity was a rather poorly fertile oasis with some lakes of brackish water lying relatively far from the irrigated and cultivated regions of the country. In some areas the government extracted salt from the ground. Apparently a caravan route passed through the oasis and it is possible that there were some rest houses along the road. The only known village in the area is a hamlet named Shiît,[6] Coptic ϢΙΗⲦ, the name of which developed in Greek sources into Σκῆτι,[7] thus giving the name to the monastic settlement after Makarios the Egyptian had started to live here.[8]

To avoid confusion, I shall briefly explain in which sense I intend to use certain words. The word 'monastery' (μοναστήριον; Latin monasterium), as we are accustomed to use it today, is unfortunately a very imprecise term. In early Christian sources it means the habitation of one single monk. The corresponding meaning has the Latin word 'cella' out of which the Greek expression 'kellion' (κελλίον) derived. A group or settlement of several monasteries or kellia inhabited by hermits is a 'laura' (λαύρα), which means a narrow street, lane, and it probably derived from the monastic settlements in Palestine, where the kellia are usually distributed as a chain on both sides of a narrow wādī. Monasteries in which the monks live according to certain defined rules, as the Pachomian monks did in close community with special living houses, named with letters taken from the Greek alphabet, and having a refectory and common working rooms and so forth, are 'coenobia' (κοινόβια). None is known to have existed in the Wādī al-Naṭrūn.

---

[6] Life of Makarios, 56.

[7] Ptolemy, On Geography, 4.5.12, uses also the name σκιατικὴ χώρα.

[8] White, Monasteries, 2:27ff, tried to find for this name a spiritual origin, which is, however, not persuading.

The modern monks who adopted certain customs from the cenobitic lifestyle practice only a semi-cenobitic way of asceticism.

The first monastic settlement in Wādī al-Naṭrūn was founded in the area now occupied by the Monastery of Baramūs or "Monastery of the Romans" (ⲚⲢⲰⲘⲈⲞⲤ), as it appears in Coptic sources. It was probably in the neighborhood of this site that the village of Shiît was located. A number of early monks' cells, being quite openly distributed, are still traceable in the ground.[9] The earliest of them, which under the present unexcavated conditions can, of course, not be distinguished from the others, were apparently not very different from the earliest monks' cells discovered in the Quṣūr ʿĪsā in Kellia (Figure 1). They were for a deep part dug into the ground[10] and covered with a kind of wooden roof from the trees surrounding the brackish lakes of the oasis.[11]

Apparently, as already said, from the very beginning these monastic cells comprised several rooms each. All early Egyptian monks' cells, of which contemporary descriptions survive in the written sources, comprise several rooms.[12] Examples of monks who had no shelter, as they are known from Syria, are rarely recorded in

---

[9] See the example surveyed by Bishop Samuel: S. el-Souriani, "Bâtiments monastiques anciens au Wâdî Natrûn," *Le Monde Copte* 21-22 (1993), 246ff and figure 2.

[10] P. Corboud, "L'oratoire et les niches-oratoires: Les lieux de la priere," in P. Bridel, ed., *Le site monastique copte des Kellia : Sources historiques et explorations archéologiques. Actes du Colloque de Genève 13 au 15 août 1984* (Geneva : Mission Suisse d'Archéologie Copte, 1986), 85-92, especially 86ff.

[11] An example of this kind in Wādī Naṭrūn, opposite the actual Dayr al-Suryān, was excavated and restored by Bishop Samuel; cf. el-Souriani, "Bâtiments," 247ff. and figure 3. The restoration of this building, as carried out by P. Badia, cannot however be accepted. The cell was dug deeply into the ground with an access by a stairway from the east. The few traces of masonry extant above ground level between the different rooms are everywhere slightly recessed from the inner sides of the rooms (not indicated in the plan), giving thus space for the bearing-surface of a number of wooden beams for the ceiling. The reconstruction of domes upon those masonry traces appears to us as erroneous.

[12] The description of a cell with several rooms in *AP* 415 (Isidor 7), since Isidor could escape into the most interior place of his *kellion* (and thus presupposing that it was composed of several rooms), appears to be something quite normal.

Egyptian sources.[13]   Apparently one of the rooms of these cells was always devoted to prayer. Makarios, as we have seen, had already established from the very beginning, a separate unit for the preparation of the eucharist. But, it might be the case that, at least in the early period, the prayer rooms of ordinary monks served simultaneously as working rooms and reception rooms to receive guests.[14]   Nowhere in the *AP*, which is an excellent source for the daily life of the early monks in Egypt, and which contains many records of the habits of the monks connected with their prayers, is it ever mentioned that monks went into another or even into a special room to perform their individual prayers. The same results from the observation that, when a visitor called on a praying monk, his visitor usually waited outside the door, which means that the prayer of the monk, who is inside of his cell, took place in the first room.

Usually the cells were meant for one monk. But soon many of these monks received disciples. Some even had several disciples. According to the *apophthegma* 526 (Markos 1) Silvanos had eleven disciples. The new comers chose their masters either by themselves, or the *hegumenos* of the community appointed the disciple to one of the elder monks. The first duty of the new comer was then to built his own cell, perhaps with the help of somebody else, in the neighborhood of his master. The *apophthegma* 486 (Makarios 33) contains some technical advice on such details as how the walls and the roof should be built. This advice was also given to the two well known newcomers, who were described as two well educated fellows, obviously not accustomed in physical labor. They are the ones who the later legend identified with the pair Dometios and Maximos. It is never recorded, except in a very few cases, whether the disciple was the physical son of the elder, or whether a disciple was going to live in the same cell as the elder. The latter might have been the case only for the very first days when the new cell was still under

---

[13] The case, recorded in the Coptic collection of the *AP* 272, that a novice was sitting in the sand for three years to receive a cell, is exceptional; see M. Chaîne, ed., *Le manuscrit de la version copte en dialect sahidique des "Apophthegmata Patrum"* (Cairo: Institut Français d'Archéologie Orientale, 1960), 153.

[14] See also H. Quecke, "Gebet und Gottesdienst der Mönche nach den Texten," in Bridel, *Le site monastique,* 93-103.

construction.[15]   In some cases, however, the newcomer could make use of an empty cell left by its former inhabitant who had either left or died.

Until the second pontificate of the Patriarch Petros II (373/75 and 378/80) when the disturbances caused by the Arian Patriarch Lucios (375-378) at the see of Alexandria during which Makarios the Egyptian, then *hegumenos* in Scetis for the first time, and several other monks were banished to Palestine, came to an end, only one *laura* of monks, surrounding the actual Dayr al-Baramūs, existed in the Wādī al-Naṭrūn.   After this event and his return to Scetis, Makarios founded a new *laura* several miles further to the south in the region of the actual Monastery of Abū Maqār (Figure 2), in the name of which the circumstances of its origin are still recorded. And it might be that the *laura* of John Kolobos, situated in the region surrounding the two monasteries Dayr Anbā Bishūy and Dayr al-Suryān was founded at about the same time. Also, numerous early monk cells are traceable in this region (Figure 3). A number of them were surveyed some decades ago by Bishop Samuel,[16] but we have no precise idea of the date of these buildings.

Meanwhile, at least to the fifth or even sixth century these three *laures* were the only monastic settlements in the region understood today as the Wādī al-Naṭrūn. A fourth one, which is mentioned in several sources of the late fouth and early fifth century and named after Moses the Black, was situated considerably further in the desert. It is not impossible to identify it with the settlement at Jabal Ḥashm al-Quʿūd[17] (Figure 4), which was discovered by Omar Toussoun several decades ago, but wrongly identified by him as the site of Kellia. The monk Pishoi or Bishūy (Greek Paesios) after whom the actual Dayr Anbā Bishūy is named, was not the founder of a *laura*. According to the fourth century sources Pišoi lived alone in the desert, far from all the other monastic settlements, as described by

---

[15] Palladios, *Lausiac History* 2, mentions a monk named Dorotheos, who built a cell every year for somebody else. This reference should not be misunderstood to mean that he needed a year's work to finish one cell.

[16] el-Souriani, " Bâtiments," 247ff. and figs. 3-7.

[17] R.-G. Coquin and M. Martin, "Jabal Khashm al-Quʿūd," in *Coptic Encyclopedia* 4:1315-1316. On the site itself, see O. Toussoun, *Notes sur le Désert lybique: "Cellia" et ses couvents* (Alexandria : Société de publications égyptiennes, 1935).

John Cassian, who visited the *laures* of Scetis during the last decade of the fourth century.[18]

"When the aged John (Kolobos), who was superior of a large monastery and a quantity of brethren, had come to visit the aged Paesios [our Pishoi] who was living in a vast desert, and had been asked of him as of a very old friend, what he had done in all the forty years in which he had been separated from him and had scarcely ever been disturbed in his solitude by the brethren,[19] he said: "Never has the sun seen me eating." No doubt only a person who really lives alone can give such an answer.

The living conditions of the monks changed drastically when the monasteries became the target of nomadic raids. All the Wādī al-Naṭrūn monasteries witnessed several attacks of this kind.[20] The monks who could flee used this chance, but many became victims of these raids, and often the area remained devastated for several years. The first method introduced to overcome such raids was to build high towers such as were already used for similar reasons by ordinary civilian inhabitants of some remote areas. These towers consisted of several floors with an entrance positioned, for security reasons at the level of the first floor, rather than ground level. Access was by a ladder or, as in later examples, via a separate staircase tower, which was connected with the proper tower by a draw-bridge, as demonstrated by the surviving examples in all the monasteries of Wādī al-Naṭrūn.[21] The erection of these towers was based on the experience that the nomadic raiders would usually not stay for long periods in the area of their plundering. Therefore, in the earlier periods at least, nothing more was needed for their defense. The earliest towers were even not provided with reservoirs of water. However, not all the monks felt the need to save their earthly lives in such towers. The story of what happened during the raid of AD 444 at the foot of the tower on the rock of Piamun, as recorded in the *Synaxarium* of the 26th Tubah (21 January) is well known. While the

---

[18] John Cassian, *Institutes* 5.27.

[19] John Cassian, *Institutes* 5.27: "... *separatus in solitudine minime a fratribus interpellatus est.*"

[20] The main raids are listed in White, *Monasteries,* 2:151ff.

[21] A general study on the towers in monasteries was given by U. Monneret de Villard, *Deyr el-Muḥarraqah: Note archeologiche* (Milan: Tip. e libreria pontifica e arcivescovile S. Giuseppe, 1928), 28ff. and figs. 3-9 and 14-25.

majority of the monks found shelter in this tower, 49 others lost their lives. The latter followed the call of an aged monk, named Anba Ionas (Younis), to receive martyrdom with him. His words, as translated by René Basset into French were, "Ils sont arrivés et ils ne veulent que notre mort: que quiconque désire le martyre se tienne avec moi, et que quiconque a peur monte dans la Tour."[22]

After the very serious raids in the middle of the ninth century which are described in detail also in the *History of the Patriarchs*, compiled by Sawīrūs ibn al-Muqaffaʻ,[23] the Patriarch Šinūdā I (859-880), who himself has been a former monk of the Makarios *laura*,[24] advised the monks of this *laura* to surround their area with a high and strong protection wall,[25] because during the occasion of this raid the towers and the walls existing until that date – even that mentioned in the life of John Khamé (eighth century) – proved to be ineffective.[26] The idea itself was not new. The Monastery of St. Catherine in Sinai had already received such a wall with the help of the Emperor Justinian I (527-565) in the middle of the sixth century.[27] The monks of the

---

[22] The whole story is recorded also by White, *Monasteries*, 2:38 and 164-167. See also the anonymous report, S.de Ricci and E.O. Winstedt, ed. and trans., "Les quarante-neuf vieillards de Scété," *Notices et extraits* 39 (1916), 323-358, especially 348 (folio 1).

[23] *History of the Patriarchs* 2:1 (fol 125r): "The Beduins did not cease pillaging the cells (κελλίον) of the monks and the monasteries, because their dwellings and their men were there in the wādī, [where] they were camping, so that they [the monks] dwelt in the keeps and the sanctuaries (σκυνή) and they built up the door-ways of their dwellings. They [the Beduins] used to lie in wait for the time when they [the monks] used to go out and to draw water, and they slew some of them and took from others what they found on them in the way of clothes and the water-skins in which they carried water."

[24] *History of the Patriarchs* 2:1.

[25] *History of the Patriarchs* 2:1 (fol. 126v): "In his great care for the Holy Desert, ... he [the patriarch] resolved to build a fortified wall round the Catholic church [of Abu Maqar]. He did this that it might become a cave and a fortress... He collected much stone and carried on the work assiduously until it was finished with towers. He made in it dwelling-places and elevated places in the shortest space of time..."

[26] See M. Davis, ed. and trans., *Life of Abba John Khamé*. Patrologia Orientalis 14 (Paris: Firmin-Didot, 1920), 317-342, especially 346 and 352ff.

[27] G.H. Forsyth, "The Monastery of St. Catherine at Mount Sinai: The Church and Fortress of Justinian." *Dumbarton Oaks Papers* 22 (1968), 1-19; see more recently my

Monastery of St. Makarios followed the advice of Patriarch Šinūdā, and several others followed their example.

Of course, the whole area of a *laura* of that time could never have been completely surrounded with a wall. Only a certain area around the church, the catholic church,[28] as mentioned in the source,[29] was fortified. The cells of the monks living outside of this area had to be abandoned and new cells of considerably smaller sizes built inside that fortification. Thus the monks had to surrender a large part of their former freedom. Instead of their previous self-sufficiency, common meals in a refectory were introduced and the different *horae* of the day were now performed in community. But by no means were all the former habits of the monks given up. They changed their style of life only to a semi-cenobitic system. On the other hand, these fortifications of the monasteries in the Wādī al-Naṭrūn were a complete success. The communities that built such walls have survived to the present day. Those who did not follow this example, such as those of Kellia and Nitria, perished.

Some remarkable facts are also observable in Wādī al-Naṭrūn with the churches. According to the written sources, at the end of the fourth century all the four *laures* in Scetis had their own churches. However, we do not know what these churches looked like. But, there is hope that at the site of the so-called Monastery of Moses the Black, to the north of Dayr al-Baramūs, where Karel Inneméé from Leiden University is undertaking excavations, remains of a fourth century church will be discovered. This site can reasonably be identified with the place where the church of Isidor stood;[30] he together with Makarios the general *hegumenos* of all the *laures* in Scetis was one of the first priests of Sketis. But the remains of such a church have not yet come to light.

At the site called Dayr Anbā John the Little (an incorrect translation of his real name, John Kolobos, which means John the

---

contribution in K.A. Manafis, ed., *Sinai: Treasures of the Monastery of Saint Catherine* (Athens: Ekdotike Athenon, 1990), 30ff. and figure 1.

[28] Which means 'general church' in the sense of 'main church.' Still today in all Greek monasteries the main church is labeled the καθολικόν.

[29] *History of the Patriarchs* 2:1 (fol. 126v) and White, *Monasteries* 2:327ff.

[30] P. Grossmann, "Zur Identifizierung des Dair al-Baramûs im Wâdî Natrûn," *Bulletin de la Societé d'archéologie Copte* 32 (1993), 85-88.

Dwarf) where for a couple of years an American Mission under the leadership of Bas van Elderen has been excavating, remains of a considerably earlier building were encountered in a sort of crypt below the floor of a rather late basilica at the center of the site (Figure 5).[31] As far as can be seen already, it consists of an apparently larger and perhaps square unit in the west and an axially placed smaller chamber in the east. Both units are connected with a relatively large centrally placed opening. Further to the north of the smaller eastern room there is another small room, which actually serves as the entrance shaft from the upper church. There is a door between both eastern rooms and there was another, now blocked, leading from this northern chamber into the larger unit in the west. According to the spatial arrangement of this earlier building, is seems rather reasonable to interpret this as a small early church. The central room in the east, if this interpretation is right, could have been the altar chamber, while the room to the north would have been the northern side chamber (*pastophorium*). It is even possible that a southern side chamber also existed.

Unfortunately no datable material has been discovered so far to be sure whether this older church could be a building from the last quarter of the fourth century. But from the architectural point of view there are no arguments to speak against such a date. In its structure, it is not very different from the early northern church of Quṣūr 'Īsā 1 in Kellia (Figure 6), which is dated to the last decade of the fourth century.[32]

If we compare these early monastic churches with some non-monastic churches from towns and larger villages (unfortunately remains from Alexandria do not survive), certain differences are immediately apparent. A town church of somewhat similar date is

---

[31] Bishop Samuel and P. Grossmann, "Researches in the Laura of John Kolobos (Wâdî Natrûn)," in S. Emmel et al., eds., *Akten des 6. Internationalen Koptologenkongresses, Münster, 20.-26. Juli 1996* (Wiesbaden: Reichert Verlag, 1999), 1:360-364, especially 360ff. and figure 2, without the indication of the underground chambers.

[32] G. Descœudres, "L'architecture des ermitages et des sanctuaires," in Y. Mottier and N. Bosson, eds., *Les Kellia: Ermitages coptes en Basse-Égypte. Musée d'art et d'histoire, Genève, 12 octobre 1989-7 janvier 1990* (Geneva : Editions du Tricorne, 1989) 33-55, especially 48 and figure 32. The plan of this church is also published in R. Kasser et al., eds., *Survey archéologique des Kellia (Basse-Égypte): Rapport de la campagne 1981* (Louvain: Peeters, 1983), vol. 1, plate 2, but without explanation.

the one in the south-eastern *suburbium* of Leucaspis (modern Marīnat al-'Alamayn) beside the Mediterranean Sea, dated by the excavators to the fourth century.[33] It is a small, accurately proportioned three-aisled basilica (Figure 7) with a vaulted apse, two side chambers and several units at the western entrance side. Everything in this church has been built of ashlar masonry. The bases of the columns, resting on a slightly elevated *stylobate*, are round and carefully profiled. Tectonic details of the architecture have been carefully observed and brought into shape at other positions also. As examples in the outer walls, the foundations are clearly distinguished from the *toichobates* and the upper portions of the walls. The churches in the monasteries, on the other hand, are rough irregular structures of unbaked brick-masonry sunk partly into the ground. There is no tectonic articulation and only some very simple cornices are to be seen. The proportions of the buildings are unbalanced and rough. This general situation also reflects the well known anecdote of Pachomios, recorded in the *Vita Altera*,[34] who, after having constructed his first church in the monastery in Pbow (Latin Pabau; modern Fāw qiblī) and realizing afterwards that it seemed too beautiful, damaged it intentionally in order that his monks would not like it too much and become proud of it. The early monks all over Egypt did not want to pray and celebrate the liturgy in richly decorated churches. In general then, the monks, or at least their abbots, did not wish their churches to be understood as monuments, but merely as roofed constructions, in which to perform their services. There are among the monasteries of Egypt only a few exceptions to this understanding of church architecture. For the main examples for the latter kind one should point out the churches of the two monasteries near modern Sūhāǧ, of Dayr Anbā Shinūdā and Dayr Anbā Bishūy.[35] In contrast, the three superimposed churches of the Pachomian monastery of Pbow are large in size, but simple in their architectural execution.[36] Until the

---

[33] E. Luzyniecka, "Architecture of the early Christian basilica in Marīna al-'Alamayn," *Architectus* 1-2 (1997), 47-57 and figure 2; redrawn recently in Grossmann, *Christlichen Architektur*, 392ff. and figure 8.

[34] *Vita Altera* 46, in F. Halkin, ed., *Sancti Pachomii vitae graecae* (Brussels: Société des Bollandistes, 1932), 166-271, especially 215.

[35] New plans of both churches are published in Grossmann, *Christlichen Architektur*, 528ff. and figs. 150-155.

[36] Grossmann, *Christlichen Architektur*, 546ff and figs. 162-163.

period of the Arab conquest it seems that no influences for the design of the town churches came from monastic churches.

But, let us return to the situation at Scetis. Apart from this single early church at the Kūm of John Kolobos, no other church was discovered so far in Wādī al-Naṭrūn, datable to the fifth or the first three quarters of the sixth century. The next dated example is building I of the 'Adhrā' church of Dayr al-Baramūs (Figure 8), erected in the time of Patriarch Damianos (577/8-606/7) probably during the early years of the seventh century and which I personally had the opportunity to excavate before the new pavement was laid. The lateral walls on the north, south and west are still standing with the remains of long sequences of wall niches,[37] now unfortunately several of them are walled up and the rest is furnished with painted modern wooden frames and doors. Also the western colonnade with its corner-pillars and engaged half-columns is still in place.[38]

The original eastern part of the church, with the sanctuary, had been demolished already in medieval times and was replaced by a new and different arrangement. But when we undertook the excavation in that church below the actual floor level, remains of the original arrangement were still in evidence. It consisted of three chambers in the east, of which the larger central one bore the altar.[39] All chambers were opened to the nave of the church, but there was originally no interconnection between them. The internal doorways, which became visible during the course of our excavation were opened only later (Figure 9). Also, a *khūrus* did not exist in the original plan. The wall now separating the *khūrus* from the nave was added at an unknown later date.

With this slightly advanced ground plan of the sanctuary having three eastern chambers and connecting openings between them, but without any traces of a *khūrus*, the church shows some similarities to a number of private monks' chapels in Kellia, of which the earliest

---

[37] White, *Monasteries*, 3:234ff. See also P. Grossmann and H.-G. Severin, "Zum antiken Bestand der al-'Adhrâ' kirche des Dair al-Baramûs im Wâdî Naṭrūn," *Mitteilungen zur Christlichen Archäologie* 3 (1997), 34ff. and figure 9; and G.J.M. van Loon, *The Gate of Heaven: Wall Paintings with Old Testament Scenes in the Altar Room and the Khurus of Coptic Churches* (Leiden: Nederlands Instituut voor het Nabije Oosten, 1999), especially 68ff. and figure 86.

[38] Grossmann and Severin, "Zum antiken," 47-51 and figs. 17-18.

[39] Grossmann and Severin, "Zum antiken," 34ff. and figure 5.

are datable to the early seventh century.[40] It seems therefore that the development of the church sanctuary followed roughly the same rules at both sites. It is also important to observe that until the beginning of the seventh century the 'Adhrā' church of Dayr al-Baramūs was not provided with a *khūrus*. Thus it can be taken for sure, that also other monastic churches in Egypt, dating to the first half of the seventh century were not equipped with a *khūrus*.

Concerning the decoration of this church, for the first time in Wādī al-Naṭrūn a little bit more than only flat walls are observable. The south-western corner-pillar with engaged quarter-columns at both sides in the western part of the church is decorated with a reused richly carved capital of stucco.[41] The pedestal of the corresponding north-western corner pillar is topped with a base which corresponds exactly with the profile of an attic base[42] as it came to be used everywhere from the Augustan period onward.[43] The triumphal arch crowning the entrance into the altar chamber and the outer doors of the church probably also received a somewhat richer decoration. In this decoration a change to a new view or a sign of an abandonment of the former attitude in the monastic architecture is recognizable.

The next step in the development can be seen in the 'Adhrā' church of Dayr al-Suryān.[44] According to al-Maqrīzī, it was constructed in the time of the Patriarch Benjamin I (627-665),[45] but it is not mentioned in the long and detailed description of Benjamin's first visit to Scetis on the occasion of the consecration of the new

---

[40] To be mentioned are the chapels of QIz 19/20, cf. Kasser et al., *Survey*, 136ff. and plates 19ff; and QIz 45 (ibid., 193ff. and plates 43ff.); while the chapel of QIz 14 (ibid., 122ff. and plate 14) was later remodeled to such a shape.

[41] Grossmann and Severin, "Zum antiken," 36f. and figure 6, and especially 47ff. and figs. 17-18.

[42] Grossmann and Severin, "Zum antiken," 36f. and figure 7.

[43] Vitruv, *On Architecture*, 3.5.2.

[44] K. Innemée et al., "New Discoveries in the al-'Adhrā' church of Dayr al-Suryān in Wādī Naṭrūn," *Mitteilungen zur Christlichen Archäologie* 4 (1998), 79-103. During the course of the actual restoration and investigation carried out by Innemée a number of new observations have been made.

[45] F. Wüstenfeld, ed. and trans., *Macrizi's Geschichte der Copten* (Göttingen: Nachdr. d. Ausg., 1845) 48, here labeled as the monastery of the Virgin of Abu Bischâi. The *History of the Patriarchs* 1:2 speaks only generally about reconstructions in the Wadi Habib (Scetis) under Benjamin without specifiing the very monuments.

church and sanctuary in the monastery of Abū Maqār,[46] as recorded by Agathon (665-681), the successor of Benjamin. It might thus have been constructed during the later part of the pontificate of Benjamin.

At the same time this church was, apparently already from its beginning, provided with a *khūrus* (Figure 10). The *khūrus* of this church is a transverse hall, in front of the sanctuary proper and separating the nave of the church from the presbytery. It is divided into three sections, separated by arches resting on engaged quarter-columns projecting out of both transverse walls. The square central section of the *khūrus* which in its full height, according to its design and the recently discovered paintings, also dates, as I was informed by Karel Innemée, to the second half of the seventh century. Even the dome is original as far as it appears from the intact original plaster. The two lateral sections of the *khūrus* are covered with half domes resting on wooden beams placed along the partition walls between the mentioned engaged quarter-columns and the outer walls.

Remains of the seventh century sanctuary do not survive. We are aware only of the fact of its division into three different chambers, of which the larger central one was with all probability furnished with the altar. Of the lateral rooms we know only the widths, but not their lengths. The entrances consisted in both cases of two little doors right in the corners. However, the width of the central chamber corresponds rather well with the width of the lateral sections of the *khūrus*. It is thus not to be excluded, that it was also shaped in the same manner, forming in this way together with those the overlapping architectural form of a triconch.[47]

The connection of the *khūrus* with the nave of the church consists of a central, tall, and arched opening, which could be closed by a door. Our former assumption that the doorjambs were decorated with engraved quarter-columns in the two frontal corners[48] could not be confirmed by later investigations. Whether a smaller second door was originally extant at the northern or southern end of the partition

---

[46] R.-G. Coquin, ed. and trans., *Livre de la consécration du sanctuaire de Benjamin.* Bibliothèque d'Etudes Coptes 13 (Cairo: Institut français d'archéologie orientale, 1975), 103.

[47] A suggestion which was communicated to me by K.C. Innemée.

[48] P. Grossmann, *Mittelalterliche Langhauskuppelkirchen und verwandte Typen in Oberägypten: eine Studie zum mittelalterlichen Kirchenbau in Ägypten* (Glückstadt: J.J. Augustin, 1982), 115ff. and figure 47.

wall, we do not know. The side of this wall of the *khūrus* facing the nave shows two half-columns flanking the central door and two engaged three-quarter-columns occupying the positions of two ordinary *antae* in correspondence with the colonnades of the nave. The arrangement of all these engaged columns offer to the visitors standing in the nave an aspect, which bears some similarities with the eastern colonnade which in earlier churches before the invention of the *khūrus* formed the eastern end of the nave.[49] It might thus have been intentionally arranged in this way, which would also explain the unusual presence of the two lateral engaged three-quarter-columns which, on the other hand, have no tradition in Egyptian architecture.[50]

This *khūrus* in the 'Adhrā' church of Dayr al-Suryān is one of the earliest examples in Egypt we know. How did it come into being? It is possible that some changes in the liturgy, concerning the movements of the clerics are responsible for this innovation. But how did this occur? The note of al-Maqrīzī is informative here, stating that the Patriarch Benjamin I was engaged in the building and consecration of this church. We know that from the time of the re-conquest of Syria and Egypt by the Roman Emperor Heraclius in 628 until the Arab conquest in 639/42 Benjamin was in hiding in the Monastery of Anbā Shinūdā near Athribis in Upper Egypt in order to avoid any encounter with the Chalcedonian Patriarch Kyros (630-643).[51] At the same time, the monks of that monastery were occupied with repairs to the damage from the Persian invasion of 619/29. These repairs were carried out in exactly the same way as the original church was built (Figure 11). The only difference was that bricks were used instead of limestone-blocks for ashlar masonry. Such a fidelity to the shape of an earlier building occurred very rarely in ancient architecture and merits special attention. It seems possible, that Benjamin who resided at that time in this monastery convinced

---

[49] Grossmann, *Christliche Architektur*, 28ff.

[50] P. Grossmann, "Altägyptische Elemente in der frühchristlichen Baukunst Ägyptens," in H. Guksch and D. Polz, eds., *Stationen: Beiträge zur Kulturgeschichte Ägyptens. Rainer Stadelmann gewidmet* (Mainz: P. von Zabern, 1998), 443-458, especially 449f.

[51] P. Grossmann, "Der Bericht Benjamins I über den Mönch Isidor und was an historischen Nachrichten in diesem Bericht enthalten ist," in Cäcilia Fluck et al., eds., *Divitiae Aegypti: Koptologische und verwandte Studien zu Ehren von Martin Krause* (Wiesbaden: Reichert Verlag, 1995), 128-133, especially 133ff.

the local monks not to make any changes, but keep the building as it was created by Shenute, the famous abbot of this monastery.[52] Such advice would suit very much the usual attitude of Benjamin, as it is known to us from several sources.[53] Only in one detail was the original design of the church changed. The eastern colonnade of the nave was not re-erected. It was replaced by a huge transverse wall, of which at the foot of the actual *khūrus* wall, some courses of bricks are still in evidence. They include two large projecting western buttresses serving as *antae* to stabilize the connection with the lateral colonnades of the nave.[54] These remains point to the fact that, together with the rebuilding of this church after the Persian invasion, a *khūrus* was introduced into the architectural program of the church, and also that Patriarch Benjamin I might have been responsible for this innovation.

Thus it appears that the introduction of the *khūrus* into Egyptian church architecture is directly connected with the personality of the Patriarch Benjamin. The idea, which stood behind this was to create a greater separation of the clerics from the lay brothers, a movement which is observable also in some contemporary liturgical innovations in the church.[55] Since the 'Adhrā' church of Dayr al-Suryān is the first church we know to have been built after the Arab conquest it is thus also the first church which was built with a *khūrus* from its beginning. The example was soon copied in other monastic churches as in the church of the monastery of Apa Jeremias at Saqqāra[56] and the 'Adhrā' church of Dayr al-Baramūs in Wādī al-Naṭrūn.[57] Until the Mamluk period which brought yet another serious change in the development of Egyptian church architecture, there exists virtually no monastic church in Egypt not provided with a *khūrus*.

On the other hand, the *khūrus* entered only slowly into the architectural program of the non-monastic churches. It is only in

---

[52] Grossmann, *Christliche Architektur*, 528-536, especially 533ff.

[53] What we know about Benjamin has been collected by C.D.G. Müller, "Benjamin I, 38. Patriarch von Alexandrien," *Le Muséon* 69 (1956), 313-340.

[54] Grossmann, *Christliche Architektur*, 534f. and figure 152A.

[55] Personal communication of Hansgerd Brakmann.

[56] P. Grossmann and H.-G. Severin, "Reinigungsarbeiten im Jeremiaskloster bei Saqqara. Vierter vorläufiger Bericht," *Mitteilungen des Deutschen Archäologischen Instituts Abteilung Kairo* 38 (1982), 155-193, especially 159ff. and figure 2.

[57] Grossmann and Severin, "Zum antiken," 42f. and figure 13.

some churches in the Baḥarīya Oasis that several examples are known.[58] One of the few examples known from Egypt proper is the five-aisled basilica at Abū Mīnā built by the Patriarch Michael I (744-768). [59]

In the Wādī al-Naṭrūn the *khūrus* is also extant in a number of more recent churches, as for example in the church of Sitt Miryam of Dayr al-Suryān[60] and in the churches of Dayr Abū Maqār.[61] The *khūrus* remained in use until the introduction of sanctuaries with several altar chambers, which occurred from the beginning of the Mamluk period (the middle of the 13th century) onward,[62] in consequence of which the *khūrus* lost its sense.[63] However, in several surviving churches only the sanctuary was changed while the *khūrus* remained unaltered.[64]

But, there are also some exceptions of this development. The church of the so-called Monastery of the Armenians, datable to the ninth century, as mentioned before, has a large altar-chamber, two openly connected side chambers, but no traces of a *khūrus*. The sanctuary is raised by two steps above the level of the nave, as is usually the case in Greek and other eastern churches.[65] Did this church belong from its beginning to a foreign congregation which did not have the tradition of a *khūrus*? I hope that some further investigations will bring light into this question.

---

[58] P. Grossmann and Zahi Hawass, "Recent discoveries in al-Haiz, Bahria Oasis," *Bulletin de la Societé d'archéologie Copte* 32 (1993), 87-110, especially 95ff. and figs. 2-3; P. Grossmann, "Ein spätantikes Gebäude in Quṣûr Muhârib (Baharîya Oase). Tempel oder Kirche?" *Bulletin de la Societé d'archéologie Copte* 36 (1997), 99-104 and figure 2; and the so-called church of St. George in al-Haiz, Grossmann, *Christliche Architektur*, 466f. and figure 83.

[59] Grossmann, *Christliche Architektur*, 404f. and figure 19.

[60] Grossmann, *Langhauskuppelkirchen*, 206ff. and figure 78.

[61] White, *Monasteries*, 3:83ff. and plates 4-5. A publication of Abdal-Rahman Abdal-Tawab and P. Grossmann, of the state of the church after its last restoration, is in preparation.

[62] A good example is the sanctuary of the church in St. Anthony Monastery, built onto the original church in the 13th century (personal communication from Michael Jones).

[63] Grossmann, *Langhauskuppelkirchen*, 196ff.

[64] Grossmann, *Langhauskuppelkirchen*, 200ff.

[65] There are only a small number of exceptions that are similarly outfitted with a raised sanctuary in Egypt.

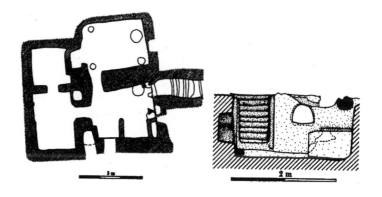

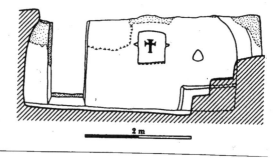

Figure 1: Early monastic cell from Kellia (after P. Corboud)

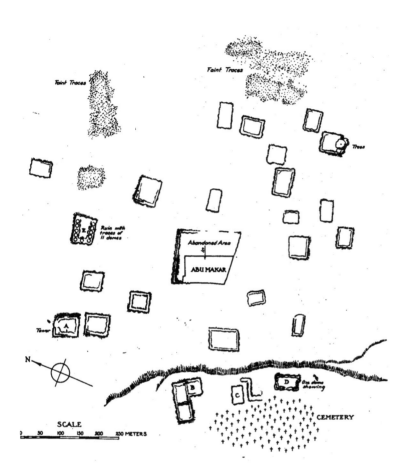

Figure 2: *Laura* of St. Makarios (after E.G. Evelyn White)

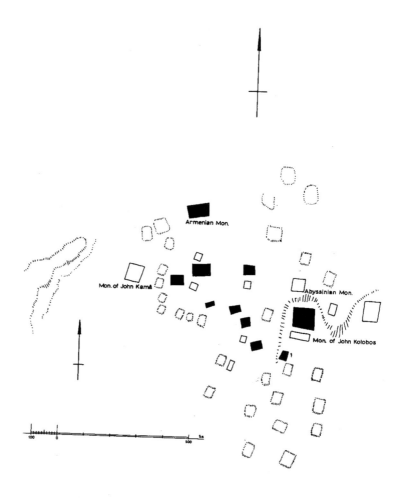

Figure 3: *Laura* of St. John Kolobos

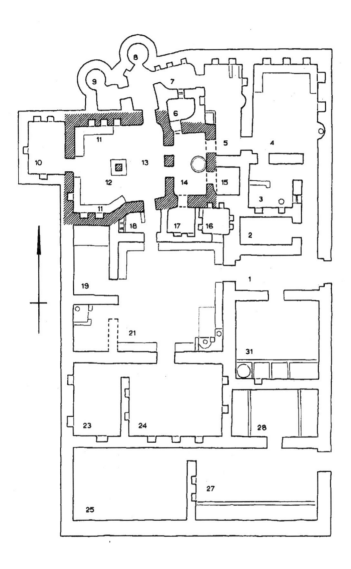

Figure 4: Main *kellion* in the laura at Ǧabal Hašm al-Qu'ūd

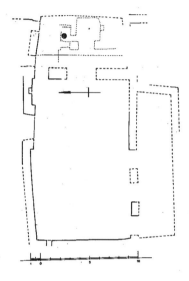

Figure 5: Earlier church at the site of Dayr Anbā John
with remains of the chapel underneath the nave

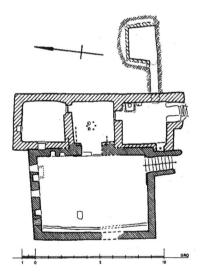

Figure 6: Early chapel of Qisa 1 in Kellia

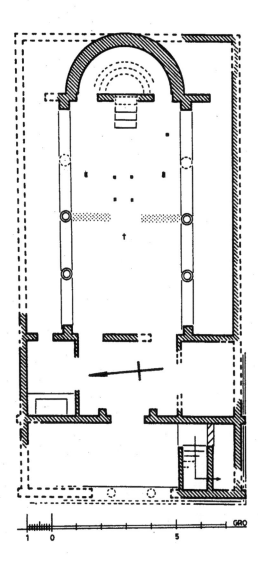

Figure 7: Town church in the eastern suburb of Leucaspis

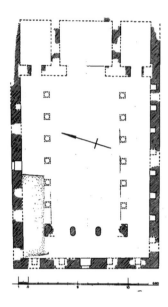

Figure 8: Original plan of the church of Dayr al-Baramūs

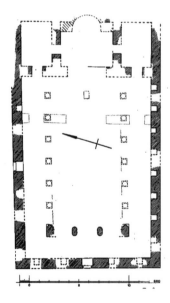

Figure 9: Later state of this church with indication
of the position of the *khūrus*-wall

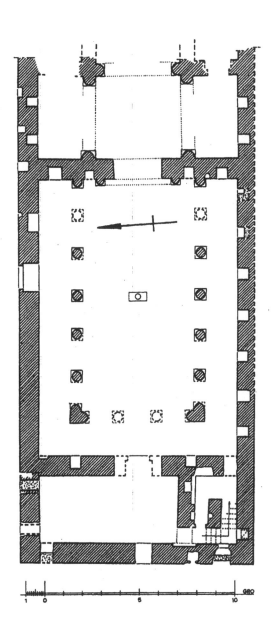

Figure 10: Original plan of the church of Dayr al-Suryān

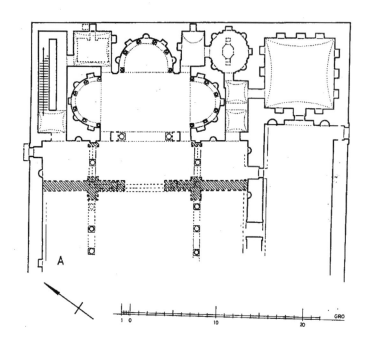

Figure 11: Eastern part of the great church in the Monastery of Anbā Šinūdā with a
tentative reconstruction of the *khūrus*-wall

The Ornamental Repertoire
in the Wall-paintings of Wadi al-Natrun:
Remarks on a Methodical Approach[*]

Suzana Hodak

"Die Bezeichnungen Ornament, Ornamentik, ornamental, Ornamentation, Ornamentierung, Ornamentist etc. leiten sich von dem lateinischen Zeitwort ornare ab. Ornare ist gleichbedeutend mit schmücken.[1] Das Ornament ist der künstlerische Schmuck; die Ornamentation oder Ornamentierung ist die Anwendung desselben; der Ornamentist ist der ornamentierende Künstler; ornamental heisst künstlerisch geschmückt oder auf die Ornamentierung bezugnehmend; die Ornamentik ist der Gesamtbegriff dieser Verzierungskunst."[2]

If one looks at the term "ornament" just from the etymology of the word, the question about its nature, the meaning field and the priority, in accordance to the above quotation, could easily be answered. Actually, however, the answer of the question does not become so simple by any means.

The Roman architect Vitruv (Vitruvius Pollio, 84–27 BC) justified in his work on architecture "De architectura libri decem" the point of view that ornament and decoration were purely luxurious accessories in art without any requirement on an own generic rank or

---

[*] The present contribution represents the revised and extended version of my lecture which I was invited to hold in February 2002 on the occasion of the Wadi al-Natrun symposium under the Auspices of His Holiness Pope Shenouda III in his residence in Dayr Anba Bishoy. I would like to express my deep thanks to His Holiness and the monks of Dayr Anba Bishoy for their cordial admission and hospitality and their assistance. For the organization of this successful symposium, I thank the St. Mark Foundation for Coptic History and the St. Shenouda the Archimandrite Coptic Society. May the Wadi al-Natrun symposium be only the beginning of following fruitful meetings.
[1] Compare the etymological relationship between "ornare" and "adornare."
[2] Quoted after F. Sales Meyer, *Handbuch der Ornamentik. Zum Gebrauch für Musterzeichner, Architekten, Schulen und Gewerbetreibende sowie zum Studium im Allgemeinen* (Stuttgart, 1993), 1.

priority.[3] In the 19th century a violent discussion around the term "ornament," its nature and its existence arose, which settled in numerous controversies theories. The large contentwise span of these theories explains itself from the broad circle of those who took part in this discussion, including art historians, archaeologists but also philosophers, psychologists, ethnologists and artists.[4] The individual theories are an important basis for a critical view of ornamental art work. Above all, however, the ornamentation moved into the center of interest – a weighting which ornamentation did not reach again since. The intention of the following remarks is not to revive this theoretical view of ornament but rather to concentrate on the question about the necessary methodical bases for a collection, documentation, and analysis of the ornamental repertoire in Coptic art.

If one wanted to describe the situation of the scientific interest in the ornamental work in Coptic art by means of a picture, one could say that the ornamental art shares the fate of an unloved stepchild, of whom one takes care in irregular distances and in uncaring manner. The reasons for this situation might be different, but can, however, in the present context be just as little discussed as can be given an overview of the ornamental treatment in all genres of art. Instead, representatively textile art is to be picked out and considered more detailed. The choice of this genre takes place not coincidentally because textile art (and more exactly said, the ornamental purple tapestries [Figure 1]),[5] directed first my attention to the ornamental

---

[3] See in particular Vitruv, *On Architecture*, 7.5.3–7. Vitruv's criticism on the "degenerate taste" was based on the excrescences of the so-called Late Second Style in the wall-paintings.   For this, see with picture examples H. Knell, *Vitruvs Architekturtheorie* (Darmstadt: Wissenschaftliche Buchgesellschaft, 1985), 161–165.

[4] A good summarized overview of the different theories in the reflection on art of the 19th century offers the monograph of F. L. Kroll, *Das Ornament in der Kunsttheorie des 19. Jahrhunderts*. (Hildesheim: G. Olms, 1987); see in particular the summary of the results on 153–156. See also E. H. Gombrich, *Ornament und Kunst* (Stuttgart, 1982).

[5] To the "ornamental Coptic purple tapestries" those textiles belong which fulfil two criteria: First, the colour scale is limited to purple and white, so that a light-darkness contrast develops; secondly, the motifs are exclusively selected from the ornamental (floral, geometrical or concrete) repertoire. An example for this kind of purple tapestry is represented in Figure 1 (a fragmentary linen textile with two purple tapestries sewn on it: a medallion, approx. 35cm × 37.5cm, as well as two fragmentary bands, each approx. 41.5cm × 3cm). The tapestries are again picked out from the photograph and presented in drawing. The textile fragment (Inv. No. 12.711) belongs to the extensive Coptic textile collection of the 'Museum Kunst-Palast' in Düsseldorf. On this collection, a catalogue is in preparation by Dr. Karl-Heinz Brune and myself. For this textile fragment, see already F. Bock, *Katalog frühchristlicher Textilfunde des Jahres*

work in Coptic art. The first contacts followed more intensive studies which resulted in a doctoral thesis with the title "De variis purpureis segmentis, paragaudis, clavis et ceteris ornamentis cum ornamento – Die ornamentalen Purpurwirkereien."[6] This work, which relies on a material basis of over 2600 tapestries, understands itself as the attempt of a basic research, a collection, documentation as well as a primary analysis of the material from different points of view. For this the collection and statement of the stock of ornamental motifs also counted, which proved to be, considering its extent (quantity) and its variety (quality), an extremely rich source for the ornamental repertoire in Coptic art.[7]

The knowledge of the significance of textiles as a source for the ornamental repertoire in Coptic art moved obviously already in the time of the large textile finds towards the end of the 19th century. In such a way Alois Riegl points out in his catalogue of the Egyptian textile collection of the Austrian museum in Vienna in 1889 that the ornamental repertoire of the textiles is of double importance because it reveals "einen ungeheuer reichen Schatz von decorativen Elementen" in a period when monumental art is predominant.[8]

In adaption and continuation of Riegl's point of view, Karl Maria Kaufmann judges the Coptic textiles even to be a possible source for the "monumental art," and therefore he demands a comprehensive investigation (of the textile art).[9]

Two years later, in the year 1924, the demands of Riegl and Kaufmann seemed to have been fulfilled because in that year Maurice Dimand published his study "Die Ornamentik der ägyptischen

---

1886 (Düsseldorf, 1887), 14 (cat. 52); and idem, *Ägypten – Schätze aus dem Wüstensand* (Wiesbaden: L. Reichert, 1996), 335–336 (cat. 384e).

[6] The work, which was accepted in the year 2000 as doctoral thesis, is in preparation for the printing.

[7] Already a first excursive confrontation of the ornamental repertoire of the purple tapestries with that of the remaining textile items (that is, the figures showing purple tapestries and the polychrome tapestries altogether), revealed that the first represent the maximum part of the ornamental repertoire in the textile art. It has to be examined in the future whether this pre-eminence is confirmed also in the comparison with the ornamental repertoire of other genres of art, that is, whether the ornamental purple tapestries must be evaluated as the primary source for the ornamental work in Coptic art.

[8] A. Riegl, *Die ägyptischen Textilfunde im K.K. Österreichischen Museum* (Vienna: R. v. Waldheim, 1889), xvii.

[9] See C.M. Kaufmann, "Altkoptische Bildwirkereien in Purpur und verwandte Funde aus den Nekropolen bei Schêch' Abâde in Oberägypten," in W. Schellberg, ed., *Sebastian Merkle: zu seinem 60. Geburtstage gewidmet von Schülern und Freunden* (Düsseldorf: L. Schwann, 1922), 152–169, especially 152–153.

Wollwirkereien. Stilprobleme der spätantiken und koptischen Kunst."
Actually, this study seems to have been undertaken, as it is
formulated in the preface, because "in den bisherigen
Veröffentlichungen überwiegen die Untersuchungen der figürlichen
Darstellungen, während das Ornament allzu stiefmütterlich behandelt
wird."[10] But with approximately 76 pages and 18 plates this study is
far from being called a hefty tome, and one doubts whether it could
be as comprehensive as its title promises. After having given a short
outline of the history of textile research, the development of textile
decoration and technique, Dimand proposes his study of the
ornamental repertoire of the textiles. Distinguishing between the
geometrical and floral ornament, he summarizes the repertoire in
several distinctive groups.[11] According to Dimand's own statement,
the aim of his work was not to present a comprehensive status quo of
the ornamental repertoire but to discuss and to solve the question
concerning the origin and the principles of style of the most important
textile ornaments.[12] In accordance to the opinion of his teacher, Josef
Strzygowski,[13] he tries to answer the question about the origin of
ornamental decoration in direction to the Orient. The study of
Maurice Dimand is the only monograph written so far solely about
the ornamental motifs of Coptic textiles. Since then the interest in the
purple tapestries, beside contributions in the various inventory and
exhibition catalogues, concentrates on a small number of essays.
Regarding their topic these studies can be divided into four groups:
(1) Studies dedicated explicitly to the ornamental repertoire but
primarily asking for their origin, their "meaning" and their

---

[10] M. Dimand, *Die Ornamentik der ägyptischen Wollwirkereien. Stilprobleme der
spätantiken und koptischen Kunst* (Leipzig: J.C. Hinrichs, 1924), iii.
[11] Dimand structures his study as follows: "1. Das geometrische Ornament: A. Die
Flächenteilung, B. Die Saummuster, C. Wellenlinie und Spiralen, D. Der Mäander, E.
Das Flechtband und die Bandverschlingungen; 2. Das vegetabile Ornament: A. Die
Entwicklung und Stilverschiedenheit der Ranke, B. Die flächenfüllende Weinranke, C.
Lebensbaum und Kandelaber."
[12] M. Dimand, *Die Ornamentik*, iii.
[13] For the disputed position of the scholar Josef Strzygowski and his scientific course
see K.-H. Brune, *Der koptische Reiter: Jäger, König, Heiliger. Ikonographische und
stilistische Untersuchung zu den Reiterdarstellungen im spätantiken Ägypten und die
Frage ihres "Volkskunstcharakters"* (Altenberge: Oros, 1999), 23–26. A critical
valuation of his role in the science history in the beginning of the 20th century is also
given by W. Kemp, *Christliche Kunst: Ihre Anfänge, ihre Strukturen* (Munich:
Schirmer-Mosel, 1994), 11–13. See the following clear judgement of Kemp:
"Strzygowskis Wirkung kann nur mit einem Paradoxon beschrieben werden: Selten hat
einer mit soviel Unsinn soviel Sinnvolles bewirkt – Sinnvoll im Rahmen einer sehr
begrenzten Fragestellung."

supraregional relationship;[14] (2) Studies that try to arrange the purple tapestries according to certain criteria in order to get, at best case, indications for dating themselves;[15] (3) Studies that ask for a continuity of the tradition of purple tapestries in Islamic time;[16] and (4) Studies that ask for a deeper meaning, going beyond the purely decorative.[17] Even this last aspect is pointed out with preference, if

---

[14] Besides the already quoted study of Dimand, compare this to the contributions of W. Holmquist, *Kunstprobleme der Merowingerzeit* (Stockholm: Wahlström and Widstrand, 1939); ibid., "Einflüsse der koptischen Kunst in Westeuropa," in *Koptische Kunst. Christentum am Nil* (Essen: F. Krupp Grafische Anstalt, 1964), 157–162, and P. Paulsen, "Koptische und irische Kunst und ihre Ausstrahlungen auf altgermanische Kulturen," in *Tribus* (Stuttgart: Museum für Länder and Völkerkunde, 1952-3), 149–187. The latter, P. Paulsen, belongs to the representatives of those who now already in the second generation led a heated discussion concerning a direct relationship between the Coptic Egypt and the Insular Continent, which focuses itself on the ornamental art, more exactly on the interlace ornament. Concerning the "Ireland-Theory," see in detail in my doctoral thesis.

[15] See for example the study of J. Trilling, "The Development of Interlace and Related Patterns," in idem, *The Roman Heritage. Textiles from Egypt and the Eastern Mediterranean 300 to 600 AD* (Washington DC: Textile Museum, 1982), 104–108 (Appendix). In consideration of the well-known research history of the Coptic textiles (robbery excavations and unsatisfactorily or less documented excavations) for the majority of them practically all archaeological basic data are missing or they are very uncertain. Thus Trilling could at least base his study only on two dated purple tapestries, which he analysed by means of strictly regarded, questionable chronologically relevant criteria (for example, the tendency towards greater complexity and suppleness of the patterns; the dividing of the surface pattern into smaller units or the lack of sense of motion). It appears to be then questionable to refine the chronology of the purple tapestries in their entirety further, relying only on two dated items.

[16] The question about the persistence of the Coptic tradition in the textile handicraft of Islamic time is treated the first time by E. Kühnel, "La tradition copte dans les tissus musulmans," *Bulletin de la Société d'archéologie Copte* 4 (1938), 79–88. In the following period this theme was discussed also by P. du Bourguet, "La fabrication des tissus coptes, aurait elle largement survécu à la conquête arabe?" *Bulletin de la Société archéologique d'Alexandrie* 40 (1953), 1–31) and E.J. Grube, "Studies in the Survival and Continuity of Pre-Muslim Traditions in Egyptian Islamic Art," *Journal of the American Research Center in Egypt* 1 (1962), 75–97. Since then the question about a Coptic influence in Islamic time is treated repeatedly in different contexts, for example in the doctoral thesis of K. el-Masry, "Die tulunidische Ornamentik der Moschee des Ahmad Ibn Tulun in Kairo," (Mainz, 1964).

[17] See for this the judgement of H. Zaloscer, *Zur Genese der koptischen Kunst*, (Vienna: Böhlau, 1991), 82: "Uns will scheinen, daß das, was wir Schmuck, Dekoration, Ornament nennen, all das, was in unseren Augen dazu dient, ein Objekt zu 'verschönern' ein modernes Konzept ist. Für die Zeit aber, da das Objekt entstand, jedoch nicht anwendbar ist. Was für uns Moderne lediglich ein ästhetisches Vergnügen ist, eine Art Delektation, ohne tiefere Bedeutung, war – unserer Meinung nach – für die Zeitgenossen des Künstlers eine deutlich lesbare und verständliche Botschaft."

the ornamentation is not completely ignored,[18] described by using phrases, as for example "geometrical/vegetal ornamentation, complex interlace pattern or ornamental design"[19] or vary rarely actually described in detail.[20] The span of the interpretations of deeper meaning reaches firstly from an apotropaic or luck-bringing aspect[21] over the reference to Christian number symbolism[22] or the cosmological meaning of special motifs, like, for example, the eight-pointed star, build by the intersection of two square elements[23] up to the postulate of an influence from the Neoplatonic philosophy.[24]

This paper does not aim to ask for the sense or to discuss the pros and cons of these theses but rather to point out that they are based on a methodically most problematic approach. The different studies (and their "results") are based by no means, as one might suppose, on a representative number of tapestries but on a very limited one, even on single items. Occasionally it appears as if the choice of the specific tapestries is made in accordance to the topic itself. The ornamental purple tapestries are endeavored for leading-on analyzing questions,

---

[18] For example, A. Stauffer, "Spätantike, frühchristliche und islamische Textilien aus Ägypten," in idem, *Spätantike frühchristliche und islamische Textilen aus Ägypten* (Bern: Bernisches Historisches Museum, 1996), 24, cat. 5.

[19] Compare for example Trilling, "Development of Interlace," *passim*; R. Shurinova, *Koptskie tkani, sobranie gosudarstvennogo muzeia izobrazitel'nykh isskustv imeni A.S. Pushkina Moskva* (Leningrad: Avrora, 1967), *passim*.

[20] See for example, A. Lorquin, *Les tissus coptes au musée national du Moyen Age* (Paris : Réunion des musées nationaux, 1992), *passim*.

[21] This interpretation is repeated almost stereotyped with reference to "secure" examples in the mosaic art. See for example, A Stauffer, ed., *Textiles d'Egypte de la collection Bouvier* (Fribourg: Musée d'art et d'histoire; Bern: Benteli Verlag, 1991), 81 (cat. 7), 94 (cat. 18), and 95 (cat. 19); see for this also the studies of H. Maguire, "Garments Pleasing for God: The Significance of Domestic Textile Design in the Early Byzantine Period," *Dumbarton Oaks Papers* 44 (1990), 215–224; and ibid., "Magic and Geometry in Early Christian Floor Mosaics and Textiles," in W. Hörandner, J. Koder, and O. Kresten, eds., *Andrias: Herbert Hunger zum 80. Geburtstag.* Jahrbuch der österreichischen Byzantinistik 44 (Vienna: Verlag der Österreichischen Akademie der Wissenschaften, 1994), 265–274.

[22] U. Horak, "Die koptischen Textilien im Johanneum/Graz," in S. Emmel et al., eds., *Ägypten und Nubien in spätantiker und christlicher Zeit. Akten des 6. Internationalen Koptologenkongresses* (Wiesbaden: Reichert Verlag, 1999), 201–208.

[23]A. Schmidt-Colinet, "Zwei verschränkte Quadrate im Kreis. Vom Sinn eines geometrischen Ornaments," in A. Stauffer, ed., *Textiles d'Egypte de la collection Bouvier* (Fribourg: Musée d'art et d'histoire; Bern: Benteli Verlag, 1991), 21–34

[24] D. Lee Carroll, "Looms and Textiles of the Copts. First Millennium Egyptian Textiles," in *Looms and Textiles of the Copts: First Millenium Egyptian textiles in the Carl Austin Rietz Collection of the California Academy of Sciences* (Seattle: University of Washington Press, 1988), 57.

although until now not even their object-immanent characteristics are acquired. In other words, the statement about the apotropaic character of a purple tapestry contributes neither to a classification of the tapestry within the context of its genre, nor to the classification of its ornamentation into the ornamental repertoire. Therefore such assignments replace neither a collection and documentation of the stock of ornamental purple tapestries nor the collection and documentation of its stock of ornamental motifs.

Even at the beginning of my analysis of the "object-immanent" characteristics of the purple tapestries it became quite obvious that the definition of an accurate methodical proceeding represents an absolute condition. The proven methodical basis should now in the following be applied exemplary to the survey of the ornamental repertoire in the Coptic wall-paintings.

Already during the studies of the ornamental purple tapestries a first excursive object-spreading view and comparison with the stock of ornaments of the remaining genres of art revealed that here a stocktaking and an analysis of the ornamental repertoire is also missing and therefore needed to be done. It should be pointed out again that methodically a stocktaking offers the only legitimate basis for leading-on questions, (for example the question about a possible transfer of motifs between genres of art by means of pattern book/sheets and the textile items themselves or, however, the contrary question about genre classifying motifs). Whether dating criteria could result here affects a far-reaching problem field, which should be discussed some other time in a different context.[25]

When the idea of a symposium in the Wadi al-Natrun took real shape and I got the invitation to deliver a paper, it was a welcome occasion to look beyond the purple textiles and to turn to a genre whose knowledge and whose stock in the churches of the monasteries of Wadi al-Natrun is continually growing, thanks to the scientific research of the past thirty years until today.[26] It is the mention of the

---

[25] For the problems of the question of dating on the basis of a comparative ornamental research see in conclusion in my doctoral thesis.

[26] A good overview of the research history and the actual state of research in the churches of the Dayr Abu Maqar, Dayr Anba Bishoy and Dayr al-Suryan until 1999 comprises the doctoral thesis of Gertrud J.M. van Loon, "The Gate of Heaven. Wall Paintings with Old Testament Scenes in the Altar Room and the Hurus of Coptic Churches," Leiden, 1999. About the ongoing research on the wall-paintings in the al-'Adra Church in Dayr al-Suryan, Karel Innemée informs regularly in detailed reports with illustrations in the electronic *Hugoye: Journal of Syrian Studies* (<http://syrcom.cua.edu /hugoye.htm>).

wall-painting. In the textile art as well as in the wall-paintings the past scientific interest primarily concentrated on the figures showing representations while the ornamentation is pushed into the background.[27] Nevertheless, there are some exceptions. For instance, there are the monograph of M. Martens-Czarnecka dedicated especially to the ornamental repertoire in the wall-paintings of the cathedral in Faras,[28] the contributions of E. Lucchesi-Palli to the stock of geometrical and floral ornaments in the wall-paintings from Bawit,[29] regarding a single motif, the so called heart-shaped leaf, in the Coptic and Nubian art,[30] and finally the contributions of M. Rassart-Debergh dedicated to the representations of crosses in the wall-paintings of the hermitages in Kellia.[31]

An iconographic study, if it cannot be accomplished using the original, depends on the published pictorial material. The problems showing here concern the possibly incomplete publication situation of the material on the one hand, on the other hand the image quality of

---

[27] Thus, even in the extremely useful concise systematic inventory of wall-paintings in monasteries and churches by G.J.M. van Loon and M. Immerzeel ["Inventory of Coptic Wall-paintings. Part one: Wall-paintings in Monasteries and Churches," *Essays on Christian Art and Culture in the Middle East* 1 (1998), 6–55; "corrections and addenda," *Essays on Christian Art and Culture in the Middle East* 2 (1999), 6–12] mainly the figures showing scenes are listed, while the independent ornamental compositions (in such an inventory the ornamental repertoire within an figures showing scene cannot be considered) are not mentioned. See for example the shallow rectangular recesses with plastered backs with painted arabesque patterns in the third register on the north wall of the *haykal* of Saint Mark in Dayr Abu Maqar. For the importance of the ornamental motifs within the repertoire of the wall-paintings, see for example the following statement of Gertrud van Loon in her doctoral thesis, "The Gate of Heaven," 193: "Decorative borders and fields play an important role in the churches studied. Wall spaces are edged with these borders, they separate scenes and it seems that they are used to fill every empty space left."

[28] M. Martens-Czarnecka, *Les éléments décoratifs sur les peintures de la Cathédrale de Faras* (Varsovie: PWN, 1982).

[29] E. Lucchesi-Palli, "Geometrische und florale Ornamente in der Wandmalerei von Bawit. Untersuchungen zu ihrer Herkunft," *Boreas* 13 (1990), 113–133.

[30] E. Lucchesi-Palli, "Forschungen zu einem Ornament der koptischen und nubischen Kunst," in M. Krause, ed., *Nubische Studien, Tagungsakten der 5. Internationalen Konferenz der International Society for Nubian Studies, Heidelberg, 22–25 September 1982* (Mainz am Rhein: P. von Zabern, 1986), 321–328.

[31] M. Rassart-Debergh, "Le thème de la croix sur les peintures murales de Kellia: entre l'Égypte et la Nubie chrétiennes," in Krause, ed. *Nubische Studien*, 363–366; ibid., "Quelques croix Kelliotes," in P.O. Scholz and R. Stempfel, eds., *Nubia et Oriens Christianus: Festschrift für C. Detlef G. Müller zum 60. Geburtstag* (Köln: J. Dinter, 1988), 373–385; ibid., "Le Christ et la croix dans l'art copte," in S. Giversen, M. Krause, and P. Nagel, eds., *Coptology: Past, Present and Future. Studies in Honour of Rodolphe Kasser* (Leuven: Peeters, 1994), 45–69.

the published one. Related to the wall-paintings of the monasteries of the Wadi al-Natrun both problems are relevant.

As far as the picture quality is concerned, this problem also occurred with regard to the ornamental purple tapestries, in so far as that the quality differed to a large extent, from illustrations on a scale 1:1 up to illustrations, which amounted to hardly more than 2cm or illustrations, which were so darkly published that it was almost impossible to identify the ornamentation of the tapestries. While in the latter case no other possibility existed than to order new photographs, in the first mentioned cases it was possible to adapt the quality of the illustrations by using Indian ink drawings instead of photographs. These drawings were scanned and thereafter worked on by means of an image-processing program, that they offer a real alternative to a photograph – up to a single difference. These differences refer to the coloring because instead of a contrasting of purple and white, this contrast is now realized by black and white (see Figure 1). Since in contrary to the purple tapestries in the wall-paintings the coloring might be important for the realizing of an ornamental pattern,[32] it is not possible to handle with black and white drawings in order to avoid the different picture quality. Therefore, one depends on the published illustrations, in the ideal case color photographs. Concerning the wall-paintings in the Wadi al-Natrun, we have in addition the alternative to use the very qualitative color copies, particularly from Pierre Laferière.[33] Regrettably, however, color photographs or at least alternatively color copies are not available for all the paintings.[34] A large portion of the wall-paintings are so far only published as black-and-white photographs.

A photographic retake of the previous stock of wall-paintings together with the documentation and collection of those wall-paintings which were uncovered since the times of Hugh Evelyn

---

[32] See the motif of the border in the south semidome in the *khurus* of the al-'Adra Church where the motif is accentuated by means of the colouring.

[33] See the wall-paintings in the Dayr Abu Maqar and in the Dayr al-Suryan: J. Leroy, *Les peintures des couvents du Ouadi Natrun* (Cairo: Institut Français d'Archéologie Orientale, 1982), *passim*.

[34] Color photographs of recent date are published by M. Capuani, *L'Égypte copte* (Paris: Citadelles & Mazenod, 1999), color plate 9.10.11 (Dayr Abu Maqar); 15–18 (Dayr al-Suryan); 21–22 (Dayr al-Baramus); and N.S. Atalla, *Coptic Art/L'art copte*, 2 vols. (Cairo, 1993), 28–29, 38–39, and 64–82 (Dayr Abu Maqar); 46–55 and 155–158 (Dayr al-Suryan); 56–63 (Dayr al-Baramus).

White,[35] Jules Leroy, and Pierre Laferière[36] is still missing,[37] completely apart from the necessity for the cleaning and/or restoration of these paintings. The importance of such a cleaning of the strongly blackened paintings has itself recently been proven in an impressive way with the wall paintings in Dayr Anba Antonius. Thanks to the cleaning nowadays, details in the picture compositions are recognizable, which remained hidden before then under the dirt of centuries.[38]

For my demonstration of the methodological approach while studying the ornamental repertoire in the wall-paintings, I selected in the following exemplary one painting from the al-'Adra Church in the Dayr al-Suryan, since Dr. Karel Innemée placed excellent photographs of the wall-paintings in the Church at my disposal. I would like to thank Dr. Karel Innemée cordially for this. The selected wall-painting shows the enthroned Virgin Galaktotrophousa in frontal view, which is located in the *khurus* of the al-'Adra Church on one of the half columns, engaged to the pier on the right side of the doorway into the *haykal* (Figure 2).

Apart from the general problem of the availability of the investigation material and its quality there are substantial problems that occur in order to reach the aim to register the stock of ornamental motifs of a genre, which require a preceding definition of the methodical proceeding. These fundamental problems can be summarized in three points: (1) the choice of a nomenclature for the ornamental motifs; (2) the choice of a written catalogue system for the ornamental motifs; and (3) the choice of an illustrated catalogue system for the visualization of the results concerning the ornamental repertoire.

---

[35] H.G. Evelyn-White, *The Monasteries of the Wâdi'n Natrûn*, vol. 3 (New York: Metropolitan Museum of Art, 1933).

[36] Leroy, *Les peintures*.

[37] During my last visit in Dayr Abu Maqar in February 2002, I noticed at several places in the church "windows" in the plaster, which revealed the view on underlying polychrome painting.

[38] The discrepancy not only in the visual effect of the paintings, but also in their "legibility," reached by the cleaning in relation to the previous condition is shown in an astonishing way by the comparison of the two recently published monographs on the wall-paintings of Dayr Anba Antonius: P. van Moorsel, *Les peintures du monastère de Saint-Antoine près de la mer rouge* (Cairo: Institut Français d'Archéologie Orientale, 1995) and E.S. Bolman, ed., *Monastic Visions: Wall-Paintings in the Monastery of St. Antony at the Red Sea* (New Haven: Yale University Press and the American Research Center in Egypt, 2002).

I. The nomenclature of the ornamental motifs

The question about an adequate nomenclature arises immediately when dealing with ornamental art because without such a system neither the clear differentiation of the individual ornamental motifs would be possible nor the practical communication about them and therefore their scientific research. In view of this necessity one usually uses a descriptive system, that is, the ornamental motifs are described, circumscribed, or provided with a clear designation. This system, although common in use, has crucial disadvantages, which make its use very questionable. One of the fundamental problems is based on the substantial measure at subjectivity that adheres to this system, since it rests on the personal perception. Furthermore, it should be pointed out that a descriptive system depends very much on the language in which it is used, i.e. one is often confronted with the problem of the "untranslatableness" of the descriptions written in one language into another. Subjective view, language barriers, and different designation conventions are the reasons why we sometimes have to handle with more than one designation for one and the same ornamental motif.[39]

With this background it appears to be reasonable to prefer, instead of a descriptive system, a more abstract and therefore less subjective nomenclature. The choice fell therefore on a designation

---

[39] To this group of motifs belong also 'popular' ones, as for instance the one in the German language so-called "Mäander Swastikamäander." The designation should be taken from the name of a river in Asia Minor, Maeandros, Maiandros, or Menderes, whose regular river course reminds one of the composition of the motif [see, for example, Meyer, *Handbuch*, 144]. In French usage one knows the motif generally under the designation "à la grecque" or in shortened form under "grecque," more rarely under the designation "méandre." The English-speaking area uses apart from the terms "(Greek) key pattern" or "Greek fret(s)/fretwork," but also designations like "ornament of meander type, meandering pattern, meander or swastika-meander." The Italian and Spanish terminology orients itself at the range of the French and English designations, so that one knows the motif in the Italian both under the designation "greche" and "meandro," according to the Spanish variants "grecas" and "meandro." The listed language variants in the nomenclature of the meander pattern do not represent thereby by any means a complete list. Rather, the most frequent designations are mentioned. Since the meander is one of the most common and well-known ornamental motifs, it becomes evident relatively fast that the different nomenclature refers to one and the same basic motif. At first sight, however, someone would probably hardly draw this conclusion. It is more probably that one would assume different ornaments behind the different nomenclature, as for example concerning the terms "key pattern" and "grecque."

system based on sigla. Even if the composition and the arrangement of the ornaments into basic motifs and their different variants cannot be free of a subjective portion, the nomenclature itself is almost neutral. Therefore it should be possible for a user to adopt it even if he does not agree with the classification of a certain ornamental motif.

In order to facilitate the access to the system of ornament-sigla, but also to reveal the criteria for assignment and ordering of the motifs, detailed explanations are attached to the sigla, but these descriptions however should not replace them.

The composition of the nomenclature of ornament-sigla

The sigla consist of maximally four. At least three components, however, contain different information:

(1) Capital letter "F-E-L": Indication of the category of the ornamental motif. The first component, the capital letter "F," "E" or "L" indicates, based on the German designations, the superordinate category to which the motif belongs, therefore whether it is a surface pattern (Flächenmotiv = F), a linear pattern (Linearmotiv = L), or a single pattern (Einzelmotiv = E).

(2) Numeral: Indication of the basic motif
The second component, the numeral, connected by a hyphen, indicates the basic motif. Starting with "1" and following in sequential numbering, each new registered basic motif receives a separate number.

(3) Small letter: Indication of the variants of the basic motif
The indication of the variant or the advancement of the basic motif is realized by means of the third component, the small letter. Each new registered basic motif is automatically marked as variant "a." The following variants of that motif are counted according to their numbers, starting with "b."

(4) Raised numeral:
The fourth and last component, the raised numeral, indicates further distinguishing features on the level of the variants of the basic motif. Depending on the quantity of distinguished sub-variants, this

information is added in sequential numbering, the indication of the variants of the basic motif.

The registration of the stock of ornamental motifs has to be separated in the first step strictly classified according to each genre, occasionally with further differentiation, as for instance the separate treatment of the wall-painting instead of painting in general. The assignment of the sigla takes place sequentially, depending on the collected material. As the material basis for each genre is of different sort, related to the quantity and quality, a preceding alignment of the material, such as for example the same ornamental motif in the textile art and the wall-painting receives from the beginning the same nomenclature, is impossible. Therefore, in the primary phase of the collection of the stock of ornaments in the individual genres one has to come to an interim solution, in order to ensure the clear identification of the ornamental motifs in the parallel nomenclatures of grammalogues. This interim solution is a concordance of sigla, and the indication of the specific genre is added to the sigla in abbreviated form (Pg = Painting) in square brackets.

II. The written catalogue system of the ornaments

Since the objective is directed to a registration as representative as possible of the ornamental repertoire, quantitatively regarded, large data sets are to be expected. Before this background the question arises, which medium is practicable for the collection, documentation and, above all, for the administration of such a large data set. Usually one uses a catalogue system in which the entries are registered in a before defined input mask, and the serial entry number, the so-called "catalogue number," ensures the identification of the entries. A later change of this input mask, be that because of a change of the formal structure or an extension or a shortening of input criteria can only be realized with substantial expenditure. Comparatively problematic, if not even usually impossible, is a later restructuring of the entries, that is, a re-organization under another criterion than, for instance, the entry number (catalogue number) or a combination of several criteria. But with regard to the background of the present basic constellation (the expected abundance of the material, its inhomogenous character, which does not make possible a secured consideration of all substantial input criteria in preliminary stages, as well as the step by step practice of registering without prior ordering of the material) this rigid catalogue comes up against limited factors.

The search for another catalogue system is even the more necessary as the registering of the stock of ornaments should take place beyond the purely quantitative level, also in qualitative regard. Apart from pure listing of records of the ornaments, an analysis of the same should be made possible, so, for example, regarding the question about the frequency of certain motifs in general or, for instance, depending on time or other aspects.

The choice fell on a data base since this catalogue system does not only secure the availability of all data of a certain motif, but offers above all a maximum of flexibility, both concerning the input mask and the entries themselves. If necessary, both the succession of the input mask can be changed (and this conversion is to be cancelled at any time) and the mask itself without restriction. The data base offers the possibility to undertake inquiries, that is, the registered material can be arranged according to individual criteria. For example, according to the sigla in order to determine as frequently a motif is used, in which context and which dating horizon, as well as according to a combination of criteria.

Therefore, the function of the database reaches far beyond a pure catalogue system because it fulfills two functions: on the one hand it administrates the registered material, on the other hand it constitutes the basis for the analysis of the registered material.

The database consists of individual data tables, meaning the input mask is arranged in tabular form. The individual entries are arranged in lines one below the other. Depending on the complexity of the material (on the quantity of criteria that are to be considered), the entry can be distributed among several data tables, which are dedicated to a certain aspect of the material as regards content. In these cases the data tables are connected among each other by the entry number, so that all the data about a specific registered item can be found by means of its individual entry number.

The database for the ornamental repertoire of the wall-paintings still consists of only one data table, which covers fifteen input columns.

In the following I would like to explain the content of these columns on the basis of the data base excerpt (Figure 3a–b) for the wall-painting of the Virgin Galaktotrophousa in the al-'Adra Church in Dayr al-Suryan (see Figure 2).

- Entry number
  This serial number serves as a code/identification key for each
  new entry in the data base. When it becomes necessary to
  distribute the data among several date tables, this entry numbers
  serve as the junction between them. The ornamental repertoire of
  the wall-painting of the Virgin Galaktotrophousa contains
  approximately ten individual motifs, which are registered under
  the entry numbers 17–26 (compare the Figure 2, where the
  individual motifs with their entry numbers are separately listed).

- Ornament-Sigla
  This column contains the indication of the ornamental motif by
  means of the nomenclature of sigla as explained above.

- Description of the ornament
  The description of the ornament, designed by means of the sigla,
  should facilitate the familiarizing with this abstract
  nomenclature, but also reveal the criteria for assignment and
  ordering of the particular ornament.

- Site
  This indication serves the spreading geographical and local
  classification of the painting, so that in detailed regard, it
  contains the information about the country, if necessary the
  region, and the general location, where the painting is to be
  found. Since the study is restricted to Egypt, this information
  needs not to be repeated. When it concerns the two remaining
  information, then the region is in the present case, the Wadi al-
  Natrun and the general location of the painting, the Dayr al-
  Suryan.

- Location of the painting
  This indication refers more precisely to the place within the
  general location where the painting which contains the ornament
  is to be found, as, for example, in the present case in the *khurus*
  of the al-'Adra Church, on the half-column, which is engaged to
  the pier on the right side of the eastern wall of the doorway into
  the *haykal*.

- Subject of the painting
  This indication refers to the painting itself, (for example, to the represented scene, the representation of the enthroned Virgin Galaktotrophousa in frontal view).

- Specific context of the ornament
  This indication refers to the ornament itself (where it is to be found within a painted scene). In the present case, for example, the ornament, entry number 19, determines the filling of the grid of the throne-like chair on which the Virgin Galaktotrophousa is sitting.

- Function of the ornament
  In contrast to the etymological derivation, which is purely based on the decorative function of the ornament, concerning the wall-paintings we have in fact to separate between two functions (two contexts of using the ornaments). On the one hand, we have the purely decorative use of the ornaments, but on the other hand, the ornaments serve to imitate something real existing.[40] The entry number 19, for example, most probably imitates the filling parts of a chair turned on the lathe. The ornament is therefore only an apparent one, because it represents the exact copy of these props.[41] In other cases, for example, the entry numbers 17–18, the facts are not so obvious at all. Therefore the double mention 'Decoration-imitation' is chosen. The two linear patterns, which decorate the vertical and horizontal borders of the throne-like chair, in fact imitate wood carving. This can be proved by the comparison with original examples of furniture strips with carved decoration.[42] In addition to the originals with realized woodcarving, there are also preserved examples of wooden furniture strips. Instead of a carved decoration the probably

---

[40] See also for this van Loon, "The Gate of Heaven," 195: "The much cheaper technique of painting is used to imitate the sculptured bands for bordering wall spaces and to accentuate mouldings."

[41] For wooden originals, see M.-H. Rutschowscaya, *Catalogue des bois de l'Égypte copte* (Paris : Ministère de la culture, 1986), 95–97, cat. 318–335 ("balustres").

[42] See for example Rutschowscaya, *Catalogue*, 137, cat. 465 (compare with the entry number 17); 106, cat. 350; 126, cat. 419–420 (variants, compare with entry number 18).

easier, less time-consuming and therefore much cheaper alternative of a painted copy is used there.[43]

- Date; Layer; Artist; Colouring, Remarks, Bibliography, Picture reference
  These last seven data columns need no further explanation.

The database represents not exclusively a documentation of the qualitative status quo of the ornamental stock of a genre, but rather also a documentation of its quantitative use within these genres. This premise means for the practice of registering in the database that each one of the ornamental records is registered by a separate entry, with two exceptions. Firstly, those records are registered *pars pro toto* by one entry, that originally belonged to a uniform ornamental context, normally to a linear band pattern. The second exception concerns the use of one and the same ornament within a picture scene in identical context (for example, the use of the beaded band pattern as a frame motif for the nimbs). As in the previous case the ornament is to be registered *pars pro toto* by only one entry. However, in the column "context of the ornamentation" this fact is to be mentioned (for example "general framing motif of the nimbs of the represented persons"). If the motif occurs in this same context in a separate picture scene, this record of the ornament has to be registered by a separate entry. If a picture scene contained several records of an ornament in different contexts, each usage in another context has to be registered by a separate entry. This distinction between the entries in the context of the ornament is important, if later one wants to make an evaluation of the ornamental stock after its use context.

---

[43] See the examples quoted above as comparisons to the entry number 18 (Rutschowscaya, *Catalogue*, 106, cat. 350; 126, cat. 419–420) with the following painted copies; see also idem, *La peinture copte* (Paris: Reunion des musées nationaux, 1992), 53–54, cat. 26–30.

III. The illustrated catalogue system of the results about the stock of ornaments – the catalogue of ornaments

The visual conversion of the results about the stock of ornaments of the wall-paintings is realized in form of an illustrated catalogue of ornaments. This catalogue is divided according to the superordinate motif categories into the three sections: "Surface patterns," "Linear patterns," and "Single patterns."

I would like to demonstrate the formal structure of this illustrated catalogue of ornaments in the following by means of an example chosen from the category of surface patterns. The starting point is given by an ornament record in the wall-painting of the Virgin Galaktotrophousa (see Figure 2). It is the surface pattern, entry number 21, which decorates the cushion on which the Virgin Galaktotrophousa is sitting. This surface pattern belongs to the isotropic surface compositions, basing on a certain grid, which is filled by the multiplication of one or more so-called unities of repeats. It illustrates a variant [Sigel "F-1c"] of the so-called "diamond-shaped grid pattern." Both the grid as well as the filling of the individual diamond-shaped fields could be carried out in different form. In the present example the grid itself is not executed, but the diamond-shaped single units consisting of four dots are arranged on the basis of an invisible grid.

This single motif record taking as a starting point the results of an analysis of the actual stock of wall-paintings in the Dayr al-Suryan and the published wall-paintings in Dayr Abu Maqar are summarized in form of an excerpt of the catalogue of ornaments (Figure 4a–b). The represented range of variation of the basic motif "F-1," the so-called 'family of the basic motif' marks only an interim balance because neither the illustrated catalogue of ornaments is to be regarded as something static nor is the data base. Depending on the state of registration, the stock of ornaments may change, be it that new basic motifs have to be defined or already existing, families of the basic motif' have to been enlarged for variants or sub-variants.

In principle each new basic motif is presented on a separate plate. The emphasized sigla are indicated at the left top margin. Depending upon the record situation the "families of the basic motif" are listed in summary on one plate, or however distributed on several plates, separated according to the variants or the sub-variants of the motif. In the cases, when several variants or sub-variants are arranged on one plate, the individual sigla are indicated over each illustration to ensure the doubtless identification of the individual record.

The sequence of the individual motif records follows the hierarchy determined by the sigla, (that is, primarily the variants of the basic motifs and secondly the sub-variants of the basic motifs). Both on the level of the variant as on that of the sub-variant the different examples which are arranged differ in most cases in the use of the subordinate filling motifs, as it is also shown in the present excerpt of the catalogue (see Figure 4a–b).

The reference indication of the individual ornamental records is given by the entry number. On the basis of these entry numbers all the information concerning the ornamental record are available in the data base.[44] The illustrated catalogue of ornaments reflects the registered status quo of the ornamental repertoire of a genre (in the present case the wall-painting). This collection of ornaments is diachronic (the repertoire does not document by any means the maximum stock at a certain fixed point of time). While in the data base the entries could be arranged flexibly also according to their dating, for the illustrated catalogue of ornaments this practise would not be useful, as the latter tries to present the maximum stock of the

---

[44] Since in the present case the complete database excerpts cannot be given, the reference indications, limited to the substantial data, are summarizes as follows: **1**: Dayr al-Suryan, Chapel of the 49 Martyrs, upper half of the east wall, above the left niche, lower part of a standing person (bishop) – decoration of the tunic; **12**: Dayr al-Suryan, Chapel of the 49 Martyrs, central niche, enthroned Virgin – decoration of the lower front of the throne-like chair; **14**: Dayr al-Suryan, Chapel of the 49 Martyrs, central niche, standing figure of a bishop or hegoumenos – decoration of his garment; **122**: Dayr al-Suryan, al-ʿAdra Church, northern semidome, painting of the dormition – decoration of the bedcover on which the Virgin is lying; **142**: Dayr al-Suryan, al-ʿAdra Church, easternmost column in the southern nave, remains of a standing figure (patriarch) – decoration of the epitrachelion; **169**: Dayr Abu Maqar, central *haykal* (*haykal* of Benjamin), upper zone (underneath the octogonal zone of transition), west wall, south-west corner – decoration of the front of the aedicule with an anonyme apostle; **179**: Dayr Abu Maqar, central *haykal* (*haykal* of Benjamin), upper zone (underneath the zone of transition), west wall, south-east corner – decoration of the front of the aedicule with Saint John the Baptist; **222**: Dayr Abu Maqar, northern *haykal* (*haykal* of St. Mark), second register, east wall (northern end), painting left to the niche, the three Youths in the Fiery Furnace – decoration of the pallium of the first Youth; **225**: Dayr Abu Maqar, northern *haykal* (*haykal* of St. Mark), second register, east wall (northern end), painting left to the niche, the three Youths in the Fiery Furnace – decoration of the pallium of the third Youth; **269**: Dayr Abu Maqar, northern *haykal* (*haykal* of St. Mark), fourth register/ octogonal zone, south-eastern wall, both spandrels, painting of the Annunciation to Zachariah – 2/3 of the background of the scene (imitation of landscape).

ornamental repertoire in clear form for the practical usage. Nevertheless, the dating of the records has to find consideration, since it is quite possible that the differences in the stock of ornaments relative to their dating are not to be explained from the selective preservation of the material, but rather as a testimony for real existing differences in the repertoire of ornamental motifs. For this reason the dating of each record is attached in square brackets to the indication of the entry number.

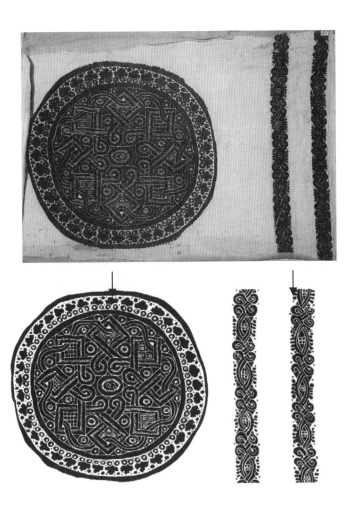

Figure 1: Coptic Textile Fragment with two Ornamental Purple Tapestries
(photograph and drawing)

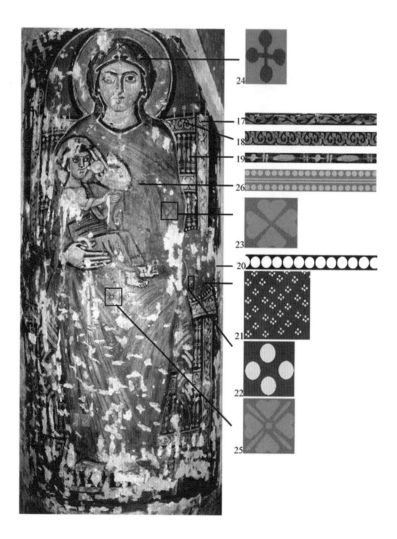

Figure 2: The Ornamental Repertoire in the Wall-painting of the Virgin
Galaktotrophousa (al-'Adra Church, Dayr al-Suryan)

Entry-Number	Ornament-Sigla (Pg)	Site	Description of the ornament	Location of the painting	Subject of the painting	Specific context of the ornament	Function of the ornament
	17L-2a	Wadi al-Natrun, Deir al-Surian,	Floral ornament: wave band with prolonged trefoils	Al-'Adra Church,khurus, eastern wall, half-column engaged to the pier on the right side of the door-way into the haykal	Virgin Galaktotrophousa enthroned in frontal view	Decor of the throne-like chair (vertical borders)	Imitation (wood carving: e.g. Rutschowscaya 1986: p. 137, cat. 465)
	18L-3a	Wadi al-Natrun, Deir al-Surian,	Floral ornament: row of sty-lized trefoils with the stem divided and returned to form circumscribing arch	Al-'Adra Church,khurus, eastern wall, half-column engaged to the pier on the right side of the door-way into the haykal	Virgin Galaktotrophousa enthroned in frontal view	Decor of the throne-like chair (horizontal borders)	Imitation (wood carving: e.g. Rutschoscaya 1986: p. 106, cat. 350; p. 126, cat. 419–420[variants])
	19L-4a	Wadi al-Natrun, Deir al-Surian,	Row of vertical spindrels and circles in alternation with pairs of horizontal lines	Al-'Adra Church,khurus, eastern wall, half-column engaged to the pier on the right side of the door-way into the haykal	Virgin Galaktotrophousa enthroned in frontal view	Decor of the throne-like chair (filling of the grid)	Imitation (parts of the chair turned on the lathe: e.g. Rutschowscaya 1986: p. 95–97, cat. 318–335):
	20L-1a	Wadi al-Natrun, Deir al-Surian,	Beaded band	Al-'Adra Church,khurus, eastern wall, half-column engaged to the pier on the right side of the door-way into the haykal	Virgin Galaktotrophousa enthroned in frontal view	Border of the cushion	Decoration/Imitation (Fringe?)
	21F-1c	Wadi al-Natrun, Deir al-Surian,	Diamond-shaped elements consisting of four dots arranged on the basis of a diamond-shaped grid	Al-'Adra Church,khurus, eastern wall, half-column engaged to the pier on the right side of the door-way into the haykal	Virgin Galaktotrophousa enthroned in frontal view	Decor of the cushion	Decoration
	22E-1b	Wadi al-Natrun, Deir al-Surian,	Diamond-shaped element consisting of four dots	Al-'Adra Church,khurus, eastern wall, half-column engaged to the pier on the right side of the door-way into the haykal	Virgin Galaktotrophousa enthroned in frontal view	Decor of the cushion: Detail of the surface pattern	Decoration
	23E-8a	Wadi al-Natrun, Deir al-Surian,	Cross-shaped flower with heart-shaped leaves	Al-'Adra Church,khurus, eastern wall, half-column engaged to the pier on the right side of the door-way into the haykal	Virgin Galaktotrophousa enthroned in frontal view	Decor of the ma-phorion	Decoration
	24E-3a	Wadi al-Natrun, Deir al-Surian,	Latin cross with round ends	Al-'Adra Church,khurus, eastern wall, half-column engaged to the pier on the right side of the door-way into the haykal	Virgin Galaktotrophousa enthroned in frontal view	Decor of the ma-phorion	[Decoration]-Cross
	25E-8b	Wadi al-Natrun, Deir al-Surian,	Cross-shaped flower with a central dot and heart-shaped leaves, in the diagonals long narrow leaves	Al-'Adra Church,khurus, eastern wall, half-column engaged to the pier on the right side of the door-way into the haykal	Virgin Galaktotrophousa enthroned in frontal view	Decor of the ma-phorion	Decoration
	26L-5a	Wadi al-Natrun, Deir al-Surian,	Linear composition: two undecorated inner bands and two outer beaded bands	Al-'Adra Church,khurus, eastern wall, half-column engaged to the pier on the right side of the door-way into the haykal	Virgin Galaktotrophousa enthroned in frontal view	Decor of the sleeve	Decoration

Figure 3a: Database Excerpt for the Wall-painting of the Virgin Galaktotrophousa (Part 1)

Entry-Number	Date	Layer	Painter	Colouring	Remarks	Bibliography	Picture reference
17	Around 8th cent. (one 2 of the first paintings in this phase)		unknown	Background/Outlines: black?/ Pattern: white	Window 57 (van Loon/ Immerzeel 1998: No. 3)	Innemée 1998(a):4 „delicately decorated throne", fig. ; ibid. 1998(b): 145, fig. 2	Karel Innemée
18	Around 8th cent. (one 2 of the first paintings in this phase)		unknown	Background/Outlines: black?/ Pattern: white	Window 57 (van Loon/ Immerzeel 1998: No. 3)	Innemée 1998(a):4 „delicately decorated throne", fig. ; ibid. 1998(b): 145, fig. 2	Karel Innemée
19	Around 8th cent. (one 2 of the first paintings in this phase)		unknown	Background: dark (blueish?)/ Pattern: white	Window 57 (van Loon/ Immerzeel 1998: No. 3)	Innemée 1998(a):4 „delicately decorated throne", fig. ; ibid. 1998(b): 145, fig. 2	Karel Innemée
20	Around 8th cent. (one 2 of the first paintings in this phase)		unknown	Background: black/ Pattern: white	Window 57 (van Loon/ Immerzeel 1998: No. 3)	Innemée 1998(a):4 „delicately decorated throne", fig. ; ibid. 1998(b): 145, fig. 2	Karel Innemée
21	Around 8th cent. (one 2 of the first paintings in this phase)		unknown	Background: red/ Pattern white	Window 57 (van Loon/ Immerzeel 1998: No. 3)	Innemée 1998(a):4 „delicately decorated throne", fig. ; ibid. 1998(b): 145, fig. 2	Karel Innemée
22	Around 8th cent. (one 2 of the first paintings in this phase)		unknown	Background: red/ Pattern white	Window 57 (van Loon/ Immerzeel 1998: No. 3)	Innemée 1998(a):4 „delicately decorated throne", fig. ; ibid. 1998(b): 145, fig. 2	Karel Innemée
23	Around 8th cent. (one 2 of the first paintings in this phase)		unknown	Background: ?/ blueish green/ Pattern: grey (=white)	Window 57 (van Loon/ Immerzeel 1998: No. 3)	Innemée 1998(a):4 „delicately decorated throne", fig. ; ibid. 1998(b): 145, fig. 2	Karel Innemée
24	Around 8th cent. (one 2 of the first paintings in this phase)		unknown	Background: ?/ blueish green/ Pattern: grey (=white)	Window 57 (van Loon/ Immerzeel 1998: No. 3)	Innemée 1998(a):4 „delicately decorated throne", fig. ; ibid. 1998(b): 145, fig. 2	Karel Innemée
25	Around 8th cent. (one 2 of the first paintings in this phase)		unknown	Background: ?/ blueish green/ Pattern: grey (=white)	Window 57 (van Loon/ Immerzeel 1998: No. 3)	Innemée 1998(a):4 „delicately decorated throne", fig. ; ibid. 1998(b): 145, fig. 2	Karel Innemée
26	Around 8th cent. (one 2 of the first paintings in this phase)		unknown	Background: ?/ blueish green/ Pattern: grey (=white)	Window 57 (van Loon/ Immerzeel 1998: No. 3)	Innemée 1998(a):4 „delicately decorated throne", fig. ; ibid. 1998(b): 145, fig. 2	Karel Innemée

Figure 3b: Database Excerpt for the Wall-painting of the Virgin Galaktotrophousa (Part 2)

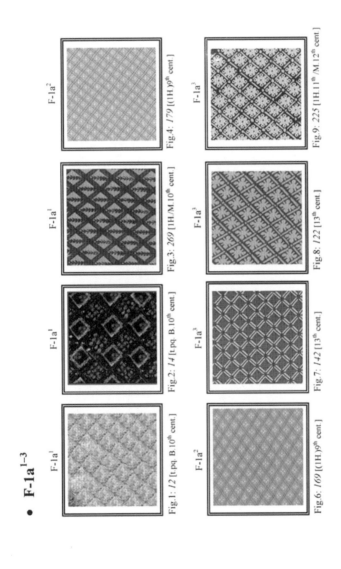

• **F-1a**$^{1-3}$

F-1a^1 — Fig.1: *12* [t.pq. B 10th cent.]

F-1a^1 — Fig.2: *14* [t.pq. B.10th cent.]

F-1a^1 — Fig.3: *269* [1H./M.10th cent.]

F-1a^2 — Fig.4: *179* [(1H.)9th cent.]

F-1a^2 — Fig.6: *169* [(1H.)9th cent.]

F-1a^3 — Fig.7: *142* [13th cent.]

F-1a^3 — Fig.8: *122* [13th cent.]

F-1a^3 — Fig.9: *225* [1H.11th/M.12th cent.]

Figure 4a: Excerpt from the catalogue of ornaments for the "family" of basic motif F-1 (Part 1)

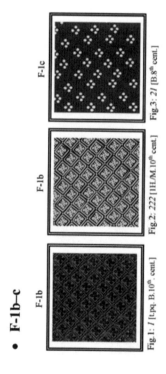

- **F-1b–c**

F-1b	F-1b	F-1c
Fig.1: *1* [t.pq. B.10th. cent.]	Fig.2: 222 [1H./M.10th cent.]	Fig.3: *2*/ [B.8th cent.]

Abbreviations

1H.	First half of...
M.	(in the) Middle of...
B.	Beginning of...
t.pq.	terminus postquem

Figure 4b: Excerpt from the catalogue of ornaments for the "family" of basic motif F-1 (Part 2)

Art in the Wadi al-Natrun: An Assessment of the Earliest Wallpaintings in the Church of Abu Makar, Dayr Abu Makar

Lucy-Anne Hunt

Introduction

The Wadi al-Natrun monasteries have a rich and diverse cultural heritage, expressive of the life and culture of the monks who have inhabited them down the ages. The visual experience has been central to monastic life and worship, manifest in wallpaintings, illustrated manuscripts and icons, as well as stucco, woodwork, stonework, and metalwork. Much of the art of the Wadi al-Natrun was made here. Other objects would have been brought to the monasteries as devotional objects or gifts, by pilgrims and travelers. Some icons, for example, can be shown to have been brought here, although it is likely that icons were also made here. Woodwork is an art form that is particularly treasured in Egypt, all the more because of its excellent preservation here, unlike so many other areas. Monastic books, used in services and private devotions, are ornamented, several with headpieces and decorated letters. Several of the monastery churches retain medieval wallpaintings and important discoveries have been made in recent years and are continuing to be made. These throw out questions, many of which beg to be answered. It is with one such example of wallpainting that this paper is concerned, those of the south *haykal* of the principal church of St. Macarius at Dayr Abu Makar. Despite their importance as being amongst the earliest works of art in the Wadi al-Natrun, the wallpaintings of the south chapel of the church of St. Macarius have never been made the object of detailed study and their broader significance remains unknown. It is proposed here to redress the balance by considering the paintings, uncovered a quarter of a century ago, in the light of the historical, archaeological, and art historical evidence. During the process it raises questions for further architectural and archaeological study.

The church of St. Macarius is now a ghost of its former self. The church is now truncated at the west end, cut down from its original

large size when the population of the monastery declined. It now
(Figure 1) comprises three *haykals* at its east end: the central *haykal*
of Benjamin, the northern *haykal* dedicated to St. Mark, and the
southern one dedicated to St. Macarius (which was uncovered during
excavations in 1976).[1] Between the central *haykal* and the southern
one lies a passageway. A short transverse section is all that remains of
the original long nave (Figure 2), which had fallen into disuse and
disrepair after the drop in the monastery's population from the mid-
fourteenth century onwards and especially during the period of the
sixteenth and seventeenth centuries.[2] By the time that W.J. Palmer-
Jones drew and photographed the building in 1911 (Figures 3-4) only
the central and north *haykal*s were visible, with the structures of the
area to the south of the passageway submerged in soil and sand, and
only the central *haykal* retaining its dome.[3] Soon thereafter
consolidation work started on the surviving section of the building.
Within two years, the dome had been rebuilt over the north *haykal*.
The two domes are visible in a photograph taken by the Englishman
Captain G.A. Auden (father of the poet W.H. Auden) in 1916, during
one of his visits to the Wadi al-Natrun monasteries while he was
stationed as a physician in Egypt.[4]

Excavation work undertaken at the church in 1976 revealed the
original floor level of the church. It was during this work, undertaken
as part of the restoration and building work on the church under the

---

[1] I am am very grateful to Father Matta el-Meskeen and the monks of Dayr Abu
Makar for facilitating my work in their monastery. I am especially grateful to Fr.
Jacoub for facilitating my work at the monastery in 1977 and for providing the original
of the plan reproduced here as Figure 3, and to Fr. Abudear for assistance during my
visit in 2002.

[2] H. G. Evelyn White, *The Monasteries of the Wâdi 'n Natrûn,* 3 vols. (New York:
Metropolitan Museum of Art, 1926), 3:31-49 (the literary sources for the history of the
monastery). For his reconstruction of the church, with its original long nave, see below.

[3] Reproduced in Evelyn White, *Monasteries,* vol. 3, plate XIXa with plan, and plate
XX.

[4] Dr. Auden's lantern slides are housed at the Orchard Learning Resources Centre
(OLRC) at the University of Birmingham. I am grateful to Mrs Meline Nielsen, the
University's Digitization and Conservation Manager, for permission to examine these
slides and the accompanying notebooks. See Meline Nielsen, "Auden Trails: from
Birmingham to Wadi Natrun" SCONUL Newsletter 24, Winter 2001, 41-42
(<http://www.sconul.ac.uk/publications/newsletter.htm>). Dr. Auden was given a leaf
from a manuscript during a visit to Dayr Abu Makar: Evelyn White, *Monasteries,*
1:216 with n. 2.

control of the Antiquities Service, that the coffin and relics of John the Baptist and Elisha the prophet were exhumed from a vault "covered with blue paint" in the northern wall of the church.[5] At the same time, fragments of non-figural painted decoration of the southern chapel emerged on the north wall, and roundels with crosses, foliage, and birds on the three levels of steps at the east end (Figure 1). Their description is as follows:

No. 1: North wall, west end: painted fragments (Figure 5).

No. 2: North wall, to the left of the doorway which gives access to the main sanctuary, and its annex. The painting here abuts a fragment of stuccowork in the door jamb (Figure 7).

No. 3: North wall, at the inner east side of the same doorway as no. 2: blue painted floral design (Figure 10); North wall, to the east of the same doorway as no. 2: painted fragment of shell niche (Figure 11).

No. 4: North wall, east of doorway: crosses (Figure 14).

No. 5: North wall, east end: multicolored panel (Figure 15).

No. 6: Roundels on the steps at the east end of the sanctuary (Figures 16-18).

No. 7: Small fragment of pigment on south wall visible in 1977.

Overall, this decoration received brief mention in a paragraph by l'Abb Jules Leroy in his study of the wallpaintings of the Wadi al-Natrun published in 1982 but has never been studied in detail and given the attention it deserves.[6]

---

[5] Fr. Jacoub el-Maqary, *An Official Account Concerning the Discovery of the Relics of St. John the Baptist and Elisha the Prophet* (Wadi al-Natrun: Monastery of St. Macarius, Wadi El Natrun, second ed. 1981), 10-11.

[6] Jules Leroy, *Les Peintures des couvents du Ouadi Natroun* (Cairo: Institut Français d'archéologie orientale, 1982), 124, with plates V-VII of decoration of the steps only, with which he drew comparison with monastic wallpainting formerly at Bawit and at Esna. Leroy gives the dimensions of the chapel as 8m²; Massimo Capuani, *Christian Egypt: Coptic Art and Monuments Through Two Millenia* (Cairo: American University in Cairo, 2002), 88, considers that the south sanctuary, also known as the little sanctuary, "probably dates from the seventh century" and reproduces two of the

Brief Survey of the Early Building History of the Church of Saint Macarius, Dayr Abu Makar

A reassessment of the building history of the church of St. Macarius and its chapels up to the eleventh century reveals three previous main building phases (in the seventh, eighth, and ninth centuries respectively).

The earliest phase is in the seventh century. The first building on the present site is associated with the rebuilding work of the Wadi al-Natrun monasteries undertaken by Patriarch Benjamin I (641-660) in the wake of the Islamic conquest of Egypt. The consecration of the church was recorded in the *History of the Patriarchs* by Agathon, syncellus and successor to Benjamin, who was with him at the time. This took place between 28 December 645 or 6 and 3 January 646 or 647.[7] While Agathon's description of the building and its decoration is imprecise, the church seems to have been divided into three sections, the sanctuary, the "dome" or choir, and the nave, with wall and column paintings of saints.[8] So the original church apparently

---

roundels on the steps. They are not mentioned in Gawdat Gabra, *Coptic Monasteries: Egypt's Monastic Art and Architecture* (Cairo and New York: American University in Cairo, 2003).

[7] This has been deduced by Ren -Georges Coquin who has reconstructed Agathon's account from various versions, including MS 207, a Bohairic collection found at Dayr Abu Makar in 1971. See René-Georges Coquin, *Livre de la Consécration du Sanctuaire de Benjamin* (Cairo: Institut Français d'archéologie du Caire, Bibliothèque d'études Coptes 13, 1975), 51 and 103. See also Peter Grossmann, *Christliche Architektur in Ägypten* (Leiden: Brill, 2002), 73 and 503. For Agathon's account recorded in the *History of the Patriarchs*, see also B. Evetts, ed. and trans., *History of the Patriarchs of the Coptic Church of Alexandria, II: Peter 1 to Benjamin 1 (991)*. Patrologia Orientalis tom. I fasc. 4 (Paris: Firmin-Didot, 1948), 504-518 [240-254]. This describes the request of the monks of Dayr Abu Makar to Benjamin to undertake the consecration, the journey to the Wadi al-Natrun, the consecration of the church of St. Macarius and Benjamin's laying down of the canons of the monastery, which had been miraculously dictated to him by a seraph. See also Evelyn White, *Monasteries*, 3:33 and 2:271-274. The church of the Forty-Nine Martyrs was built at the same time, before 655 AD: Evelyn White, *Monasteries*, 3:33-34.

[8] *History of the Patriarchs* 2.510 [246] states that "Then, when he [Benjamin] had completed the consecration of the dome, he went out into the body of the church, to consecrate its walls and columns; and at the end he returned and sat in [*sic*] the dome." Evelyn White, *Monasteries*, 3:33, envisaged the building like that of Abu Sarga in Old

included a sanctuary (today's central sanctuary), domed choir, nave, and colonnaded aisles. Other construction took place in the seventh century, including the building of the church of the Forty-Nine Martyrs, built at the same time, and monastic cells continued to be built throughout the seventh century.[9]

Evelyn White suggested that the eighth century was an infertile one for building at the monastery despite the fact that cell rebuilding by the monks continued and, most importantly, the relics of St. Macarius were returned to Dayr Abu Makar during the patriarchate of John IV (790-799). He went as far as to say that "There is no reason to suppose that the recovery of the remains of Saint Macarius by the monks ... led to anything more than embellishment of the church built by Benjamin."[10] But this embellishment could have included wallpainting, even though it did not attract the specific attention of chroniclers.

The ninth century was both a destructive and productive time in the history of the church. A couple of years before the death of the patriarch Mark II in 819 the monasteries of the Wadi al-Natrun suffered a devastating attack by the Arabs during which churches and cells were burnt and monks were killed or dispersed.[11] Evelyn White, who dated the devastation ca. 817, considered that "the seventh-century Church of Saint Macarius, the cells, and all the other buildings of the monastery were either totally destroyed or reduced to gutted ruins."[12] The sanctuary of Benjamin was subsequently rebuilt after 825, and probably in 830, by patriarch Yakûb (James) who,

---

Cairo. For the wallpaintings, see Coquin, *Livre*, 34, and the review of Coquin's work by Khalil Samir in *Orientalia Christiana Periodica* 46 (1980), 218.

[9] Evelyn White, *Monasteries*, 3:33-34.

[10] Evelyn White, *Monasteries*, 3:34. For the translation of the body of St. Macarius, see Evelyn White, *Monasteries*, 1:131-34 (the Coptic MS text recording the events is dated 830) and ibid., 1:292-94. The body had been stolen from Dayr Abu Makar before the end of the fifth century and had been housed in churches in two locations in Egypt before its return.

[11] B. Evetts, ed. and trans., *History of the Patriarchs IV: Mennas I to Joseph (849)*. Patrologia Orientalis, tom X fasc. 5 (Paris, Firmin-Didot 1959), 438 [552] under Mark III states that "the Arabs plundered it [Wâdî Habîb], and took the monks captive, and demolished the churches and cells there. And the holy seniors were scattered in every part of the world." There is further mention under James 50th patriarch (819-830), 440-441 [554-555] of the devastation as having taken place before the death of Mark III. See also Evelyn White, *Monasteries*, 2:297-98.

[12] Evelyn White, *Monasteries*, 3:35.

having previously constructed a sanctuary of saint Shenûdeh to the
south of the church, then also "adorned it with every kind of
ornament."[13] The church of St. Shenûdeh (St. Sinuthius) (later
incorporated as a chapel into the larger church complex; marked "E"
in Figure 2), was previously built to the south of the Sanctuary of
Benjamin by James, before his elevation in 819, to provide a focus
for the monks worshipping in the various ruined churches.[14] It was
because this new church did not prove big enough to house the
community of monks that James decided to rebuild the Sanctuary of
Benjamin itself which "was in a state of decay" according to the
History of the Patriarchs.[15]

Evelyn White suggested that the passageway today between the
central sanctuary and the (present) south chapel – the "cell of the
Council" as it was known in the fourteenth century – was built in the
ninth century (Figure 1, Figure 2C).[16] He postulated that it formed
one of two small rectangular-shaped chapels flanking the central
haykal of Benjamin at the time of the ninth-century rebuilding. He
suggested that a gap was left between the *haykal* of Benjamin and the
haykal of Shenûdeh which was only filled with the documented
building of a church of St. Macarius in the early eleventh century
(Figure 1, Figure 2D).[17] Since the main sanctuary, known as the
haykal of Benjamin was itself dedicated to St. Macarius the Great,
this one would have been dedicated to another saint of the same
name, either St. Macarius of Alexandria or Macarius Bishop of
Tkôou.[18]

---

[13] *History of the Patriarchs* IV, 459-460 [573-574]; Evelyn White, *Monasteries*,
3:35. Evelyn White here suggests (note 3) that the Coptic MS account of the late
eighth-century translation of the relics, dated 830 and found in the monastery, was
written for the installation of the relics in the new church.

[14] *History of the Patriarchs* IV, 452-453 [566-567] states that "In the days of his
priesthood he [James] had begun to build a sanctuary in the name of Sinuthius, to the
south of the sanctuary of Saint Macarius; and there the monks began to assemble
instead of the ruined churches. Now he finished it, and restored the other churches";
Evelyn White, *Monasteries*, 2:300.

[15] *History of the Patriarchs* IV, 459-450 [573-574]; Evelyn White, *Monasteries*,
2:300.

[16] Evelyn White, *Monasteries*, 3:33.

[17] Evelyn White, *Monasteries*, 3:3 and 46; 2:343.

[18] Evelyn White, *Monasteries*, 3:36.

It may be suggested, however, that the chronology may be more complex than Evelyn White proposed. First, it is not known what, if anything, survived from the seventh-century church. The *History of the Patriarchs* statement that the Sanctuary of Benjamin was "in a state of decay" – rather than totally destroyed, for example – leaves open the possibility of some structures, or parts of structures, remaining from the original building phase. Is it possible that part of the structure of the southern passage might even date from the seventh century? And why, in the ninth century, would such a neat gap be left between the new church/chapel of Shenûdeh and the Sanctuary of Benjamin? Is it not more likely that the positioning of the new sanctuary of St. Shenûdeh was dictated by an existing structure between it and the Sanctuary of Benjamin? This building could then have been rebuilt or refurbished as a chapel in 1005. It is true to say, however, that such a chapel is not mentioned in any of the sources before 1005, and without further study of the archaeology and architecture of the building it would be impossible to be categorical on these points.

Evelyn White was right to highlight the importance of the ninth century for building work at Dayr Abu Makar and in the monasteries of the Wadi al-Natrun. The restoration work on the great church at Dayr Abu Makar would have continued after 830 under Patriarch Joseph (830-849), together with other building work, including the construction of another church, by the steward of the monastery at the time, Shenûdeh.[19] By the mid-ninth century the monastery had four churches.[20] This building work can be shown to have been taken further. The *History of the Patriarchs* records that Joseph's patriarchate saw "the monasteries in every place grow and increase every day...above all the monasteries of the Wâdi Habîb were like the Paradise of God, especially that of Macarius."[21] Nor was Abu Makar the only monastery in the Wadi al-Natrun to benefit from building work in the ninth century. The church of al-'Adra at Dayr al-Suryan too saw building work at the same time. An additional stimulus to restoration activity here may have been the visit in 829-

---

[19] *History of the Patriarchs* IV, 539 [653]. The church, dedicated to the Fathers and Disciples, was to the north of the Great Church, was "adorned with every kind of ornament"; Evelyn White, *Monasteries*, 2:300-301; 3:35.

[20] Evelyn White, *Monasteries*, 3:35.

[21] *History of the Patriarchs* IV, 538 [652].

830 of Dionysius, Patriarch of Antioch to Egypt.[22] The closeness of
the stuccowork fragment in the south chapel at Dayr Abu Makar
(Figure 7) with the lavish arguably ninth-century stuccowork of the
square east ended sanctuary of the church of al-'Adra at Dayr al-
Suryan indicates a direct connection between the two monasteries.[23]
The rebuilding of the church of 'Adra at Dayr al-Suryan was
undertaken by monks from Takrit in Iraq in 818-819 according to an
inscription on the north wall of the church.[24] It is likely that the
stuccowork in both the church of St. Macarius and that of al-'Adra
was added later in the ninth century. This is on the basis of the close
similarity of both with that in the mosque of Ibn Tūlūn in Cairo of
265AH/879AD and at the Iraqi city of Samarra, inhabited between
221/836-269/885.[25] The abstract "Style C" in particular is
comparable, an example being that of the excavator Ernst Herzfeld's
ornament 94.[26] This adds further to the suggestion that the ninth-
century work extended beyond the outside wall of the rectangular
"cell" to include a structure in the supposed "gap" between the *haykal*
of Benjamin and the church of Shenûdeh. If so, perhaps it was
undertaken following the pillaging of Dayr Abu Makar in 866 after

---

[22] Michael the Syrian, *Chronicle*, XII, 17: J-B. Chabot, ed. and trans., *Chronique de
Michel le Syrien, Patriarche Jacobite d'Antioche* (Paris: Ernst Leroux, 1899-1910) tom
III, especially 79-80; Gregory Bar-Hebraeus, *Chronicon ecclesiasticum ed. Joannes
Baptista*, 3 vols. (Louvain: Peeters, 1872-77), 1:375-376 (cols). Dionysius criticised the
Egyptian monks for their lack of learning and their baptismal practices. Evelyn White,
Monasteries, 2:301, refers to this visit, Dionysius' criticisms and, in note 5, he voices
his suspicion that "the restoration of the Syrian monastery was in some way connected
with this visit of Dionysius." Neither Michael the Syrian or Bar Hebraeus specifically
refers to a visit to Dayr al-Suryan, however. To combat the renewed harassment by
Arab marauders, Dayr Abu Makar was walled in the late ninth century (Evelyn White,
Monasteries, 3:36).

[23] Lucy-Anne Hunt, "Stuccowork at the Monastery of the Syrians in the Wādī
Natrūn: Iraqi-Egyptian Artistic Contact in the 'Abbasid Period," in David Thomas, ed.,
Christians at the Heart of Islamic Rule: Church Life and Scholarship in 'Abbasid Iraq
(Leiden: Brill, 2003), 99 and 104-105, with figure 15 compared to Figures 7A and B.

[24] Lucas van Rompay and Andrea B. Schmidt, "Takritans in the Egyptian Desert:
The Monastery of the Syrians in the Ninth Century," *Journal of the Canadian Society
for Syriac Studies* 1 (2001), 50-51, inscription D.3.

[25] Hunt, "Stuccowork," 93-127.

[26] Ernst Herzfeld, *Der Wandschmuck der Bauten von Samarra und seine
Ornamentik* (Berlin: Verlag Dietrich Reimer, 1923), 69 n. 96, Tafel XXXIII (Ornament
94).

which Dayr Abu Makar was walled in the late ninth century, in ca. 870.[27] The building of the exterior wall indicates concern to protect the refurbished monastery, including the church and its sanctuaries.

The eleventh century saw the building of the chapel of St. Macarius in 1005, as already mentioned. Also it is known that by 1007, the time of the persecution by the caliph al-Hakim, there was a chapel to the north of the Great Church dedicated to St. Onuphrius, although it is not known when this chapel was built.[28] The emphasis further switched to the north side of the church with the construction of the northern sanctuary of St. Mark on the occasion of the (temporary) acquisition of the head of St. Mark in the eleventh century.[29] Now the number of sanctuaries at the east end had grown to four. All four chapels – St. Mark to the north, the central sanctuary of Benjamin, the chapel of St. Macarius, and the chapel of St. Shenûdeh – were referred to in a text of the consecration of the Chrism in 1167.[30] They are mentioned again in the fourteenth-century text of the Book of the Holy Chrism which describes the procession taken by Benjamin II in 1330 plan of the church (here reproduced as Figure 2).[31] At this time the door in the north wall of St. Macarius' chapel was sealed, as it had also been in 1305 when the patriarch John could not gain access to the sanctuary of St. Macarius from the central sanctuary.[32] As already mentioned, the "cell of the Council," identifiable with the passageway between the central *haykal* and that of St. Macarius, is referred to in the account of 1330.[33]

This summary of the history of the church identifies four potential times for wallpainting and other decorative work to have been undertaken in the church prior to the eleventh century. These are: 1) the original decoration completed by 645-6 or 646-7; 2) the refurbishment of the church on the return of the relics of St. Macarius in the 790s; 3) substantial building work undertaken in the ninth century following the destruction of c. 817 during which the rebuilding of the central sanctuary was complete by 830, with other

---

[27] Evelyn White, *Monasteries*, 3:35-36; Peter Grossmann, "Zur Datierung der ersten Kirchenbauten in der Sketis," *Byzantinische Zeitschrift* 90 (1997), 377-388 with note 78.

[28] Evelyn White, *Monasteries*, 3:37.

[29] Evelyn White, *Monasteries*, 3:37.

[30] Evelyn White, *Monasteries*, 3:38.

[31] Evelyn White, *Monasteries*, 3:39-46, with restored plan, p. 42.

[32] Evelyn White, *Monasteries*, 3:43-44.

[33] Evelyn White, *Monasteries*, 3:44.

building work and refurbishment continuing after that date; and 4) the documented building of the sanctuary of St. Macarius in c. 1005. It is now time to examine the surviving fragments in detail to ascertain where they belong in this timeline and what they contribute to the discussion of the chronology of the Church complex.

The Fragmentary Wallpainting

The layers of wallpainting along the north wall of the sanctuary will be described with reference to the plan (Figure 1), from the lowest layer upwards.

1. First Fragment (Figure 5, from top to bottom)

> 1a= lowest layer. A few very faint vertical lines indicate the earliest phase. Scrapings slightly to the east on the same stretch of wall indicate how the wall was prepared to receive this earliest phase of plastering.

> 1b=middle layer. The second layer is characterized by a pale blue cross enclosed within a blue freely drawn cartouche frame. The lower left side of the left arm of the cross is beaded

> 1c=higher layer. The third layer is an ornamental fragment imitating marbelling, measuring 52cm x 52.5cm across. Within a red surround is a black-bordered wave pattern undulating around sets of three dots, seemingly in imitation of a vine scroll, against a green ground. This same border design, with only the dots, extends inward in arcs from the frame in two places. Between is an area of beige with a paler sketchy design of a diagonal a circular and a semicircular shape painted over. Comparison can be drawn with a wavy tendril border and a black pearled border in one of the baths at Samarra of the ninth century.[34]

> 1d=modern. There are traces of recent replastering, as on the west wall of the sanctuary and elsewhere.

---

[34] E. Herzfeld, *Die Malereien von Samarra* (Berlin, D. Reimer, 1927), 81-84, for bath ornaments, with, especially, Tafel LVIII. The ornament is here derived from Sassanian art.

2. Second Fragment: North of jamb, opening towards the middle of the north wall of the sanctuary, measuring 62cm x 34.5cm across (Figures 6 and 7).

2b=middle layer. To the left of the door jamb there is a blue cross from the second layer. Leaves and buds shoot from the ends of the arms that are preserved. There are berries at the end of the subsidiary arms. This floral cross with its budding ends finds a comparison in panels on the east wall on either side of the apse niche of Hall 1 at Bawit, dateable to the eighth century.[35]

2c=higher layer. To the left of the door jamb, projecting 1.75cm from the stucco layer is a fragment of the third "marbelling" layer, with the black and green meandering border.

Stucco door jamb fragment: Apparently contemporary with the blue painted layer (2b) is a stucco door jamb fragment. A vertical beaded border runs down the left of the main panel which has carved circles, with their centers drilled with a single hole, and with four small drill holes around each. To the right the main panel has a "teardrop" motif drilled with "eyes." There has been some damage to this panel since the photograph (Figure 7) was taken in 1977, and the plaster has been consolidated at the outer edge. This damage also obscures parts of the level 2c, evident over the stucco fragment in the photograph.

The stucco can be compared with stucco from the church of al-'Adra in the nearby Dayr al-Suryan, as already discussed. Both can be related to ninth-century stuccowork at the 'Abbasid city of Samarra in Iraq.

3. North East side of inner doorway, North wall: This inner doorway leads from the south sanctuary into the corridor linking with the central sanctuary.

---

[35] Alexander Badawy, *Coptic Art and Archaeology: The Art of the Christian Egyptians from the Late Antique to the Middle Ages* (Cambridge and London: Massachusetts Institute of Technology Press, 1978), 259, fig. 4.33 for a painted reconstruction.

3b=middle layer. Blue painted flowers design within geometric grid (Figure 10). The chrysanthemum-type flowers, in a vase, are contained within a wavy design which itself occupies a six-sided frame. This framework projects to right and left in squares, with triangles on the other sides. The wavy design is then continued in each of these. Measured facing the inner doorway to the east, the fragment measures 77.8cm x 201cm up; 7cm from right edge of doorway, 9cm from left.

4. North wall, towards east from doorway: This starts 9.5cm from the doorway, running 83cm high, going along the wall below the window at the east end (approximately 265cm in length). The main elements are fragments from the middle and upper layers.

4b=middle layer. A shell niche design on the "blue" layer is surrounded by a geometric frame (Figure 11). Such a shell is reminiscent of sculpted panels and architectural sculpture. It compares with earlier examples in Coptic monuments, including the shell canopy over a wreath containing a cross, next to a cross on steps, on a marble relief reused in the ambo of the church of al-Mu'allaka in Old Cairo which has recently been dated to the sixth-seventh centuries (Figure 12).[36] It is also reminiscent of the sculpted shell niches within conches in the main apse of Dayr al-Ahmar at Sohag of the seventh-eighth centuries (Figure 13).[37]

An intermediary layer of blue plaster.

4c=upper layer. Upper layer or "dado." This consists of a rectangular framework, predominately in green and black, with a

---

[36] Antje Middeldorf Kosegarten, "Die Mittelalterlichen Ambonen aus Marmor in den koptischen Kirchen Alt-Kairos," *Marburger Jahrbuch für Kunstwissenschaft* 27 (2000), 50 with Abb. 23-25. The author speculates as to whether this relief formed part of the original ambo of the church.

[37] H.-G. Evers and R. Romero, "Rotes und Weisses Kloster bei Sohag: Probleme der Rekonstruktion" in K. Wessel, ed., *Christentum am Nil, Internationale Arbeitstagung zur Austellung "Koptische Kunst," Essen, Villa Hügel, 3-25 Juli 1963* (Recklinghausen: Verlag Aurel Bongers, 1964), 188 with Abb. 80. For a watercolor of painted in 1903 of the apse's painted decoration, see U. Monneret de Villard, *Les Couvents près de Sohâg* (Milan: Tipografia pontificia arcivescovile S. Giuseppe, 1925), 2, 131 with fig. 212.

cross in terracotta in each diamond shape (Figure 14). The crosses have globular ends and the intermediary arms with dots on the ends. The medallions themselves have dotted frames.

This upper design continues approximately 222cm to the east, to the right of an opening at the east end of the north wall. Here the main layers (the blue and the dado) peter out with the blue layer predominant in the corner, with some traces of red.

5. Panel at the East end of the North Wall: A panel of an imbricated multi-colored design measuring approx. 115cm up x 49.5cm across (Figure 15). The design appears above the level of the steps of the east wall, at a right-angle to it. There is a green/black outer border and a brick-colored inner border. The panel itself comprises green, dark red and copper red "flame" like motifs arranged to form a design of repeating triangles.

This imbricated design is widespread amongst the ninth-century paintings at Samarra in various contexts.[38] The illusionistic effect of the design is also reminiscent of examples in earlier Coptic art – the imbricated panels in yellows, blue, and red-browns on the cupola over the inner hall of the fifth-century chapel 25 at Bagawāt, located above the pendentive depicting phoenixes standing on globes.[39] This chapel may have been monastic in context, as two of the figures represented are identifiable as Sts. Paul and Thecla.[40] While such a design ultimately derives from Hellenistic and Roman Egyptian mosaics, it also occurs elsewhere in monastic contexts, including at Bawit. A niche is the east wall of the room designated by the excavators as "25 bis."[41]

---

[38] For example, the fruit bowl motif between the two dancers in the domed building in the harem. For this see Herzfeld, *Der Wandschmuck*, 9-12 with Tafel I-II for which, amongst the parallels, Herzfeld cited a Coptic textile, Abb 302b, of a pineapple between a pair of palmettes. The imbricted design also appears on several representations of textiles, in the harem, as, illustrated for example, in Tafel XXIV, painted in blue on white.

[39] Ahmed Fakhry, *The Necropolis of El-Bagawāt in Kharga Oasis* (Cairo: Government Press, 1951) plate VII; Badawy, *Coptic Art*, 245 with fig. 418.

[40] Badawy, *Coptic Art*, 245.

[41] J. Maspero and E. Drioton, *Fouilles exécutés à Baouît*. Mémoires publiés par les membres de l'Institut Français d'archéologie orientale du Caire, tom. 59 (Cairo: Institut Français d'archéologie orientale, 1931-1943), plate XXXIX (b).

It is difficult to locate the level of this panel in relation to the others but apparently at the top of the steps the blue is broken through to the multicolored layer making this panel the earliest of the sequence.

6. Painted roundels on steps at the east end of the south chapel (Figures 16-18): On the East wall of the south chapel is a set of painted roundels on three steps, each roundel measuring c20-30cm high.[42] These contain crosses, birds with leaves, flowers or fruit, or foliage motifs with delicate floral motifs in between. One roundel contains a vase/bowl with fruit. The designs within the roundels vary considerably, some having additional clusters of dots. Some of the roundels also have an inner beaded ring. The colors used are red, green, yellow, and white. Some of the motifs are fluidly painted while others, including some of the crosses and animals, are quite stolid. In 1977 there was a tiny plaster fragment painted with green and red paint visible in the southwest corner of the *haykal*, at the return of the wall from the steps (Figure 1, no. 7). This suggests that the south wall of the *haykal* was also originally decorated.

It is difficult to relate the roundels on the steps to the painted layers on the east wall. Some brickwork projects into the eastern niche with two or possibly three painted layers evident. The lower one has some fragments of a wavy line with green which could conceivably be the same as the upper layer on the north wall (see no. 1c above). If true, this would mean that the roundels were added after the north wall painting was completed. This would tie in with the date of 1005, following the substantial ninth-century reworking of the central part of the church. But with only such a small fragment exposed, it is difficult to be categorical about this.

At first sight the general format of the roundels is reminiscent of textile designs. Indeed, for example, the motif of birds within foliage roundels does appear in fifth-early sixth century textiles (Figure 19).[43] But the closest parallels are to be found in wallpainting itself. The use of clusters of dots within the roundels, as well as the delicate, wispy, floral motifs found between the roundels are not unlike those found

---

[42] Leroy, *Les Peintures*, 124, surmised that these are the earliest paintings. He referred to these as "une suite de tableaux ... inspireés de la flore et de la faune stylés, qui ajoutent une note éclatante." He compared them with paintings at Bawit and at Dayr al-Fakhoury at Esna.

[43] G. Egger, "Koptische Wirkerei mit Figuralen Dartellungen," in K. Wessel, ed., *Christentum am Nil* (Essen: A. Bongers, 1963), 245 with 241, Abb. 106.

between the large foliage roundels containing foliage stars in the room designated cell J at Saqqara, of between the early sixth and the late seventh centuries.[44] The fleshier foliage motifs (Figure 18) are strongly reminiscent of the vegetal mosaics decorating the octagon of the Dome of the Rock in Jerusalem, of the late seventh century.[45] A tomb cover excavated at Karâra in Egypt and now in Heidelberg, painted with medallions of peacocks and floral motifs that displays a similar combination of Umayyad motifs and Sassanian-inspired floral design, has also been dated to the Umayyad period 658-750, when Egypt was ruled by governors.[46] Art of the Umayyad period is also the most likely inspiration for the more Sassanian-inspired of the cross motifs.[47]

The crosses in roundels here have a decorative function, as opposed, for example, to those at the hermitages at Esna, for example, which accompany inscribed commemorative prayers.[48] The "Maltese" cross design of Figure 16 (centre, between affronted birds) is similar

---

[44] J.E. Quibell, *Excavations at Saqqara* (Cairo: Institut Français d'archéologie orientale, 1908), plate LIII. This is also reproduced by Badawy, *Coptic Art*, 266, fig. 4.42. See also C.C. Walters, *Monastic Archaeology in Egypt* (Warminster: Aris & Phillips, 1974), 296 and 301-2.

[45] As a parallel for Figure 18 see S. Nuseibeh and O. Grabar, *The Dome of the Rock* (London: Thames and Hudson, 1996), 94-95, photograph of a detail of the outer octagon arcade. The Abu Makar roundel imitates the curving fronds, the longest of which are similarly ornamented with white dots in the Dome of the Rock, as well as the triangular motif issuing at the centre top. For another example of a roundel at Dayr Abu Makar, see Leroy, *Les Peintures*, plate VII, lower left roundel reproduced.

[46] H. Ranke, *Koptische Friedhöfe bei Karâra und der Amontempel Scheschonks I bei el Hibe, über die badisch Grabungen in Ägypten in den wintern 1913 und 1914* (Berlin, 1926), frontispiece; Badawy, *Coptic Art*, 275-76 with fig. 4.53 and references.

[47] Compare, for example, the roundel containing the eight-pointed star in the roundel reproduced by Leroy, *Les Peintures*, plate VI (middle), with the drawing of Sassanian designs reproduced in the context of paintings of textile motifs at the harem in Samarra (Herzfeld, *Der Wandschmuck*, 70, n.23).

[48] For those of the oratory of Hermitage 3 at Esna, see Serge Sauneron and Jean Jacquet, *Les Hermitages chrétiens du désert d'Esna* (Cairo: Institut Français d'archéologie Orientale, 1972), 1:91 with plate XXIV (inscription no. 28, prayer of Phib), 1:92-93 with plate XXXV (inscription no. 29), and 2:24 with plate CXX (inscription No . 29). Sauneron and Jacquet, *Les Hermitages*, 1:vii, date these hermitages to the late sixth-early seventh century.

to that in sanctuary area of basilica Qls 366 at Kellia, dateable between the second half of the seventh to early eighth centuries.[49]

Inhabited vine scrolls with birds and animals are found in rooms D and K, as well as the sanctuary decoration of the area of the kôm at Kellia known as Qls 366. This has itself has been compared to decoration uncovered in the west wall of the small church at Karm al-Ahbârîya near Abu Mena and therefore not far from the Wadi al-Natrun. There are several similarities of both with Dayr Abu Makar, although the Kellia paintings are distinctive in their use of blue, and also the more classical handling of the fauna.[50] White dots in the border roundels at Karm al-Ahbârîya are directly similar to Dayr Abu Makar.[51]

But the closest parallel is with painting formerly at Bawit, specifically the roundels painted as the dado in the north wall of room 40 (Figure 20), a vaulted chapel, in the convent to the south of the monastery of Apa Apollo.[52] Occupying the border below standing saints and archangels, the roundels contain eight-pointed rosettes similar to those amongst the Dayr Abu Makar painting (compare Figures 17, 20). Also similar are the delicately heart-shaped shoots arising from the foliage between each roundel (see Figures 16-18), the groups of tiny white dots surrounding central dots to form stars (see Figures 16-18), and the white beaded borders framing the roundels (see Figure 18).[53] The shoots between the roundels echo the

---

[49] Gerhard Haeny and Annalis Leibundgut, *Kellia: Kôm Qouçoûr 'Isa 366 und seine Kirchenlagen* (Louvain: Peeters, 1999), 5:49, 50, 60, 61, cat. nos. 2-5, especially Tafel 11 (3); 12 (2), 13 (1). For the dating, see conclusion, 79-83, especially 80 (phase I of the basilica).

[50] Haeny and Leibundgut, *Kellia*, 69, with Tafel 18.2, 20.2. These are compared with Karm al-Ahbârîya, Tafel 26, 1a-b. The main difference is that blue is a more prominent color in the Kellia paintings than at Dayr Abu Makar and the fauna more realistic. A comparison between the fat bird in Figure 15 and that in Tafel 18.2 makes this point clear. These paintings are contemporary with phase 1 of the basilica (see previous note above).

[51] See Haeny and Leibundgut, *Kellia*, Tafel 26 (1a-b).

[52] Maspero and Drioton, *Fouilles*, xiii-xiv, 140-142 with plates XLVII-L. Although without elaboration, it was Leroy who first drew attention to this link with Bawit (see no. 29 above). Maspero and Drioton (*Fouilles*, vi, xiv, 140-142) supposed that the convent was dedicated to St. Rachel as she appears, inscribed as the mother of the convent (that is, the abbess), in the painting above the lower border, which continues around the other walls.

[53] See especially Maspero and Drioton, *Fouilles*, plates XLIX-L.

fragment 2b (Figure 7) above, already compared with painting elsewhere at Bawit. The colors are also close, with predominately red, green, and yellow appearing in the sequence at Bawit.[54] Generally, Bawit paintings are dated to the seventh and eighth centuries.[55] Although under Islamic rule, the eighth century was certainly an active one at Bawit. An early eighth-century graffitto even attests to a rare example of conversion of an Arab to Christianity, being written in Greek by George, son of Sergios, previously Mâlek 'Abdallah, son of 'Amr. Graffiti at Bawit suggest visitors came there from all over Egypt including the Fayyum, Akhmim, and the Delta.[56] This similarity of the painting of the roundels at Dayr Abu Makar with the Bawit painting betokens a continuing monastic artistic tradition.

While there is a strong awareness of this monastic tradition, the paintings of the roundels are not incompatible with an eleventh century date, especially when the rich repertoire of Fatimid Egypt is taken account of. Lustreware bowls depicted birds and animals within medallion and other shapes, including bowls now in the Museum of Islamic Art in Cairo.[57] The bird in profile facing right (Figure 18), seemingly a grouse, is not unlike the bird carved on a rock crystal ewer in the Museo degli Argenti, Palazzo Pitti, Florence dated 100/8 and probably from Egypt.[58]

7. South East corner of Chapel: Traces of wallpainting were visible in 1977, in blue with an ochre/green border (Figure 1, n. 7).

---

[54] Maspero and Drioton, *Fouilles*, plate XLVIII.

[55] See, for example, H. G. Severin, "Bāwīt," in A.S. Atiya, ed., *The Coptic Encyclopedia* (New York: Macmillan, 1991), 2:364.

[56] Maspero and Drioton, *Fouilles*, x.

[57] Richard Ettinghausen and Oleg Grabar, *The Art and Architecture of Islam* (New Haven: Yale University Press, 1987), 191 with illustrations 175 (period of al-Hakim) and 176. For the Fatimid use of decorated background compartments in ceramics, see Venetia Port, *Medieval Syrian Pottery* (Oxford: The Ashmolean Museum, 1981), 14-15 with note 12.

[58] Ettinghausen and Grabar, *Art and Architecture of Islam*, 193 with illustration 179.

Conclusion

The painting on the north wall seemingly predates that of the steps in the south chapel. Discounting the faint vertical lines of fragment no. 1a, the panel no. 5 with the imbricated design is apparently the earliest painting on the north wall and therefore the chapel as a whole. This precedes the middle layer, which arguably dates to the ninth century. Much of this layer is painted in china blue, including the cross (no. 1b), the blue cross to the left of the door jamb (no. 2b), the flowers in the vase (no. 3b), and shell niche (4b) on the east side of the doorway. Above it the upper layer includes the fragments of marbelling design (no. 2c) to the left of the door jamb and the dado (4c) with crosses in a rectagular framing. This might well have been painted in 1005, the year of the documented construction of the chapel. The lower painted layer of the painted steps, which perhaps functioned as a synthronon, is possibly contemporary with this upper layer. The exposed painted roundels relate to designs in other media, especially textiles, and can be shown to derive from art of the Umayyad period, although it is likely that they date from slightly later in the eleventh century. The chronology suggested here proposes that the painting on the north wall was undertaken when the central part of the Great Church was remodeled from ca. 830. The key evidence here is the Samarra C style stucco fragment which is comparable to the stuccowork at Dayr al-'Adra at Dayr al-Suryan and probably undertaken by the same artists, possibly from Takrit in Iraq. This argues against Evelyn White's view that there was a "gap," the perfect size of the chapel, left between the Sanctuary of Benjamin and the chapel of St. Shenuda. There must have been a chapel or other structure which was replaced in 1005, leaving the earlier phases of painting on the north wall. This chapel was itself then decorated with painting, and the steps again subsequently. The hypothesis proposed here throws into sharp relief the need for further research on the Great Church of St. Macarius, one of the most important churches of the Wadi al-Natrun monasteries. The developments of both the ninth and the eleventh centuries are worthy of further reflection. The drawing together of the various elements of the church as a complex in the eleventh century, a process referred to by Evelyn White as "coalescence," is of its time and reminiscent of the remodeling of the Church of the Holy Sepulchre in Jerusalem by the Byzantine emperor shortly before the mid-eleventh century.[59] Study of the early wallpaintings also draws attention to a vital and virtually ignored aspect of the church's decoration, also of interest in themselves as reflecting Egypt's monastic tradition through the prism of secular art.

---

[59] See, most recently, Martin Biddle, *The Tomb of Christ* (Stroud: Sutton, 2000), 74-88 with references.

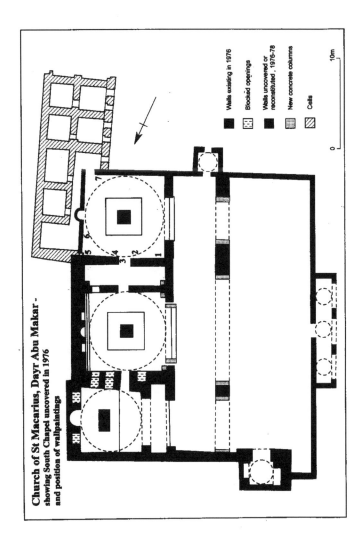

Figure 1: Plan, Church of St. Macarius, Dayr Abu Makar (after 1976)
(Courtesy of Dayr Abu Makar; redrawn by Nigel Dodds)

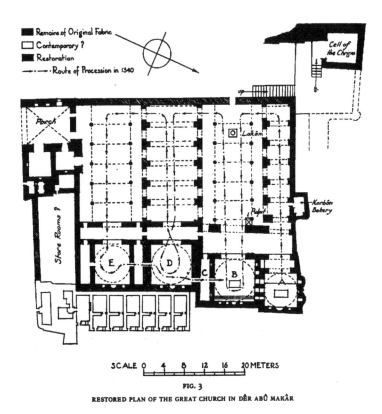

SCALE 0   4   8   12   16   20 METERS

FIG. 3

RESTORED PLAN OF THE GREAT CHURCH IN DÊR ABÛ MAKÂR

Figure 2: Reconstructed Plan of the Church of St. Macarius in the 14th century
(after: Evelyn White, *Monasteries*, 3:42)

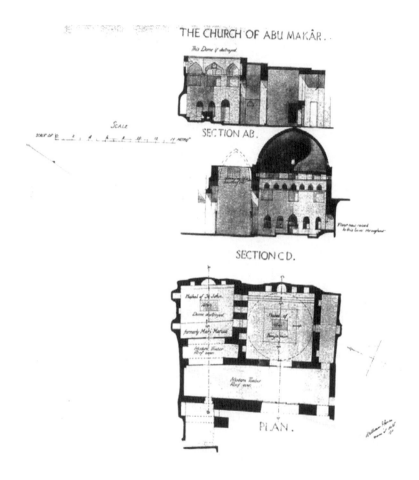

Figure 3: Plan of Church of St. Macarius, Dayr Abu Makar, 1911 Palmer Jones
(Palmer-Jones after Evelyn White, *Monasteries*, 3: plate XX)

Figure 4: Church of St. Macarius, Dayr Abu Makar
(after Palmer-Jones in Evelyn White, *Monasteries*, 3: plate XIXa)

Figure 5: Painted fragment (Fragment 1)
North wall, west end.
South chapel, Church of St. Macarius, Dayr Abu Makar.
(photo by L.-A. Hunt)

Figure 6: Doorway in North wall, with stucco and painted fragments
South chapel, Church of St. Macarius, Dayr Abu Makar.
(photo by L.-A. Hunt)

Figure 7: North wall, painted and stucco fragment to west of doorway
South chapel, Church of St. Macarius, Day Abu Makar.
(photo by L.-A. Hunt)

Figure 8: Wallpainting, Saqqara, cell J
(photo after Quibell, *Excavations at Saqqara*, plate LIII)

Figure 9: Stucco from Samarra (style C), ornament 94
(photo after Herzfeld, *Der Wandschmuck*, Tafel XXXIII)

Figure 10: Blue painted floral design, inner east side of North doorway (Fragment 3)
South chapel, Church of St. Macarius, Dayr Abu Makar.
(photo by L.-A. Hunt)

Figure 11: Painted fragment of shell niche (Fragment 4b)
Inner east side of North doorway.
South chapel, Church of St. Macarius, Dayr Abu Makar.
(photo by L.-A. Hunt)

Figure 12: Al-Mu'allaqa Church, Old Cairo
Sculpture on ambo.
(photo by L.-A. Hunt)

Figure 13: Sculpted shell niche
Church, Dayr Al-Ahmar.
(photo after Evers and Romero, "Rotes und Weisses Kloster bei Sohag," Abb. 80)

Figure 14: Crosses, east of doorway, North wall (Fragment 4c)
South chapel, Church of St. Macarius, Dayr Abu Makar.
(photo by L.-A. Hunt)

Figure 15: Painted panel of multicolor imbricated design
East end of north wall, South chapel, Dayr Abu Makar.
(photo by L.-A. Hunt)

Figure 16: Roundels with crosses and birds
Presbyterium steps, east side of south chapel,
Church of St. Macarius, Dayr Abu Makar.
(photo by L.-A. Hunt)

Figure 17: Detail of roundels on presbyterium steps
East side of south chapel, Church of St. Macarius, Dayr Abu Makar.
(photo by L.-A. Hunt)

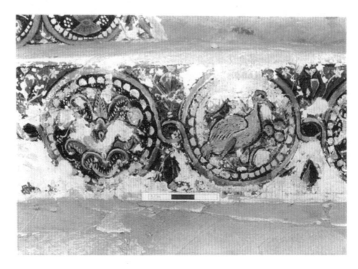

Figure 18: Detail of roundels on presbyterium steps
East side of south chapel, Church of St. Macarius, Dayr Abu Makar.
(photo by L.-A. Hunt)

Figure 19: Bird, detail of woven textile fragment
Vienna, Museum für angewandte Kunst (T. 624).
(photo after Egger, "Koptische Wirkerei," Abb. 106)

Figure 20: Bawit, Room 20
Lower north wall, painted roundels.
(photo after Maspero and Drioton, *Fouilles*, plate XLIX,
courtesy Bodleian Library, Oxford)

A Play of Light and Shadow: The Stuccoes of Dayr al-Suryan and their Historical Context

Mat Immerzeel

"Une description toute verbale, comme celle tentée par E. White, complique les choses et égare l'esprit dans le jeu de toutes ces lignes combinées avec des éléments de décors floraux stylisés et reproduits en à-plat ou en léger relief qui permettent aux ombres et aux lumières de s'insinuer entre les éléments ornementaux pour les éclairer ou les faire disparaître selon les heures du jour ou la position prise par le spectateur."[1] This impression of the stuccoes in the Church of al-'Adra in Dayr al-Suryan dating from the early 10th century was written down by Jules Leroy in 1974. Indeed one is tempted to limit himself to admiring these remarkable reliefs, but in spite of Leroy's doubts concerning the adequacy of a purely formal approach, an accurate description certainly helps to understand them, and to assign them their place in the history of the monastery and its rich artistic past.

Reliefs in plaster were a cheap and locally easily available substitute for stone sculpture, and had the advantage of allowing the covering of large surfaces. The technique of decorating walls and ceilings with stuccoes goes back to classical antiquity.[2] The Sasanian neighbors of the Roman Empire too adorned their palaces and houses with decorated plasterwork, such as in Ktesiphon and Kish (Mesopotamia).[3] This tradition was held high by the Umayyads, the new rulers of the Near East from the seventh century onwards,[4] and their Abbasid successors

---

[1] J. Leroy, "Le décor de l'église du couvent des Syriens au Ouady Natroun (Egypt)," *Cahiers archéologiques* 23 (1974), 161.

[2] F.T.E. Godin, "The Multiple Use of Stucco and Plaster in Classical Antiquity," *Essays on Christian Art and Culture in the Middle East* 3 (2000), 63-79.

[3] J. Kröger, Sasanidischer Stuckdecor (Mainz am Rhein: P. von Zabern 1982) and idem, *Hofkunst van de Sassanieden. Het Persische rijk tussen Rome en China (224-642). 12 februari - 25 april 1993* (Brussels: Koninklijke Musea voor Kunst en Geschiedenis, 1993), 63-65.

[4] R.W. Hamilton, "Carved Plaster in Umayyad Architecture," *Iraq* 15 (1953), 43-55; D. Talbot Rice, *Islamic Art* (London: Thames and Hudson, 1975), 22-24; R. Ettinghausen and O. Grabar, *The Art and Architecture of Islam: 650-1250* (Harmondsworth, England and New York: Penguin, 1987), 56-71; Qasr al-Hayr al-Garbi: D. Schlumberger, *Qasr el-Heir el Garbi* (Paris: P. Geuthner, 1986); Khirbat al-Mafjar (Israel): K.A.C. Creswell, rev.

(see below). Stuccoes in churches were found in Europe, in particular in France, Germany, Spain, and Italy (e.g. Ravenna and Cividale),[5] but hardly in Egypt. The best-preserved Coptic example is a curious stucco capital in the Church of al-'Adra in Dayr al-Baramus.[6] In the Kellia simple reliefs were applied on the walls, or plaster was used to mould columns.[7] This was also the case in the seventh-century architecture of the church in Dayr al-Suryan.

Our possibilities to compare the stuccoes of the monastery with other examples are restricted. Stuccoes conserved *in situ* are rare, as the material is vulnerable and could easily be reused. This makes the reliefs of Dayr al-Suryan even more exceptional. They have resisted the teeth of time mainly because the monastery was almost permanently inhabited. Meanwhile, in spite of several restoration campaigns, its church has remained relatively well intact over the ages.

The stuccoes are present in the *haykal* and the *khurus* of the Church of al-'Adra (Figure 1a-b), as well as in the adjoining Chapel of the Forty-Nine Martyrs (Figure 1c). In the 18th century a damaged part of the over eight centuries-old decoration in the *haykal* was replaced. At this occasion new panels with coarse motifs were added to this room as well as to the *khurus* and the nave.

Description[8]

The rectangular *haykal* (length 4.09m; width 4.17m; height ca. 10m) is covered with a dome resting on an octagonal zone. A central niche dominates the east wall, and is flanked by two smaller ones. Similar

J.W. Allan, *A Short Account of Early Muslim Architecture* (Aldershot: Scolar, 1989), 195-199 and figures 113-116.

[5] C. Sapin, "Les stucs de Saint-Jean-de-Maurienne," *Cahiers Archéologiques* 43 (1995), 67-100.

[6] H.G. Evelyn White, *The Monasteries of the Wâdi 'n-Natrûn*, vols. 2-3 (New York: Metropolitan Museum of Art, 1932-1933), 3:236-237 and plates LXXXIVB, LXXXVA.

[7] Catalogue 1989. *Les Kellia. Ermitages Coptes en Basse-Egypte. Musée de l'art et d'histoire Genève, 12 octobre 1989-7 janvier 1990*. Genève, in particular figs. 30, 31.

[8] See also Evelyn White, *Monasteries*, 204-206; S. Flury, "Samarra und die Ornamentik der Moschee des Ibn Tulun," *Der Islam* 4 (1916), 421-432; C.C. Walters, *Monastic Archaeology in Egypt* (Warminster: Aris and Phillips, 1974), 192-194; M. Immerzeel, "The Crowned Altar. The Stuccoes of Deir al-Surian and their historical background," *Essays on Christian Art and Culture in the Middle East* 3 (2000), 40-45; and idem, "The Stuccoes of Deir al-Surian: a *Wafq* of the Takritans in Fustat?" in *Acts of the Seventh International Congress of Coptic Studies. Leiden, 28 August-2 September 2000* (Leiden: Peeters, in print).

niches and doorways giving access to the neighboring rooms are present in the north and south walls.

The stuccoes are applied at two levels (Figure 2). At eye level, the niches and doorways are framed with rectangular fields, the one around the central niche being the most elaborate. At a level of about three to four meters panels alternate with windows consisting of a stucco framework (Figures 3, 5, 8, and 9).[9] Below this zone runs a frieze (width 0.4m), which is interrupted only by the framework of the central niche. As the adjacent rooms are fairly lofty, the windows in the north and south walls do not let in daylight, while those in the east wall have been closed and covered with stucco panels in the 18th century (Figures 4 and 5; see below). Hence, daylight only enters through windows in the octagonal zone and the dome.

On the east wall the spandrels of the frame of the central niche contain a circle. Vine scrolls cover the remainder of the surface (Figure 6). The jambs are figured with narrow leaves in low relief. A slightly protruding frame consisting of two half-columns and a stilted arch surrounds the niche. The capitals show leaf ornaments, and on top of them a vase containing flowers is rendered. Both elements are in high relief. The arch consists of two parts, the outer one being decorated with undulating stalks, connecting a continuous pattern of palmettes and alternating with leaves, while the inner is decorated with diagonally crossing lines (Figures 4 and 6). At the sides shafts with bases and capitals carry a secondary arch with a lozenge pattern. Vertical bands with a flat foliated scroll border the frames (Figure 7).

At the upper zone both corner panels are decorated with an undulating leaf pattern (Figure 5). On the two panels between the former windows a central vine-like stem rises, culminating in a flower or fruit at the top, while curving stems, tendrils, leaves and fruits fill the background. Two crosses flank the stem. The three later panels overlapping the former windows are in low relief. The central one has an encircled cross in the centre, while the outer panels are provided with a tree ornament (Figures 4 and 5). To these elements more crosses and objects such as small trees, a vessel and a cup are added.

On the north and south walls the four narrow panels to the extreme left and right are decorated with a straight vegetal ornament ending at the top in a chalice-like object (Figures 3 and 8). At intervals along the stems symmetrical excrescences terminate in leaves. The two panels between the windows are conceived in a plant form with a central stem.

---

[9] For these windows and their likeness with stucco windows in the *haykal* of Benjamin in Dayr Abu Maqar, see Evelyn White, *Monasteries*, 95, 97, and 200-201.

The leaves are five-lobed palmettes, with additional leaves, pointed and rounded fruits or clusters (Figures 3, 8, and 9).

The frieze shows a continuous pattern consisting of a palmette motif in high relief upon a double stalk, which curves outward and then upward inclosing a bunch of fruit and dominates the leaves filling the background (Figures 6, 8, and 9). A fruit alternates with this motif. The left part on the north wall has been replaced by an 18th-century coarse imitation with a cross (Figure 3).

The small niches have rectangular frameworks in low relief surrounding their upper half, with circular ornaments and scrolls in the spandrels, and slender shafts surmounted by an arch. The frameworks on the north and south walls resemble those of the niches in the east wall, but the spandrels of the doorways show a protruding floral element instead of a circular ornament. A decorated panel at the top of the niche in the north wall has partly survived.

The jambs of the doors or altar screens between the *khurus* and the *haykal* are inserted into narrow walls to the left and the right. These do not belong to the original architecture, but were without any doubt added to support the wooden construction. The narrow walls are covered with a layer of plaster bearing flat decoration at the front inside the *khurus* consisting of a repeated motif including a stylized vase and vegetal ornamentation. The plaster on the right wall partly covers an encaustic painting of a standing soldier-saint (perhaps Saint Sergius) on the bordering half-column. Hence this painting must be older then the stucco layer and the woodwork.[10]

The Chapel of the Forty-Nine Martyrs consists of three parts from different periods, the *haykal* being the oldest. Its east wall has three niches, the outer ones being framed by rectangular fields (Figure 10). In the 13th century the insides of the niches were painted with the images of two apostles (left and right) and the Virgin with the Child (center; painted over a similar older representation). According to their stylistic features these murals can be attributed to the painter who worked in the Church of al-'Adra of Dayr al-Baramus.[11] The frameworks show

---

[10] K.C. Innemée, K.C., P. Grossmann, K.D. Jenner, and L. van Rompay, "New Discoveries in the al-'Adra Church of Dayr as-Suryan in the Wadi al-Natrun," *Mitteilungen zur christlichen Archäologie* 4 (1998), 88 and figs. 10-11.

[11] G.J.M. van Loon, *The Gate of Heaven: Wall Paintings with Old Testament Scenes in the Altar Room and the Khurus of Coptic Churches* (Leiden: Nederlands Instituut voor het Nabije Oosten, 1999), 73, 74, 194, 195, and 198.

elements comparable to those in the church. In the spandrels a large leaf curves outwards, while the remainder of the surface is filled with an undulating stem and leaves. The architectural framing consists of two half-columns with bases and capitals on which an arch with a floral pattern is placed. A rectangular field in high relief, filled with leaves and palmettes, is applied on top.

Abbasid Stuccoes: Style and Architectural Application

Assessing their style the stuccoes in Dayr al-Suryan belong to an oriental group of purely ornamental plasterwork from the ninth and tenth centuries. Their affinities with other stuccoes in Egypt, in particular those in the late ninth-century Mosque of al-Maydan, better known as the Mosque of Ibn Tulun, was noticed by Joseph Strzygowski in 1901 and Samuel Flury in 1916.[12] Flury also pointed at the similarities between the stuccoes in Egypt and the many plaster ornaments that Ernst Herzfeld had discovered some years earlier at the site of Samarra in present Iraq.[13] For a while this Mesopotamian city had been the political centre of the Islamic world; it was the capital of the Abbasid rulers between AD 836 and 892, and the stuccoes must have been made in this time span. Although Herzfeld had published the Samarran material in 1923 already, Hugh Evelyn White did not work out the obvious 'Mesopotamian connection' in his detailed studies of the Wadi al-Natrun monasteries (1932/1933), and also in later publications this wider context was never fully explored.[14] Given the fact that the

---

[12] J. Strzygowski, "Der Schmuck in der älteren el-Hadra Kirche im syrischen Kloster der sketischen Wüste," *Oriens Christianus* 1 (1901), 357-358; see also Evelyn White, *Monasteries*, 206-207, plates XCIIb, XCIII. For the mosque see Creswell, *Early Muslim Architecture*, 392-406; Ettinghausen and Grabar, *Art and Architecture of Islam,* 92-94 and figure 68.

[13] Flury, "Samarra," and idem, "Die Gipsornamente des Der es-Surjani," *Der Islam* 6 (1916), 71-87.

[14] Evelyn White, *Monasteries*, 197, 204-206, and plates LXIV-LXII; M.S. Dimand, *A Handbook of Muhammadan Art* (New York: Metropolitan Museum of Art, 1958), 89-90; G. Kühnel, *Islamic Art and Architecture* (Ithaca, NY: Cornell University Press, 1966), 58; J.M. Fiey, "Coptes et syriaques. Contacts et échanges," *Studia Orientalia Christiana, Collectanea* 15 (1972-73), 342-344; Leroy, "Le décor de l'église" 161-162 and figs. 6-7; Walters, *Monastic Archaeology*, 192-194; P. Grossmann, "Dayr al-Suryan. Architecture," in *The Coptic Encyclopedia*, ed. Aziz S. Atiya (New York: Macmillan, 1991), 3:878, 880; M. Zibawi, *Orients chrétiens. Entre Byzance et l'islam* (Paris: Déclées de Bouvier, 1995), 163 and figure 122; T.K. Thomas, "Christians in the Islamic East," in H.C. Evans and W.D. Wixom, eds., *The Glory of Byzantium. Art and Culture of the Middle Byzantine*

monastery was populated with monks from Syria for centuries there are enough reasons to turn our view eastward.

The reliefs in the mosque and the monastery are not the only stuccoes in the Abbasid style in Egypt. Another example *in situ* is a modest fragment in the *haykal* of Saint Macarius in Dayr Abu Maqar, to the left of the entrance in the north wall (Figure 12). Many fragments came to daylight at the site of Fustat near Old Cairo. These remained unstudied so far; a few elements only are on permanent exhibition in the Islamic Museum in Cairo. Outside Egypt and Iraq the Abbasid style is represented in Iran, such as in the Friday Mosque in Isfahan[15] and in the Mosque of Nayin (about 960),[16] while in Afghanistan stuccoes fill the walls of the ninth-century mosque of Mashid-I-Ta'rikh at Balkh.[17] All these were obviously inspired by the art of Samarra, which is more or less situated in the centre of the distribution area.

Herzfeld made a first attempt to distinguish three styles, which he argued represent a chronological sequence, but as combinations appear on several occasions the formal diversity reflects differences in fashion rather than in time. Herzfeld's classification is still valuable, but Creswell reversed his sequence.[18] The so-called Style A (Herzfeld Style 3) includes carved vine ornaments in the tradition of late antique and early Christian art, rendered in a very plastic and naturalistic manner, while Style B (Herzfeld Style 2) is characterized by anti-naturalistic, more stylized vegetal compositions. Style C (Herzfeld Style 1) shows an abstract beveled ornamentation, and seems to be derived from Central Asian ornamental art.

These styles are represented in Dayr al-Suryan as well. Ornaments of Style A dominate, while, for example, the panels between de windows on the north and south walls in the *haykal* contain elements of Style B (Figures 3, 8, and 9). The outermost panels at window level on these walls are typical representatives of Style C (Figures 3 and 8), just

---

Era. A.D. 843-1261 (New York: Metropolitan Museum of Art, 1997), 367-368. A recent elaborate study is Immerzeel, "The Crowned Altar."

[15] Creswell, *Early Muslim Architecture*, 347.

[16] Dimand, *Handbook*, 89-90; Kühnel, *Islamic Art*, 58; Ettinghausen and Grabar, *Art and Architecture of Islam*, 212-213 and plates 210, 212, and 213.

[17] Creswell, *Early Muslim Architecture*, 348-349, and plate 225; J.D. Hoag, *Islamic Architecture* (Milan: Electra Editrice, 1975), 28-30, and figure 36, III; L. Golombek, "Abbasid Mosque at Balkh," *Oriental Art* 15 (1969), 173-189; Ettinghausen and Grabar, *Art and Architecture of Islam*, 214 and plate 216; R. Hillenbrand, *Islamic Art and Architecture* (London: Thamesand Hudson, 1999), 46 and figure 30.

[18] Creswell, *Early Muslim Architecture*, 374-376; see also Talbot Rice, *Islamic Art*, 32-34 and figs. 24-26; Ettinghausen and Grabar, *Art and Architecture of Islam*, 101-105, figs. 78-80; Hillenbrand, *Islamic Art*, 43 and figs. 25-27.

like the fragment in Dayr Abu Maqar (Figure 12). Yet the stylistic classification of the Abbasid stuccoes is not the most important item for their characterization; the almost unrestricted possibilities to combine different elements according to their architectural functionality also have to be taken into account. In the palaces and houses at Samarra stuccoes served as a covering of mud-brick walls.[19] In the mosque in Cairo, on the other hand, they mainly emphasize the stone arcade structure (Figure 11). Friezes consisting of continuing strips of undulating patterns frame the pointed arches over the piers and the windows at a higher level. In addition, ornamental panels are applied at their soffits. The limitation to border decoration is repeated consequently on the piers, at the corners of which engaged colonnettes with stucco capitals seem to support the arches although they are entirely decorative.

If we turn to look at Dayr al-Suryan again, the decoration has affinities with both concepts. The Samarran layout of surface-filling characterizes the higher level of the altar room of the church, while the border decoration of the mosque can be found mainly in the edges of the niches. In the central niche of the *haykal* the half-columns and capitals are variants on those in the mosque, while the border of its arch is filled with a similar undulating vegetal ornament.

One particularity in the church is the contrasting difference between the protruding high relief above eye level and the flat design of the lower parts. At this point we have to turn again to Leroy's impressions about the typical play of light. Seen from a higher level the protruding elements bench slightly towards the beholder inside the *haykal* (Figure 9). Obviously the relative darkness in the room inspired the stucco-workers to profit at maximum of the daylight entering through the windows. To this purpose they have sought to produce an optical illusion to give more depth to the reliefs. The constantly changing light fall emphasizes the protruding parts more than would have been the case if their relief has been low, and consequently seems to play with the shapes. In the chapel the same concept has been repeated: the relief of the frameworks is fairly flat, that of the fields at the top high.

[19] Hillenbrand, *Islamic Art*, 43: "The labour-saving properties of the moulded beveled style were ideally suited to the mushroom growth of Samarra, and the humble mud-brick of which even the palaces were mostly built was cheaply and effectively disguised by this mass-produced decoration."

Christian Aspects in the Decoration

Apart from the crosses on the east wall strictly spoken nothing in the decoration makes the stuccoes typically Christian (Figures 4 and 5). It is true that vegetal ornaments such as vine scrolls as well as vases or vessels from which vegetation sprouts belonged to the traditional Christian repertory, but these motifs had their origin in antiquity while they were also familiar to Islamic art. More puzzling is what is absent in the plasterwork: there are no figurative elements. This is even more striking if we take into consideration the presence of Christ Emmanuel, the Virgin and several saints, with Coptic inscriptions and composed of inlaid bone or ivory, on the doors inside the church, which appear to be more or less contemporary to the stuccoes (dated AD 914 and 926/927),[20] and the many wall paintings in the *khurus* which must have been visible, or perhaps painted, when the stuccoes were made.[21] This choice for a non-figurative programme was very likely not inspired by theological reflections. Iconoclasm was no longer a hot issue at that moment and likely never was at that place, and can therefore not have been of any influence. Either the stucco-workers were not skilled in representing human figures, or they and the people who commissioned the work preferred to remain faithful to the entirely ornamental repertoire of Abbasid reliefs.

What qualifies the Christian contents of the reliefs is the overall design, in particular in the *haykal* of the church. In the Mosque of Ibn Tulun the plastered edges of the arcades emphasize the structure of the building with their consequently repeated ornamentation. As far as the borders and columns of the niches and doorways are concerned the situation in Dayr al-Suryan is similar, but the composition as a totality is more the expression of a particular religious function than is the case in the mosque. The design in the *haykal* was worked out to give a spatial effect paying respect to the increasing importance of orientation towards the East that is inherent in church architecture and liturgy. Seen from the entrance the altar seems to be surrounded with a subtle play of daylight, as if it has a nimbus, or crown, while pertinently the decoration accumulates at the central niche. The effect is an almost metaphysical atmosphere. This brings us to the symbolic meaning of the decoration.

---

[20] Evelyn White, *Monasteries,* resp. 197-200, plate LXIV and 187-190, plates LVIII-LX; Leroy, "Le décor de l'église," 153-154, 159-161, and figs. 3-5.

[21] K.C. Innemée, L. van Rompay, and E. Sobczynski, "Deir al-Surian (Egypt): Its wall-paintings, wall-texts, and manuscripts. *Hugoye: Journal of Syriac Studies* 2.2 (1999), 2-3 (<http://syrcom.cua.edu/hugoye>).

In many churches the image of Christ, or a cross, appears in the apse, which Paul van Moorsel has called "...the place where the Divine can manifest itself."[22] The altar room is the place where one is allowed to look straight into heaven, and in this context the 'crown of light,' with its rich vegetation, could very well be considered a creative alternative to render the heavenly paradise.

The artistic *language* of the stuccoes in Dayr al-Suryan has its roots in the Christian tradition, which, in its turn, was derived from that of late antiquity. Nevertheless, the *vocabulary* of the plasterwork – the isolated motifs – is that of other Abbasid works. The artists made use of the decorative fashion of their time, but they simultaneously fully respected the Christian function of the building.

The Date of the Stuccoes

The similarities between the stuccoes in the monastery and those in Samarra as well as in the Mosque of Ibn Tulun are indicative for a dating in the ninth or tenth century. Samarra was founded as the capital of the Abbasid rulers in AD 836, but the city was deprived of its most prominent inhabitants from AD 892, when the court was moved to Baghdad, and hence lost its importance. The Mosque of Ibn-Tulun was inaugurated in AD 879, which means that its stuccoes were made when Samarra was still flourishing. Although the ninth century was the main period of the Abbasid style the example of the reliefs in the Mosque of Nayin in Iran demonstrates the continuity in its development during the next century.

The first Syrian monks settled in the monastery in the first half of the ninth century. One of the first activities of this group, of which the names of the Fathers Mattay and Ya'qub from Takrit are known, was to carry out some necessary rebuilding work in the seventh-century church.[23] A recently discovered Syriac inscription on the northern wall

---

[22] P. van Moorsel, "The Vision of Philotheus (on Apse-Decorations)," in M. Krause, ed., *Nubische Studien. Tagungsakten der 5. Internationalen Konferenz der International Society for Nubian Studies. Heidelberg, 22.-25. September 1982* (Mainz am Rhein: P. von Zabern, 1986), 337 (reprint in idem, *Called to Egypt. Collected Studies on Painting in Christian Egypt* (Leiden: Nederlands Instituut voor het Nabije Oosten, 2000), 107.

[23] U. Monneret de Villard, *Les églises du Monastère des Syriens au Wâdi en-Natrûn* (Milan: Tipografia pontificia arcivescovile S. Giuseppe, 1928), 5; Evelyn White, *Monasteries*, 309-311; K.C. Innemée and L. van Rompay, "Le monastère des Syriens au Ouadi Natroun (Egypte). A propos des découvertes récentes de peintures et de textes muraux dans l'Eglise de la Vierge du Couvent des Syriens," *Parole de l'Orient* 23 (1998),

of the nave mentions the Seleucid year 1130 (AD 818/819) as the year of (re)construction.[24] But what was the architectural situation at the eastern part of the church at their arrival in the monastery?

Certainly the present *haykal* is not part of the original construction. In 1995 Innemée suggested that the *khurus* originally had the shape of a *triconcha* consisting of three apses with half-domes of which only the northern and southern ones have remained.[25] His assumptions were based on the programmatic particularities of the 13th-century wall paintings in the extant half-domes and in that at the western end of the nave. The cycle includes the Annunciation and Nativity together in the southern half-dome, the Ascension in the one in the nave, and the Assumption of the Virgin in the northern half-dome. The discovery of a second Annunciation scene underneath the painting in the nave demonstrated that this cycle had replaced an earlier programme. According to Innemée's hypothesis the location of original Annunciation implied the presence of the Nativity in the northern half-dome of the *khurus*, the Ascension in the hypothetical eastern half-dome, and Pentecost on the south side of the *khurus*. Fieldwork executed in 2002 has pointed out that at least a part of this suggestion is correct, as traces of the Nativity were discovered underneath the 13th-century Dormition in the northern half-dome.[26]

The question is now when the supposed eastern apse was replaced with the square altar room. Although it is still far from clear if the original construction was extant in the early ninth century, the present *haykal* cannot be written on the account of Mattay and Ya'qub. A Syriac inscription on the lintel and the left jamb of the doors or altar screens giving access to the room suggests a second rebuilding campaign about one century later:[27]

To the praise and magnification and glory and exaltation of the venerable, and holy, and consubstantial Trinity. Moses [of Nisibis]

184-186; L. van Rompay and A.B. Schmidt, "Takritans in the Egyptian Desert: The Monastery of the Syrians in the Ninth Century," *Journal of the Canadian Society for Syriac Studies* 1 (2001), 41-60.

[24] van Rompay and Schmidt, "Takritans," 50-51.

[25] K.C. Innemée, "Deir al-Sourian – The Annunciation as part of a cycle?" *Cahiers Archéologiques* 42 (1995), 129-132.

[26] K.C. Innemée and L. van Rompay, "Deir al-Surian (Egypt): New discoveries of 2001-2002," *Hugoye : Journal of Syriac Studies* 5.2 (2002) (<http://syrcom.cua.edu/hugoye>), in particular 11.

[27] Evelyn White, *Monasteries*, 197; see also Strzygowski, "Der Schmuck," 365, and Leroy, "Le décor de l'église," 154.

the Abbot took pains and built and raised up this altar of the Church
of the Mother of God, in the days of the patriarchs, Mar Gabriel and
Mar John, in the year 1225 of the Greeks, in the month of Iyor,
upon the fifteenth of the same; that God, for whose holy Name's
sake (he did this), may be unto him a recompenser for good, and
unto every believer who has obtained a lot in this altar and this holy
monastery, for the saving of his life and its preservation, and for the
blotting out of (the sins) of his departed ones, and for the
forgiveness of his (own) sins.

The inscription refers to the consecration of a new altar on *Iyor* (May)
15 in the Seleucid year 1225 (AD 914),[28] but in fact it tells us more.
Leroy has remarked that *madbho*, the Syriac expression for altar, is also
used for the altar room in general.[29] This puts the inscription in a
different light: it seems to be related to the construction of the entire
haykal followed by the official inauguration in 914. The initiator of this
prestigious project was the illustrious Abbot Moses of Nisibis, whose
name also appears in manuscripts and in a Coptic inscription just below
the dome of the *khurus*.[30]

The year mentioned in the inscription helps to date the stuccoes as
well, mainly because of the decorated panels on the narrow walls, which
were constructed to support the doorjambs.[31] Yet fieldwork executed in
June 2002 has revealed a more complicated situation. When
investigating into the plaster behind the doors and the stuccoes on the
doorjambs Innemée did not find a direct stratified link between the
construction of the doors and the erection of the *haykal*. He suggests that
the present altar room may be of a later date.[32] How much later is a
matter requiring further investigation, but the chronological gap cannot
be very large. The context suggests that at the moment of consecration
there was already an altar behind the doors. The rebuilding could have
been executed in several phases and rounded off with the application of
the inscription after the consecration. In anticipation of further research
a provisional dating in the first quarter of the tenth century can be
accepted for the stuccoes.

For the later reliefs a dating about 1780 is ascertained, as the most
recent layer of plaster covering the walls of the church was applied in

---

[28] Innemée, van Rompay, and Sobczynski, "Deir al-Surian (Egypt)," 15.
[29] Leroy, "Le décor de l'église," 161.
[30] Grossmann, "Dayr al-Suryan."
[31] Immerzeel, "The Crowned Altar," 50-52; see also my "The Stuccoes."
[32] Innemée and van Rompay, "Deir al-Surian (Egypt)," 16.

this period.[33] Stuccoes comparable to the additions in the *haykal* are included in the same layer in the nave - on several columns and above the entrance to the *khurus* - and on the western wall of the *khurus* itself. Exceptional is a small pedestal with stucco decoration showing an angel in the nave, to the left of the entrance of the *khurus* (Figure 13). It does not belong to the 10th-century ornamentation, nor to that from the 18th century; according to Innemée this representation is applied on a 13th-century layer of plaster.

The Takritan Connection

The first Syrian inhabitants in the monastery originated from Takrit in the southern Tigris valley (Mesopotamia), about 100km north of Baghdad. By that time Syrian monks had already been living within Egypt for centuries, but monks were not the only Mesopotamians in this country. Many fellow countrymen had moved to Fustat, amongst whom a number of Takritan Christians.[34]

The relationship between the monks and the Christian Takritans must have been tight, in particular that with the colony in Fustat.[35] It has been suggested that the influence of this community was the real reason for the Syrian presence in the monastery. In three texts the purchase of the monastery by Takritans from Fustat on behalf of the Syrian monks living in Egypt is quoted. The man behind this project was Marutha, son of the high-ranking functionary Habbib.[36] But the texts concerned are suspect because they are rather late: one is dated AD 1562, another AD 1607, and the date of the third is uncertain. So far no contemporary evidence justifying this claim has been found.[37] On the contrary, in all likelihood the monastery fell under the Coptic Patriarchate without interruption, and had a mixed Coptic-Syrian population for ages.

Another event illustrates the importance of Dayr al-Suryan to the Syrians in the Tigris valley. Although Abbot Moses came from North

---

[33] According to the data presented by Bishop Martyros in his contribution to the *Acts of the Seventh International Congress of Coptic Studies. Leiden, 28 August-2 September 2000* (in print).

[34] Fiey, "Coptes et syriaques," 326-327.

[35] Evelyn White, *Monasteries*, 311-312.

[36] Evelyn White, *Monasteries*, 312-315.

[37] Evelyn White, *Monasteries*, 317-321, has suggested that the purchase dates from the seventh century, but this early dating is unlikely; see Fiey, "Coptes et syriaques," 325-326; Innemée and van Rompay, "Le monastère des Syriens," 191-193; van Rompay and Schmidt, "Takritans," 41-42, and 53.

Syria, he continued the existing contacts with Mesopotamia. Shortly after the finishing of the doors between the nave and the *khurus* in AD 926/927 he traveled to Mesopotamia and North Syria from where he returned in 932 with 250 manuscripts in his luggage.[38] This was more than just an enrichment of the library. The donors must have had good reasons to confide them to the monks: they must have considered Dayr al-Suryan their own monastery, worthy of keeping these precious treasures.

To fit the stuccoes within this Mesopotamian connection we have to turn again to Samarra, which was situated in between Baghdad and Takrit. The inhabitants of the three cities were practically neighbors and those who had moved to Egypt must have maintained close contacts with each other. Some were merchants, others had administrative duties, but in particular the arrival of Ibn Tulun from Samarra in AD 868 must have led to an influx of court functionaries and soldiers as well as architects, artists and craftsmen.

Several architectural elements of the mosque erected on Ibn Tulun's orders point to Samarra. Creswell described it as "a foreign, 'Iraqi building planted down on the soil of Egypt."[39] Cogently, the plasterwork was certainly not made by local workmen, but by stucco-workers from Samarra. After accomplishing their task in Cairo these specialists very likely did not return, but successfully continued to exploit their expertise in Egypt, in particular in Fustat.

Apparently the Christians from Mesopotamia did what was in their power to strengthen the infrastructure of the monastery, not only by supporting its library, but also by financing building activities. The reference in the lintel inscription to "every believer who has obtained a lot in this altar[room] and this holy monastery" is indicative of external support. Consequently, the possibility of the stuccoes being part of a donation by Syrian benefactors, perhaps Takritans from Fustat, in the form of a pious donation (*waqf*) has to be considered seriously.

This hypothesis, tempting though it is, does not answer all questions. The time span of several decades between the making of the stuccoes in the mosque and those in the monastery makes it unlikely that both were produced by the same team of artists. The work in Dayr al-Suryan must have been executed by a next generation of stucco-

---

[38] Monneret de Villard, *Les églises du Monastère*, 29; Fiey, "Coptes et syriaques," 340-341; Leroy, "Le décor de l'église," 152-153; Innemée and van Rompay, "Le monastère des Syriens," 187-188.
[39] Creswell, *Early Muslim Architecture*, 406; see also Ettinghausen and Grabar, *Art and Architecture of Islam*, 92-94.

workers, perhaps under the direction of an experienced master, who had continued the tradition of their forerunners in Egypt. The general concept demonstrates that at least some of them must have understood the decorative language of Christian buildings, not to speak of the possibility that they were Christians.[40]

A final matter is the reason why this, in the case of an eastern church building unconventional, decoration was chosen for this particular monastery. In the introduction the presence of decorative plasterwork in churches in Europe has been mentioned, but any direct European influence on the reliefs in Dayr al-Suryan is unlikely. While the affinity of Christian Egyptians with plaster reliefs seems to be negligible, at least at this scale and in such important places as altar rooms, the Syrians had their centuries-old tradition in decorating (secular) buildings. From this point of view the stuccoes in the monastery could be considered a typical Syrian item in a partly Syrian, partly Coptic environment, as if the Syrian community aimed at leaving their mark as an expression of their identity in their most important monastic settlement abroad. The coincident availability of stucco-workers from their homeland, who now had the opportunity to work in a monastery, might have been helpful to realize this desire. Eventually the presence of these specialists led to cultural interaction, as the fragment in Dayr Abu Maqar demonstrates that Copts were also sensible for the charm of their craftsmanship.

---

[40] Several (later) written sources mention that the architect of the Mosque of Ibn Tulun was also a Christian. The oldest reference can be found in al-Balawi's *Sirat Ahmat ibn Tulun* from the early 11th century (ed. Kurd 'Ali 1939, 182; see Creswell, *Early Muslim Architecture*, 392, n. 4). In view of the Samarran elements in the architecture this person might have been a Mesopotamian Christian.

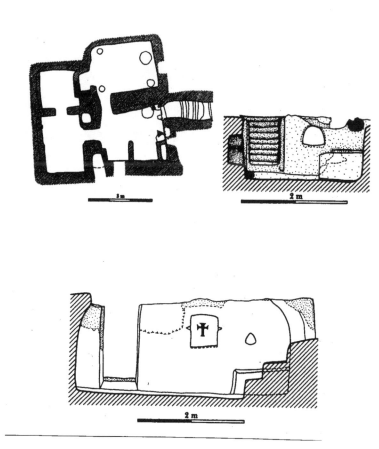

Figure 1: Eastern Part of the Church of al-'Adra and the Chapel of the Forty-Nine Martyrs

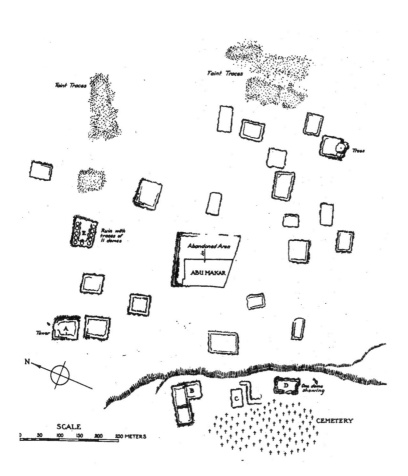

Figure 2: The Stuccoes in the *haykal* of the Church (after Evelyn White, *Monasteries*,
plates LXVII and LXIX; and Immerzeel, "The Crowned Altar," fig. 3)

Figure 3: North Wall of the *haykal*: upper zone

Figure 4: East Wall: centre of the upper zone

Figure 5: East Wall: southern part of the upper zone

Figure 6: East Wall: central niche

Figure 7: East Wall: border to the left of the central niche

Figure 8: South Wall: upper zone

Figure 9: South Wall: upper zone seen from a higher level

Figure 10: Right Niche in the Chapel of the Forty-Nine Martyrs
(before the discovery of the paintings)

Figure 11: Mosque of Ibn Tulun: section of the arcade

Figure 12: Dayr Abu Maqar: stucco fragment

Figure 13: Pedestal with an Angel in the Nave of the Church

Results of the Recent Restoration Campaigns (1995-2000) at Dayr al-Suryan

Ewa Parandowska

Introduction

Since 1995 I have had the opportunity to work as a conservator with the Dutch-Polish-Egyptian team directed by Dr. Karel Innemèe of Leiden University on the discovery and protection of Christian wall paintings in the Holy Virgin Church at the Syrian Monastery. In spite of the relative shortness of the seven seasons that have taken place (from two to six weeks) and the limited number of team members (between two and five), the results of our investigations are significant. Our research has revealed that under the smooth grayish undecorated plaster on the church interior walls there are traces of several successive architectural alterations and many murals from different periods, decorating the walls, columns, and domes of the building. During the exploratory phase in 1995, over fifty "windows" were opened in the eighteenth century plain plaster on different walls. Once the underlying coats had been exposed it became clear that all the major parts of the church had been decorated with wall paintings. We were able to estimate the number of successive decorated layers (from three to five) and determine what the character of each had been. Now, having uncovered about 100m^2 of decorated surfaces, we can safely say that almost the entire interior of the church had been covered with colorful paintings and inscriptions.

Each working season adds to the known iconographic repertory of painting themes, the history of the architectural modifications, and their chronology. Nonetheless, another 300m^2 of the eighteenth century plaster sill remains to be removed before all the concealed murals will have been revealed, preserved, and prepared for display, which is the chief aim of the project.

Not only will knowledge of Dayr al-Suryan's history benefit from our investigations, we shall also learn important data about the workshop, style, and technique of Coptic and specifically Syrian artists, while the conservation of the church interior will undoubtedly improve the aesthetic impression left by this church, which should thus become one of the most valuable Coptic monuments in Egypt.

Thanks to the kind hospitality of His Holiness Pope Shenouda III and to the invaluable assistance of the monks from Dayr al-Suryan, we have been able to pursue our work in an atmosphere both pleasant and fascinating.

Stratigraphy of the Decorated Layers

As it has been said already, the objectives of the project are to discover, consolidate, preserve and study all of the wall paintings inside the church. Dr. Karel Innemèe has published interim reports, concentrating especially on the iconography, while Luc van Rompay and Peter Grossmann have additionally published their observations, respectively, on the inscriptions and the nature and dating of the architectural alterations in the Monastery.

As a consequence of previous campaigns it has been possible to identify the original context of the murals and inscriptions. We have been able to estimate the extent of the paintings in the major parts of the church, to trace the stratigraphy of painted layers and the technology of each individual coating, as well as its date.

At present, three historically different phases of renovation have been identified on most of the uncovered surface. It has been suggested, however, based on extant data, that the church (or at least some parts of it) had been redecorated at least five times between the seventh and eighteenth centuries. The fact that four phases of decoration on the upper walls of the *khurus* and five layers of plaster appear on the partition wall between the nave and the *khurus* indicates that the most important (and exposed) walls of the church had been replastered and repainted more often that the other walls, not to mention rebuilding.

Firstly, this partition wall, which originates from the second half of the seventh century, had a door inserted in it in the tenth century; the inscription that appeared next to the doorway, partly covering the earlier painting, has helped to date this phase. Next, during the thirteenth-century renovation, additional walls were constructed in front of the two niches covered with eight-century murals; these new walls were also decorated. Finally, the entire interior of the church was replastered in the eighteenth century. In order to do this all the previous layers of decorated plaster had to be removed from the walls and dome, the debris being dumped largely into the hollow space behind the new wall and inside the niches. Fragments recovered from this space were sent to the laboratory for examination. The provisional laboratory test results regarding pigment and plaster structure have been helpful in letting us determine the composition of mortars applied, the kind of coloring agents and binding media, the technique of execution, which has also had an influence on the state of preservation of particular layers.

Characteristics of the Paint Layers and Mortars

The coatings represent different techniques, style, and artistic value. The first layer with decoration dates back to the second half of the seventh century. On a coarse, sand-lime yellow mortar covered with white limewash, there is a red and orange pattern of lines and crosses, and geometrical motifs, all painted *al secco* (distemper technique). There is much in favor of the decoration of this coating never having been finished.

The second phase of the decoration, beginning in the eight century, used as background a light gray limewash, thickly applied straight on top of the earlier paintings. It is represented in the whole church. The lower part of the nave and the *khurus* walls, to a height of two meters, were decorated with a *dado* of marble columns and an architrave, topped with a geometrical freeze and a red frame that divides the wall at mid-height. In the upper half there were numerous framed representations of different saints, as well Coptic and Syriac inscriptions (Figure 1).

The colorful scenes were executed in the encaustic technique or mixed with distemper directly on the thick gray limewash, already damaged in places. Several of the murals were painted on a black primary ground. The heterogeneity of this decoration phase, both technical and stylistic, suggests the hand of different artists and a certain span of time. Several artists used the same pigments and painting conventions (deep bright colors mixed with wax and red-black frames around each representation. The remains of the decoration found in the dome and on the upper walls of the *khurus*, dated to the tenth century (third phase), were applied on a thin new layer of white gypsum, which was very friable and loosely adhering to the ground.

At first glance, the similar character of the geometric and floral border gives an impression of a single artistic program. Details of style and technique, however, prove that the murals were added on gradually after the eighth century and before the renovation in the thirteenth, when a major rebuilding of the church was undertaken. The fourth layer of decoration, the so-called "Syriac" layer, was applied after the interior of the church had been renovated (windows and niches were blocked, some of the doors changed, and new supporting beams for two half-domes mounted). The plaster was light, gray on the surface, composed of lime-gypsum mortar with some fine sand added.

The decoration of this layer has survived almost intact in three of the half-domes: two in the *khurus* still in place, the third one transferred to a new support and displayed temporarily on the eastern corner of the nave. Some other fragments have so far been uncovered on the southern and eastern wall of the nave and on the columns. In the *khurus*, the only minor fragments have been revealed – testimonies to the stratigraphy on the capitals and above the blocked windows.

Most of the decoration has been removed before a new layer (fifth) of plain thick pinkish plaster composed of lime, sand, and crushed brick was applied over almost the entire church interior, obscuring the original shape and giving new profiles to architectural elements. The thickness of this last layer is not constant and varies from 0.8cm to 12cm, hiding from view the carelessly removed remains of the two earlier decorated layers.

State of Preservation

The redecoration as well as the various building activities practically always resulted in some mechanical damage to the painted layers, such as pitting the hammering, which were intended as a means of preparing the surface for replastering. The decoration of the second and third phase, undoubtedly the most important from the point of view of both artistic and iconographic value, was replastered twice, first in the thirteenth and then in the eighteenth century. Despite intentional mechanical damages, the encaustic technique, which is resistant to chemical changes, was instrumental in saving a significant percentage of this historical layer (Figure 2).

Overall, the thirteenth-century murals are in the worst condition. This plaster was easy to detach from the waxy, greasy surface underneath. The technique (tempera on gypsum calcitic plaster) explains the heavy contamination with salts (carbonates and chlorides) and, in effect, the "discoloration" of some parts of the painted surface, replastered with wet eighteenth-century mortar. Some of the representations cannot be uncovered completely in view of structures that were introduced attached to the columns and walls which were meant as reinforcement of the pillars supporting the barrel-vaults.

The condition of this layer on three of the half-domes is different as the destruction was more of a natural aging process than mechanical damages, meaning the surface was covered with dirt that accumulated over a period of 800 years, dimming the colors substantially. Some sections have become very pale, this due to changes of humidity and environmental conditions, as well as a complete disintegration of the binding medium.

Much of the serious damage took place in more recent times, especially from the nails that were driven through all the layers when the electric installation was installed and when lamps and icons were hung, and from the new niches that were cut in the walls to accommodate chests for books and offerings.

Reconstruction of the Paint Layers (Chiefly Second and Third Phase)

To reiterate, the objective of the conservation work was to uncover and restore the original polychromed decorations and to improve the aesthetic value of the church interior. Originally, it has been envisaged that the discovery, documentation, and consolidation of successively appearing representations would precede the restoration of architectural elements and the retouching of the murals, which were to be left for the final stage. However, considering the relative shortness of our seasons at Dayr al-Suryan, it would have taken the project several years to be completed. That would have meant that the unretouched murals would determine the decorative character of the church for a long time. Obviously, the hundreds of small light-colored lacunae cannot but have a disturbing effect on viewers (Figure 3), who are furthermore unable to understand the painting. At the insistence of the bishop and monks, a policy was adopted to leave none of the paintings uncovered during a given season unfinished. Final decisions concerning the reconstruction and retouching of the second layer were preceded by many discussions. Even our team was not in agreement, Karel Innemèe objecting to any interference with the eight-century relic of historical value. Thus, an attempt was made to reduce to a minimum the intervention of a restorer, involving only actual integration of the missing parts and restoring the legibility of the original forms, wherever possible (Figure 4).

The decision in favor of retouching the paintings was prompted by the following factors:

1. The church remains in active use, serving liturgical purposes on an everyday basis. Hence, it cannot be treated as merely an archaeological testimonial of the past;

2. Despite two episodes of hammering and replastering, most of the paintings have survived in a condition that was sufficiently good to allow for particular representations to be reconstructed in their entirety;

3. The surviving parts of the paintings permit the palette used by the artist in executing particular images to be reconstructed with considerable exactness. Colors do not fade in the encaustic technique. They appear just as bright as on the day that they were applied, hence, the opportunity to restore them faithfully; and

4. Our retouching work, executed with professional "Wincolor & Newton" waterpaint colors, not only fills in exactly all the damaged fragments, but also assures quick and complete correction or removal of the retouching, if necessary, using a moist tampon. Another advantage of this technique is its high resistance to light (no change of color over time, as in the case of oil-based paints, coupled with complete reversibility).

The reconstruction was limited to fragments, which could be restored based on surviving evidence. A lime-sand mortar was used to fill in the other big lacunae even with the surface.

Not the least in our discussions was the choice of retouching technique. Of the various methods proposed by conservators around the world, *trateggio* requires the missing parts of a mural to be restored with a thin line or dots in order to make apparent the difference between the original and the restored fragment. The differences should be visible from close-up, but indiscernible to the eye from afar. It is recommended particularly for lime techniques of wall painting, especially in monumental-size paintings. In easel-paintings, retouching has to be invisible to everything but laboratory methods, which can discern between the original and the restored parts of a painting using UV, IR, or RTG photography, or pigment study. With regard to the Dayr al-Suryan murals, the application of the wax technique makes things easier. The retouching imitates the original color of the pigments and their laying on (in a number of layers) as closely as possible, but at close quarters the difference between the shining impasto original and the flat and mat retouching is quite evident. The final effect has been found to be satisfying.[1]

---

[1] Further discussion is in the following publications: K.C. Innemée, P. Grossmann, K.D. Jenner, and L. van Rompay, "New discoveries in the al-'Adrâ' Church of Dayr as-Suryân in the Wâdî al-Natrûn," *Mitteilungen zur christlichen Archäologie* 4 (1998), 79-103; K.C. Innemée, "Recent discoveries of wall-paintings in Deir Al-Surian," *Hugoye: Journal of Syriac Studies* 1.2 (1998) (<http://syrcom.cua.edu/hugoye>); K.C. Innemèe, "The Wall Paintings of Deir al-Sourian. New Discoveries of 1999." *Hugoye: Journal of Syriac Studies* 2.2 (1999) (<http://syrcom.cua.edu/hugoye>); K.C. Innemée, and L. van Rompay, "La présence des Syriens dans le Wadi al-Natrun (Égypte): À propos des découvertes récentes de peintures et de textes muraux dans l'Église de la Vierge du Couvent des Syriens," *Parole de l'Orient* 23 (1998), 167-202; K.C. Innemée, and L. van Rompay, "Deir al-Surian (Egypt): New discoveries of January 2000," *Hugoye: Journal of Syriac Studies* 3.2 (2000) (<http://syrcom.cua.edu/hugoye>); and L. van Rompay, "Deir al Sourian: Miscellaneous Reflections," *Essays of Christian Art and Culture in the Middle East*, vol. 3. Leiden: Leiden University, 2000.

Figure 1: Fragment revealing three stages of the redecoration

Figure 2: Uncovered fragment before conservation
revealing the mechanical damages (pitting and hammering)

Figure 3: Painting before retouching: small lacunae
have been filled with lime-chalk putty

Figure 4: The same painting during retouching

Indigo and Madder,
Finger Prints and Brush Strokes:
Notes on Six Byzantine Great Deesis Icons of
Wadi al-Natrun Monasteries
and their Egyptian Origin

Zuzana Skalova

Six large Deesis portraits of unknown provenance are preserved in the Coptic monasteries in the Wadi al-Natrun. Five, which are of serial nature, formed a part of a majestic Great Deesis set of 11 icons. There is also a portrait of St. John the Baptist, painted by another painter but demonstrating the same local technical characteristics. Analogous Deesis icons, dated to the twelfth and thirteenth century, survive in the collection of the Greek Orthodox Monastery of St. Catherine at Mount Sinai. The size and style of the portraits as well as the typical grey-blue and reddish wavy decoration on the reverse of both groups imply a link between the Greek (Melkite) and Coptic icon workshops in the country. This investigation in technical art history reconstructs the set and traces the origin of the Wadi al-Natrun icons painted in Byzantine style on locally made sycamore panels to Coptic patronage in Cairo.[1]

Part One

The Thirteenth-Century Interceding St. John the Baptist from a Trimorphon Set

At least two Byzantine Deesis portraits reached the Monastery of the Syrians: the remaining *Interceding St. John the Baptist*[2] (91cm x

---

[1] For medieval icons on sycamore panels with reverse wavy decoration in the Coptic collection, which were re-restored in the frame of the joint Egyptian-Netherlands Coptic Icons Conservation Project 1989-1996, see the present author's chapter "Medieval Icons in Arab and Mameluke Times" and "Catalogue," in Z. Skalova and G. Gabra, *Icons in the Nile Valley* (Cairo, in print), 2:110-119 and cat. nos. 7-16.

[2] Published in a Dayr al-Suryan's pamphlet. For color reproduction, see Skalova and Gabra, *Icons of the Nile Valley,* 2: cat. no.7.

65cm x 1.5cm) (Figure 1.1) and the now lost *Interceding Virgin Mary*, whose measurements are not documented but whose replica[3] and photos[4] exist (Figure 2). It can be assumed that both icons originated from the same set of three icons (in Greek: Trimorphon), comprising of the central panel with a frontally depicted Christ, flanked by his human mother, the Virgin Mary, and St. John the Baptist, the first witness to his divinity. The Trimorphon became the core of so-called Great Deesis composition — developed from the liturgical prayers of intercession — flanked by varying number of archangels, evangelists, apostles and locally venerated saints, all depicted in praying position.[5]

Extended Deesis sets were placed on the Byzantine sanctuary screens, dividing the sanctuary from the nave, by the twelfth century. Professor Sharon Gerstel connects in her study, *Beholding the Sacred Mysteries: Programs of the Byzantine Sanctuary*, the alteration in the sanctuary division with liturgical changes which concealed the clergy behind the high altar screen (Greek iconostasion). Becoming higher, these icon-partitions "obscured the mysteries from the gaze of the unconsecrated." By the end of the thirteenth century, the practice of screening the sanctuary by high barriers topped with icons (inserted into the inter-columnations or placed in rows) was widespread in the Empire,[6] and, as the Deesis icons made in Egypt indicate, beyond its political frontiers.

The fate of the Egyptian Trimorphon of yet unknown provenance demonstrates vicissitudes that beset the medieval icons which were taken down from their screens: the central icon of Christ vanished; the panel with the *Interceding Virgin* was consumed in 1980s by the flames of a candle placed too close; and the surviving panel on with *Interceding John the Baptist* was at some time partly consumed by termites (?).[7] It is sycamore panel with alternating gray-blue (indigo) and reddish (madder?) lines of finger prints (Figure 1.2). [8]

---

[3] The icon, painted by Father Yusab, can be seen in the Church of the Holy Virgin.

[4] Unpublished. My supposition is based on a color slide, made probably by Mr. Nabil Selim Atalla, now in the archives of the Societé d'Archeologie Copte, Cairo, which kindly gave permission to include this photo in my research.

[5] A.P. Kazhdan, ed., *The Oxford Dictionary of Byzantium* (Oxford: Oxford University Press, 1991), 1: 599.

[6] S.E.J. Gerstel, *Beholding the Sacred Mysteries: Programs of the Byzantine Sanctuary* (Seattle and London: University of Washington Press, 1999), 9-10. This fine study concerns the sanctuary decoration of 27 churches in Macedonia, spanning the period 1028-1328.

[7] The panel's central part was almost consumed by wood-eating insects, but not necessarily in the monastery. This damage might be earlier. Two thirteenth-century

Note on the Regional Technique of the Interceding St. John the Baptist

The appalling damage to the support on which the *Baptist* is painted allows us to look through the icon and to scrutinize otherwise hidden carpentry, peculiar to the Nile valley, where trees were scarce and ancient beliefs, techniques, and workshop practices continue to exist. It would seem that the timber from sycamore fig tree (*ficus sycomoros*), plentiful in the country since Pharaonic times, was used up to the Middle Ages also for its sacred connotations.[9] The *Baptist*'s support is made of three vertical planks of sycamore wood, heavy and coarse, held together with three horizontal half-round traverses on reverse and with a narrow board nailed from the front. It was made carefully: the nails do not protrude and there are no rifts between the planks (characteristics typifying some medieval icons firmly attributed to Coptic patronage, such as the twin beams in the Church of St. Mercurios Abu Seifein discussed below). The priming on front side and the thick plaster layer on reverse camouflage planks whose irregularities are filled in with chunks of raw gypsum, from locally available deposits in the "White" Western desert (Figure 1.3), their joints smoothed with pounded soaked reeds or date-palm fronds,[10] applied one upon another in an effort to produce a regular surface. The patchwork of these local materials was glued together with proteinous glue and covered with linen cloth. Then gypsum priming layer was skillfully applied. The artist's palette was lead white,

---

beam icons in the Church of St. Mercurios in Cairo mentioned below were also affected in this way.

[8] For the wavy bands on the reverses of the Nile valley icons were most probably used madder (the root of *Rubia tinctorum*) and indigo plant (macerated leaves of the plant *indigogera argentea* growing wild in Nubia and Ethiopia) known to Egyptian artisans from textile industry (M.-H. Rutschowscaya, "Coptic Textiles: Manufacturing Techniques," in Aziz S. Atiya, ed., *Coptic Encyclopedia* [New York: Macmillan, 1991], 7:2215). The occurrence of indigo and madder on the reverse of the Wadi al-Natrun *Baptist* is subject of an ongoing research and has been confirmed thanks to W. Hesterman, Muiden.

[9] For cultural and spiritual dimensions to the sycamore fig tree in the Nile valley, where, since the Pharaonic period divinatory properties have been attributed to it, see Z. Skalova, "New Evidence for the Medieval Production of Icons in the Nile Valley, in *Historical Painting Techniques, Materials, and Studio Practices*," in A. Wallert, E. Hermens, and M. Peek, eds., *Historical Painting Techniques, Materials, and Studio Practice: Preprints of a Symposium, University of Leiden, the Netherlands, 26-29 June 1995* (Marina Del Rey, CA: Getty Conservation Institute, 1995), 87-88.

[10] These are the materials typical for local industries, such as basketry, as practiced also in the Coptic monasteries. See R. Krawiec, *Shenoute and the Women of the White Monastery* (New York: Oxford University Press, 2002), 18.

carbon black, yellow and red ochres, finely ground azurite and vermillion, mixed in egg-yolk as binding medium. This technology is typical of all medieval icons on sycamore panels of the Nile valley, which all have a common feature: their reverse side is plastered and decorated with alternating grey-blue and reddish wavy lines The blend of traditional Egyptian carpentry and materials with refined Greek painterly technique and styles is unique characteristic of this regional school of icon painting, producing sacred pictures for Melkite and Coptic patrons. Consequently, the icons of Byzantine era, made in Egypt, are more appropriately treated by restorers as fragile gilded wooden Pharaonic art objects or so called Fayyum portraits than as European icons.[11]

Despite the disfiguring damage to the support, lacunae in preparation and paint layers and the obscuring resinous varnish, John the Baptist's imposing portrayal is of outstanding quality. On the solidly primed and gilded front side the image is painted into sketchy incised contours, filling the space, with the saint's right hand and nimbus, jeweled with white, red and blue pearls, extending into the border. Along the inner side of this nailed border a jeweled band of black lozenges alternating with white pearls can be discerned – a characteristic of Crusader painting.[12] The saint is identified in red Greek letters O A[γιος] IO[αννης] left, and O ΠΡΟ[δρομος], right. We see the saint half length, turned to his left, with his hands held in prayer. He is dressed, as usual, in prophet's pallium and the fur mantle. His unusually broad contemplative face is almost hidden by mass of dark disheveled hair and beard, the formula invented to depict *pathos* of his inner suffering since he foresaw the suffering of

---

[11] Findings of the scientific analysis of another medieval icon *Seven major Feasts,* painted in Cairo, testify to use of similar local materials and technique. I am indebted to Peter Hallebeek (Institute Collection Netherlands, Amsterdam) for valuable consults concerning the materials, techniques and suitable conservation methods of medieval icons in the Coptic collection, generously given since early 1990s. The ground layer on icons from the Middle Ages painted in Egypt is invariably gypsum, weakly-bound, or even without binding medium, and therefore particularly vulnerable to humidity; see Z. Skalova, "'Traced by Incense': A Thirteenth-Century Epistyle in the Church of the Holy Virgin, Harat Zuwayla in Cairo," *Bulletin of the American Research Center in Egypt* 180 (2001), 21 and 22 with note 8.

[12] This is the only icon of the Nile valley, I found up to date, with such inner decorative framing. However, parallels can be found on many art works as far as Italy and Greece, and on numerous so-called Crusader icons at the Monastery of St. Catherine at Sinai (for example on *St. Nicolas with scenes from his life,* dated by Doula Mouriki to the third quarter of the thirteenth century); see the November page in the *Calendar of the St. Catherine's Monastery for 1991.*

Christ. In a pale face, modeled in ochres from dark greenish basis and highlighted on the cheeks and forehead with white strokes, his elongated eyes with light brown pupils and narrow nose are delineated with dark lines and the mouth is red. Although more detail cannot be discerned this seems to be the work of the same workshop, perhaps even of the same master who painted the icon of the enthroned Virgin and Child wearing nimbi jeweled with white, red and blue pearls, which is still displayed in its Coptic woodwork stand in the Church of St. Barbara in Old Cairo.

The *Enthroned Virgin and Child* (125cm x 76cm x 2cm) is also painted on sycamore panel with alternating grey-blue and reddish lines of brush strokes (Figure 3.1). The icon was photographed (before its over-cleaning in 1988) and published in 1989 by Lucy-Anne Hunt as the thirteenth-century work of a Greek painter on the basis of comparison with Sinai icons.[13] During its re-restoration in 1990-1991 I came to conclusion that the image was painted on locally made sycamore board that was almost certainly the product of a Coptic workshop in Cairo (Figure 3.2).[14] Not surprisingly, full-sized images of the Virgin Mary and the Christ Child enthroned on a high-backed wooden throne can be found in the thirteenth–century Coptic monumental art, the closest parallels being those in the Old Church of the Monastery of St. Antony near the Red Sea, dated by an inscription to 1232/1233.[15]

The reverse decoration of these panels consisting of superimposed grey-blue and reddish bands of finger prints or brush strokes deserves our attention, as it occurs on numerous Middle

---

[13] L.-A. Hunt, "Iconic and Aniconic: Unknown Thirteenth and Fourteenth Century Byzantine Icons from Cairo in their Woodwork Settings," *Poikila Byzantina* 6 (1989), 68-94 with nos. 35-36 and figs. 18-20.

[14] This icon was re-restored with assistance of Manal Fahmy, in the frame of the Netherlands-Egyptian Coptic Icons Conservation project, in cooperation with the Church of St. Barbara. In 1990, Dorothea Pechova competently provided scientific determination of the materials. See Z. Skalova, "Conservation problems in Egypt: Icons Preliminary Classification and Sopme Case Studies," in *Preprints of the IXth Triennial Conference, ICOM CC* (1990) 2:777-782 with figs. 1-4; idem, "A Little Noticed Thirteenth-Century Byzantine Icon in the Church of St. Barbara in Old Cairo 'The Virgin with Child Enthroned,'" *Bulletin de la Societé d'archéologie Copte* 30 (1991), 93-103, plates I-VIII; and idem, in Skalova and Gabra, *Icons of the Nile Valley,* 2: cat. no. 8

[15] For these images of the enthroned Virgin and Child, recently restored, see E.S. Bolman, *Monastic Visions: Wall Paintings in the Monastery of St. Antony at the Red Sea* (New Haven: Yale University Press and the American Research Center in Egypt, 2002), figs. 4.23 and 4.28.

Byzantine icons in the region, and particularly in the collection of
icons in the Greek-Orthodox Monastery of Saint Catherine at Mount
Sinai.[16] The majority of these "made in Sinai" icons, of varied sizes,
forms and styles, attest to the mobility of the cosmopolitan fleet of
monk-painters of the era, when the Crusaders patronized the
monastery during their presence in the Holy Land (1098-1187),
Constantinople (1204-1261) and Cyprus (from 1190s on). The
arcaded beams and Deesis portraits dating to the prolific twelfth and
thirteenth centuries are the most relevant for this survey. Many have
been attributed by Kurt Weitzmann to a Cypriot atelier.[17] Among the
Deesis portraits recently published by Mary Aspra-Vardavakis[18] as
the work of a Cypriot workshop operating at Sinai in early thirteenth
century,[19] that of the *Interceding St. John the Baptist* painted in
emotional Komnenian style, is interesting; here is a well-preserved
portrait of the Baptist of size and iconography, that suggests close
parallels with our icon in Wadi al-Natrun; both the affinities and the
differences are striking (Figures 4.1 and 4.2).

---

[16] The reference on Sinai icons on panels with similar decoration in this survey has to
remain limited. For published items see D. Mouriki, "Icons from the Twelfth to the
Fifteenth Century," in K.A. Manafis, ed., *Sinai: Treasures of the Monastery of Saint
Catherine* (Athens: Ekdotike Athenon, 1990), 105, nos. 25, 68, 70 and 72; and A. Weyl-
Carr, "Templon Beam with the Deesis and Feast Scenes," in H.C. Evans and W.D. Wixom,
eds., *Glory of Byzantium* (New York: Metropolitan Museum of Art, 1997), 377, cat. no.
248 (back).

[17] K. Weitzmann, "A Group of Early Twelfth-Century Icons attributed to Cyprus," in
idem, *Studies in the Arts at Sinai* (Princeton: Princeton University Press, 1982) and
idem, *The St. Peter Icon of Dumbarton Oaks* (Washington, DC: Dumbarton Oaks,
1983).

[18] M. Aspra-Vardavakis, "A Thirteenth Century Sinai Grand Deesis," in
Drevnjerusskoe Iskusstvo: Rus, Vizantija, Balkany, XIII vek (St. Petersburg, 1997),
106-113, figs 1-2; and idem, "Three Thirteenth-Century Sinai Icons of John the Baptist
Derived from a Cyprus Model," in N. Paterson-Ševčenko and C. Moss, eds., *Medieval
Cyprus: Studies in Art, Architecture, and History in Memory of Doula Mouriki* (Princeton:
Princeton University Press, 1999), 181, text fig. 3 and fig. 12. There is another icon of
the Baptist (54.4cm x 45.6cm) from late twelfth/thirteenth century Deesis A, consisting
today of Trimorphon flanked by *Archangels Michael* and *Gabriel* (lost) and *Apostles
Peter* and *Paul*, all with reverse wavy decoration.

[19] The fine panel of imported wood is decorated with the familiar alternating grey-blue
and reddish lines of brush strokes, here elaborately executed in imitation of a richly
embroidered liturgical textile.

1. Sinai *Baptist* (from Great Deesis set B of 5 icons)	97.5cm x 66.5cm (Figure 4)
2. Wadi al-Natrun *Baptist* (from a Trimorphon set)	91cm x 65cm (Figure 1)
3. Wadi al-Natrun *Gabriel, John, Matthew, Mark* and *Paul* (from Great Deesis set of 11 icons)	89cm x 55.3cm (Figures 6-10)

To sum up: The Wadi al-Natrun *Baptist* can be ascribed to the hand of a Greek or Byzantine-trained master working in Egypt, probably in Cairo. It looks contemporary with the St. Barbara's *Enthroned Virgin and Child*, attributed to the thirteenth-century artist with Cypriot connection. The fact that both panels' reverse sides are marked with wavy lines strengthens presumed Coptic-Byzantine cooperation. While such reverse finish was noted by leading Byzantinists on twelfth- and thirteenth-century icons from Sinai, Cyprus, and Mount Athos,[20] its occurrence on 25 icons of the Nile valley, is little known.[21] When studying this Egyptian group of medieval icons in detail (some during their restoration), I come to conclusion that such consistent technical feature attests to prolonged production of icons in the country, and emerged as a trademark of workshops in which local carpenters and painters cooperated with itinerant Byzantine-trained masters, active in the eastern Mediterranean during the prolific thirteenth century; such arrangements would go a long way to explain why this phenomenon did not posses a clearly-defined style. Besides, it should not be overlooked that sycamore panels made in Egypt vary in quality of workmanship.

To the group of Byzantine icons painted in Egypt on skillfully crafted sycamore panels with reverse wavy decoration belong five Great Deesis portraits of equal size (89cm x 55.3cm), divided between Wadi al-Natrun monasteries (Figures 5 and 6-10). Also these large icons have parallels in Sinai, particularly the portrait of Apostle Paul of which numerous icons are still extant.[22]

---

[20] Gerstel, *Beholding the Sacred Mysteries*, 10 with nos. 14 and 31.
[21] For the list of 50 medieval icons of which 25 are on sycamore panels with wavy decoration, see my "List of Icons in the Nile valley dating to the Middle Ages," compiled in 1996, in Skalova and Gabra, *Icons of the Nile Valley,* 2:118-119 and ills. 27a, 28, 37f and cat. no. 8b.
[22] See Weitzmann, *The St Peter Icon*, figs. 33-39 and 41-48.

Part Two

Five Palaiologan Serial Portraits from the Great Deesis[23]

Monastery of St. Macarios	*Archangel Gabriel* AP[χαγγελος] | [γα]BP[ιηλ] 89cm x 55.3cm	Figure 6
	Mark the Evangelist O AΓIOC MAPKOC 89cm x 55.3cm	Figure 7
	Matthew [o] | [α]Γ[ι]O[ς] MAΘAIOC 89cm x 55.3cm	Figure 8
	Apostle Paul O A[γιος] ΠAYΛOC 89cm x 55.3cm	Figure 9
Monastery of the Romans	*John the Theologian* O AΓ[ιος] IΩ [αννης] O ΘEOΛOΓOC 89cm x 55.3cm	Figure 10

On all five icons were glued square pieces of thick hand-made paper identifying in Arabic the saints who are inscribed in Greek, and providing translations of the gospel texts in the hands of the evangelists. The handwriting is that of the learned hegumenos 'Abd al-Masih Salib al-Mas'udi (1848-1935), monk at the Monastery of the Romans.[24] However, documentation about the acquisition of icons of such majestic size and quality has not yet been found.

The icons were published for the first time by Dr. Meinardus, who assigned them to the sixteenth/seventeenth century Cretan School.[25] But these saints were painted on sycamore panels fashioned

---

[23] This part is a follow-up to my lecture and contribution "Five 13th Century Great Deesis Portraits in the Wadi al-Natrun: Their Origin," delivered at the Seventh International Congress of Coptic Studies, 27 August – 2 September 2000, Leiden University; see *Abstracts of Papers* 103. Forthcoming in the *Acts* of the Congress.

[24] Dr. Nessim Youssef recognized this handwriting during the symposium. It is not recorded when the monasteries acquired these beautiful icons and they are not mentioned by the learned travelers, until (possibly) Johann Georg zu Sachsen in 1913; see Skalova, "Five Deesis Icons in Wadii Natrun," forthcoming. Abd al-Masih Salib al-Mas'udi worked in the Library of the Monastery of St. Macarios, and served later in Cairo in the administration of the patriarchate (Aziz S. Atiya, "'Abd al-Masih Salib al-Masu'di," in *Coptic Encyclopedia*, 1:7).

[25] O. Meinardus, "The Collection of Coptica in the Monastery of St. Macarius," *Bulletin de la Societé d'archéologie Copte* 19 (1970), 235-248, plates IV.A, IV.B and V.A; idem, "The Byzantica of Scetis," *Bulletin de la Societé d'archéologie Copte* 22 (1976), 177-181, plates I.A, I.B, II.A, II.B and III.B; and idem, "Byzantine Treasures

in the same typically regional Egyptian way as the *John the Baptist*'s support (described in detail above), which makes them attributable to a local medieval workshop.[26]

The panels, with 3cm narrow integral borders, remained well preserved and flat thanks to the nature and the thickness of sycamore wood (the fact that their both sides are coated being of less influence). On each reverse a solid layer of white plaster is decorated with alternating wavy grey-blue and reddish lines consisting of finger prints. Such standardized reverse-finish (which might have originated as imitation of marble revetments[27] on Middle Byzantine altar barriers or of liturgical hangings (see Figure 3), indicates that the icons were once inserted in a screen where they would be also viewed from the sanctuary.

The state of preservation of the portraits differs considerably and the faces and draperies appear rather schematic under the dusty yellowed varnish, so that stylistic analysis should wait until they are professionally cleaned. Some preliminary observations can be made. The Byzantine-trained artist painted the five portraits in the refined egg-yolk tempera technique, using the same limited palette, available locally, as the master who created the Wadi al-Natrun *Baptist*: white, black, ochres, azurite blue, and vermilion red. The paint was applied in layers on white, partly gilded gypsum priming into incised contours. The incised nimbi are just delineated with thin red lines. On the greenish bases and pale complexions, bright red has been employed for the saints' mouths, cheeks, outlining their aquiline noses and, significantly, the inner-corners of their almond-shaped and deeply shadowed eyes with light irises. Dark brown lines and white brush strokes accentuate the facial features and small hands.

---

in Coptic Churches," *Coptic Church Review* 16 (1995), 108-116, figs. 3-5. Dr. Meinardus published also the *Archangel Gabriel* but did not add it to the set. His photos from the 1960s show the icons darker than in 1989 when I saw them for the first time. For his late dating see note 61.

[26] As yet, there has been no analysis of the wood on which the Wadi al-Natrun portraits were painted. However, although these boards have integral borders, the local workmanship and use of materials can be discerned. Suggestion that these panels are fashioned from sycamore wood are based on my previous conservation work on medieval icons with this reverse decoration, scientifically confirmed by Prof. Dr. J. Baas (Onderzoeks-instituut, Rijksherbarium, University of Leiden), published in Skalova, "New Evidence," 87-88, as well as by C. Vermeeren (BIAX, University of Leiden, communication dated 1996, unpublished). See also note 42.

[27] Gerstel, *Beholding the Sacred Mysteries*, 10 with n. 30. In Egypt, this kind of ornament also can be found, for example, on recently discovered murals in the *khurus* of the Church of the Virgin in the Monastery of the Syrians.

These provincial masterpieces demonstrate a blend of Middle and Late Byzantine features, which suggests that they still might belong to the thirteenth century. *Archangel Gabriel*'s androgynous face, among the refined Palaiologan-looking New Testament protagonists, gives the impression of being more hieratic (Figure 6). The exceptionally well-conserved *St. Mark the Evangelist*, the *Apostle of Egypt*, is individualized as a mature, handsome broad-faced man with a neat coiffure and a short brown beard (Figure 7). The unconventional modeling of his mantle with V-shaped folds has parallels on icons in Cairo.[28] *St. Matthew*'s poor condition nevertheless, allows us to recognize him as a vigorous elder (Figure 8). *St. John the Theologian* is a partly bald, white haired, long-bearded scribe with inkpot and pen (Figures 9.1 and 9.2). The *Apostle Paul* was portrayed as a formidable bald-headed thinker with a pointed black beard holding the codex with both hands (Figures 10.1 and 10.2).

In the collection of St. Catherine's Monastery at Mount Sinai, among a considerable number of large-scale Great Deesis icons (that they were intended for an iconostasion is certain): six portraits of St. Paul holding the codex with both hands should be mentioned, as they provide an impressive range of this unchangeable iconographical representation. They were published by Kurt Weitzmann in his comprehensive study of the thirteenth-century icon of St. Peter of Dumbarton Oaks.[29] While iconographically the Wadi al-Natrun *Paul* derives from similar representation as the early thirteenth–century Sinai icon from a so-called master set, stylistically it is different, filling a gap in our knowledge of the icon painting of the region. Two replicas of this Komnenian Sinai *Paul*, one from the second half of fifteenth century, second from the sixteenth century Cretan work strengthen an earlier dating for the Wadi al-Natrun *Paul*.

Closest stylistic parallels to this grand-scale Wadi al-Natrun *Paul* and *St. Mark the Evangelist* can be found in Cairo in tiny depictions of these apostles on the Pentecost scene occurring on two arguably thirteenth-century "Byzantine-Coptic" narrative icons. Refined *Apostle Paul*, cleaned under the microscope, on the majestic beam

---

[28] Such V-shaped folds can be seen on three medieval icons, all also painted on sycamore panel with reverse wavy decoration: *Twenty-four Priests of the Apocalypse* (73cm x 106cm x 1cm) and *Scenes from the Life of the Virgin and Christ*, Church of St. Mercurios, and on the icon of the *Assumption of the Virgin with the Episode of her Girdle* in the Coptic Museum but originally from the Hanging Church; see Skalova and Gabra, *Icons of the Nile Valley,* 2: cat. nos. 12, 15, and 16.
[29] See Weitzmann, *The St Peter Icon*, figs. 34, 36, 38, 42, 44, 46, and48.

icon with the *Seven Major Feasts* (55cm x 305cm x 2cm) in the Church of the Holy Virgin in the Convent of the same name, in Haret Zuweila, is strikingly similar to the Wadi al-Natrun *Paul* (Figures 9 and 11). Another portrait, not yet cleaned, is on the remarkable panel with *Scenes from the Life of Christ and the Virgin* (73cm x 190cm x 3.2cm), in the Church of St. Mercurios.[30]

Reconstruction of the Great Deesis set from which the Wadi al-Natrun portraits originated

Deesis sets are recognizable because of the serial nature of icons which composed them. How were our five icons displayed and how did they function? Based on the direction in which each figure is turned and by comparing the analogous series, the following order of eleven icons can be reconstructed[31] (Text Figure 1):

[Peter],
St. John the Theologian,
St. Mark the Evangelist (whose position in this Deesis set attests to local preference[32]),
Archangel Gabriel,
[Virgin],
[Christ],
[John the Baptist] (the icon preserved in the Monastery of the Syrians described in Part One?)
[Archangel Michael],
[Luke],
Matthew
Paul

In their original locations within the Great Deesis set, high on the screen, the bent position of the Wadi al-Natrun praying saints' heads would have caused them to gaze down towards the beholders in the

---

[30] For this dating, which is based on extensive research, see Skalova, "'Traced by Incense'"; Z. Skalova and S. Davis, "A Medieval Icon with Ten Scenes from the Life of Christ and the Virgin in the Church of Abu Seifein, Cairo," *Bulletin de la Société d'archéologie Copte* 39 (2000), 211-238 with plate XVIII; and Skalova and Gabra, *Icons of the Nile Valley*, 2: cat. nos. 16 and 17.

[31] A. Cutler, "Under the Sign of the Deesis: On the Question of Representativeness in Medieval Art and Literature," *Dumbarton Oaks Papers* 41 (1987). 145-154.

[32] I am indebted to Prof. Dr. Bastiaan van Elderen for suggesting after my lecture that St Mark is positioned within the Deesis set according to the Alexandrian theological tradition.

nave. As each icon measures about 89cm in height and 55.3cm in width,[33] all together they would need to occupy at least a space of 6 and a half meters. If some kind of inter-spacing was used, such as columnets (in accordance with Byzantine usage) and if the Trimorphon icons above the entrance were wider, the set would fit on a screen approximately 7 m wide.

Such a sophisticated Great Deesis set of 11 portraits in Byzantine style on typically Egyptian but carefully fashioned sycamore panels, must have been commissioned for an important shrine in the country. There, these icons could survive, darkened, *in situ*.[34] The ancient Coptic church of St. Mercurios Abu Seifein in the monastery of the same name located in the former Fustat near the Roman fortress of Babylon, today known as Christian Old Cairo, is considered here as the original venue.

Part Three

The Church of St. Mercurios Abu Seifein in the Monastery of St. Mercurios, Old Cairo

The Sanctuary Furnishings
The main sanctuary screen of the once patriarchal Church of St. Mercurios is a remarkable structure. It is not an iconostasion but a typically Coptic higab which evolved from the chancel barrier. It is a solid but composite structure of elements dating to various eras. Between two early-Byzantine columns, which flank the holy doors of the sanctuary, "strengthened," probably also in the thirteenth century, with full-size images of the *Virgin and Child* and *Christ Pantocrator*,[35] are inserted three medieval ivory-inlaid panels, each approximately 187cm, 186cm, and 192cm wide. These columns carry

---

[33] Thickness of the board with the frame: 4-4.5cm; width of the border: 3cm.
[34] The patriarchal churches in cosmopolitan Cairo deserve consideration, as their screens were not modernized until the mid-eighteenth century. The catholicon of the Greek Orthodox Patriarchate dedicated to St. Nicolas the Traumaturg can be dismissed. It has new gilded iconostasion (with 65 westernized Russian icons, donated in the nineteenth century), unsuitable for the proposed Great Deesis set. For the origin of these Russian icons, see Volkoff, *Voayers Russes* 111, and Skalova, "Vicissitudes of Icons in Modern Period," in Skalova and Gabra, *Icons of the Nile Valley*, 2:143.
[35] For the thirteenth-century Byzantine instruction for the priest to bow in front of icons flanking the holy doors of the sanctuary in penance (*metanoia*), see Gerstel, *Beholding the Sacred Mysteries*, 9.

the "entablature" into which two rows of eighteenth-century icons, 11 portraits and arcaded beam with 21 histories, were fixed between five cornices[36] (Figure 12). Four cornices are inscribed in Coptic and Arabic with biblical quotations, painted or carved but today all over-painted and therefore difficult to date.[37] In the middle-section runs a medieval balk, decorated with carved *mukarnas* (comparable *mukarnas* can be seen on the eleventh/twelfth rebuilt cupola above the screen),[38] to which are fastened 12 projecting wooden consoles for lamps and ostrich eggs. Altogether, these elements form an "epistyle," buttressed from behind by the arcaded "bridge of masonry"[39] (Text Figure 2). Similar Fatimid-style arcaded masonry, also resting on Byzantine columns, divides the western part of the nave from the narthex.

The screen contains two features relevant to this research: firstly, it has the necessary width; secondly, the upper row of sacred pictures is a Great Deesis set composed of 11 icons measuring together 7.88cm; they portray the same saints who can be seen on the reconstructed set from which the five Wadi al-Natrun icons originated. Here was the required space into which our medieval portraits would fit (Text Figures 1 and 3, and Figure 12).

To strengthen this argument about existence of a medieval Great Deesis set in the church, it should be mentioned that in this venue survive six large icons of serial nature, painted on heavy and coarse sycamore boards with the reverse wavy decoration, which I perceive

---

[36] It can be mentioned briefly that adjacent at right angles is a second eighteenth-century Deesis set of nine icons depicting Christ the High Priest flanked by two archangels and six apostles, on the southern side of the former splendid men's chamber, the ancient screens of which, described by A.J. Butler in ca. 1880, were since removed. The function of this second Deesis set and its Ottoman setting (partly visible on Figure 12) deserve further research.

[37] The caution is necessary since in the northern side chapel, dedicated to the Virgin Mary, an arcaded beam is placed on the medieval screen; on the beam *Virgin and Child flanked by Twelve Apostles* were painted by Yuhanna al-Armani. The panel, which looks reused, rests on a cornice inscribed in Coptic. Into this carved cornice's right end an older painted fragment was inserted. See Z. Skalova, in collaboration with M. Mansur and Y. Nessim Youssef, "Three Medieval Beam-Icons from Coptic Patriarchal Churches in Cairo," in *Actes des Fouilles Coptes, Le Caire 7- 9 Novembre 1996* (Cairo, 1998), 110-111, n. 34 and plates XXIXa-c.

[38] P. Grossmann, *Mittelalterliche LanghausKuppelkirchen und verwandte Typen in Oberägypten* (Glückstadt: J.J. Augustin, 1982), 45-46, n. 181. Dr. Grossmann noted that the screen had been fitted into the nave, which was reduced in 1176, at the time of Patriarch Mark (1166-1189).

[39] This medieval arcaded bridge is on its eastern side decorated with painted ornament and cherubim, probably Ottoman.

as a group made sometime in the thirteenth century. They are imaginable as *membra disiecta* of an extensive medieval furbishing of this sacred space once divided by screens into *haykal* and *khurus* for sacred services by clergy and second *khurus* (or Butler's "men's chamber"[40]) for lay offices. This eastern part of the church would be later twice modernized: in 1750s and around 1900. Due to their traditional Coptic iconography, integrated by painters into imported models to emulate Byzantine effects, these six icons can be best described as "Coptic-Byzantine."[41] Their patronage by Coptic hierarchy is further attested by sources used, which include theological writings of the prominent Coptic-Arabic authors of "the golden age." Those of Bishop Bulus al-Bushi,[42] Ibn Kabar, and Ibn Sabba have already been recognised.

Two re-restored arcaded beam icons on sycamore panels with wavy decoration are particularly interesting as, due to their form and size as well as commemorative iconography, they would fit into the existing sanctuary screen: The *Enthroned Virgin and Child, Prophets, Archangels, Holy Bishops and Monks* (43cm x 252cm) (Figure 13); and its shortened pair beam *Christ at Second Coming with Archangels, Prophets and Six* [originally ten] *Equestrian Martyr-saints* (now 43cm x 165cm, but originally ca. 280cm long (Figure 14).[43]

Both beams represent the vital continuation of earlier Coptic art, particularly friezes of locally venerated monks, bishops, and equestrian martyrs carved in stone, woven in textile as well as painted on the walls of desert monasteries either excavated (the Monastery of St. Jeremiah in Saqqara and St. Apollo in Bawit), or still existing (the Monastery of St. Antony at the Red Sea).[44] The frontal hieratic images of holy monks and bishops, clad in liturgical vestments, on

---

[40] Term coined by A.J. Butler, derived from the church's division, as in the 1880s when women were assigned a place in the nave.
[41] The joint Egyptian-Netherlands *Coptic Icons Conservation Project* established between 1990 and 1996, in cooperation with the SCA, one of its workshops in the Church of St. Mercurios in Old Cairo, with the aim to re-restore the medieval icons on panels with reverse wavy decoration. All six medieval icons of serial nature are painted on panels of noticeably inferior workmanship, which have been identified as sycamore fig – the beams by Prof. Dr. P. Baas, other four icons by Dr. C. Vermeeren. The icons are listed in Skalova and Davis, "A Mediaeval Icon," 216, plates XVIII-XXIIa, and in color in Skalova and Gabra, *Icons of the Nile Valley*, 2: cat. nos. 9-13 and 16.
[42] See Davis' ground-breaking contribution in Skalova and Davis, "A Mediaeval Icon," Part Two.
[43] Skalova, "New Evidence."
[44] Bolman, *Monastic Visions.*

beam A, would reflect, when *in situ*, commemorative ceremonies taking place in the Church of St. Mercurios when it functioned in its heyday as a mausoleum and housed burials of Coptic hierarchy as attested by the sources and tombs of bishops.[45] The intercessory function of the Deesis set on the *khurus* screen would complement the commemorative function.

The Great Deesis Set of 11 Portraits by Ibrahim al-Nasikh and Yohanna al-Armani

A dedicatory Arabic inscription on the icon of Apostle Paul quotes Acts of Apostles 9:3-5; 22:6-8 and dates the set to 1751/2 (Figure 15). It reads:

1   And then, suddenly, a light came from heaven,
2   shining upon him. Then he felt on the ground,
3   and heard a voice saying to him, Saul,
4   Saul, why do you persecute me? He asked, "Who
5   are you, O Lord"? And the Lord said to him: "I am
6   Jesus of Nazareth, whom you are persecuting."
7   O Lord [...] +++
8   Remember everyone who strived and worked together with them to paint (taswir) these
9   ten (sic) icons for the holy (mukades) sanctuary (iradyun)
10 [which is] in the church of Abu Seifein. They were consecrated by the hand
11 of the Father and Patriarch, Anba Murqus,[46]
12 the 106th Patriarch of Alexandria, in the year 1165 AH/1468 AM[47]
13 The painting is from the hand of the wretched Ibrahim
14 Ibn Samaan al-Nasikh, and Yuhanna al-Armani al Kudsi.

Each portrait is approximately 70cm x103cm (inclusive a 2cm frame), except the central icon of *Christ the High Priest*, which is wider, measuring 88cm x 103cm, thus taking together 7.88m. The icons were clearly painted for an existing screen to be fixed in 1751/2 (in an archaic mode) between five older or replicated cornices.[48]

---

[45] For Byzantine parallel see Gerstel, *Beholding the Sacred Mysteries*, 20 with note 35.
[46] AD 1745-1769; see A.S. Atiya, "Mark VII," in *Coptic Encyclopedia* 5:1537-8.
[47] In *abuqti* numerals. For scholarly advice and translation of Arabic I am indebted to Joost Hagen, Dr. Hans Jansen, and Dr. Jos van Lent (Leiden University).
[48] See note 37.

This Ottoman Deesis set on the screen of the St. Mercurios Church is the lofty witness to the first post-medieval reflorescence of the Coptic community keen to refurbish (after almost a half millennium) their most venerable churches in the metropolis. However, this revival in icon painting had also lamentable consequences: The survival of so few old icons in these remaining Cairene churches is arguably attributable less to the (well-documented) tribulations that beset them and their diminishing parishes in the long Middle Ages than to the improving circumstances of the Christian communities under the Ottoman empire during the eighteenth century and the widespread (but undocumented) replacement of the timeworn and darkened medieval icons, which no one knew how to "revitalise."[49] For example, Ibrahim and Yohanna reused some medieval panels for their creations. More obliteration would follow in the modern era!

The eastern section of the Church of St. Mercurius' interior as we see it today is so altered that it is necessary to remark on the changes which the edifice underwent in the Middle Ages and than again in the modern times.

Reconstruction of the Medieval Sanctuary Space

The placing and function of the Great Deesis set on the sanctuary screen of the Coptic patriarchal church of St. Mercurius in Cairo would appear Greek in inspiration.[50] However, some typically Egyptian features should be recalled again: carved and inlaid, geometrically patterned, woodwork panels and doors, Coptic and Arabic sacred texts accompanying the icons, and, especially, the existence of two special spaces, a *khurus* (choir)[51] behind this screen, and a "men's chamber" in front of it.

A.J. Butler described the *khurus*-screen in his book as follows: "Passing inside, one remarks that the inner as well as the outer face of the screen is inlaid with ivory [...] On this (inner, eastern) side of the screen too are many pictures and some Coptic writings." He saw another splendid inlaid screen, the *haykal*-screen dividing the apsidal

---

[49] See Skalova, "'Traced by Incense,'" 19, and idem, "Patriotic Icon Painting: Ibrahim Al Nasikh and Yohanna Al Armani (1740-1780)," in Skalova and Gabra, *Icons of the Nile Valley*, 2:137-141.

[50] As note 7.

[51] In this article I do not always use Butler's terminology, preferring Dr. Gertruud van Loon's more accurate descriptive and functional Coptic/Arabic naming. Butler's 'choir' is here 'khurus' (some authors write 'khurus') and 'choir-screen' is 'khurus-screen.' See van Loon, *The Gate of Heaven*, 109-124.

haykal with the altar from the typically Coptic *khurus* (choir-chamber) still *in situ*: "The centre part of this, the iconostasis, resembles in style the choir-screen, and is doubtless of the same period [...]. The screen, of course, ends upwards with a row of pictures."[52] Icons were displayed everywhere: on the *haykal*-screen, on the shelves round the walls of the *khurus*, on both sides of the *khurus*-screen (Text Figure 4).[53] This double screening of the altar in the medieval Coptic churches seems a uniquely Coptic phenomenon (arguably reflected by ancient rectangular churches in Ethiopia).[54]

Let us recall the external circumstances of Christian life in Muslim Egypt. From the Arab conquest of the seventh century on, the Copts were not allowed to build new churches, and from the eleventh century their religious life became constrained to their walled compounds. One imagines that gradually the Fatimid interior of the Cairene patriarchal church became a fortified enclose — "the union of temple and fortress" — which housed the divine service from the start to the finish (the supposed secondary function of so many screens as physical and spiritual protection of the Holy of Holies from intruders cannot be ignored).

The Copts, in their striving to represent truthfully God and heaven, based their churches on Old Testament architecture "as a fulfillment of scripture." Their double sanctuary space (*khurus* and *haykal*) reflects the two rooms of the scriptural Tabernacle of the synagogue:[55] *khurus*, narrow space before the altar room (*haykal*), is the Holy Place, symbolizing Paradise, where, in words of Ibn Sabba

---

[52] A.J. Butler, *The Ancient Coptic Churches of Egypt*, 2 vols. (Oxford: Clarendon Press, 1884), 1:99ff, particularly 105-108. Butler's description shows that the sanctuary of this Coptic church in Old Cairo (and others), was divided into the *khurus* and *haykal* sections, separated by wooden partitions, all carrying medieval icons. He saw these icons covered with darkened varnish, and yet he was still able to appreciate their value and date them fairly accurately. However, the fact that the beam icon with the *Six Equestrian Martyr-saints* was not anymore intact, warns us to assume that the icons were ca. 1880 still *in situ*.

[53] In the Church of the Transfiguration, Monastery of St. Catherine at Mount Sinai, the icons are displayed in archaic mode on the shelves round the walls of the aisles. The archival photos of Coptic churches demonstrate that this usage was common in Cairo until the 1920s.

[54] In Ethiopia, this division, which could have been borrowed from Egypt, still works: The sanctuary, "Holy of Holies" (in geez: *gedussa gedudusan*), as in the Bible, is separated by a "Holy" space (in geez: *geddest*) from the nave (in geez: *gené mahelét*), where the cantors stand. At certain liturgical parts the curtains are drawn. While there are not screens, painted walls close partly the way. Father Ugo Zanetti, who read the draft of this paper, kindly suggested this connection.

[55] van Loon, *The Gate of Heaven*, 110-116.

"the souls of righteous await the Last Judgment in order to ascend to heaven." From there only the consecrated men could approach God by entering the *haykal*, containing the altar hidden behind yet another screen; as an image of the Old Testament Tabernacle, a Holy of Holies, the earthly Jerusalem.[56] As in the Byzantine churches, withdrawal of the Coptic clergy behind the altar barrier (away from the lay beholder) must have been connected with liturgical changes enhancing the religious mysteries.

The division of the eastern section of the church into *haykal* and *khurus* by two screens, *haykal*-screen and *khurus*-screen, was a medieval feature which moved out undocumented from urban churches around 1890s. Prior to 1890s the existing screen, Byzantine and Coptic in inspiration, did not function as an altar screen (iconostasion) but as the *khurus*-screen; behind it there was a second screening with icons in front of and probably also round the altar, now lost (Text Figures 5.1 and 5.2).

Reverend Butler himself commented in 1902 (when Egypt was under the British, *ergo* Christian rule) on the ongoing modernization within Babylon, lamenting the disappearance of unique architectural and artistic heritage during the renovation of the ancient churches of that little-changed sacred area by Coptic benefactors, "with the British occupation came a sense of security which has led to a most deplorable destruction. The need for a fortified enclosure having vanished, Copts, Greeks and Jews vied together in demolishing the walls."[57]

Clearly, such liberated feelings were valid also for the "spiritual" barricades within the church edifice itself, especially the partitions around the altar, perceived by traditional Copts as the Old Testament Holy of Holies, while the zealots of modernization wished to call a finish to the oppressive past symbolised by the windowless temple/fortress of Mamluk era, labyrinth of screens and black icons, and change it into modern place of worship. Yet by "modernizing" the Copts "westernized" their ancient churches inspired by newly built Uniate, Catholic, Protestant, and Coptic churches in Cairo: such as the new patriarchal church, Morqosseia (built after 1800 without *khurus*), or later, the church of the Butrus-Ghali family, Butrusseia.

---

[56] Ibn Sabba as quoted by van Loon, *The Gate of Heaven*, 117.
[57] Butler, *Arab Conquest*, 238, as quoted by P. Sheehan, "The Roman Fortification," in P. Lambert, ed., *Fortifications and the Synagogue: The Fortress of Babylon and the Ben Ezra Synagogue, Cairo* (London: Weidenfeld and Nicolson, 1990).

The surviving worn-out medieval icons taken off their screens, by loosing their liturgical place and function and not yet being valued as art objects, became a "theological embarrassment"; they could not be used for prayer nor destroyed, being sacred with divine word written upon them.[58]

In 1994, when working in the Dumbarton Oaks Library, Washington DC, I was informed that the Wadi al-Natrun Deesis portraits were a gift to the monks by the Russian Tsar.[59]

The argument can be summarized as follows:

- In Wadi al-Natrun monasteries are preserved six locally-made majestic Great Deesis portraits which testify that the Middle Byzantine practice of screening the sanctuary by high barrier topped with such icons reached also the Nile valley.

- All six icons – painted on typically Egyptian sycamore wood panels with reverse finish consisting of superimposed grey-blue and reddish bands of brush strokes or finger prints – date to the era when in the Byzantine *koine* icons were painted on panels with similar reverse decoration. They should be added to the notable number of comparable large-size twelfth- and thirteenth-century Deesis icons at Sinai, Cyprus, and elsewhere in the eastern Mediterranean, deriving from the Late Komnenian/Early Palaiologan models, or being a synthesis of both styles. Their preliminary dating to the prolific thirteenth-century (or extending to the early fourteenth-century) needs to be confirmed, or refuted, by professional cleaning.[60]

- Thirteenth-century Cairo must have been a vivid cosmopolitan center of icon painting, where itinerant painters (arriving via

---

[58] See the author's chapter "The Sign Language of Religious Practices," in Skalova and Gabra, *Icons of the Nile Valley*, 2:76-81.

[59] Personal communication by Dr. Natalia Teteriatnikova.

[60] Another case in point, later but still relevant for our survey, is a Great Deesis set of 17 icons, in the iconostasion of the St. Neophytos Monastery in Cyprus. It is dated 1544 and signed by Iosif Chouris, believed to be a "hellenized" Syrian Cypriot. Interestingly, while *Christ, Archangels*, and *Apostle Peter* hold books and scrolls inscribed in Greek, on the pages of the books, held slightly open in the hands of *Apostle Paul* and *Evangelists Matthew* and *Mark*, the texts are in Armenian script. Surely, when viewing these Italianate mid-sixteenth-century Cypriot icons, painted by an Armenian artist, the dating of the Great Deesis portraits in Wadi al-Natrun to the same period (see note 21) should be refuted.

Jerusalem and Sinai) and Byzantine-trained lay Copts worked side by side in workshop painting icons for both Melkite and Coptic patrons.[61] It is proposed here that the Wadi al-Natrun Deesis icons were painted for the patriarchal Coptic Church of St. Mercurios in Christian Old Cairo.

- Five portraits surely originate from Great Deesis set of 11 icons, in which the best preserved *St. Mark the Evangelist* was prominently positioned according to the Alexandrian (Coptic?) tradition. The medieval sanctuary screen of the Church of St. Mercurios carries the Great Deesis set of 11 portraits by Ibrahim al-Nasih and Yohanna al-Armani from 1751-1752, which look as though they might be replicas of an older set of the same saints (being comparable with the surviving Wadi al-Natrun "prototypes"). The original Deesis icons were most likely in a Byzantine style, iconography, and technique akin to another six medieval icons on sycamore panels with wavy reverse decoration, still preserved in this church (which could be *membra disiecta* of a larger sanctuary programme).

- When the Copts modernized their ancient churches in Cairo around 1900, they abolished the *khurus* and dismantled haykal and nave screens and discarded the icons framed within them. Until then the lofty screen in the Church of St. Mercurios functioned as *khurus*-screen, forming part of the enclosed chamber (the second *khurus* for lay services).

- Finally, the medieval arrangement of two rows of icons (Ottoman narrative beams below and a Deesis set above) on the former *khurus*-screen in Cairo, deserves more research, as it might be a unrecognised Coptic record of how icons were positioned on Middle Byzantine templon in the region, and particularly at St. Catherine's Monastery, before it was replaced by higher iconostasion.

---

[61] Bishop Samuel, ed., and Mina al-Shamaa, trans., *Abu al-Makarim, History of the Churches and Monasteries in Lower Egypt in the Thirteenth Century*, (Cairo, 1992), f. 13b. Later, one such early occasion for direct transfer of new models from the Byzantine capital to Cairo could be the arrival of new Melkite patriarch in 1262 to Mameluke Cairo; see A.-M. Talbot, "The Restoration of Constantinople under Michael VIII," *Dumbarton Oaks Papers* 47 (1993), 252.

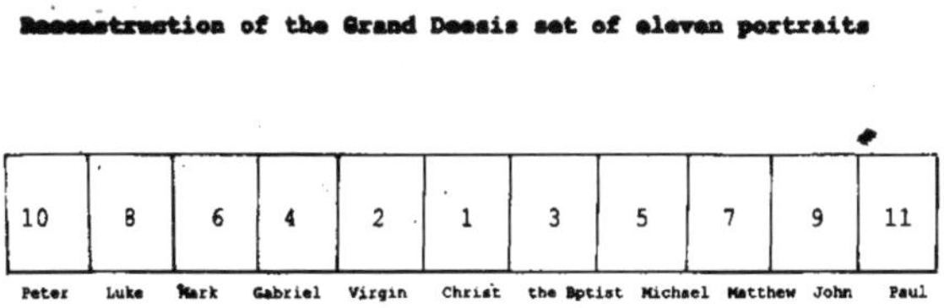

Reconstruction of the Grand Deesis set of eleven portraits

10	8	6	4	2	1	3	5	7	9	11
Peter	Luke	Mark	Gabriel	Virgin	Christ	the Bptist	Michael	Matthew	John	Paul

Text-figure 1: Reconstruction of the Great Deesis set from which the Wadi al-Natrun portraits of *Gabriel*, *Mark*, *Mathew*, *John*, and *Paul* originated. (drawing by Z. Skalova, 2000)

solid stone partition

altar

Text-figure 2: The arcaded "masonry bridge" supporting the icons.

Text-figure 3: Reconstruction: The Wadi al-Natrun icons "inserted"
into the *khurus*-screen of the St. Mercurios Church.

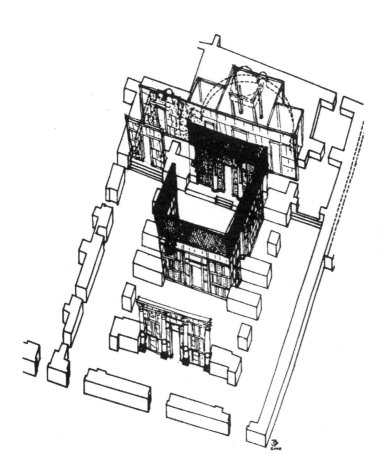

Text figure 4: Reconstruction.
The sanctuary area divided by high screens in *haykal*, *khurus*, and men's section.
(drawing by Jaroslav Dobrowolsky)

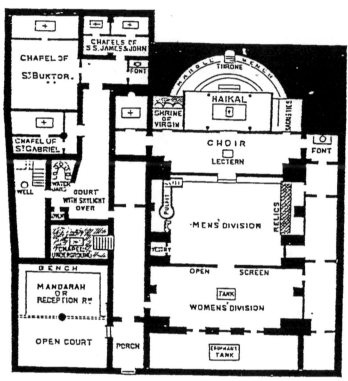

Text figure 5.1: Ground plan of the Church of St. Mercurios,
Monastery of St. Mercurios, Cairo, in ca. 1880.
(after Butler, *Ancient Coptic Churches*, 1: fig. 3)

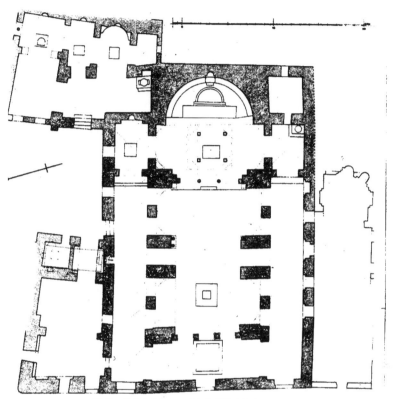

Abb. 15. Die Merkurioskirche von Dair Abū Saifain in Fusṭāṭ
A. Heutiger Zustand

Text figure 5.2: Ground plan of the Church of St. Mercurios,
Monastery of St. Mercurios, Cairo, in 1980s.
(after P. Grossmann, *Mittelalterliche Kuppelkirchen*, fig. 15)

Figure 1.1: Wadi al-Natrun, Monastery of the Syrians.
Icon of *St. John the Baptist*
(photo by Z. Skalova)

Figure 1.2: Reverse.
(photo by Z. Skalova)

Figure 1.3: Gypsum formations in the Western White Desert, Egypt.
(photo by Romani Sobhi)

Figure 2: Wadi al-Natrun, Monastery of the Syrians.
Icon of *Interceding Virgin*
(photo by Nabil Selim Atalla)

Figure 3.1: Cairo, Church of St. Barbara. Icon of *Enthroned Virgin and Child.*
(photo by Z. Skalova)

Figure 3.2: Reverse.
(photo by Z. Skalova)

Figure 4.1: Mount Sinai, Monastery of St. Catherine.
Icon of *St. John the Baptist,* early thirteenth-century
(photo by Z. Skalova)

Figure 4.2: Reverse.
(photo by Z. Skalova)

Figure 5: Wadi al-Natrun, Monastery of St. Macarios, Church of St. Claudius.
Four Deesis portraits

Figure 6: Wadi al-Natrun, Monastery of St. Macarios.
Icon of *Archangel Gabriel*
(photo by Emad Nasry)

Figure 7: Wadi al-Natrun, Monastery of St. Macarios.
Icon of *St. Mark the Evangelist*
(photo by Emad Nasry)

Figure 8: Wadi al-Natrun, Monastery of St. Macarios.
Icon of *St. Matthew*
(photo by Emad Nasry)

Figure 9.1: Wadi al-Natrun, Monastery of St. Macarios.
Icon of *Apostle Paul*
(photo by Emad Nasry)

Figure 9.2: Reverse.
(photo by Z. Skalova)

Figure 10.1: Wadi al-Natrun, Monastery of St. Bishoi.
Icon of *St. John the Theologian*
(photo by Emad Nasry)

Figure 10.2: Reverse.
(photo by Z. Skalova)

Figure 11: Cairo, the Church of the Holy Virgin,
Monastery of the Holy Virgin in Haret Zuwayla.
Apostle Paul (detail from Pentecost) on the beam icon with *Seven Feasts*
(photo by Z. Skalova)

Figure 12: Cairo, Monastery of St. Mercurios, Church of St. Mercurios.
(Former) *khurus*-screen with the eighteenth-century *Great Deesis*
and men's section today
(photo by Hisham Labib)

Figure 13: Cairo, Monastery of St. Mercurios, Church of St. Mercurios.
The beam icon *Enthroned Virgin and Child, Prophets,*
Archangels, Holy Bishops and Monks
(photo by Z. Skalova)

Figure 14: Cairo, Monastery of St. Mercurios, Church of St. Mercurios.
The beam icon *Christ at Second Coming with Archangels, Prophets and Six* [originally
ten] *Equestrian Martyr-saints*
(photo by Z. Skalova)

Figure 15: Cairo, Monastery of St. Mercurios, Church of St. Mercurios.
Icon *Apostle Paul* with the dedicatory inscription
(photo by Z. Skalova)

History through Inscriptions:
Coptic Epigraphy in the Wadi al-Natrun[1]

Jacques van der Vliet

The painter Theodore, active in the monastery of Saint Antony near the Red Sea in the thirteenth century, inscribed on one of the walls of the church of this monastery the following proverb: ⲦⲈⲒⲬ ⲚⲀⲦⲀⲔⲞ ⲦⲈⲤⲈⲀ[Ⲓ Ⲛ]ⲀⲘⲞⲨⲚ Ⲉ[Ⲃ]ⲞⲀ, that is: "the hand will perish, what is written will remain."[2] It is the almost exact Coptic counterpart of the well known Latin saying: *vox audita perit, littera scripta manet.* Man writes to survive. The painter Theodore, too, wished to be remembered beyond his earthly existence. The quotation above is from the opening lines of a commemorative inscription which he wrote next to one of his paintings and in which, addressing the readers, he asks for their prayers.

The desire to save from oblivion persons or events was the motivating force behind much of the traditional source material of *epigraphy*, the study and, in particular, the decipherment and interpretation of ancient inscriptions. The scholarly discipline of

---

[1] I wish to thank my colleagues Mat Immerzeel and Brian P. Muhs for their friendly assistance.

[2] Painter's memento in the nave; Text: R.-G. Coquin and P.-H. Laferrière, "Les inscriptions pariétales de l'ancienne église du monastère de S. Antoine, dans le désert oriental," *Bulletin de l'Institut Français d'Archéologie Orientale* 78 (1978), 279-280, no. 14, ll. 3-9; reproduced in P. van Moorsel, *Les peintures du monastère de Saint-Antoine près de la mer Rouge.* La peinture murale chez les Coptes, 3. Mémoires de l'IFAO, 112/1-2 (Cairo: Institut Français d'Archéologie Orientale, 1995-1997), 1:182, n. 2 (cf. II, pl. 82); the latest edition is by B.A. Pearson, in E.S. Bolman, ed., *Monastic Visions: Wall Paintings in the Monastery of St. Antony at the Red Sea* (Cairo: American Research Center in Egypt; New Haven: Yale University Press, 2002), 229, under N35.3 (cf. 38, with fig. 4.2), who failed to understand both beginning and end of the inscription. For the painter Theodore and his work, see now Bolman's beautiful book. Some further examples of this proverb in Coptic: W.E. Crum, "Inscriptions from Shenoute's Monastery," *Journal of Theological Studies* 5 (1904), 555 (no. A 1, ll. 26-27); 561 (no. A 8) with 562, n. 2; 563 (no. A 9); in Arabic: A. Hebbelynck and A. van Lantschoot, *Codices coptici Vaticani, Barberiniani, Borgiani, Rossiani.* Tomus I: *Codices coptici Vaticani* (Vatican: Bibliotheca Vaticana, 1937), 427.

epigraphy developed within the context of classical studies and was originally concerned primarily with Latin and Greek commemorative and funerary inscriptions. The study, for example, of hieroglyphic Egyptian, Aramaic, or Coptic inscriptions is a later development, and even at present these disciplines retain some of the aims and methods of traditional, classical epigraphy. The object of Coptic epigraphy in a broad sense can be understood as the surviving inscriptional material from Christian Egypt and Nubia.[3] As such, it comprises much more than just Coptic inscriptions in stone. It is characterized by a wide variety of media (stone, plaster, wood) and purposes (funerary, dedicatory, didactic) as well as by great linguistic diversity (in addition to Greek, Coptic and Arabic, the principal languages of Christian Egypt, Old Nubian, Syriac, Armenian, and Ge'ez may also be found). Moreover, much of this Coptic epigraphic material bears a monastic stamp.

Egyptian monasteries, whether still inhabited or long deserted, have produced large ensembles of inscriptions of all kinds. Often, these are an important source for reconstructing the history of a particular establishment. The monastic chronicles of Latin Europe are virtually unknown in Egypt and in quite a number of cases the only written evidence is inscriptions and stray documents. Striking examples of such a predominantly epigraphic documentation are offered by the Monasteries of Jeremiah in Saqqara[4] and Hatre (Hadra) near Aswan.[5] Therefore, the most valuable scholarly contributions in the field of Coptic epigraphy are precisely those publications which do not stop at the more or less satisfactory edition of a handful of inscriptions but try to integrate the epigraphic source material into a broader vision of the general history and culture of a particular site or cluster of sites. Although more recent examples are not lacking, the monumental three-volume set of Hugh G. Evelyn White's *The Monasteries of the Wâdi 'n Natrûn* does remain an outstanding example of such an integrative approach.

What, then, would be the role of inscriptions in a future reworking of Evelyn White's panoramatic study? Admittedly,

---

[3] For a useful overview of Coptic epigraphy, see M. Krause, "Inscriptions," in *The Coptic Encyclopedia*, ed. Aziz S. Atiya (New York: Macmillan, 1991), 4:1290-1299.

[4] See C. Wietheger, *Das Jeremias-Kloster zu Saqqara unter besonderer Berücksichtigung der Inschriften*. Arbeiten zum spätantiken und koptischen Ägypten, vol. 1 (Altenberge: Oros Verlag, 1992).

[5] Cf. S. Timm, *Das christlich-koptische Ägypten in arabischer Zeit*. TAVO Beihefte, Reihe B 41/1-6 (Wiesbaden: Ludwig Reichert, 1984-1992), 2:664-67.

epigraphic material is certainly not the principal source of information for the history of the Wadi al-Natrun. Even if important inscriptions are not lacking, the epigraphic record does not match other sources, either from the Wadi itself or of external origin, for their number and wealth of information. Funerary inscriptions on tombstones, for example, abundant at many other monastic sites in Egypt, are practically absent in the Wadi al-Natrun.[6] This may be connected with local usage: also the site of the Kellia produced only one small funerary stela.[7] It should, moreover, be remembered that excavations are the classical source of inscriptions. The Wadi al-Natrun, although an ancient and a monumental site, is not primarily an archaeological site. It is dominated by four big monasteries which are very much alive and whose communities are much more concerned with the future than with the past. In fact, excavations in the area are generally of a recent date and modest in scale. Also the current Dutch restoration project in Dayr al-Suryan, which greatly increased the number of known mural inscriptions, is modest in scale. Nevertheless, epigraphy does have a lot to offer to the historian of the Wadi al-Natrun and I hope to be able, in the following pages, to give an idea, first, of the variety and richness of the epigraphic sources, and then of their importance.

As was remarked above, the epigraphic material from Coptic monastic sites is as a rule much more varied than the formal stone-inscriptions of classical epigraphy. This variety can be observed in the monasteries of the Wadi al-Natrun too and will be briefly illustrated in the following paragraphs.

Although the area did not produce an extensive corpus of funerary stelae, monumental inscriptions on stone are by no means entirely lacking. It may suffice to mention two examples, both inscribed on marble slabs and both kept at present in Dayr al-Suryan. The first is a Bohairic text which commemorates the demise of Saint John Kame in A.D. 858;[8] the second, a bilingual (Greek-Old Nubian)

---

[6] Cf. H.G. Evelyn White, *The Monasteries of the Wâdi 'n Natrûn*. Publications of the Metropolitan Museum of Art Egyptian Expedition, vols. 2, 7, and 8 (New York: Metropolitan Museum of Art), 3:53.

[7] R. Kasser et al., *Kellia: Topographie*. Recherches suisses d'archéologie copte, 2 (Genève: Georg, 1972), 82, no. 58, 5/20, fig. 33.

[8] Evelyn White, *Monasteries,* 3:193-94 (with an incorrect date A.D.), plate LV, B; presently mounted in a case in the *khurus* of the Church of the Virgin Mary.

epitaph of the Nubian King George (Geôrgi, Geôrgios) of A.D. 1157.[9] These two monuments provide important historical information, but it is unfortunate that both were detached from their original contexts long ago.[10]

For another group of inscriptions the situation is, in this respect, much more favorable. They would never have survived outside their original contexts, since they are inseparable from the walls and other architectural elements of the monastery buildings themselves. These are the more or less formal mural inscriptions which have been painted upon or scratched into monastery walls from the earliest days of their existence until the present day. They bear a direct physical relationship to the architecture of the holy place to which their fate is linked.

For our purposes, several kinds or genres of mural inscriptions can be distinguished. The most informal and familiar of these is certainly the *graffito*: a usually short inscription often mentioning merely the name of its author, sometimes accompanied by a prayer.[11] The author may be a visitor, a pilgrim for example, or a local. So-called graffiti may be scratched in (as their name suggests), but they are perhaps even more often painted or, nowadays, written with a ballpoint or felt-tip pen. They can be found everywhere, from pharaonic temples to subway stations, but certain spots are more privileged than others. In the Wadi al-Natrun monasteries, a noteworthy concentration of them can be found, for example, in the chapels on the second floor of the *qasr* of Dayr Abu Maqar. The clouds of crude graffiti, in Coptic, Syriac, Armenian, Arabic, and French, hardly enhance the esthetic effect of the medieval

---

[9] Published in F.L. Griffith, "Christian documents from Nubia," *Proceedings of the British Academy* 14 (1928), 118-128, plate. I; cf. Evelyn White, *Monasteries*, 3:215-217, plate LXXVI; D.A. Welsby, *The Medieval Kingdoms of Nubia: Pagans, Christians and Muslims along the Middle Nile* (London: British Museum Press, 2002), 89-90 and 260 (all give an incorrect date A.D.); presently exhibited in the museum of the monastery.

[10] Presumably both were brought in from neighbouring monastic sites; see Evelyn White, *Monasteries*, 3:193 and 217.

[11] On ancient Christian graffiti, see now W. Eck, "Graffiti an Pilgerorten im spätrömischen Reich," in *Akten des XII. internationalen Kongresses für christliche Archäologie. Jahrbuch für Antike und Christentum. Ergänzungsband* 20/1 (Münster: Aschendorffsche Verlagsbuchhandlung, 1995), 206-222; for a representative ensemble from a Coptic monastery, S.H. Griffith's chapter in Bolman, *Monastic Visions*, 185-193.

wallpaintings in these rooms.[12] Still, they are born not out of mischief or lust for destruction, but out of a desire to remain present, to "survive," within a certain sacred space and thereby to partake of its *baraka*. What distinguishes them from other inscriptions is their informal and personal character.

Less informal in character are *dipinti*, full-fledged texts that are painted on the walls with considerable care and usually on a fairly large scale. Most of the recently discovered Syriac inscriptions at Dayr al-Suryan are actually dipinti, some of them quite monumental ones.[13] Unlike graffiti, they certainly cannot have been made without the permission of the local authorities. It takes considerable time, skill and technical means to produce them. Their contents, too, are much more varied: they may be commemorative in character, but also, for example, didactic. In spite of being more formal, dipinti are nevertheless usually "incidental" in the sense that they do not belong to the planned decoration scheme of a building. In this respect they differ from a third category of painted mural inscriptions, those which intimately belong to the painted decoration of the building, usually a church or chapel.

Ancient and modern wall paintings and even icons may bear a whole series of inscriptions that are functionally related to the picture. In the main, three types can be distinguished: *legends, founder's mementos*, and *painter's mementos*.[14] The latter two usually contain a prayer, respectively, for the sponsor and the painter of the scene. As regards their form, such prayers often resemble those written, with similar purpose, in the colophons of manuscripts. The legends which accompany so many paintings, although the most familiar as a genre, are actually perhaps the least well understood. They may seem a rather unsophisticated way of identifying, for an ignorant audience,

---

[12] For these graffiti, see Evelyn White, *Monasteries*, 3:75-76, 79-80, plate XVI; J. Leroy, *Les peintures des couvents du Ouadi Natroun*. La peinture murale chez les Coptes, 2. Mémoires de l'IFAO, 101 (Cairo: Institut Français d'Archéologie Orientale, 1982), 45-49, plates 91-103.

[13] See, for example, K.D. Jenner and L. van Rompay's contribution in K. Innemée et al., "New discoveries in the al-'Adrâ' Church of Dayr as-Suryân in the Wâdî al-Natrûn," *Mitteilungen zur christlichen Archäologie* 4 (1998), 96-103; K. Innemée, and L. van Rompay, "La présence des Syriens dans le Wadi al-Natrun (Égypte): À propos des découvertes récentes de peintures et de textes muraux dans l'Église de la Vierge du Couvent des Syriens," *Parole de l'Orient* 23 (1998), 174-180.

[14] See the slightly different classification by Pearson in Bolman, *Monastic Visions*, 217-19.

the actors, events or other elements of a painted scene. That is why they are often invaluable for modern scholars when facing damaged, incomplete or indistinct scenes.[15] In fact, the aim of the legends is entirely pedagogical: while identifying the elements of the picture, they invite its beholder to activate his or her knowledge of the Holy Scriptures, of sacred literature, or even of major theological issues. Thus, the biblical texts on the prophets' scrolls in the Annunciation scene in the Church of the Virgin at Dayr al-Suryan evoke the mystery of the Incarnation as adumbrated in the Old Testament.[16] Rather than attesting to ignorance, legends appeal to erudition. All three elements (legends, a founder's memento, and a painter's memento) can be found together in a typical form in a recently discovered, but as yet unpublished monument of the Wadi al-Natrun, a painted hermitage in the surroundings of Dayr Abu Maqar, which will be provisionally presented below.

Finally, there are other bearers of inscriptions which can be easily overlooked but which nevertheless have their own importance within monastic epigraphy and particularly in the monasteries of the Wadi al-Natrun. The category in question is that of moveable objects, like furniture and ecclesiastical implements. These too may bear legends and/or commemorative inscriptions. A striking example, again from Dayr al-Suryan, is the bronze flabellum (ceremonial fan) with a Syriac inscription, dated A.D. 1202, now in the Museum of Mariemont in Belgium.[17]

These three categories of inscriptions – the monumental stone inscriptions, those painted upon or scratched into the walls, and finally those adorning moveable objects – constitute the subject of monastic epigraphy in its breadth and variety. As I hope to show, they are a source of information which the historian of the Wadi al-Natrun would be unwise to neglect, even if they do not always write History with a capital letter. In what follows, I will be referring in particular

---

[15] See, for example, K. Innemée and L. van Rompay, "Deir al-Surian (Egypt): New discoveries of 2001-2002," *Hugoye : Journal of Syriac Studies* 5 (2002), 13-14 and 28-40 (<http://syrcom.cua.edu/hugoye>) on the scenes with Constantine and Abgar in the *khurus* of the Church of the Virgin at Dayr al-Suryan and their Syriac legends.

[16] Cf. P. van Moorsel, "La grande annonciation de Deir es-Sourian," in *Called to Egypt: Collected Studies on Painting in Christian Egypt*. Publication of the "De Goeje Fund"; 30 (Leiden: Nederlands Instituut voor het Nabije Oosten, 2000), 211.

[17] Published by J. Leroy, "Un flabellum syriaque daté du Deir Souriani (Egypte)," *Les Cahiers de Mariemont* 5-6 (1974-75), 31-39.

to the Coptic, that is to say Bohairic Coptic, inscriptions that have been discovered since 1990 near Dayr Abu Maqar and in the Church of the Virgin at Dayr al-Suryan,[18] and are still only partly published.[19] These can be approached from various angles, each apt to throw light on a particular aspect of past life in the monasteries concerned. Here I will limit myself to only three aspects of the recent finds, namely their historical, linguistic, and cultic implications.

The importance of inscriptions may be purely historical, in the narrow sense of "documenting local history." They produce names and dates for persons or events from the monastery's history. Thus, the conventional prayers accompanying wall-paintings may acquaint us with the names of artists and donors. In Dayr al-Suryan, for example, two big ornamental crosses painted on the north wall in the north-eastern corner of the nave of the Church of the Virgin (Figure 1, n. 2) are the work of an artist Solomon.[20] Two brief and entirely conventional prayers request God's mercy for Solomon but, at present, provide no further information beyond his name and his activity as an artist. It is therefore also difficult to say whether the crosses painted by him were made to order, as part of the planned decoration of the Church, or a merely tolerated product of his personal devotion.

The painted panels in a room hewn into the rock to the south of Dayr Abu Maqar and discovered in the autumn of 1990 have certainly been made to order.[21] One wall shows Saint Menas with his camels and Christ standing to his right, while another wall shows the Virgin Mary feeding the Logos next to a much damaged representation of Christ Pantokrator upon the Four Living Creatures. The paintings are provided with conventional legends in Greek, whereas colophon-type prayers for the founder and the painter of the ensemble are conceived in Bohairic Coptic. The painter's memento is much damaged and the

---

[18] For the latter, see the accompanying plan.

[19] The new inscriptions from the Church of the Virgin will be published in full in the final publication of the Leiden Dayr al-Suryan project; for preliminary publications and discussions, see the footnotes and the bibliography in the Appendix.

[20] Both crosses are visible on the photo in L. van Rompay and A.B. Schmidt, "Takritans in the Egyptian desert: The Monastery of the Syrians in the ninth century," *Journal of the Canadian Society for Syriac Studies* 1 (2001), 60, to the right. More about this wall below.

[21] The ensemble was recorded immediately after discovery by the late Professor Paul van Moorsel and his team; this documentation is kept in Leiden and its publication is forthcoming.

artist's name lost. Fortunately, enough survives to date his work to the year 943-44 (A.M. 660). According to the other memento, it was an ascetic called Father Mena Panau who ordered and paid for the construction and decoration of the "cave" (it is called thus in the inscription, with the Greek word σπη′λαιον) and possibly the adjoining hermitages as well. There is a good chance that the same person is mentioned as the spiritual father of a Deacon Gabriel who appears as the scribe of a Vatican manuscript of A.D. 978-79.[22] Around the middle of the tenth century, he must have been a person of some importance within the monastic community and we may expect to find more traces of him.

Of an entirely different nature is the great commemorative inscription running beneath the painted decoration adorning the central dome above the *khurus* of the Church of the Virgin in Dayr al-Suryan (Figure 1, n. 5). This text, which has gradually been uncovered since 1999,[23] consists of one line of tall decorative letters and mentions, in addition to a deacon John, two priests, namely *papa* Moses and *papa* Aaron;[24] the former, Moses, is furthermore styled *higoumenos* and *oikonomos*. Judging from similar inscriptions, for example those running underneath the eleventh century apse-composition in the church of the monastery at Naqlun (Dayr al-Malak) in the Fayyum,[25] the persons commemorated here were the monastic authorities in whose period of office and under whose supervision the dome above the *khurus* was refurbished. They may

---

[22] Scribal colophon edited by Hebbelynck and van Lantschoot, *Codices coptici*, 472-73; reproduced in H. Hyvernat, *Album de paléographie copte* (Paris: Leroux; Rome: Spithoever, 1888; repr. Osnabrück: Zeller Verlag, 1972) plate XL, 2. Note, however, that there is a two letter lacuna in the name (**MHNⳈ Ⲡ[ⳈN]ⳈⲨ** is my own reconstruction) and that the manuscript, although acquired at Dayr Abu Maqar, was originally written for a church outside the Wadi al-Natrun.

[23] See K. Innemée et al., "Deir al-Surian (Egypt): Its wall-paintings, wall-texts, and manuscripts," *Hugoye: Journal of Syriac Studies* 2.2 (1999) (<http://syrcom.cua.edu/hugoye>), 8 (with illustrations 3 and 4; cf. 37.e and 46); L. van Rompay, "Deir al-Surian: Miscellaneous reflections," *Essays on Christian Art and Culture in the Middle East* 3 (2000), 87 and plate 3. It is not yet fully uncovered. For the most recent discoveries in the *khurus*, see now Innemée, "Deir al-Surian (Egypt): New Discoveries of 2001-2002."

[24] For the title *papa*, see T. Derda and E. Wipszycka, "L'emploi des titres *abba*, *apa* et *papas* dans l'Egypte byzantine," *Journal of Juristic Papyrology* 24 (1994), 54-56.

[25] Partly visible in W. Godlewski, "Les peintures de l'église de l'Archange Gabriel à Naqlun," *Bulletin de la Société d'Archéologie Copte* 39 (2000), 93 and figure 2.

have been the sponsors of the operation as well, but this is by no means necessary and as yet not borne out by the extant remains of the text. We are rather dealing here with the kind of dedicatory inscription which "dates" important construction works according to the ecclesiastical and, sometimes, worldly authorities of the time.[26] Indeed, as my colleague Lucas van Rompay acutely observed, the Moses and Aaron of the inscription have a good chance of being identical to the Moses and Aaron mentioned, as "priests and directors of the monastery of the Syrians," in the undated colophon of a Syriac manuscript from Dayr al-Suryan.[27] Karel Innemée, on the other hand, proposes to identify the Moses of the inscription with the famous Abbot Moses of Nisibis (first half of tenth century).[28]

Although at the present moment the evidence provided by this inscription does not appear conclusive, it may in the near future enable us to fit the works undertaken in the course of decorating and refurbishing the Church of the Virgin into a broader picture of the life and history of the monastic community some 1000 years ago. Already it raises the question, simply by being conceived in Coptic, of language within the community, a question for which, as becomes more and more evident, no easy and clear-cut answers can be expected.[29] The close proximity of Syriac, Coptic, Greek, and Arabic on the walls of the Church of the Virgin poses not so much, to my mind, the question of ethnicity but primarily that of domains or registers and, only secondarily, that of the historical circumstances which may have determined the criteria for code selection and their changes. I prefer not to dwell on this theme but will rather turn to Coptic as it is used in the recently discovered inscriptions of the Church of the Virgin.

---

[26] Compare the Naqlun inscription just mentioned, which dates the refurbishment of the apse to the periods of office of Archbishop Zakharias of Alexandria, of Bishop Severos of al-Fayyum, and of a local abbot (archimandrite), Papnoute, a local archpriest, Kabri, and two more local dignitaries whose names and functions are lost (upper line of text; edition by the present author forthcoming in W. Godlewski's publication of the church of the Naqlun monastery).

[27] See van Rompay, "Deir al-Surian," 84.

[28] K. Innemée, "Deir al-Surian (Egypt): Conservation work of Autumn 2000," *Hugoye: Journal of Syriac Studies* 4/2 (2001), 10 (<http://syrcom.cua.edu/hugoye>); Innemée and van Rompay, "Deir al-Surian (Egypt): New discoveries of 2001-2002," 12.

[29] See the cautious remarks by van Rompay, in Innemée et al., "Deir al-Surian (Egypt)," 44-50, and van Rompay, "Deir al-Surian."

Coptic, as is well known, is not a uniform language. Several varieties of Coptic can be recognized, often unhappily styled "dialects," some of which had only a limited, local or regional, currency. Not so Bohairic Coptic, which was used in a wide area which included the Wadi al-Natrun. Bohairic, however, is not a unity either. Again, several varieties of Bohairic can be distinguished. Thus, the variety found in most of the literary manuscripts from Dayr Abu Maqar is traditionally called Nitrian Bohairic. Although well attested thanks to a great number of hagiographical and homiletic texts, it has been little studied.[30] The situation is even worse for non-literary Bohairic,[31] that is Bohairic as it is found, for example, in documents and inscriptions, and which, we may think, must at a certain period have been close to the living language as it was used for every day purposes in a particular region. In fact, witnesses of non-literary Bohairic are relatively scarce[32] and therefore the recent inscriptional finds in Dayr al-Suryan are, next to the texts discovered by the French and Swiss expeditions on the walls of the Kellia, welcome additions to the repertoire.[33] A few examples may explain the interest of the new Dayr al-Suryan inscriptions.

On the south wall of the nave, next to the later painting of the Three Patriarchs, a dipinto of nine lines in Bohairic Coptic has come to light (Figure 1, n. 6).[34] The painting partly overlaps the inscription

---

[30] See, however, the provisional remarks by L. Th. Lefort, "Littérature bohairique," *Le Muséon* 44 (1931), 115-135, and A. Shisha-Halevy, "Bohairic," in *Coptic Encyclopedia* 8:58.

[31] Cf. Shisha-Halevy, "Bohairic," 58: "nonliterary Bohairic is still a complete mystery."

[32] Although the list of Bohairic inscriptions given by Roquet a quarter of a century ago (G. Roquet, "Inscriptions bohaïriques de Dayr Abû Maqâr," *Bulletin de l'Institut Français d'Archéologie Orientale* 77 [1977], 163-64) can be considerably expanded now, the corpus is still not impressive.

[33] For the Bohairic of the Kellia inscriptions, see now R. Kasser, "L'épigraphie copte aux Kellia et l'information qu'elle donne sur l'importance de la langue bohairique *B5*," *Bulletin de la Société d'Archéologie Copte* 37 (1998), 15-48, and idem, "Langue copte bohairique: Son attestation par les inscriptions des Kellia et leur évaluation linguistique," in S. Emmel et al., eds., *Ägypten und Nubien in spätantiker und christlicher Zeit: Akten des 6. Internationalen Koptologenkongresses, Münster, 20.-26. Juli 1996.* Sprachen und Kulturen des Christlichen Orients, vol. 6 (Wiesbaden: Reichert Verlag, 2:335-346).

[34] For the inscriptions on this wall, see van Rompay, in Innemée and van Rompay, "Deir al-Surian (Egypt): New discoveries of January 2000," *Hugoye: Journal of Syriac Studies* 3/2 (2000), 17-32 (<http://syrcom.cua.edu/hugoye>). The present text is no. 1

and there is no connection between them. The text is predominantly of a didactic character – epigrammatic exhortations to modesty are followed by a short prayer for the author, a certain Jacob. Similar dipinti, which must have been meant to bear out the wit and erudition of their authors, can be found on several monastic sites throughout Egypt.[35] Here we are concerned rather with the state of language reflected in the text. Most remarkably, it shows a clear tendency towards devoicing of the labial /b/ not only in final but in initial position as well. Thus the name of the author, Jacob, is written ⲓⲁⲕⲱⲡ (1.7),[36] but also ⲡⲟⲗ- for ⲃⲟⲗ- (properly, ⲃⲉⲗ-) is found (1.6).[37] The latter phenomenon is quite rare,[38] whereas final devoicing of /b/ occurs occasionally both in mural inscriptions from the Kellia[39] and in Wadi al-Natrun literary manuscripts.[40] Its conspicuous presence in such a short text as the Dayr al-Suryan dipinto of Jacob suggests that it may have been a characteristic of non-literary Bohairic of the Western Delta. In the same dipinto, it is, in a sense, mirrored by another phenomenon, which is much more common in non-literary Wadi al-Natrun Bohairic, namely the "occlusivefication"

---

in fig. 1; cf. furthermore Innemée and van Rompay, "La présence des Syriens," 171; Innemée et al., "Deir al-Surian (Egypt)," 40f.

[35] For a very similar dipinto in the Monastery of Phoibammon in Western Thebes, see H.E. Winlock and W.E. Crum, *The Monastery of Epiphanius at Thebes*. Publications of the Metropolitan Museum of Art Egyptian Expedition, vols. 3 and 4 (New York: Metropolitan Museum of Art, 1926), 1:12-13; W. Godlewski, *Le monastère de St Phoibammon.* Deir el-Bahari, vol. V (Warsaw: PWN, 1986), 150-51, no. 27 (who dates it to the 7th-8th century). The typical exhortation "may a wise man (ⲥⲟⲫⲟⲥ) solve this saying" (here 1.6) recurs in the dipinti which a certain Ananias left on the west wall of the church of the Red Monastery, Sohag (undated and unpublished).

[36] Note also ⲕⲱⲡ for ⲕⲱⲃ (1.5); ϫⲱⲡ for ϫⲱⲃ (1.7).

[37] The text offers no real examples of initial ⲃ-. For the vocalisation of the nominal state form, see Shisha-Halevy, "Bohairic," 58, who refers to H.J. Polotsky, *Collected Papers* (Jerusalem: Magnes Press, 1971), 344.

[38] Some scarce Sahidic examples in W.E. Crum, *A Coptic Dictionary* (Oxford: University Press, 1939; several times reprinted), 27a, and P.E. Kahle, *Bala'izah: Coptic Texts from Deir el-Bala'izah in Upper Egypt* (London: Oxford University Press, 1954), 93, under 65A.

[39] Thus ϫⲱⲡ / ϫⲟⲡ for ϫⲱⲃ, see R. Kasser, "L'épigraphie copte," 41.

[40] Several examples in Crum, *Coptic Dictionary*, 27a. Especially ⲕⲱⲡ for ⲕⲱⲃ is not rare, see ibid., 98-99, also for example a memento of A.D. 1025 in codex Vat. copt. 58[4], f. 35v (Hebbelynck and van Lantschoot, *Codices coptici*, 390), it may have influenced the spelling ⲓⲁⲕⲱⲡ here.

of the intervocalic glide /w/ into /b/. Thus we find, in addition to the almost commonplace **MЄBI** for **MЄYI** (1.9),[41] also **ЄBON** for **ЄYON** (1.8).[42] A possibly related phenomenon, that is a doubling of the intervocalic glide /w/, can be observed, be it only once (**ЄYOYⲱNI**), in the legends of the great Annunciation in the western semi-dome of the Church of the Virgin in Dayr al-Suryan (Figure 1, n. 1).[43] The same double phonological shift that occurs in the dipinto of Jacob (/w/ becoming /b/ and /b/ becoming /p/) would appear to be reflected in the spelling **BⲱTЄⲠ** for **OYⲱTЄB** in the memorial inscription of Saint John Kame, mentioned above (1.13). This inscription, shows, in addition, a spelling **OYBⲱTЄⲠ** (1.4), with a doubling or reinforcement of the labial in word-initial position (single **OY-** or **B**-becoming **OYB**-) that occurs more often in texts from the region, as well as in literary "Nitrian" Bohairic.[44] Here a whole pattern of shifts in the notation of labials can be detected which is characteristic of a greater group of texts from this general region and deserves further study.[45]

The texts which, in the Dayr al-Suryan Annunciation, the four Old Testament prophets exhibit on their scrolls offer some additional interest. They correspond neither in their textual nor in their linguistic

---

[41] **MЄBI** also occurs in the Kellia inscriptions (Kasser, "L'épigraphie copte," 36 and 30); other examples in the Church of the Virgin at Dayr al-Suryan are a graffito below the Galaktotrophousa in the *khurus* (unpublished) and a graffito on the capital of a column in the southern nave (see Innemée and van Rompay, "Deir al-Surian (Egypt): New discoveries of January 2000," 33-35; van Rompay, "Deir al-Surian," 87, plates 4-5; cf. 84).

[42] **BON** for **OYON** also once in the Kellia (Kasser, "L'épigraphie copte," 39 and 30). Both **MЄBI** and **BON** occur passim in the colophons and readers' notes of the Vatican Bohairic codices from Dayr Abu Maqar.

[43] van Moorsel, "La grande annonciation," 214, l. 10; 218, fig. 6.

[44] Thus in the Kellia: **OYBON** for **OYON** (cf. Kasser "L'épigraphie copte," 39 and 30: "cumul"). More frequently in "Nitrian" literary texts: Crum, *Coptic Dictionary*, 467a (**OY** "supplemented" by **B** and conversely); Lefort, "Littérature bohairique," 123 (under I.c), and e.g. **OYBЄPϢЄNOYϭI** (spelling of the proper name Barsanuphius; cf. J. van der Vliet, "Un évêché fantôme: **NIOYBЄPϢЄNOYϭI**," *Göttinger Miszellen* 120 [1991], 109-111; codex Vat. copt. 62[12], Hebbelynck and van Lantschoot, *Codices coptici*, 445-46).

[45] See, provisionally, Kasser's remarks ("L'épigraphie copte," 30 and 31-32) on part of the Kellia material, although I would prefer to avoid the misnomer "Bashmuric."

form to those of the Bohairic Bible. They are nonetheless Bohairic and certainly not "Bashmuric" as has been claimed.[46] However, especially in its so-called "sahidizing" aspect, their language is closer to the local, "Nitrian" variety of literary Bohairic than to classical "biblical Bohairic." Thus ϫ I is found for Ϭ I.[47] This aspect of the texts is perhaps most clearly visible in the treatment of the /h/-sounds which is remarkable for the total absence of the Bohairic ϩ. The latter is replaced by either Ⲭ (once)[48] or Ⲯ (twice).[49]

Although the relatively small amount of material makes all theories very fragile, it would appear that the recently discovered inscriptions in the Wadi al-Natrun can afford us a glimpse of a regional variety of "living" Bohairic. In this respect they resemble the colophons and readers' notes found in the Coptic literary manuscripts produced in the Wadi al-Natrun.[50] These "marginal" texts are also by nature and contents close to much of the inscriptional material and deserve to be studied together with it. Both inscriptions and colophons might well appear to represent a similar brand of "subliterary Nitrian" Bohairic which occasionally also surfaces in the far more regular local form of "literary Nitrian" Bohairic. If this observation would prove to be correct, it would strongly militate against the view that "literary Nitrian" Bohairic is a merely artificial dialect which derives its specific character from heavy contamination with literary Sahidic.[51]

---

[46] So-called "Bashmuric" is supposed to be characterized first of all by the absence of specifically Coptic (Demotic) graphemes (cf. R. Kasser, "Bashmuric," in *Coptic Encyclopedia* 8:47-48; R. Kasser and A. Shisha-Halevy, "Dialect G (or Bashmuric or Mansuric)," in *Coptic Encyclopedia* 8:74-76. This is not the case here, as it is in occasional reader's notes in Wadi al-Natrun literary manuscripts (e.g. codex Vat. copt. 59[1], f. 29v; Hebbelynck and van Lantschoot, *Codices coptici*, 401).

[47] van Moorsel, "La grande annonciation," 214, l. 10; 218, fig. 6 (Ϭ only occurs in the compendium Ⲡ̅Ⲟ̅Ⲥ̅). Cf. Shisha-Halevy, "Bohairic," 58.

[48] van Moorsel, "La grande annonciation," 214, l. 8; 218, fig. 5: ⲚⲬ Ⲏ ⲦϤ; contrast next example.

[49] Ibid., 213, l. 6; 217, fig. 4: Ⲉ Ⲯ Ⲟ Ⲩ Ⲛ Ⲛ Ⲯ Ⲏ ⲦϤ; cf. Lefort, "Littérature bohairique," 124 (under II); Shisha-Halevy, "Bohairic," 58.

[50] Although it is to be regretted that the Bohairic sequel to van Lantschoot's collection of Sahidic colophons never appeared, rich material can be gleaned from Hebbelynck and van Lantschoot, *Codices coptici*.

[51] The classic statement of this view is Lefort, "Littérature bohairique."

When inscriptions are particularly apt to throw light upon the living local vernacular, it is because they are as a rule firmly tied up with a particular spot or site. They do not travel, as books so easily do. This connection with a certain spot, brings us to another important aspect of epigraphic material, to wit its relationship with its surrounding space. The legends of paintings, of course, are – we may say - glued to the picture in which they have their logical place. The position of graffiti and dipinti on church walls must correspond to a certain logic as well. Unfortunately, such logic as there once must have been in putting an inscription in a certain place is not always easily reconstructed. To quote just one example, I am unable to suggest why the nine line dipinto of Jacob on the southern wall of the nave in the Church of the Virgin was situated just there and nowhere else. A similar dipinto in the Monastery of Phoibammon in Western Thebes was inscribed on a doorpost.[52] What inspiration can have guided the hand of the epigrammist Jacob?

There are, however, also more telling examples. On the eastern part of the northern wall of the nave (near nos. 2-3 in Figure 1), a cluster of graffiti and dipinti has been discovered, in several layers and in different vernaculars: Syriac, Coptic, and Arabic. For this reason, Karel Innemée baptised it "the Palimpsest Wall."[53] Such clustering suggests that this particular spot enjoyed the favor of passers-by and visitors on account of its venerability and *baraka*. One Coptic graffito of an otherwise quite ungratifying appearance permits us to be more precise (Figure 1, n. 3).[54] These four short lines written by a certain Michael, who may have been a visitor,[55] comprise a short prayer asking "the God of the Holy James the Persian (ⲡⲓⲁⲅⲓⲟⲥ

---

[52] See above, note 35.

[53] K. Innemée, "Recent discoveries of wall-paintings in Deir Al-Surian," *Hugoye: Journal of Syriac Studies* 1/2 (1998), 21 (<http://syrcom.cua.edu/hugoye>). See, furthermore, idem, "The iconographical program of paintings in the church of al-'Adra in Dayr al-Sourian: Some preliminary observations," in M. Krause and S. Schaten, eds., *ΘΕΜΕΛΙΑ: Spätantike und koptologische Studien Peter Grossmann zum 65. Geburtstag*. Sprachen und Kulturen des Christlichen Orients; vol. 3 (Wiesbaden: Reichert Verlag, 1998), 148; Innemée and van Rompay, "La présence des Syriens," 177-78; Innemée et al., "Deir al-Surian (Egypt)," 40c-d.

[54] Not on figure 2 in Innemée and van Rompay, "La présence des Syriens," 178, but partly and vaguely visible on figure 5 in van Rompay and Schmidt, "Takritans," 60 (extreme lower right-hand corner).

[55] The inscription mentions his place of origin (end of l.3, now largely lost) which, however, does not necessarily imply that he did not live in the Wadi al-Natrun.

ιλ[ΚѠΒΟС] ΠΙΠЄΡСΙС)" to have mercy on the author. In Coptic literature but also in Coptic epigraphy, the invocatory formula "God of Saint so-and-so" is very frequent. One might say that it invokes God while at same time engaging a particular saint as the supplicant's mediator. Therefore the saint in question is never an arbitrary one, but always the one topically most relevant; he or she is at this particular place or in that particular situation the most appropriate mediator.[56] There can therefore be little doubt that wherever God is invoked as "the God of James the Persian," James the Persian himself must have been near at hand.

In fact, James the Persian, or James the Sawn Asunder, is no foreigner in the monasteries of the Wadi al-Natrun. The only complete Coptic account of his martyrdom and of the translation of his relics is extant in a tenth century Bohairic manuscript from Dayr Abu Maqar.[57] The same monastery, too, produced a fragment of another copy.[58] That in the late eleventh century relics of Saint James the Persian were kept in the Wadi al-Natrun is known through Mawhub Ibn Mansur Ibn Mufarrij's notice in the *History of the Patriarchs of Alexandria*.[59] Other sources suggest their presence in Dayr al-Suryan at an even earlier date.

An inscribed piece of church furniture from Dayr al-Suryan, the well known inlaid reliquary, now in the museum of the monastery, represents among other saints a standing figure in military attire. A legend in Greek calls him "the Holy James: Ο ΑΓΙΟС ΙΑΚΟΒΟС."[60] On account of a far later inventory of the contents of this shrine which mentions, among other relics, those of Saint James the Persian,

---

[56] Cf. J. van der Vliet, "The Church of the Twelve Apostles: The Earliest Cathedral of Faras?" *Orientalia* 68 (1999), 93.

[57] Codex Vat. copt. 59[1], edited in I. Balestri and H. Hyvernat, *Acta Martyrum* II. Corpus Scriptorum Christianorum Orientalium, vol. 86. Scriptores coptici, t. 6 (Paris: CSCO, 1924; reprinted Louvain, 1953) 24-61; an annotation would seem to date the manuscript to A.D. 883-84, but see Hebbelynck and van Lantschoot, *Codices coptici*, 402. The interesting translation story (Balestri and Hyvernat, *Acta*, 50-60) was studied by O. von Lemm, *Iberica*. Mémoires de l'Académie Impériale des sciences de St.-Pétersbourg, series 8, vol. 7, no. 6 (St. Petersburg: Academy of Sciences, 1906), 2-19; it links the Saint with the Oxyrhynchite nome, not (yet?) with the Wadi al-Natrun.

[58] See Evelyn White, *Monasteries*, 1:75, no. XIV.

[59] Discussed by Evelyn White, *Monasteries*, 2:363-64.

[60] The reliquary is decribed and discussed in Evelyn White, *Monasteries*, 3:194-196, with plate LXIII. On the figure of Saint James ("attired in a short, skirted tunic"), ibid., 195. Cf. Innemée et al., "Deir al-Surian (Egypt)," 33.

already Evelyn White had concluded that the figure called James on the front of the chest represents James the Persian and that from the outset the reliquary was destined to contain the latter's relics.[61] Moreover, the object itself shows a strong family resemblance to the wooden screens which Moses of Nisibis had erected in front of the *haykal* and the *khurus* of the Church of the Virgin in the early years of the tenth century. It can be inferred that the reliquary dates from the same time and had originally been intended for this same church. Evelyn White suggested that its original place might have been in the *khurus*.[62] However, by invoking "the God of James the Persian," the humble Coptic inscription of Michael contradicts the latter point of view. Instead, it confirms what my colleague Karel Innemée had surmised already on the basis of the reliquary's measurements, that it had stood originally in the niche of the short east wall adjacent to the northern wall of the nave (Figure 1, n. 4),[63] that is precisely next to the spot where Michael's graffito was uncovered. Here the textual and the archaeological evidence combines to pinpoint a local cult of the relics of Saint James the Persian, at least as old as the tenth century, to the north-eastern corner of the nave of the Church of the Virgin.

The inscriptions briefly discussed above represent a mere selection from the epigraphic material in Coptic discovered in the Wadi al-Natrun during the last fifteen years. They nevertheless suffice to show two things. First, that the Wadi al-Natrun has considerable potential for exciting finds, also in this field. Secondly, those inscriptions, even quite insignificant ones, can be interesting as historical sources on their own account. They are able to shed light on a wide variety of aspects of the life of a monastic community through the ages: on the patronage of art and artists, on local language politics and language variety, and on local cults and their "topography." Each of these aspects deserves further study in the years to come. There can be little doubt that in a future rewriting of the history of monasticism in the Wadi al-Natrun, the epigraphic evidence will prove to be as crucial as that of literary, liturgical or archaeological sources.

---

[61] Evelyn White, *Monasteries*, 3:196, where also the document in question ("a paper formerly affixed to the wall of the church") is translated.

[62] See ibid., 194, 196, and caption to plate LXIII ("from the choir (?)").

[63] Cf. Innemée, "The iconographical program," 148; idem, "Recent discoveries of wall-paintings," 21.

APPENDIX

Bibliography of publications relating to Wadi al-Natrun epigraphy that have appeared after 1924 (date of demise of H.G. Evelyn White). Although fairly complete as far as major publications are concerned, the list does not pretend to be exhaustive. Brief annotations are meant to be indicative of the epigraphic relevance of each title.

Evelyn White, H.G. *The Monasteries of the Wâdi 'n Natrûn*. Publications of the Metropolitan Museum of Art Egyptian Expedition, vols. 2, 7, and 8. New York: Metropolitan Museum of Art, 1926-1933: vol. III quotes and discusses the epigraphic sources available to the author.

Griffith, F.L. "Christian documents from Nubia." *Proceedings of the British Academy* 14 (1928), 117-146: edition of the epitaph of King George (Dayr al-Suryan: 118-128).

Hunt, L.-A. "Eternal light and life: A thirteenth-century icon from the Monastery of the Syrians, Egypt, and the Jerusalem paschal liturgy." *Jahrbuch der Österreichischen Byzantinistik* 43 (1993): 349-374; reprinted in: *Byzantium, Eastern Christendom and Islam*, vol. II. London: The Pindar Press, 2000: 127-152: brief Greek legends (reprint, 128).

Hunt, L.-A. "The fine incense of virginity: A late twelfth century wallpainting of the Annunciation at the Monastery of the Syrians, Egypt." *Byzantine and Modern Greek Studies* 19 (1995): 182-232; reprinted in: *Byzantium, Eastern Christendom and Islam*, vol. I. London: The Pindar Press, 1998: 158-204: due attention is paid to the legends (but see now van Moorsel, "La grande annonciation," below).

Immerzeel, M. "Discovery of wall-paintings in Deir anba Bishoi (Wadi'n Natrun)." *Newsletter/Bulletin d'information International Association for Coptic Studies* 30 (1992), 8-11: mentions (unpublished) Coptic inscriptions ("Chapel of Benjamin").

Innemée, K.C. "The iconographical program of paintings in the church of al-'Adra in Deir al-Sourian: Some preliminary observations." In *ΘΕΜΕΛΙΑ: Spätantike und koptologische Studien Peter Grossmann zum 65. Geburtstag*, ed. M. Krause, S. Schaten. Sprachen und Kulturen des Christlichen Orients; vol. 3. Wiesbaden: Reichert Verlag, 1998: 143-153: refers *passim* to legends and other inscriptions.

Innemée, K.C. "Recent discoveries of wall-paintings in Deir Al-Surian." *Hugoye: Journal of Syriac Studies* 1.2 (1998) (<http://syrcom.cua.edu/hugoye>): refers to legends and other inscriptions (Coptic, Greek, Syriac) in the Church of the Virgin.

Innemée, K.C. "New discoveries at Deir al-Sourian, Wadi al-Natrun." In *Ägypten und Nubien in spätantiker und christlicher Zeit: Akten des 6. Internationalen Koptologenkongresses, Münster, 20.-26. Juli 1996*, ed. S. Emmel et al., vol. 1. Sprachen und Kulturen des Christlichen Orients, vol. 6. Wiesbaden: Reichert Verlag, 1999: 213-222: refers to legends and other inscriptions (Coptic, Greek, Syriac) in the Church of the Virgin.

Innemée, K.C. "Deir al-Surian (Egypt): Conservation work of Autumn 2000." *Hugoye: Journal of Syriac Studies* 4.2 (2001) (<http://syrcom.cua.edu/hugoye>): discusses i.a. the Coptic inscription in the dome above the *khurus*, Church of the Virgin (10).

Innemée, K.C., Grossmann, P., Jenner, K.D., van Rompay, L. "New discoveries in the al-'Adrâ' Church of Dayr as-Suryân in the Wâdî al-Natrûn." *Mitteilungen zur christlichen Archäologie* 4 (1998), 79-103: occasional discussion of Greek legends (Innemée, 79-90); four Syriac dipinti (Jenner and van Rompay, 96-103).

Innemée, K.C., and van Rompay, L. "La présence des Syriens dans le Wadi al-Natrun (Égypte): À propos des découvertes récentes de peintures et de textes muraux dans l'Église de la Vierge du Couvent des Syriens." *Parole de l'Orient* 23 (1998), 167-202: chiefly on the Syriac texts (174-180).

Innemée, K.C., and van Rompay, L. "Deir al-Surian (Egypt): New discoveries of January 2000." *Hugoye: Journal of Syriac Studies* 3.2 (2000) (<http://syrcom.cua.edu/hugoye>): mural inscriptions in Coptic and Syriac, Church of the Virgin.

Innemée, K.C., and van Rompay, L. "Deir al-Surian (Egypt): New discoveries of 2001-2002." *Hugoye : Journal of Syriac Studies* 5.2 (2002) (<http://syrcom.cua.edu/hugoye>): Coptic and Syriac legends; Syriac graffiti, Church of the Virgin.

Innemée, K.C., van Rompay, L., Sobczynski, E. "Deir al-Surian (Egypt): Its wall-paintings, wall-texts, and manuscripts. *Hugoye: Journal of Syriac Studies* 2.2 (1999) (<http://syrcom.cua.edu/hugoye>): references to legends and other inscriptions (section I, Innemée); discussion of Syriac and

Coptic inscriptions in the Church of the Virgin (section II, van Rompay).

Leroy, J. "Le décor de l'église du couvent des Syriens au Ouady Natroun (Égypte)." *Cahiers archéologiques* 23 (1974), 151-167: quotes legends (Syriac, Greek, Coptic); facsimile copies of Syriac dedicatory texts (154).

Leroy, J. "Un flabellum syriaque daté du Deir Souriani (Egypte)." *Les Cahiers de Mariemont* 5.6 (1974-75), 31-39: Syriac inscription on a flabellum (A.D. 1202).

Leroy, J. *Les peintures des couvents du Ouadi Natroun.* La peinture murale chez les Coptes, 2. Mémoires de l'IFAO, 101. Cairo: Institut Français d'Archéologie Orientale, 1982: quotes *passim* legends and other inscriptions.

Martin, M.J. "A Syriac inscription from Deir al-Surian." *Hugoye: Journal of Syriac Studies* 5.2 (2002) (<http://syrcom.cua.edu/hugoye>): dedicatory text on a marble column.

Meinardus, O.F.A. "The Museum of Dair as-Surîân also known as the Monastery of the Holy Virgin and St. John Kame." *Bulletin de la Société d'Archéologie Copte* 17 (1963-64), 225-234: several inscribed objects, most of them previously known.

Meinardus, O.F.A. "The collection of coptica in the Monastery of St. Macarius." *Bulletin de la Société d'Archéologie Copte* 19 (1967-68), 235-248: several inscribed objects; some texts are given.

Monneret de Villard, U. *Les églises du monastère des Syriens au Wâdî en-Natrûn.* Milan: privately printed, 1928: quotes legends from the screens of Moses of Nisibis (30-31; cf. Evelyn White, *Monasteries*, 3:180 ff.; Leroy, "Le décor de l'église").

Martyros El-Souriany. "The youngest layer of plaster in the Church of the Holy Virgin Mary in El-Sourian Monastery." In *Seventh International Congress of Coptic Studies: Abstracts of Papers.* Leyden: Faculty of Arts, Leiden University, 2000: 73: the full paper, which is partly based upon Arabic graffiti, is forthcoming in the proceedings of the congress.

Roquet, G. "Inscriptions bohaïriques de Dayr Abû Maqâr." *Bulletin de l'Institut Français d'Archéologie Orientale* 77 (1977), 163-179: dedicatory inscriptions in the "Haykal of Benjamin"; cf. Leroy, *Les peintures des couvents*, 124-25, plates III-IV, and *SB Kopt.* I, nos. 495-97.

van Loon, G.J.M. *The Gate of Heaven: Wall paintings with Old Testament scenes in the altar room and the ḫûrus of Coptic churches.* Publications de l'Institut historique-archéologique néerlandais de Stamboul, vol. 85. Istanbul: Nederlands Historisch-Archaeologisch Instituut, 1999: quotes *passim* the legends of the paintings discussed, many of them from the Wadi al-Natrun monasteries.

van Moorsel, P.P.V. La grande annonciation de Deir es-Sourian. *Bulletin de l'Institut Français d'Archéologie Orientale* 95 (1995), 517-537: replaced by citation below.

van Moorsel, P.P.V. "La grande annonciation de Deir es-Sourian." In *Called to Egypt: Collected Studies on Painting in Christian Egypt.* Publication of the "De Goeje Fund"; 30. Leyden: Nederlands Instituut voor het Nabije Oosten, 2000: 203-224: text of the legends (Greek and Bohairic; 213-14); replaces citation above.

van Rompay, L. "Art and material culture of the Christian Syriac tradition: Some current projects." *Hugoye: Journal of Syriac Studies* 1.1 (1998) (<http://syrcom.cua.edu/hugoye>): preliminary remarks on Syriac text finds in Dayr al-Suryan, Church of the Virgin (7-8).

van Rompay, L. "Deir al-Surian: Miscellaneous reflections." *Essays on Christian Art and Culture in the Middle East* 3 (2000), 80-87: includes discussion of mural inscriptions in Coptic and Syriac, Church of the Virgin.

van Rompay, L., and Schmidt, A.B. "A new Syriac inscription in Deir al-Surian (Egypt)." *Hugoye: Journal of Syriac Studies* 4.1 (2001): wooden beam, A.D. 1285-86.

van Rompay, L., and Schmidt, A.B. "Takritans in the Egyptian desert: The Monastery of the Syrians in the ninth century." *Journal of the Canadian Society for Syriac Studies* 1 (2001), 41-60: includes discussion of the new mural inscriptions in Syriac, Church of the Virgin (49-51).

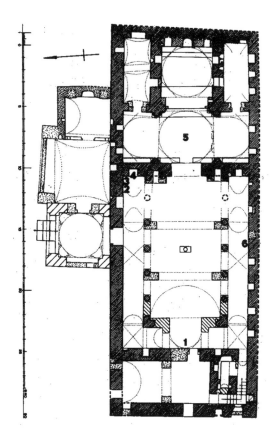

Figure 1: The Church of the Holy Virgin, Dayr al-Suryan: plan, after P. Grossmann,
     showing the location of some of the recently discovered inscriptions

     1: the great Annunciation
     2: Solomon's crosses
     3: graffito of Michael
     4: presumed original position of tenth-century reliquary
     5: commemorative inscription in the dome above the *khurus*
     6: dipinto of Jacob